About the Author

Sam Crompton, holding a powder horn, poses by the Soldier's Memorial in Northampton, Massachusetts. (*Photo: Dieu Etinde*)

Samuel Willard Crompton teaches history at Holyoke Community College in Massachusetts. He is the author or editor of many books, including one on Ulysses S. Grant.

Crompton studied "The Civil War in Trans-National Perspective" at a National Endowment for the Humanities summer seminar, and has contributed many individual articles to the *American National Biography*. He lives in the Pioneer Valley of western Massachusetts, where he sometimes takes walks that lead to the white stone by the side of a country road that announces this was the birthplace of "Fighting Joe" Hooker.

i

Also from Visible Ink Press

The Handy African American History Answer Book
by Jessie Carnie Smith
ISBN: 978-1-57859-452-8

The Handy American History Answer Book
by David L. Hudson Jr.
ISBN: 978-1-57859-471-9

The Handy Anatomy Answer Book
by James Bobick and Naomi Balaban
ISBN: 978-1-57859-190-9

The Handy Answer Book for Kids (and Parents),
    2nd edition
by Gina Misiroglu
ISBN: 978-1-57859-219-7

The Handy Art History Answer Book
by Madelynn Dickerson
ISBN: 978-1-57859-417-7

The Handy Astronomy Answer Book, 3rd edition
by Charles Liu
ISBN: 978-1-57859-190-9

The Handy Bible Answer Book
by Jennifer Rebecca Prince
ISBN: 978-1-57859-478-8

The Handy Biology Answer Book, 2nd edition
by Patricia Barnes Svarney
ISBN: 978-1-57859-490-0

The Handy Dinosaur Answer Book, 2nd edition
by Patricia Barnes-Svarney and Thomas E. Svarney
ISBN: 978-1-57859-218-0

The Handy Geography Answer Book, 2nd edition
by Paul A. Tucci
ISBN: 978-1-57859-215-9

The Handy Geology Answer Book
by Patricia Barnes-Svarney and Thomas E. Svarney
ISBN: 978-1-57859-156-5

The Handy History Answer Book, 3rd edition
by David L. Hudson Jr.
ISBN: 978-1-57859-372-9

The Handy Investing Answer Book
by Paul A. Tucci
ISBN: 978-1-57859-486-3

The Handy Law Answer Book
by David L. Hudson Jr.
ISBN: 978-1-57859-217-3

The Handy Math Answer Book, 2nd edition
by Patricia Barnes-Svarney and Thomas E. Svarney
ISBN: 978-1-57859-373-6

The Handy Ocean Answer Book
by Patricia Barnes-Svarney and Thomas E. Svarney
ISBN: 978-1-57859-063-6

The Handy Personal Finance Answer Book
by Paul A. Tucci
ISBN: 978-1-57859-322-4

The Handy Philosophy Answer Book
by Naomi Zack
ISBN: 978-1-57859-226-5

The Handy Physics Answer Book, 2nd edition
By Paul W. Zitzewitz, Ph.D.
ISBN: 978-1-57859-305-7

The Handy Politics Answer Book
by Gina Misiroglu
ISBN: 978-1-57859-139-8

The Handy Presidents Answer Book, 2nd edition
by David L. Hudson Jr.
ISB N: 978-1-57859-317-0

The Handy Psychology Answer Book
by Lisa J. Cohen
ISBN: 978-1-57859-223-4

The Handy Religion Answer Book, 2nd edition
by John Renard
ISBN: 978-1-57859-379-8

The Handy Science Answer Book®, 4th edition
by The Science and Technology Department
    Carnegie Library of Pittsburgh, James E.
    Bobick, and Naomi E. Balaban
ISBN: 978-1-57859-140-4

The Handy Sports Answer Book
by Kevin Hillstrom, Laurie Hillstrom, and Roger
    Matuz
ISBN: 978-1-57859-075-9

The Handy Supreme Court Answer Book
by David L Hudson, Jr.
ISBN: 978-1-57859-196-1

The Handy Weather Answer Book, 2nd edition
by Kevin S. Hile
ISBN: 978-1-57859-221-0

Please visit the "Handy" series website at www.handyanswers.com.

THE
HANDY
CIVIL WAR
ANSWER
BOOK

THE HANDY CIVIL WAR ANSWER BOOK

Visible Ink Press®
43311 Joy Rd., #414
Canton, MI 48187–2075
Visible Ink Press is a registered trademark of Visible Ink Press LLC.

Most Visible Ink Press books are available at special quantity discounts when purchased in bulk by corporations, organizations, or groups. Customized printings, special imprints, messages, and excerpts can be produced to meet your needs. For more information, contact Special Markets Director, Visible Ink Press, www.visibleinkpress.com, or 734–667–3211.

Managing Editor: Kevin S. Hile
Art Director: Mary Claire Krzewinski
Typesetting: The Graphix Group
Proofreaders: Shoshana Hurwitz and Barbara Lyon
Indexer: Larry Baker

Cover images: Portrait of General Robert E. Lee, portrait of Major–General Ulysses S. Grant, print depicting Battle of Gettysburg, and rebel fortifications in Atlanta, Georgia, all Library of Congress.

Library of Congress Cataloging-in-publication Data

Crompton, Samuel Willard.
  The handy Civil War answer book / Samuel Willard Crompton.
    pages cm. – (The handy answer book series)
  ISBN 978-1-57859-476-4 (pbk.)
  1. United States–History–Civil War, 1861-1865–Miscellanea. I. Title.
  E468.C93 2014
  973.7–dc23   2013044594

10 9 8 7 6 5 4 3 2

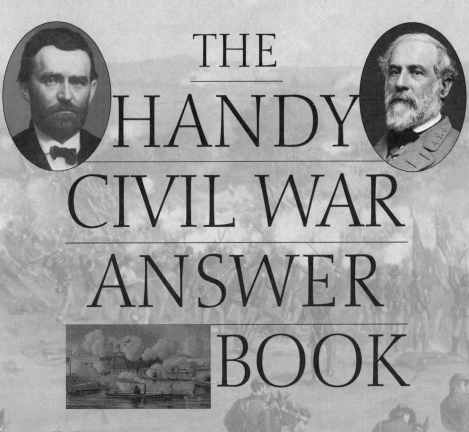

THE
HANDY
CIVIL WAR
ANSWER
BOOK

Samuel Willard Crompton

VISIBLE
INK
PRESS

Detroit

Contents

Dedication

For my beloved Charlotte, who came from a foreign land that has also been tested in civil war. May her home country and her adopted one both know the blessings of peace.

Acknowledgements

Special thanks to Davis Abbott for all the Avalon Hill war games, and to John S. Bowman, who helped cut my teeth in the writing of popular history. Great memories to Nicholas Racheotes, the inspirer-in-chief, as well as to Bradley Nutting, who showed me the path of a conscientious historian. Locally, thanks to the staffs of all the libraries in the Pioneer Valley but especially to those of Smith College, where so many Civil War facts were found. And many thanks to the Book Expo of America because that is where I met Roger Jänecke and Kevin Hile, the forces behind the pages of Visible Ink.

Photo Credits

Dean Franklin: p. 339.

Hal Jesperson: pp. 209, 213, 220, 221, 253, 275, 278, 279, 294, 318, 319

Nat Bocking: p. 345.

Norman B. Leventhal Map Center: p. 7.

Silver2k12: p. 293.

Shutterstock: pp. 4, 36, 37, 72, 73, 92, 106, 125, 136, 137, 148, 149, 188, 202, 206, 217, 230, 264, 347.

Introduction

The men and women of 1861 lived in the long shadow cast by the events of 1776. Eighty-five years had passed since the writing of the Declaration of Independence, but that document—and the repercussions it caused—echoed for the people about to enter the American Civil War. Even their children, once past the age of nine or ten, were acutely conscious of their American Revolution heritage.

The reason is not hard to find: the grandparents, and in come cases great-grandparents, of the people of 1861 had indeed achieved something remarkable by establishing a true republic against great odds. Whether it was a full-scale democracy could be debated—and still is—but the basis for government by the people had been established. Americans—North, East, South, and West—were justifiably proud of what their ancestors had accomplished. But the interval of three generations had seen visible cracks in the edifice of the young republic, and sectionalism had become nearly as strong as devotion to the Union.

The Union of the thirty-three states, in 1861, was a mystical and marvelous thing, but it was also ineffable: it was neither seen nor heard. The state governments, by contrast, were visible to the average person, and the ramifications of the decisions of local lawmakers were more readily felt. Therefore, when challenged to choose between the two, many people—especially from the Southern states—went with their states, rather than favoring federal power. But even the millions of people who lived in the North and admired the Union often showed their state and sectional loyalties: virtually all the regiments raised in the Civil War belonged to an individual state: the 10th Minnesota or the 27th New York, for example. What it boiled down to, at least for the average white American, was whether his or her loyalty to the Union was as great as the allegiance to the particular state. It was no easy choice.

Many Northerners accurately recalled that between 1776—the year of independence—and 1787—the year the Constitution was written—there had been no serious federal or central government: the state governments held virtually all the power. In the North, the large majority of persons believed that it had been for the common good that those state sovereignties were ceded to the federal government; in the South, by contrast, a significant majority believed that the states never *had* yielded their sovereignties. At its essence, the conceptual division came down to this: Northerners believed the Union was a solemn compact between the people that must endure regardless of the rights of states, while Southerners saw the Union as a gentleman's agreement that could be altered, or abrogated, if serious conflicts arose. Lincoln, in his first inaugural address, likened the situation to that of a husband and wife: "Physically speaking, we cannot separate," he declared.

No one knows exactly why the South—with its vast agricultural land and commitment to the institution of slavery—was perceived as female, or why the North—personified both by the rolling farms of the Midwest and the commercial houses of the East Coast cities—was seen as male, but once the identification was made, it lasted. Thus, the South, which had a powerfully masculine code of dominance by the white man as well as deference to the opinion of the woman of the house, was defined as the rebellious wife, while the North, which had moved little closer to gender equality, was identified as the possessive husband who wanted his wife back. Quite possibly it was the British caricature artists—who had honed their trade for decades—who first framed the conflict in terms of gender; once they did so, the idea stuck. This understanding naturally leads us to an important question: Why not let the woman of the house depart?

To Lincoln, looking from the portico of the Executive Mansion, as the White House then was known, it was obvious that this marriage must endure. If the lady of the house were allowed to leave, the man would soon languish and decay because the home would become a mere boarding-house. Likewise, if the man should leave, the wife would find it impossible to remove all the weeds and till the soil.

But when one added the power of geography to the equation, the necessity of union was even more abundantly clear. Had the Appalachian Mountains run from east to west, or if the Mississippi River flowed west to deposit its silt into the Pacific Ocean, *then* some sort of division could be made. But given the lay of the land and waters, it was imperative that the two houses of the republic—the husband and wife—remain in concert.

To the average Southerner—and, of course, that term is inadequate in describing many of the people of 1861—the situation was quite different. Whether he saw his nascent nation as male or female, the Southerner was determined to allow it time to breathe. To the Virginian planting tobacco, it seemed an unjust betrayal of the principles of 1776 to prevent any state, or combination of states, from departing the Union. Had the Union itself not been created by separation from Great Britain? And the farther west one traveled, the more aggressive a temperament one found. The Virginia and Carolina gentlemen were insistent enough, but those of Arkansas and Mississippi were even more vehement, and those of Texas even more so. Texas, after all, had been the Lone Star Republic for nine years before joining the federal union: its right to independence was the clearest of all.

And so, in the spring of 1861, North and South came to blows.

Both sides believed the conflict would be intense but gentlemanly, bloody but short. The typical Southerner knew he could lick any three Yankees, while the average Northerner knew he could bring more tools and weapons to bear than his foes had ever seen. And in those early clashes—whether at Bull Run, Wilson's Creek, or Ball's Bluff—the war was mostly about the single question of Union or disunion. The men from the North were certain that they must fight to hold together that wonderful, even magical thing which had now grown to a total of thirty-four states (Kansas the most recent), while those of the South were adamant that their new confederacy of eleven states must become a free and independent nation.

The conflict became much worse as the year progressed.

There were battles in which people behaved like gentlemen and skirmishes in which they did not. There were surprising acts of chivalry, as well as occasional outbursts of savagery. We can, quite precisely, name the time at which the conflict became bloodier and more intense, however: it was during the spring of 1862. One year into the war, things became more savage at the Battle of Shiloh, a contest almost unrivaled in intensity. The fierce weather, the rain pelting the wounded as they lay on the ground only added to the misery. And, just three weeks later, if we can credit the report of one eyewitness, Confederate cavalrymen fired into a group of New Orleans civilians who dared to cheer when the Stars and Stripes were raised over the Crescent City. That was the month—April of 1862—when the conflict truly escalated.

Lincoln, as usual, read the signs better than most. Though he issued a call for 300,000 more volunteers in the summer of 1862, he knew that the morale of the Union armies was wavering. Despite numerous Northern successes—at Shiloh, New Orleans, and elsewhere—the Confederates fought with an increased level of willpower. If the war had continued in this vein, the North might eventually have tired, and, like a henpecked husband, allowed his wife to depart. Then too, there were outsiders—personified by Britain and France—that seemed to delight at the prospect of a divorce: they had their own reasons for that feeling. Lincoln never used this exact expression (at least not in public), but the only answer was to "double the size" and "double the motivation" for the war. In order to bring a war that had already claimed perhaps 150,000 lives to an end, he was willing to up the ante.

So Lincoln took up his pen and drafted a plan, but he could not act until he learned of the Battle of Antietam. It was not the crushing victory he sought, but it was enough to allow Lincoln to release his preliminary Emancipation Proclamation to the public. Once he did that, the character of the war changed.

To be sure, there were some Northern soldiers who deserted in the aftermath of the proclamation. Some of them said to a British observer that they had enlisted to fight for the Union, not for the "n*****s." At least ninety percent of the Northern men remained in the field, however, and over the next few months they came to see their mission as two-fold: they were there to preserve the Union created by their ancestors *and* to fulfill the promise of freedom that was in one of the opening lines of the Declaration of Independence: "that all men are created equal." There it had been contained in those words all along, but it was not until the early part of 1863 that many people began to truly believe it.

Once the question of slavery or freedom was added to that of Union or disunion, the triumph of the North was only a matter of time. Lincoln, who already possessed the bigger armies and the better technology, now added his double motivation for prodding the soldiers forward, and they moved with increasing speed. There still are Confederate admirers who claim that this moment or that would have created the turnaround, but they are all whistling Dixie. Even if Pickett's Charge had succeeded and Robert E. Lee had won the Battle of Gettysburg, the North would not have yielded. Even if Jubal Early had captured Washington, as he attempted to do in the summer of 1864, the Union would not have been imperiled. By 1863, the Union had become doubly strong: it now anchored its cause on the solid rocks of Union and emancipation, while the Confederacy teetered on the shoals of slavery and disunion. And if all that were not enough, the North had new reinforcements on the way: the first black men to serve their nation in war.

There had, of course, been blacks who served in the Revolutionary War—some on the side of independence and others with the British—and there had been those who sought their freedom by joining the British in the War of 1812. Virtually none of these military endeavors had paid off for them, however; on almost every occasion, the blacks who served were defrauded. Some served the cause of revolution only to be returned to their masters when all was over; others served King George III only to be sent to chilly Nova Scotia or the sweltering West Indies. In 1863, for the first time ever, there was a real chance for empowerment. The first major use of black soldiers was on a windswept beach in South Carolina, and though they did not capture Battery Wagner, their sacrifice made all the difference.

By the end of 1863 the war was as good as won, except that the Confederates would not admit defeat. Something deeply stubborn, almost perversely defiant, lived within the hearts of many Confederates. Even when Sherman marched through Georgia, his men noted the contempt with which old women sometimes looked upon them; and even when Lee and his men were bottled inside Richmond and Petersburg, the Southern men fought on. No matter how poorly we may rate their cause, many of them served it with superb devotion.

In the winter of 1865, as the last drama was about to be enacted, Lincoln met with his top commanders and told them to not treat the Southern people harshly. Never in the history of the republic had defeat been so total; it would take everyone years to adjust, he said. By then, Lincoln had fully become the emancipator-in-chief, a role he embraced reluctantly, but in that very reluctance was an authenticity that many black Americans admired. Father Abraham had come through for them.

Was it really just happenstance that Lee surrendered to Grant on Palm Sunday? Was it truly mere coincidence that Holy Week saw the beginnings, however small, of reconciliation between victor and vanquished? And to carry the analogy to its ultimate conclusion, who could ignore the symbolism of Lincoln being shot on Good Friday? To those who believe we overdo our appreciation of Lincoln, think of what the scene might have been like had he lived.

Would North and South have been reconciled if Lincoln had not been assassinated? We cannot say for certain, but we know—deep in our hearts—that there was a decent chance, as long as Lincoln was calling the shots. Was there a chance that blacks would have found a way to truly integrate themselves into the life of the former Confederate states? However slim, there was a chance; lacking Lincoln—especially his spirit of magnanimity—it was nearly impossible.

What made this farmer's son, this splitter of rails, this failed shopkeeper so great a leader of men? Though thousands of books have been written, and thousands more will come, we may never fully know the answer. Lincoln was, and remains today, a profound mystery. At the time of his death in 1865, he had risen to a level seen only once before: he could be compared only to George Washington. After his death, the nation would not see a leader of his stripe again until Franklin Roosevelt, who, even with all his brilliance, was not as multi-faceted as the man from Springfield, Illinois. Did Lincoln have his faults? Of course he did, not the least of which was his inability to console his wife in the aftermath of Willie Lincoln's death. Such lapses only underscore Lincoln's humanity, his availability to us, his spiritual descendents. But we cannot ignore that the situation, in the generation after Lincoln's death, left much to be desired.

Union had been achieved, and would be questioned or threatened no more. Seven hundred and fifty thousand men—by the most recent estimate—had given their lives that the nation and the ideals behind it became one and the same. Union, which had been so ineffable in 1861, was now transparently real, so real that the word was used much less frequently. The proof was so clear that the word did not have to be employed.

Emancipation, too, was an accomplished fact. More than four million blacks who had previously worked for slaveholders were now free human beings. Though the majority would wind up working for someone—perhaps former masters—in the agricultural South was not indicative of total failure; rather, it served to underscore how difficult it was to take freedom on paper and translate it into material reality. The Russian serfs, by curious coincidence, had been emancipated in 1861, but they, too, would take at least two more generations to attain economic independence.

Along with the obvious successes, however, we have to recognize the failures.

Peace without friendship was the immediate legacy for relations between North and South. Lincoln, in his first inaugural address, had pled for friendship between the two peoples, but it was not accomplished in his lifetime or even that of his sons. The wounds were too deep, and the Northern victory was too obvious for Southerners to shrug it off. Then too, the South was economically prostrate for a full generation.

Citizenship without equality was another legacy, and it lasted even longer than peace without friendship. Citizenship, within the boundaries of what that word meant to the founding fathers, had been the aim of most black Americans. By virtue of the Emancipation Proclamation and the thirteenth and fourteenth amendments, they obtained citizenship, but not the consequent admission of equality. That would take a very long time.

We have to ask ourselves the ultimate question having to do with the Civil War. Was it worth it?

For the Northern soldier who died, and for his grieving wife or sweetheart, the answer was often, but not always, yes. Men and women of the 1860s had a rather different approach to life than we experience today; lacking the wonders of modern medicine, they viewed life as one continuously hazardous adventure. To claim that Billy Yank had died to save the Union and to free the slaves was enough for many to say he had not died in vain. For his children, perhaps the four that formed the statistical average of the time, the question could usually be affirmed in the positive. Our modern-day mindset recoils from the notion, but the great majority of orphaned children—and there were many—proudly spoke of what their fathers had done.

For the Southern soldier who was wounded but lived to tell the tale, the answer was divided about half and half. To be sure, he was proud of his regiment and the burdens they had carried, but he mourned the loss of so many comrades and the collapse of the Southern cause, the dream of Southern freedom. It might be consoling to him to know that his great-great-grandchildren would re-enact his battles, and that people would visit his grave on Memorial Day.

For the black soldier who saw the worst that war had to offer, and who then returned to civilian life, the realities of life were, perhaps, the cruelest. Many a person who proudly carried a rifle and fought under the Star-Spangled Banner later had to sweat away his days on a ruined plantation, where the master awarded him a share of the crop. Even so, we do not imagine that he regretted his experience: only that he lamented the after effect.

The men, women, and children of 1861 were much older in 1865. They had lived, in four years, through events that might have, in more normal times, required the transit of twenty. Many of them continued to revere the events of 1776, but they had to know that the maelstrom that they had endured was at least as great as that faced by the founding fathers.

By 1865 the American landscape and the American character had been remade. The people that Alexis de Tocqueville had described as footloose and unmilitary had become the grimmest, most formidable of "stayers." The concept of total war had been stamped into the American character, as the nation's twentieth-century foes would learn to their dismay. Along with the tragedies and the hyper-militarism came something else: a new "birth of freedom" that would echo around the world.

The great crisis of 1861 brought an invigorated patriotism, one that would endure for many years. No subsequent conflict until the Second World War would demand so much from so many Americans, and even that conflict would not claim so many American lives. There is a pathway, though, that can be seen by tracing the events of 1776 and 1861, as well as to 1941. In both of the latter cases, the generation believed it was taking action to fulfill what an earlier generation had not.

The American G.I. who fed candy to starving children in Belgium, Germany, and Japan, as well as the American businessman who attempted to introduce democratic capitalism in Czechoslovakia and Rumania, echoed the men in blue and the warriors in gray. They were all descendants of the great travail of 1861, which was itself descended from the great struggle of 1776.

AMERICA IN THE 1850s

1850

What was life in the United States like in 1850?

A decade prior to the Civil War, the nation looked much as it had throughout the nineteenth century: a land of sprawling landscape, increasing population, and vast opportunity. Of course the opportunities were more evident if a person was white, male, and Protestant.

In 1850, the majority of white Americans considered themselves especially blessed by Providence. They knew that their nation was more peaceful and prosperous than many. The average white American could end up, at the end of his or her lifetime, with a great deal of land, the most commonly agreed-upon measure of wealth. Of course there were hazards on the way to that status. Many Americans died early deaths from cholera, typhus, smallpox, and yellow fever, but the same could be said of people in other nations. When they compared their lot to that of their neighbors, Americans were especially confident that they lived in the best of all possible worlds. Very few Americans envied the Mexicans to the south, or the British-Canadians to the north.

What was the lifespan of the white American at this time?

It is much more difficult to say than, for example, the lifespan of an average person today. The reason for this is that there were several great "bars" or "hurdles" to cross on the way to a good old age. Quite a few Americans did make it to their seventies or eighties, but they had to make it past the childhood illnesses that came on at around the age of three. Assuming one made it through chickenpox, measles, and the like, there was another great time of hazard for women: the childbearing years. Even if a woman did not die while giving birth, she often succumbed to complications after the fact. But assuming that she made it past that barrier, the next big one was the time of accidents, trips, and

1

falls. These were especially prevalent in the lives of men, and the risk was compounded by how much "frontier life" they were exposed to. Cutting down trees, sawing wood, building log-frame houses, not to mention fording streams and breaking in animals, all took their toll, and it was a rather rare person who made it to middle age without enduring real wounds and accidents. One affliction that befalls modern-day Americans was not very prevalent in their time: heart attacks. The vigorous labor they performed, plus the relatively clean food they ate, kept heart attacks at bay. High blood pressure and strokes were another matter, however: many Americans were felled by what was at that time called a "fit of apoplexy."

What did the American family look like in 1850?

This question is more difficult to answer numerically and statistically because the census takers were much more interested in individual and national statistics than family ones. We can, however, take a stab at it by turning to the anecdotal record, in this case the words of Alexis de Tocqueville.

"In America, the family, in the Roman and aristocratic signification of the word, does not exist," de Tocqueville began. "All that remains of it are a few vestiges in the first years of childhood, when the father exercises, without opposition, that absolute domestic authority, which the feebleness of his children renders necessary.... As soon as the young American approaches manhood, the ties of filial obedience are relaxed day by day: master of his thoughts, he is soon master of his conduct. In America, there is, strictly speaking, no adolescence: at the close of boyhood the man appears, and begins to trace out his own path."

How much credence can we give to de Tocqueville on this and other observations?

Like any observer, de Tocqueville was mistaken on some things; unlike most observers, he was a careful witness of all that he saw. Literally thousands of American historians, philosophers, and sociologists have spent extended time with his writing, and they have, perhaps, required millions of their students to do the same. And so, while we would not wish to accept everything de Tocqueville says without considering it for ourselves, the balance inclines us to favor many of his observations.

Alexis de Tocqueville (1805–1859) was a French historian, political thinker, and author of *Democracy in America*.

What de Tocqueville meant was that conditions in American society allowed far greater freedom to the young man than to his counterparts in Europe. The reason can be quickly found: the availability of cheap land. Given that, the twenty-year-old man could quickly establish a new homestead and start a new family. Exceptions to the rule always exist, however, and we will soon see how the many sons of John Brown remained deeply loyal—almost to an extreme—long after they had passed the boundary into maturity.

What did de Tocqueville say about girls and women?

His observations on the American female are one of the most sympathetic, and touching, of all his writings. As de Tocqueville saw it, the young American girl—somewhere between the ages of eight and sixteen—enjoyed more freedom and joy than the girls of any other nation. The American girl performed her household chores without complaint, and when the work was done, she went for long picnics, horseback rides, or walks in the woods, and all these she performed without fear of being molested. All this changed on the day of her wedding, however.

From the moment she married, the American female became burdened with a hundred different tasks, most of which never seemed to be done. She knitted, sewed, cooked, cleaned, cared for her husband and children in all manner of ways, and never seemed to have a moment for herself. Even so, she seemed—to de Tocqueville—to be content, knowing her value and worth. He concludes his chapter on the subject with these lines: "If I were asked, now that I am drawing to the close of this work, in which I have spoken of so many important things done by the Americans, to what the singular prosperity and growing strength of that people ought mainly to be attributed, I should reply—to the superiority of their women."

What did the nation look like in terms of boundaries and geography in 1850?

The United States had just increased its size by a full quarter. The War with Mexico cost the United States rather little and brought it rich rewards. In return for a sixteen-month conflict that indicated the prowess of American arms, the United States gained California, New Mexico, Arizona, and much of what is now Utah. The acquisition of these territories seemed like an unmitigated blessing, but it also opened the door to a renewed debate on the merits and demerits of the institution of slavery.

Why did it take so long for Americans to get around to a full-scale debate on slavery?

Many Americans hid their heads in the sand where slavery was concerned. Its presence had long been an embarrassment to those who claimed the young republic was the freest place in the world; it had long been a source of discomfort to white Southerners, who rejected the notion that slavery was evil, but admitted it presented complex problems. Foreigners, generally, were able to see into the debate more skillfully than those who were caught up in its heat, but even they sometimes shrugged their shoulders, saying that this was an American problem that required an American solution.

A newspaper notice announcing the sale of five black slaves. Such ads in classified sections of newspapers were common.

As late as the autumn of 1849, there were still plenty of Americans who found a way not to talk about slavery, but the events of the winter of 1850 finally removed this possibility. In that winter, the Territory of California applied for statehood, and in a special election its voters confirmed that they wished to enter the Union as a free state, one where slavery was specifically and intentionally forbidden.

What was life in California like in 1850?

The territory that would soon become the Golden State was a rather wild place, where fortunes were made and lost in the blink of an eye or the turn of a hand at cards. The federal census of 1850 numbered 92,597 persons in California, the great majority of whom were recent immigrants, drawn there by the gold that had been found in the hills near Sacramento. That California would furnish the United States with riches was believed by most, because the territory possessed vast agricultural, as well as mining, resources.

Many Northerners feared that the slave-holding South would expand, reaching the Pacific Ocean, but the supremacy of the North, where transportation hubs were concerned, made all the difference. In the two years since gold was discovered, far more Northerners than Southerners had moved to California, a move made possible by the steamships that carried them to Panama, the mule trains that carried them over the Isthmus, then the other set of steamboats that took them up to California. To be sure, there were quite a few Southerners who had made this migration, but they were—for the most part—outnumbered.

What happened when California's bid for statehood reached Washington, D.C.?

As one might expect, there was a political firestorm. For many years, as much as three decades, there had been a rough equality between the Northern and Southern states, allowing for parity in the United States Senate. If California entered as a free state, that balance or equality would be destroyed, and there was no telling what the South might do.

Men and women of the South looked back two generations, to the time of Thomas Jefferson and James Madison, remembering when their political power exceeded that of the North. Four out of the first six presidents of the United States had come from the South, and there had been times when the South dominated Congress as well. This was clearly a thing of the past, however, as could be seen by anyone who examined the federal census of 1850.

What did the census of 1850 reveal about the difference between the North and the South?

The census of that year clearly indicated that the population of the Northern, free states was fast exceeding the rate of growth in the Southern slave states. This could have been predicted a decade earlier, but the tide of immigration had greatly increased, bringing many new persons to the cities of the North. Boston, Baltimore, Philadelphia, and Newport had all grown, but the big winner was clearly New York City. Not only was it already the most populous place in the nation, but it bid fair to outdistance all its rivals, to become *the* metropolis of the country.

The census of 1850 also indicated the strength of New York State as a whole. The Empire State—the term had already appeared—increased from a population of 2.4 million in 1840 to 3.1 million in 1850. Such growth had never before been seen. Other Northern states showed similar patterns of growth. Pennsylvania, for example, increased from 1.7 million persons in 1840 to 2.3 million in 1850. In terms of free population, but also of total population, the Northern states were clearly winning the race against the Southern ones.

SLAVERY AND SECTIONAL ANIMOSITY

Did people feel there was a race between the North and the South? Was there already that much competition?

There was. Americans, in 1850, were a deeply, profoundly sectional people. They tended to identify first with the state where they lived and then with the geographic section to

5

which that state belonged. This type of sectional thinking and identification had been around almost since the beginning of the republic, but it had truly accelerated since 1815, the year the War of 1812 ended. The conclusion of that conflict with Great Britain allowed Americans to expand in new directions, most of them westward. As they moved west, or did business with concerns in western areas, Americans attempted to bring the culture to which they belonged to new areas. For example, a Massachusetts man who moved to Illinois, and there were many who did, tended to bring his Northern, Yankee type of identity. And a South Carolina man who chanced to move all the way to Texas— as quite a few did—tended to bring his Palmetto State ideas and ideals with him. Perhaps because there was so much geographic mobility, Americans began talking about their "sections" of the nation as if by second nature.

How restless, or movement-oriented, were the Americans of 1850?

They were extremely restless. Fifteen years earlier, the astute Frenchman Alexis de Tocqueville noted that an American had no sooner finished the roof on his house before he tried to sell it, and that he had no sooner planted his garden than he wanted to hire other men to harvest the crops. There were, of course, some exceptions to the rule. A Bostonian often remained a Bostonian for life, and the same could be said for a resident of Charleston, South Carolina. But these cities, as interesting and evocative as they were, did not represent the fullness of the American experience, which was much better explained by a look at New York City and New Orleans.

If Manhattan demonstrated the restless energy of the immigrant from overseas, then New Orleans did the same for the immigrant from elsewhere in the nation. By 1850, New Orleans was very prosperous, thanks to the ever-increasing number of steamboats that plied the Ohio and Mississippi Rivers. No one predicted that New Orleans would overtake Manhattan in terms of population—the latter had a strong head start— but in terms of commercial energy, the two places had much in common.

One can clearly see that there was a difference between the North and the South. Was there also a perceived West?

Yes. When we examine the language and speech of the 1850s, it is clear that Americans thought of themselves as belonging to one of three sectional groups: the commercially inclined North, the agriculturally inclined South, and the West, which was a combination of these two impulses.

The West, as people defined it in 1850, started somewhere in the Buckeye State of Ohio and moved toward the setting sun, culminating somewhere in the state of Iowa. The population of all the states in this area—which we now label the Midwest—were surging, and the number of horses, cattle, and sheep were growing apace. Indiana, for example, went from a population of 686,000 in 1840 to one of 988,000 a decade later. And Illinois made truly exceptional progress, increasing from 476,000 in 1840 to 851,000. Anyone who spent time in the Western states during the 1850s decade noted the energy and willpower of their people.

Was there a center to the West?

Cincinnati, Louisville, Indianapolis, and Detroit all coveted the title, but things were headed in Chicago's direction. In 1860, the Windy City had 109,260 inhabitants and was already receiving the largest share of the agricultural wealth of the Western states.

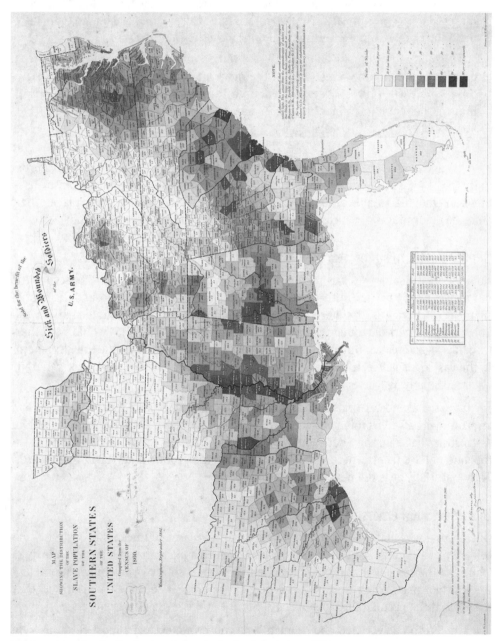

This map shows the the distribution of slaves in the South in the year 1861.

What would most of us today, if transplanted into the 1850s, feel about slavery and other matters of concern back then?

Given the power of social conformity, it is quite possible that many of us would view slavery as a bad thing, even a wicked one, but agree that it could not be removed by political means. The North, we might argue, *had* the power to make the South behave differently, but it did not have the right to do so.

Of course some of us would be out-and-out abolitionists, demanding that the peculiar institution be removed. But the more we conversed with people of that time, and learned how slavery had endured through three, almost four generations of the republic, we might be dissuaded from action.

Chicago benefited both from its position on the Great Lakes and its relative proximity to the Mississippi River. Then, too, it had ambitious and aggressive politicians—Stephen Douglas notable among them—who relentlessly promoted the place. Their outsized descriptions of Chicago may have led to its being named the "Windy" City.

Did the Southern states also have a "West"?

Not in quite the same way. The reason is that cotton—which had replaced tobacco as the number-one crop in the South—thrived especially well in the areas close to the Mississippi River. There was, therefore, less reason and less pressure to migrate farther west. Some Southerners did, of course, do so; the Lone Star State of Texas would not otherwise have been created. But Texas was the standout, the exception to the rule. Except for it, the vast areas between Virginia in the east and Louisiana in the west were generally regarded simply as "the South."

As to social and cultural aspects, it is difficult to say whether a Texas gunslinger was as prominent as a Virginia gentleman, or if a Georgia planter was the same as one in Arkansas. What held the South together, though, at least conceptually, was that it was the land of hard labor, where human hands broke the ground and reaped the rewards. That, naturally, begs the next question.

Did white Southerners regard slavery as morally wrong?

One naturally hesitates to make too strong a claim because of the possibility that other evidence will emerge. But for the most part, it seems plain that the large majority of white Southerners did not regard slavery either as an absolute wrong or as a moral failure on their part. When white Southerners spoke of their "peculiar institution," they meant that the peculiar circumstances of Southern life made slavery necessary.

The South had very few abolitionists, and those who existed almost certainly kept their mouths shut. At the same time, the South had a great many people whose lives were not connected to the institution of slavery; only 350,000 of 1.3 million families owned any slaves whatsoever. These two numbers naturally make it seem as if slavery stood on a narrow platform, and that most white Southerners did not have a reason to fight for it. Yet, oddly enough, many white Southerners would, indeed, fight for an institution that brought them no special benefit.

Did white Northerners regard slavery as morally wrong or the South as morally degenerate?

As late as the year 1850, most white Northerners were willing to let white Southerners do what they wanted with their peculiar institution. Was it really the right of the North to tell the South what to do? Most Northerners would argue that it was not. There was a small but growing number of people in the North that accused the South of moral degeneracy, however, and this number would only increase during the decade to come.

Moral degeneracy is not quite the same as evil or absolute wrong. White Northerners often accused their Southern cousins—an expression of speech—of having degenerated over the previous two generations. There had been a time when it seemed that the white Southerners would voluntarily free, or manumit, their slaves, but that day was long past, and it seemed—to men and women of the North—that the South was less conscious of evil, sin, and wrongdoing than in the past.

THE COMPROMISE OF 1850

What happened with the proposal that California enter the Union?

Three great statesmen of the republic rose in the Senate to deliver remarks on the subject. John C. Calhoun of South Carolina, Henry Clay of Kentucky, and Daniel Webster of Massachusetts were old, but they were the only persons who had the moral and political stature to make powerful statements. Calhoun, who had become much more bitterly opposed to any form of federal intervention, warned the North to leave the South alone. Clay, who had long been seen as the great compromiser in the Congress, asked for his fellows to make one more arrangement. And Daniel Webster, whose

South Carolina Senator John C. Calhoun (1782–1850), a former U.S. vice president under John Quincy Adams and Andrew Jackson, as well as former secretary of war and secretary of state, vehemently opposed the Compromise of 1850.

constituents had loved him for many years, earned political disfavor in the North by arguing in favor of compromise.

Calhoun was ill when the debates began, and he died in March 1850, another mark of the passage of an era. All official business was suspended till his funeral was over; the congressmen then began debating once more. Despite the best efforts of Clay and Webster, the debates were deadlocked till a second death acted like the break of a logjam.

What role did President Taylor play in events before the Civil War?

President Zachary Taylor (1784–1850) was a Southern man, born and bred; he also owned slaves. Taylor was an ardent nationalist, however, a sentiment brought on by many years of service in the U.S. Army. Taylor showed great frustration with the political infighting, and at one point he threatened to use executive action to bring both California and New Mexico into the nation at the same time. And then, on July 9, 1850, Taylor died.

The timing was so mysterious—or fortuitous, depending on one's point of view—that Taylor's body was exhumed in 1991. At that time it was found that there had been no foul play; the worst that could be charged was that the president had eaten a bowl of bad fruit on the Fourth of July, perhaps helping to bring on his death. Taylor's place in the White House was taken by Vice President Millard Fillmore, who was more open to compromise. As a result, the Compromise of 1850 was hammered out in July and August, and the nation as a whole learned the news in September.

What did the Compromise of 1850 entail?

In several different pieces of legislation, shepherded through Congress by Henry Clay (1777–1852), the Compromise of 1850 attempted to settle the slave question for once and for all.

California was admitted as the thirty-first state of the Union. California entered as a free state, in which slavery was expressly forbidden. The slave trade in the District of Columbia was abolished (slavery itself was not). It had long been a source of embarrassment that men and women were bought and sold within a few blocks of the White House and the Capitol. New Mexico and Utah were organized as territories, and it was agreed that when they were ready for statehood, the people of those territories would exercise popular sovereignty, meaning they would vote whether to enter as slave or free states. Finally, perhaps most importantly, a new, much tougher Fugitive Slave Law was written.

How was the Compromise of 1850 received?

With enthusiasm and rejoicing. North and South, East and West, Americans believed that this set of congressional actions would settle, perhaps bury, the slave question for good. There were fireworks in some cities and towns, and parties in which Northern and Southern men and women congratulated each other for having saved the republic. Almost everyone agreed that the question of California's admittance had brought about a serious crisis *and* that Congress had risen to the occasion.

The only people who seemed displeased or unhappy were the abolitionists, and even in 1850 it was difficult to say how many of them there were. Longtime leaders of the abolition movement like William Lloyd Garrison and newer members, such as Frederick Douglass, warned their listeners and readers that no compromise, however clever, could ever end the problem of slavery. It was a moral question and could only be settled when the institution was destroyed. As to *how* it might be destroyed, the abolitionists differed among themselves.

Was there any chance that the Compromise of 1850 could have worked?

No. Northern and Southern persons of good will deceived themselves, hoping that the differences could be papered, or smoothed over. In fact, the difference between two economies—one commercial and the other agricultural—and between two increasingly different societies—one heading in the direction of urban life, the other remaining rural—was difficult enough. Once one added slavery to the mixture, it became far too combustible for any compromise, however well designed, to prevent trouble.

Then, too, there was the matter of the rising slave population. There were, in 1850, about 3.4 million slaves in the United States, as well as about 400,000 free persons of color. If the slave population continued to grow at this rate, the Southern states might one day resemble the sugar-rich islands of Cuba and Jamaica.

What was the first sign that the Compromise of 1850 was headed for failure?

It came in the reaction of the abolitionist groups in the North. Never, they declared, would any member of their community join in a posse or other kind of group to seize and return fugitive slaves. The new Fugitive Slave Law, written by Congress, required Northern sheriffs and constables to assist the slave-catchers, but they would have no part of it.

Even these early statements inflamed the passions of some Southerners, who claimed that the Yankees—as they labeled the people of the North and the West—could never be trusted to fulfill their obligations. In the first two years following the Compromise of 1850, two cities became the standout places, or homes, for the hardliners. That Boston would be the home of many abolitionists was no surprise: this was the city of Lexington, Concord, and Bunker Hill. Boston also had a significant community of free persons of color and an increasing number of white residents who stood with them. That Charleston, South Carolina, would be the hardline city in the South was a little more surprising, but when one examines its position in the South, as the city that had received the largest number of enslaved Africans, the position of its people is more profoundly understood.

11

UNCLE TOM'S CABIN

Where was *Uncle Tom's Cabin* published?

As one might expect, the blockbuster novel of the decade, indeed of the nineteenth century, was published in Boston. On March 20, 1852, publisher John Jewett brought out 5,000 copies of the two-volume work *Uncle Tom's Cabin; or, Life among the Lowly*. Both he and the author feared all the copies would not sell, but 3,000 sold in the first week, and within the month subsequent printings and editions were ordered. *Uncle Tom's Cabin* was on its way to becoming the literary sensation of the era.

Written by Harriet Beecher Stowe (1811–1896) of Maine, *Uncle Tom's Cabin* depicted the lives of a handful of slaves as they moved through some of the "best" as well the some of the "worst" aspects of slave life. The overall effect was extremely powerful, combining the eye of the novelist with the skill of a researcher.

How was *Uncle Tom's Cabin* received?

The question can perhaps best be answered by quoting from the *New York Times*. The *Times* was not yet the premier American newspaper; it played a distant third to the *Herald Tribune* and the *New York Post*. But when it came to reporting the reception of *Uncle Tom's Cabin*, no one did better than the *New York Times*:

> "Have you seen it?" asked a neighbor the next morning after a late arrival from California.
>
> "No," was our reply, "but have you!"
>
> "Yes, I was up last night, and read the first volume."
>
> "Where did you get it?"
>
> "I must not say, twenty-five names are now on the list."
>
> "We concluded there was no chance for us until the next arrival, if this copy must be thumbed by twenty-five readers."

How many people had their minds changed by *Uncle Tom's Cabin*?

There were no opinion polls in 1852, and anecdotal evidence is generally considered less than reliable, but it seems possible that

Harriet Beecher Stowe was the author of *Uncle Tom's Cabin*, which vividly portrayed the plight of slaves in the South. Some even believe her novel helped spark the war.

How did Harriet Beecher Stowe become the most famous woman of her time?

Born in Connecticut in 1811, Harriet Beecher was the daughter of the nation's most prominent Protestant minister, Lyman Beecher. Not surprisingly, all of her brothers became men of the cloth. And when it came time to marry, Harriet Beecher joined hands with Calvin Stowe, yet another Protestant minister.

The couple lived for a time in Ohio, where they came to know people escaping along the Underground Railroad. Harriet Beecher Stowe interviewed a number of escaped slaves and compiled the nucleus of what later became her novel. The turning point came, however, when she learned of the new Fugitive Slave Law, enacted by Congress. This persuaded her to seek the publication of her work. It was first published in serial form by a magazine in Washington, D.C., then brought out by the Boston publisher John Jewett. It is no exaggeration to say that American literature was never the same again. Mrs. Stowe certainly had her critics; they claimed she sensationalized her material, but on the other hand they accused her of being a dry journalist. Literary style was never the strongest element of *Uncle Tom's Cabin*; rather, it was the moral tone that paved the way to its success. Within a few years of its publication, Harriet Beecher Stowe was known all over the transatlantic world; when Lincoln first met her, he is said to have exclaimed: "So you're the woman who wrote the book that started this great big war!"

half a million people in the Northern states had their minds altered by the book. Roughly 300,000 copies were sold that first year, and for every person who read the book, there were probably two others who heard it in oral form.

Harriet Beecher Stowe was a novelist, not a reporter, but her words struck a chord with her Northern readers. The book spilled over international boundaries and was read by many English men and women, especially those from working-class origins. When Stowe later toured Europe, she found her reputation already made; among those who entertained her were British Prime Minister Lord Palmerston and the well-known author Charles Dickens.

1854

If 1852 was the "year of the book," then why is the year 1854 so well known?

Two reasons why 1854 became so well known in the annals of the Civil War are as follows. The first has to do with a piece of legislation; the second has to do with an escaped slave.

In January 1854, Senator Stephen Douglas of Illinois brought the so-called Kansas-Nebraska Act to the congressional floor. Born in rural Vermont, Douglas had gone West at an early age, and by 1854 he was the single most-important booster for the City of Chicago and the State of Illinois. Douglas' desire was to ensure that whenever a transcontinental railroad was built (people already discussed the possibility) it would be routed through Chicago, leading to a great increase of prosperity for the Windy City. Toward that end, Douglas was willing to make all sorts of sacrifices, including the concepts under which the Missouri Compromise of 1820 had been made. Although that congressional action asserted that slavery would never exist north of the line of 36 degrees and 30 minutes north latitude, Douglas brought his new bill, under which the people of the Kansas and Nebraska territories would later employ popular sovereignty to decide whether to enter the Union as free or slave states.

Illinois' Senator Stephen A. Douglas (1813–1861) proposed the Kansas-Nebraska Act, which would effectively make the Missouri Compromise outdated. Many historians regard the passage of the Act as a major factor in leading the country into war.

How was Stephen Douglas' bold proposal for the Kansas-Nebraska Act received?

Almost everyone in Congress—the House and the Senate—recognized the implications of the Kansas-Nebraska Act. If it passed, and its provisions became law, the Missouri Compromise would be outdated, and there was a possibility—however slim—that slavery would come to dominate in the eventual states of Kansas and Nebraska. Many historians believe that the introduction of the Kansas-Nebraska Act was the single most-explosive event that helped bring on the Civil War; even if they are mistaken, no doubt exists that it was one of the most important.

Neither the House nor the Senate wished to rush this bill through, and President Franklin Pierce (see sidebar) was cautiously in favor. As a result, the Kansas-Nebraska Act moved with glacierlike slowness, and it was not until the fourth week of May that it was passed by both Houses. In that same week occurred the other major event that insured 1854 would long be remembered.

Who was Anthony Burns?

Born in Virginia in 1834, Anthony Burns was the youngest of eleven slaves born to his master's slave mistress. Burns' early life was no picnic—to say the least—but he does not appear to have been singled out for any especially negative treatment. In the winter of 1853, Burns escaped slavery and made his way to Boston, where he began working any number of odd jobs to survive. It was there, in Boston, that he was apprehended by a slave catcher on May 25, 1854.

A handbill went around Boston the next day with the words "A MAN WAS STOLEN LAST NIGHT" on its masthead. Thanks both to Harriet Beecher Stowe's novel and to the terms of the Fugitive Slave Law, Boston had been on edge for some time. The arrest of Anthony Burns proved to be the explosion that set off the powder keg.

How could the incarceration or freedom of one man, Anthony Burns, make such a difference in the abolition debate?

We naturally ask this question because we are aware that 3.5 million of Burns' compatriots were still enslaved. But to the abolitionists of Boston, and their growing list of supporters, Burns was not a number: he was the manifestation of an evil that was right in front of them. Most Bostonians had not seen the plantations of the South;

Born a slave in Maryland, Anthony Burns fled north to Boston in 1853, where he was arrested a year later under the Fugitive Slave Act. Tried and sent back to his owners, Burns' court case caused protest riots in Boston.

in Anthony Burns, they saw a cause they could rally around. Therefore, when Burns had his trial, he was defended by none other than Richard Henry Dana Jr. (1815–1882), the man who had written the well-known *Two Years before the Mast* a decade earlier. Just as important, a crowd of several thousand Bostonians gathered outside the courtroom, hoping to influence the result.

What eventually happened to Anthony Burns and his defenders?

A tragedy occurred when several dozen Bostonians attempted to break in to the lockup and free Burns. In the excitement of the moment, they killed a man who was serving as a volunteer for those who defended the jail. He quickly became a martyr for the cause of law and order, and Burns' defenders began losing their popularity. Even so, three regiments of Boston militia and Regular U.S. Army soldiers were required to get Burns down the street to a steamer that took him to a Virginia ship off the coast. Days later, Burns was back in slavery in Virginia, and the affair, as it was called, appeared to be over.

Burns' slavemaster soon found that a man who had tasted freedom made a rather poor worker on being returned to slavery, and he put him up for sale. The $1,300 price

15

What was a dough-faced Democrat?

The expression was coined sometime in the 1850s and applied to politicians like President Franklin Pierce (in office 1853–1857) and President James C. Buchanan (in office 1857–1861). A dough-faced Democrat was a party regular who came from the North, but who favored the politics of the South.

Franklin Pierce did not fit the bill entirely, but he was a Northern man who believed that compromise was essential to holding the Union together, and if he had to accommodate the South on the slave issue, then so be it. Pierce sent quite a few federal troops to Boston to make sure that Anthony Burns was returned to slavery. James C. Buchanan, elected president in 1856, fit the stereotype much more closely than his predecessor. Throughout a distinguished, sometimes even brilliant, career in diplomacy and administration, Buchanan had made a point of befriending the Southern states. When he was inaugurated in 1857, Buchanan continued that trend and eventually became known as the worst president of his time (some historians believe he has been maligned). Even though "dough-faced Democrat" was a rather silly expression, "black Republican," which emerged a few years later, was even worse.

was soon raised by a group of Bostonians, and Burns became a free man. While he showed gratitude to those who had released him, Burns was not eager to return to Boston; he found both its climate and its people rather chilly. He moved to Ohio and studied at Oberlin College before moving to Canada just before the Civil War began. Burns died in Ontario in 1863.

Why do historians generally consider the Anthony Burns affair a turning point?

Until May 1854, many Northern men and women were opposed to slavery in the abstract, without having witnessed any of its effects. After June 1854, the month when Burns was returned to Virginia, a significant number, perhaps even a majority of well-bred Northern men and women, began to speak about what "must" one day happen. If a man could be "stolen" from the streets of Boston and sent to slavery, even worse things might occur. Therefore, the abolitionist cause began to gain ground in Boston and in the neighboring countryside. The best evidence for this is the anger, then the hatred that many Southerners declared for the "damn Yankees" who thought they knew more about the slaves than the people who possessed them.

On its own, the Anthony Burns case was not sufficient to turn the tide, and the Bostonians might eventually have forgotten. But when coupled with the Kansas-Nebraska Act, signed by President Pierce in the same week that Burns was incarcerated, this was enough to bring many Northerners to a new appreciation of just how malicious the so-called "Slave Power" was.

What did Northerners mean when they used the expression the "Slave Power"?

To the historian, the Southern states in the 1850s look beleaguered. Their population growth lagged behind that of the North, and their percentage of the national wealth was slipping. But to Northerners, the South of the mid-1850s looked big and powerful, with possibilities for its becoming even mightier. From this fear came the idea of the Slave Power.

There were, it is true, some Southerners who believed that the production of cotton, with the attendant use of slaves, was an unstoppable thing; these men said that the South should expand into the Caribbean and even the northern part of South America in order to ensure its success. The average white Southerner had no such thoughts; to him, it was sufficient to run his farm and keep his slaves in line. But white Northerners began to develop the idea that the "Slave Power" was on the rise and that it had corrupted many levels of the U.S. government, including the executive branch.

1855 THROUGH 1858
AND JOHN BROWN

What was the state of the nation—to employ a twenty-first-century expression—in 1855?

The United States was in a curious, even odd, position. On one hand, the nation had never been so powerful or so prosperous. Sometime during the middle of the decade, foreign observers began looking on the United States with more respect and even a touch of fear. Anyone watching the population figures or the commercial exchanges could see the raw vitality of the Americans. But there was a flip side to the equation.

Americans were anxious about the state of the Union, as opposed to the state of the nation. The two things may sound synonymous to us, but enough differences exist to make it worthwhile to examine them. A nation takes a long time to be formed (ask the Germans or Italians of the nineteenth century), while a political union can be more readily effected. The Union which many Americans looked upon as a rather sacred thing was really a fragile one, born of a number of compromises between the North and the South. When, therefore, one asked Americans of 1855 about the state of the nation, they usually answered the question in terms of the *Union*. And in that year, the Union seemed imperiled by the increased tension over the subject of slavery.

What was "bleeding" Kansas in 1855? Does it deserve the term "bleeding"?

Affairs in Kansas were heading in a negative direction, but it had not yet become the bloody battleground later described. The key fact, in 1855, was that the newly formed Territory of Kansas held its first election.

17

Given that Northern and Southern men alike saw Kansas as a potential battleground, it made sense that the former would win the race, if only because the North and the West now had so many people. But the territorial elections of 1855 went the Southern, pro-slavery way, thanks to a one-day invasion by men from Missouri. Called the Border Ruffians, these men galloped over the border into Kansas and voted illegally. As a result, the first territorial elections returned a pro-slavery governor and legislature, both of which were recognized as legitimate by President Franklin Pierce.

Was there anything else that President Pierce could have done for Kansas?

No. He could, perhaps, have called for a second election, but even that might have caused more troubles than it solved. Operating from a distance, President Pierce saw the potential for chaos in Kansas and decided to let a bad thing alone. What Pierce underestimated, however, was the willingness, even the eagerness, on the part of other Northern men to act.

Henry Ward Beecher, the brother of Harriet Beecher Stowe, was a well-regarded clergyman in Brooklyn, New York. Beecher claimed that the North and the West had to meet the threat by the South by all means available, and men who took him seriously soon packed six-shooters and rifles as they headed for Kansas (the weapons were labeled "Beecher's Bibles"). One of those men was John Brown.

THE EMERGENCE OF JOHN BROWN

Who was John Brown, and what had he accomplished up to this point in life?

Born in rural Connecticut, Brown (1800–1859) came from a deeply religious family that claimed descent from the early Puritans. He moved west with his family to Ohio at a young age and spent several years on the frontier, which was where he developed his lifetime loathing for the institution of slavery. At some time during the War of 1812 (we cannot be more precise) Brown saw a militia captain badly mistreat his black slave, who was about Brown's age. The scene was so ugly and violent that Brown became a lifetime opponent of slavery, even though he had little opportunity to fight it.

Brown's first wife died and he quickly remarried; between them, his wives bore him twenty children. Most of Brown's energy was spent tending to his large family, but sometime in the 1840s he took up the abolitionist cause with fervor, and when he first met Frederick Douglass in 1847, Brown proposed a plan for freeing the slaves.

How did Frederick Douglass become the best-known African American of his time?

Like Anthony Burns, Frederick Douglass (1818–1895) was born into slavery in Maryland, and like Burns, Douglass knew that his slavemaster was also his father. Douglass escaped slavery and made his way to Massachusetts, where he soon became the darling of abolitionist groups. Handsome, cultivated, and self-assured, Douglass defied many of the stereotypes concerning blacks, black men in particular.

By 1847, the year he met John Brown, Douglass was well known both for his fine speaking style and for his autobiography, which described slave life in considerable detail. Douglass now lived in Syracuse, New York, and was the editor of *The North Star,* one of the first publications run by an African American. If there was one person John Brown wished to persuade, it was Frederick Douglass.

What did John Brown propose to Frederick Douglass?

As they sat in the living room of Brown's home in Springfield, Massachusetts, Brown described to Douglass his plan for

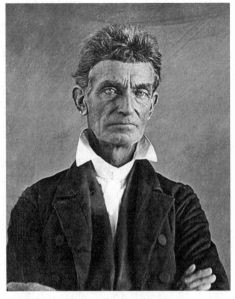

Stern-faced and clean-shaven John Brown was a noted abolitionist who believed only armed conflict could end slavery. He was active in "Bleeding Kansas" during the late 1850s.

freeing the slaves of Northern Virginia. He, naturally, wished to free all the others, too, but one had to begin somewhere. Brown showed Douglass a map of the Appalachian and Allegheny Mountains and claimed that the Almighty had placed those mountains there as a perfect place of refuge for escaped slaves. Using guerrilla-style tactics, Brown and perhaps one hundred men would help slaves escape plantations in Northern Virginia and bring them to the mountains, where they could hold off any and all enemies.

Douglass was dubious. Did it not make more sense to persuade the slaveholders that they participated in a failed system that would eventually perish, he asked. Brown, in Douglass' recollection, shook his head and said that he knew the heart of the slaveholders: they were too proud to accept that truth. They would have to be forced to yield their slaves, and he intended to make that happen.

Why had John Brown taken so long to get around to his project?

It was not from a lack of self-confidence or belief. Brown found it nearly impossible to launch anything during the early 1850s. Until he had the assistance, or at least moral support, of some prominent abolitionist such as Douglass or perhaps William Lloyd Garrison, he could not be heard on a larger stage. No such person came forward to assist Brown, and it was the trouble in Kansas, rather than anything special in Northern Virginia, that allowed him to take action. In the fall of 1855, Brown set out for the Kansas territory, taking several of his sons and a wagonload of repeating rifles with him.

Why did John Brown have so many nicknames and titles?

To look at him, one would think that one or two nicknames would be sufficient. Five feet ten inches tall, Brown looked taller because of his ramrod-straight posture. He did not yet possess the full gray beard that later made him so recognizable, but his features were so stern and plain that one can imagine the men calling him "Old" John Brown as well as "Captain." These were but the beginning of a slew of titles and nicknames that would be bestowed upon him.

The "why" can only be answered by saying that Brown was a complex person who presented different aspects of himself to different people. He liked to present the no-nonsense Yankee appearance, but there was the feel of a Romantic-era hero about him as well. And though he quoted the Bible more than Shakespeare, Brown was clearly a literate person in the powerful sense of the word: he could use words to great effect.

Did Brown start the troubles in Kansas all on his own?

John Brown was that kind of messianic believer, but even he could not pull that off. Instead, Brown just happened to be in the Kansas Territory at a propitious time, one when the fight between pro-slavery men and abolitionists was picking up speed. By the spring of 1856, there were two governments in the Kansas Territory: a pro-slavery government based at Lecompton and a Free-Soil government based at Lawrence. Recognizing the potential for deadly conflict, Brown organized a militia company at his home, twenty miles out of Lawrence. He became "Captain" John Brown to them, one of his ever-increasing list of names.

What happened in Lawrence, Kansas?

On May 21, 1856, a large group of pro-slavery men rode in and sacked Lawrence, the Free-Soil capital of the Kansas Territory. The pro-slavery men especially had it in for the *Lawrence Telegraph*, the Free-Soil newspaper: they set fire to the building and destroyed the printing press. Brown, as it turned out, was not far away.

On learning that Lawrence was under attack, Brown mustered his militia company and marched. He did not reach Lawrence in time, and his men were demoralized to learn that the town had been sacked. Brown had some trouble holding them together until they learned that an attack of another kind had been made, and this one was committed in broad daylight, in the United States Senate.

Who was Charles Sumner?

Born in Massachusetts in 1811, Charles Sumner was the junior senator from that state (he occupied the seat formerly held by the renowned orator Daniel Webster). From his debut, he showed himself an enemy to the institution of slavery. An ardent abolitionist, Sumner was horrified by the events in Kansas, and even before he knew that Lawrence had been attacked, he rose in the Senate to make a condemnatory speech. Titled "The Crime against Kansas," Sumner's speech made some *ad hominem* attacks against Senator Andrew Butler of South Carolina, who was not present to defend himself. Sumner truly went over the line when he suggested that this senator, as well as many other Southern gentlemen, was more interested in having sex with his slaves than with the well-being of black people in general.

Very likely, Sumner knew he had crossed a line, but he was a *Northern* gentleman, and to him the worst that could be expected was that he would be pilloried in the newspapers. Like William Lloyd Garrison and other abolitionists, Sumner was willing to endure that kind of attack. He did not expect the purely physical one that came his way on May 22, 1856.

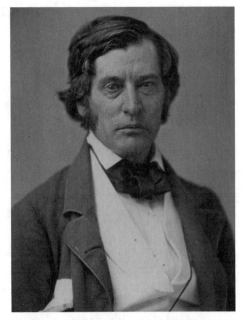

Senator Charles Sumner (1811–1874) of Massachusetts was strongly opposed to slavery. His *ad hominem* attack against Southerners, particularly Senator Andrew Butler of South Carolina, drew such outrage from Butler's relative Preston Brooks that he beat Sumner senseless with his cane.

Who was Preston Brooks and what did he do?

Preston Brooks (1819–1857) was a twenty-eight-year-old member of the U.S. House of Representatives and a nephew of Senator Butler. On the afternoon of May 22, 1856, Preston Brooks strolled into the Senate chamber and spied Charles Sumner at his desk, presumably writing the text of his next speech. Official business was over for the day, and only two dozen persons were in the chamber; they were mostly over to the left, about thirty feet away from where the action was about to begin.

Brooks approached Sumner and attempted to speak, but the New England man merely looked up and told him to go away (very likely, he did not realize Brooks was Butler's kinsman). Brooks then patiently explained that he was a Southern gentleman, and where he came from *ad hominem* attacks were not allowed to go unpunished. Thoroughly irritated, Sumner repeated his demand to go away. That was the moment when Brooks raised his cane and began beating Sumner on the head.

Had there ever been a physical attack like this before in the House or Senate?

Not in the U.S. Senate and not in the House of Representatives. This attack was something quite unprecedented. Perhaps that is why the dozen-odd persons in the chamber

21

did nothing to help Sumner; they watched with horror as Brooks hit him on the head, time and again.

Sumner attempted to rise, but was prevented by the iron bolts that connected the writing desk to the floor. In a few minutes, he keeled over and fell to the floor, unconscious. No one precisely described how Preston Brooks looked, but one suspects that he straightened his suit, tucked his cane back under his arm, and strode away with a look of self-satisfaction.

What happened to Preston Brooks?

The better question might be: What happened *for* Preston Brooks? Over the next few months, he received hundreds of canes in the mail, many from distinguished Southerners. The implication was clear: hit the Yankees where it hurts.

No charges were ever brought against Brooks, who died of natural causes a year later (had he lived longer, charges might have been brought). Charles Sumner spent the next three years as a convalescent. His fellow Republicans intentionally left his Senate chair empty during all that time, a testament to how far sectional division had come. When he finally returned to the Senate, in 1859, Sumner was, not surprisingly, among the toughest of congressional leaders where the South was concerned.

How soon did the nation—and people like John Brown—learn of Preston Brooks' attack on Charles Sumner?

Just a decade earlier, it would have taken a week, perhaps even ten days, for the news to reach people in the Kansas Territory. That timetable had changed, dramatically, as the result of the overland telegraph.

Samuel F. B. Morse had perfected the telegraph, and the first message had flashed across the wires in 1844. Since then, the telegraph companies had spread their poles across much of the nation, and even people as "removed" or distant as John Brown learned the most important news in a matter of hours. Therefore, on May 23, 1856, Brown knew what had happened in Washington, D.C. He quickly made up his mind to have revenge.

Which of the many sectional aggressions did John Brown respond to?

This is difficult to say because Brown—at this point in life—did not always explain himself clearly or thoroughly. The Sack of Lawrence, on May 21, clearly influenced him, as did the attack on Charles Sumner. But when Brown was asked directly, he often replied that his action was in response to the death of five Free-Soil men killed in Kansas earlier that spring. Whatever combination of events pushed Brown to the brink, he went beyond all reason.

On the evening of May 24, 1856, Brown and several of his sons entered the pro-slavery settlement of Osawatomie, along the banks of the Pottawatomie Creek. Without warning, the Brown family members entered several households and removed five men, often with the screams of wives and children echoing as they departed. Bringing these men to the banks of the creek, Brown stood by while his sons hacked them to death with swords. Whether some or all of the men were killed by rifle fire before the sword hacking commenced remains open to dispute. Most accounts concur that Brown did not participate in the killings, but there is not—or was not—the slightest doubt that this action was his. He made it happen.

What was the response to the killings at Osawatomie?

The reaction was one of stunned horror, followed by widespread condemnation of John Brown and all his family. What made this Northern man, who had accomplished rather little in life save the creation of a large family, believe that he was an avenging angel? To Southerners, it was even worse; to them, Brown was a vicious demon. And in the weeks that followed, damning evidence turned up in all sorts of places. The Brown family legacy—a number of his ancestors

By 1859 John Brown had grown his distinctive beard and was about to launch an audacious attack on the arsenal at Harpers Ferry.

and relatives were judged insane—surfaced, and the pictorials—or caricatures—that were drawn depicted Brown as a snakelike individual, possessed by demons.

Like Preston Brooks—at whom many fingers could also be pointed—John Brown escaped trial. He was in the Kansas Territory, a place that now had two separate governments, each of which looked on the other as illegal. The pro-slavery government at Lecompton was, naturally, outraged, but Brown and his family were in Free-Soil territory and could claim that their area had been attacked with the Sack of Lawrence. The large majority of persons on the East Coast and in the South roundly condemned Brown, but some people in the West, and quite a few in Kansas, began to look on him as a kind of savior.

Who wrote the first commentary favorable to John Brown?

James Redpath was a Scottish journalist who had moved first to New York City and then to Kansas. Like most journalists, he was in search of a good story, and he found it in John Brown. About ten days after the Massacre at Pottawatomie, Redpath came across Brown and his men in the Kansas wilderness. They were perfectly aware of what they had done, and the possible consequences, but they were also jubilant over having struck the first blow against slavery in the Kansas Territory. Redpath quoted John Brown as follows:

This question cannot be answered with one hundred percent surety because so many people in so many places laid claim to the honor. What we can say for certain is that the Whig Party and the Know-Nothing Party had both evaporated by 1854, and there was a power vacuum in American politics. Many people in the Western states favored the new Free-Soil Party, but when it lost the presidential election of 1856, they turned their allegiance to the even newer Republican Party.

Perhaps it was in a Wisconsin log cabin on a cold winter night; then again, it may have been alongside a riverbed on a warm Ohio evening. What matters is that the Republicans—basing their political philosophy on the life of the early Republic—became a political force during the mid-1850s. They were not as adamantly antislavery as the Free-Soil men, at least not at first. But as they grew in number, the Republicans gained attention on the East Coast, and it was the combination of the two groups (Western farmers and Northern men of commerce) that made the party so formidable. Then, too, it helped that the party had stalwarts such as the rising Abraham Lincoln.

"I would rather have the small-pox, yellow fever, and cholera all together in my camp, than a man without principles. It is a mistake, sir, that our people make, when they think that bullies are the best fighter, or that they are the men fit to oppose these Southerners. Give me men of good principles, God-fearing men; men who respect themselves; and with a dozen of them, I will oppose any hundred such men as these Buford ruffians." Of course, a truly objective journalist would have inquired of Brown why men of such strong principles would carry out a massacre, but in times like Kansas 1856, some things were better left unsaid.

How did John Brown escape prison or a worse fate?

He was indicted in Kansas, but the sheriffs were loyal either to the Lecompton government or the Lawrence government. Brown easily skated between the two and left Kansas for a time. In 1858, he conducted a major cross-state raid into Missouri, where he freed a number of slaves and sewed terror among a number of plantation owners. Soon after that success, Brown grew a long gray beard as a disguise; this became one of his trademarks.

By 1858, Brown had earned a small host of nicknames. He was "Captain" John Brown to his militia. He was "Old" John Brown to poets. He was a legend in the making.

Who ran in the presidential election of 1856?

The 1856 election was a contest between the Democratic Party, led by James C. Buchanan, and the Republican Party, led by John C. Frémont (1813–1890). A more interesting contrast would have been difficult to find.

Born in Pennsylvania in 1791, James C. Buchanan had been in politics so long that he sometimes referred to himself as the "Old Public Functionary." He had been ambassador to France, to Russia, secretary of state, and a U.S. Senator for many terms. Buchanan was a "dough-faced" Democrat, meaning that though born and raised in the North, he often supported policies that favored the South.

Born in Savannah in 1813, John C. Frémont was the son of a French immigrant. Much of Frémont's career had been spent as the leader of federal exploratory expeditions in the Far West, and his name was known to many, if not most, Americans. Frémont was a political opportunist, but he was genuine enough on the subject of slavery: he was dead set against it.

Who won the presidential election of 1856?

James C. Buchanan won, but the contest was tougher than expected. It was a three-way race, between Buchanan and the Democrats, Frémont and the Republicans, and former President Millard Fillmore and the so-called American Party. Buchanan clearly won the election with 1.8 million popular votes to 1.3 for Frémont and 800,000 for Fillmore, but when one probes more deeply he or she finds a very divided electorate. In the "free" states, for example, Frémont won the most popular votes, and had he been on the ballot in all the "slave" states the result might have been different. In the entire slave-holding South, however, Frémont was on the ballot in only four states—Maryland, Delaware, Kentucky, and Virginia—and he won only a trifling vote in all of them combined.

That Buchanan and the Democrats had won was undeniable; that American politics was now severely fractured was equally impossible to deny. For the first time in the history of the republic, a party had been kept off the ballot in a large section of the nation, and the losers could—with some justification—claim to have been robbed. This was not all, however: a Supreme Court decision with major ramifications was about to be handed down.

THE DRED SCOTT DECISION AND ITS IMPACT

Who was Dred Scott?

He was, perhaps, the single best-known African American of the mid-nineteenth century. Born in slavery in Missouri, Dred Scott sued in federal court for his freedom, based on the fact that his master had taken him to other "free" states. Scott's master was a physician, and he had taken Scott to Illinois and Wisconsin. Given that these were free states, where slavery was expressly forbidden, Scott now sued. The case went all the way to the Supreme Court.

On March 4, 1857, James C. Buchanan was inaugurated as the fifteenth president of the United States. Buchanan had been tipped off, a day or two earlier, to the Dred Scott

25

Dred Scott was a slave who sued for his and his family's freedom when his owner took them all to Illinois and the Wisconsin Territory. But the U.S. Supreme Court, in *Dred Scott v. Sandford* (1857) ruled that slaves were not U.S. citizens and also ruled against Scott based on the Missouri Compromise.

decision, but he wisely said little about the case, referring only to the fact that the decision would soon be handed down. In his inaugural address, James C. Buchanan emphasized the nature of political compromise: it had, in fact, been the guiding motif of his long political career. Buchanan was a very savvy politician. One thing he did not realize was that men like himself, whose careers had commenced shortly after the War of 1812, were being replaced by those whose careers had risen out of the War with Mexico.

How did the Mexican War influence Americans of the 1850s?

The War with Mexico (1846–1848) was such a dramatic victory for the United States that it led many citizens to believe there was nothing their nation could not achieve. Even the Duke of Wellington, the victor over Napoleon at the Battle of Waterloo, freely confessed his opinion that General Winfield Scott was the greatest living soldier.

Politicians like Henry Clay, Daniel Webster, and John C. Calhoun witnessed the conclusion of the War with Mexico, but it was their last hurrah. Such men had either retired from Congress or were now in the grave. They were replaced by a more aggressively sectional group of men in Congress, persons such as Charles Sumner of Massachusetts and Louis T. Wigfall of Texas. Buoyed by their country's victory in the Mexican War, believing in Manifest Destiny, this new generation of politicians did not fully realize how dangerous their sectional politics were; if a new war were to commence, it would be fought between the sections of the young nation, rather than against a foreign foe.

THE SUPREME COURT DECIDES

Who was Roger Taney?

Born in 1777—the year that George Washington and the Continental Army went to Valley Forge to spend the winter—Roger Taney was a Maryland lawyer who became chief justice of the Supreme Court in 1836. He was nominated by Andrew Jackson.

Taney brought an intriguing mixture of qualities and qualifications to his work. He was born into a slave-holding family that profited handsomely from the "peculiar" institution, but he freed his slaves in his middle years. Though it was the Western man Andrew Jackson that brought him to the Supreme Court, Taney was really an East Coast aristocrat. He married a sister of Francis Scott Key, the man who wrote "The Star-Spangled Banner." By 1857, Taney had been Chief Justice for twenty-one years, and he had seen questions and agitations over the slave issue disturb the nation several times. Given his longevity and his perspective, it was likely that Taney would be able to render a more clear-eyed decision than almost any other jurist. Yet he fumbled completely.

What was the Supreme Court's decision in *Dred Scott v. Sandford*?

The physician who previously owned Dred Scott had passed away; the court case was therefore named for the plaintiff and for the heirs of the physician's estate.

Chief Justice Roger Taney read the lengthy decision aloud on March 6, 1857. The decision began with the ruling that Dred Scott was not a citizen of the United States and could not sue in federal court. This necessarily required some explanation. Taney went on to say that the founding fathers—those who established the nation in 1787—had never envisioned blacks as equals, much less citizens. There was no precedent for black persons being treated as social or political equals, and that type of discrimination (the word did not have the strictly pejorative feeling that it possesses today) allowed the Supreme Court to reject the plaintiff's suit. That should have been it.

Taney went further, much further, however. He went on to say that the rules under which the nation had been founded—the federal constitution—did not allow Congress to regulate slavery where it existed. Therefore, the congressional compromises that had been achieved by such lengthy debate and argument—such as the Missouri Compromise of 1820 and the so-called Great Compromise of 1850—were unconstitutional. *That* was unexpected.

Why did Chief Justice Taney go so far in the landmark decision?

The chief justice was not accustomed to explaining his decisions beyond what was handed down in the ruling. Roger Taney was not a diarist, either, and we moderns have to guess what influenced him in 1857.

Roger Taney was chief justice of the U.S. Supreme Court from 1836 to 1864, including presiding over the Dred Scott case.

Taney was from Maryland, a state that would play an outsized role throughout the Civil War, including the assassination of Abraham Lincoln. Taney may have believed he was striking a blow for his fellow Marylanders, but his keen jurist's mind should have enabled him to rise above such parochial concerns. Much more likely is that Taney saw himself as the last person on the scene from the time of the founding fathers and that he intended to speak on their behalf. This supposition on our part naturally begs a follow-up question.

Was Justice Taney correct in his assertion about the beliefs and attitudes of the founding fathers?

At the minimum, he was half correct, and he may have actually been closer to three-quarters. Almost none of the founding fathers, from what we see in their records, believed that blacks were, or would become, the equals of whites.

It is important, here, to draw a distinction between the *beliefs* and the *sympathies* of the founding fathers. Many of the founding fathers of the nation sympathized with black Africans. Many of them believed it was a terrible thing that people had been seized, brought to America, and enslaved. This is different from saying that blacks and whites would one day be equals, however. In the debates at the constitutional convention of 1787, which culminated in the writing of the federal constitution, many sympathetic expressions were made by highly literate, culturally sophisticated men. Almost none of them ever declared that blacks were citizens, however. Does this alter our perception of the founding fathers of our nation? It has the potential to do so.

How was the Dred Scott decision received?

In the Northern and Western states, it was received with the deepest gloom. In this one ruling, Chief Justice Taney appeared to open the way for slavery to reach every part of the Union. The Republican Party had been growing in strength, but the Dred Scott decision lifted its energy enormously. In the North, too, compromise political parties, such as the American party, received their death knell. The division between pro-slavery and Free-Soil beliefs had grown too large for compromise.

In the South, the Dred Scott decision was hailed as the best of all possible news. The South had felt under assault ever since the Pottawatomie Massacre by John Brown and his sons; now it appeared that the South was on the rise, or comeback. In between the North and the South, in the so-called Border States, the Dred Scott decision was generally considered bad news. The people of Maryland, Delaware, Kentucky, and Missouri rightly suspected that any future conflict between the North and the South would take place on their soil(s).

Who was James Henry Hammond?

Born in South Carolina, James Henry Hammond (1807–1864) was an unrepentant defender of the institution of slavery; indeed, on several occasions he declared that slav-

Who were the so-called "Fire-Eaters"?

James Hammond was a fine example of a political type: the aggressive, unrepentant Southern politician. Unlike many of his fellow Southerners, the Fire-Eaters did not apologize for slavery or its effects on the African American population. They claimed slavery was a positive good, because without it millions of African persons would have no exposure to Christianity or Western capitalism.

Men like James Hammond, Robert B. Rhett, and others went even further, however, declaring that they would perform the magician's trick of secession without war, akin to a circus performer sticking fire down his throat without being burned. This, they said, was possible because the Northern states needed cotton and peace, far more than the Southern states needed peace or Northern materials. Therefore, when the day of secession came, the Northerners would accept Southern secession, and two nations would emerge: one North and the other South. The latter would continue to sell cotton to the highest bidder and would outdo the North in material prosperity. The Fire-Eaters gave Southerners a bad name.

ery was not merely acceptable, but that it represented a positive good. Hammond had an unsavory personal history; in his diary he admitted both to a homosexual relationship and to his "familiarities and dalliances" with his four nieces, all in their teens.

On March 4, 1858, a year to the date since the inauguration of James C. Buchanan, Hammond rose in the U.S. Senate to deliver a speech subsequently known as "King Cotton." Hammond extolled the material and commercial success of the Southern states and ridiculed the holier-than-thou critics in the North. Northern men should be glad slavery existed, Hammond asserted, because the wealth produced by cotton fed their industries. He was, to be sure, not completely wrong. Rather, it was the emphasis of the speech that made some people—then and now—cringe. The most famous, or infamous, words were as follows: "No, you dare not make war on cotton. No power on earth dares to make war upon it. Cotton is king."

Was there any truth to the idea that "Cotton is king"?

At the time, quite a few people concurred that there was something to it. Cotton was so important to the economy of the United States, indeed of the transatlantic world, that it seemed possible foreign powers—the British and French, especially—would intervene to prevent any subjection of the Southern American states by the Northern ones. In retrospect, however, Hammond's claim runs up against the same troubles as the claims by today's Arab nations that the world could never live without Middle Eastern oil.

In both cases—the cotton of the Confederacy and the petroleum of the Arab nations—the initial claim looks impressive, but it overlooks the dynamic creativity of Western capitalism. If cotton could not be obtained from the Southern states, it would be obtained from somewhere else; if the Arab nations attempted to blackmail the Western powers, oil, or some other form of energy, would be found. Then, too, Hammond's bold claim overlooked the incredible prosperity that already existed in the Northern states.

ABRAHAM LINCOLN APPEARS ON THE SCENE

When did Abraham Lincoln appear on the political scene?

Born in Kentucky in 1809, Lincoln had moved to Indiana and then Illinois. A person of great ambition, he slowly worked his way up the ladder of life in the American West, becoming a store owner, a captain of militia, and eventually a successful attorney. His marriage to Mary Todd, who came from a prominent Kentucky family, undoubtedly assisted his rise, but some of the stories about the young Lincoln are true. He was honest to a fault and a friend for life.

Lincoln had served a term in the U.S. House of Representatives during the Mexican War, but he really rose to prominence as an astute, middle-of-the-road member of the new Republican Party. In 1858, he challenged Stephen A. Douglas, the author of the Kansas-Nebraska Act, for the open U.S. Senate seat from Illinois.

Why was this political match-up between Douglas and Lincoln given so much attention?

Douglas was a formidable politician: friends called him the "Little Giant." Lincoln was a relative newcomer, but between them, these two candidates indicated the strength of

the State of Illinois in particular and the Western states in general. People were already paying attention, but when Lincoln challenged Douglas to a set of debates, the observations increased.

The format was determined well in advance. The man who opened the debate did so with a one-hour speech. His opponent then had an hour and a half in which to respond, and the man who had started the whole thing was allowed a half-hour response to that rejoinder. This clearly was not a "sound-bite" type of debate; the issues could be explored in great detail. At the same time, politicians of that time knew how to "spin" a long argument and to fill time.

Lincoln's family home in Springfield, Illinois, is on the National Register of Historic Places.

Where were the Lincoln–Douglas debates held?

The first was held in Ottawa, Illinois (all the locations were in the state of Illinois), on August 21, 1858. Douglas led off that day; Lincoln had his one-and-a-half-hour rejoinder; and Douglas then concluded with his half-hour response.

The second debate was held at Freeport on August 27, 1858. This time it was Lincoln who opened, Douglas who made his rejoinder, and Lincoln who concluded with a half-hour response. The third debate was at Jonesboro on September 15, and this time Douglas opened. The fourth debate was at Charleston on September 18, and Lincoln opened. The fifth debate was at Galesburg on October 7; the sixth was at Quincy on October 13; and the seventh and final debate was held at Alton, on October 15, 1858.

What was the level, or style, of speechmaking at the Lincoln–Douglas debates?

There were moments and times when it was rather high, and times and moments when it was quite low. Neither man proved above the fray: each threw all sorts of pot-shots at the other.

There was an almost equal division of "high" and "low" moments, meaning that there were days and debates in which Lincoln was clearly better rested and more clear on the stump, and vice versa. Neither man really won great plaudits, because they were both playing a political game, and one that included increasingly high stakes. But on the whole, those who listened believed that Douglas was the "stronger" orator, who made his points more forcefully, and that Lincoln was the "sounder" one, using logic more effectively. Neither man achieved a high level of oratory during the debates. The long time frame meant that both had to employ rhetorical tricks just to make it through the three-hour debates.

What role did slavery play in the Lincoln–Douglas debates?

A much higher level than most people expected. Going into the debates, many people believed they would revolve primarily around taxation, railroad issues, and the growth and development of the State of Illinois. All of these matters were touched upon, sometimes at considerable length, but the issue of slavery reared its head time and again.

First, it is important to say that Lincoln was no abolitionist, not even a lukewarm one. Time and again during the debates and the election campaign, he declared his belief that slavery, while abhorrent on a personal level, was protected by the federal constitution. Another way of saying this is that there was no constitutional remedy for slavery, no way for the federal government or any other power to bring about its end. Douglas sometimes employed race-baiting, including taunting Lincoln on the subject of African American equality. Time and again, Lincoln asserted his belief that blacks were not equal to whites and that they might not be so for as long as a century into the future.

Why, then, do we so frequently think of Lincoln as the Great Emancipator?

Because he *became* that person and filled that role. In 1863, Lincoln would set over four million people free. But he arrived at that point through a long, sometimes convoluted,

31

process. If Lincoln was truthful in 1858—and many historians believe he was—then he was, at that time, a rather typical man from the Western states. He did not dislike black people, and he thought it a terrible thing that they were enslaved, but he had no black friends and no basis for comparison.

What were the election results in 1858?

The Republicans won more popular votes, but the state legislature, which made the final decision, decided for Douglas. Lincoln had lost again.

Tradition has it that Lincoln, the night he learned of his election defeat, tripped and almost fell while going home. The story also goes that Lincoln, who had been despondent, reminded himself that this was a small trip, and not a serious fall, and that the analogy regarding his political career might also be true. Whether this story is precisely true is less important than what it reveals about Lincoln: he was a powerful fighter and seldom gave up. He needed that quality because there had been plenty of failures earlier in life. He lost his first political election at the age of twenty-three; the store in which he worked had gone bankrupt.

Where did American politics stand at the beginning of 1859?

The political scene was neither happy nor hopeful. Ever since Preston Brooks' attack on Charles Sumner, members of the U.S. House and Senate had been apprehensive of a repeat. Some senators and congressmen even carried concealed weapons into the chambers.

There was acrimony on both sides of the aisle, with Republicans accusing Democrats of false policies and vice versa. President Buchanan was the only person with the power and authority to bring both parties to heel, but he was singularly ill-prepared for that role. During his long political career, Buchanan had proven adroit at subtle negotiations and persuasion: he was not adept at using raw political power. 1859 was, quite possibly, the year in which more Americans used words like "crisis," "danger," and "extremism" when referring to their politics and political leaders.

Where, meanwhile, was John Brown?

Little had been heard of John Brown for some time. In the aftermath of his successful raid into Missouri in 1858, Brown had gone underground, hiding in different places. The safest of his safe places was the settlement he had established at North Elba, New York, just a few miles shy of the Canadian border. There Brown had set up a small community of the extended Brown family and escaped slaves. In keeping with Brown's beliefs, the community was run on strictly egalitarian lines. Everyone worked and everyone ate together, with no special favors or treatment for anyone.

Brown could easily have remained at North Elba, allowing events to take their course, but he was still determined to have a larger impact on history. Toward that end, he went to Boston and neighboring Concord—the town where the Revolution had begun

Where did the American economy stand in 1859?

It was in reasonably good shape. There had been a sharp economic downturn in 1857, but things were improving throughout 1859. Cotton, not surprisingly, was the single biggest export, but there were all sorts of new businesses. One of the most successful of American products sold within the nation were pianos and piano-fortes. An advertisement in the *Evening Journal Almanac,* published in Albany, New York, lists elegant pianos, made by Boardman, Gray, and Company, for $150.

in 1775—seeking help from the well-to-do and famous. Brown was especially eager to recruit the assistance of the literary and cultural community in Concord, which included Ralph Waldo Emerson, Amos Bronson Alcott, and Henry David Thoreau. Virtually all of them listened to Brown's appeal, but none were ready to make a strong public stand. Frustrated and irritated, Brown departed Massachusetts, penning a sarcastic note to the latter-day descendants of the Puritans as he departed.

Wasn't Brown himself a Puritan?

He was indeed. Brown's strange and remarkable life pointed forward, to a new kind of America, but he also harkened backward, to earlier and more difficult times. Those who knew Brown best considered him a new type of Oliver Cromwell, the hero of the English Puritans during their Civil War in the 1640s: a stern, inflexible person who demanded that other people view the world with his set of eyes (as well as values).

After the rejection of Brown by the literary leaders of Massachusetts, Brown disappeared from sight for a while. His supporters in the North—who were rather small in number—knew only that the "Old Man," as they called him, had contracted with a weaponmaker to produce 1,500 pikes (shades of Oliver Cromwell!).

JOHN BROWN AND HARPERS FERRY

What was so important about Harpers Ferry?

In the first few years of the nation's history, President George Washington spoke with Secretary of War Henry Knox about the need for an independent arms establishment. To that point, all of America's rifles and muskets had either been made by private contractors or had been imported from overseas. Determined to change this state of affairs, Washington and Knox decided upon Springfield, Massachusetts, and Harpers Ferry, Virginia, as the places for the new federal arsenals.

The Springfield armory was established first: its location was chosen by the fact that enemy ships would not be able to pass the Connecticut River at that point. The Harpers Ferry location was established around 1797; its site was chosen for the abundance of

33

U.S. Marines surround Brown and his men at Harpers Ferry in this illustration from *Harper's Weekly* magazine.

fresh water running through and for the fact that arms manufactured there could quickly be distributed to the people of four states: Pennsylvania, Maryland, Delaware, and the District of Columbia. Thomas Jefferson penned a stirring essay on the physical location. "The passage of the Potomac [River] through the Blue Ridge [Mountains] is perhaps one of the most stupendous scenes in nature," he wrote. In 1850, the federal census indicated that there were 1,747 persons at Harpers Ferry, broken into 806 white males, 745 white females, fifty free black men, thirty-seven free black women, thirty-seven male slaves, and seventy-two female slaves.

How and why did John Brown decide upon Harpers Ferry?

The nucleus of his plan could be detected as early as 1847, the year in which he spoke to Frederick Douglass about the importance of the Appalachian and Allegheny Mountains (see page 19). The precise date or time at which Brown resolved upon a capture of Harpers Ferry is unknown, but it seems to have been sometime during the spring of 1859. Disappointed by the reception he got in New England, Brown decided on something bold, even revolutionary. He would arm and free the slaves, even if he had to do it all himself.

During the summer of 1859, Brown did some quiet recruiting in New York State, and toward the end of that summer he appeared in southern Maryland, where he rented the house of a man named Kennedy. Neighbors knew only that a man who called himself "Mr. Isaac Smith" appeared around the Fourth of July and that he had friends who visited on occasion. When "Isaac Smith" met locals, he was invariably polite, saying he had come to the region because of a lack of work in the North.

How many recruits did John Brown find?

Accounts vary, and not all men who volunteered eventually took part in the great revolt, but the number was no fewer than twenty and was perhaps no more than thirty. This was a very small group for so ambitious a plan, but Brown did not appear downcast. He was accustomed to tackling great goals with slender means.

The men came from various backgrounds and towns; what they shared was the belief that a blow against slavery must be struck. They did not delude themselves as to the hazardous nature of the task before them; then again, Brown did not reveal all of his plans. Clearly, it was his intention to arm the slaves, but as some people pointed out, the slaves had no training in the use of firearms. That was why Brown paid for and had 1,500 pikes, which could be used with a minimum of training, brought to his location on the Kennedy farm.

Where, meanwhile, was Frederick Douglass?

Twelve years had passed since he first met John Brown, and in that time Frederick Douglass had become even more successful and well known. He had never forgotten John Brown, of course, and when Brown sent an urgent message, asking to meet, Douglass left the relative safety of Syracuse, New York, and went to southern Pennsylvania. The plan was for him to meet John Brown at a point just on the Pennsylvania side of the Maryland border, where they could confer.

In the conversation—held along the side of the road—Brown asked, nearly begged, Douglass to join him. To have someone of Douglass' stature would enhance the rebellion, he said, and the slaves would flock to him. Douglass shook his head, saying that it was the slaveholders who would flock to Harpers Ferry and they would kill everyone, including Brown, who, he said, was walking into a "perfect steel-trap."

When Brown found he was unable to persuade Douglass to join him, he made ready to depart. A former black slave by the name of Shields Green had been listening. He decided to go with Brown, whose tiny force was now increased by one.

When did the raid on Harpers Ferry commence?

At 8 P.M. on October 16, 1859, Brown told his twenty-one accomplices, "Men, get on your arms, we will proceed to the Ferry."

Minutes later, the little band set out. They went two by two on their march to Harpers Ferry, and on arriving they found the gate guarded by only one man. He was astounded by their demands, and on his refusal, the accomplices simply climbed over the wall and took possession. On their way from the Kennedy farm, the accomplices had cut the telegraph wires; they did this so well that no messages got out for the next twenty-four hours. To this point all was going according to Brown's plan. He now sent out six men on a very special mission: their task was to capture George Washington's great-grandnephew.

Who was Lewis Washington, and why was he so important?

Forty-six-year-old Lewis Washington was a colonel in the Virginia state militia and a great-grandnephew of President George Washington. Lewis Washington had long known the importance of his family name, but it came to haunt him on the night of October 16–17, 1859. Here is how he described what happened (when questioned by a congressional investigative committee):

> I was in bed and asleep. As I opened the door there were four armed men with their guns drawn upon me just around me. Three had rifles and one a large revolver. The man having a revolver held in his left hand a large flambeau, which was burning. The person in command turned out to be Stevens. He asked me my name, and then referred to a man of the name of Cook, who had been at my house before, to know whether I was Colonel Washington. On being told that I was, he said, "You are our prisoner."

35

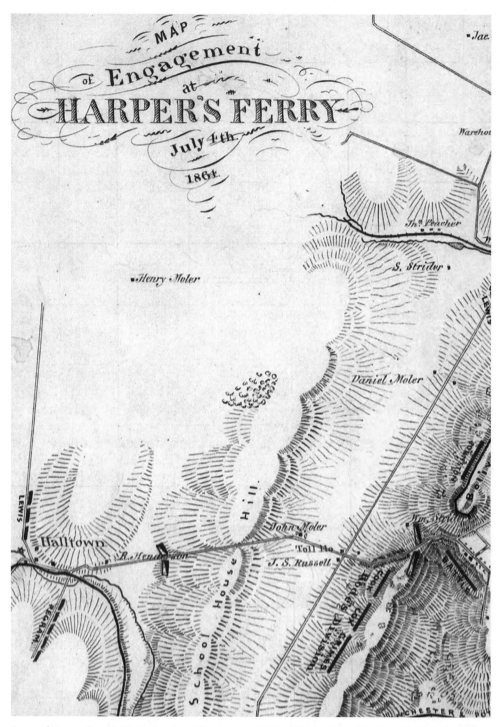

A map of Harpers Ferry in Virginia as drawn for a report of the 2nd Corps, Army of Northern Virginia. The federal arsenal is on the far right of the map on page 37.

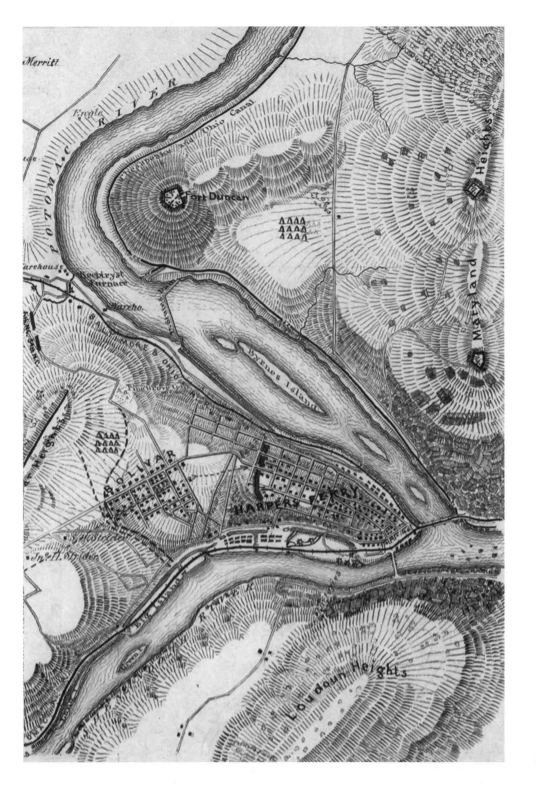

What did the accomplices do to, or with, Colonel Washington?

Astonished by the intrusion, Washington asked many questions, but received few answers. Soon, the men who had seized his house set free several of his slaves and brought Washington outside, saying they would take him to Harpers Ferry. Not knowing what John Brown had yet accomplished, Washington marveled at this, wondering how it would help their cause. But soon enough, they pushed him into his own carriage and headed for the Ferry (previous to this they had taken his sword).

On the way to the Ferry, Washington still continued to think that the whole thing might be a joke, but on arriving, he found that the gate was open and other accomplices were standing guard. The whole business was still strange to him, and it was only when they brought him in to meet John Brown that any of it began to make sense. Like many other people, Lewis Washington found John Brown, in person, both more compelling and sane than he was portrayed in the newspapers.

What did Brown say to Washington?

Washington was led into the engine-house of the federal armory, where Brown was waiting for him. Brown began the conversation by remarking that it was cool that morning (it was about 3 A.M.) and that Washington might enjoy a place by the fire. Brown then declared that he had taken great care to make sure Washington was his prisoner. As Lewis Washington later described it to an investigative committee, Brown said:

> I shall be very attentive to you, sir, for I may get the worst of it in my first encounter, and if so, your life is worth as much as mine. I shall be very particular to pay attention to you. My particular reason for taking you first was that, as the aid to the governor of Virginia, I knew you would endeavor to perform your duty, and perhaps you would have been a troublesome customer to me; and, apart from that, I wanted you particularly for the moral effect it would give our cause, having one of your name as a prisoner.

Did John Brown explain what was meant by "our cause"?

That was one of the first questions posed to Lewis Washington by the investigative committee. He replied that Brown was not very specific, saying only that "this thing must be put a stop to."

Of course, John Brown meant slavery.

LINCOLN'S ELECTION, SOUTHERN SECESSION: 1860 TO APRIL 1861

JOHN BROWN'S FAILURE

Was John Brown as important a figure as we sometimes hear? Or was he a delusional person who just happened to be in the right place at the right time?

That Brown has an aura of romance, even of godliness, about him cannot be denied. That he was "lucky" in some respects is also accurate. But there was very little that happened to him by way of accident. He was one of those truly self-determined individuals who make things happen.

What was so important about George Washington's sword?

Almost as soon as he arrived in John Brown's presence, Colonel Lewis Washington saw that Brown had taken his sword—which had once belonged to his famous relative—strapped to his body. Colonel Washington did not speak of the matter; very likely, he did not realize the importance that Brown attached to it.

Like the vast majority of Americans in 1859, Brown had a profound reverence for George Washington. Almost no American—North, South, East, or West—had anything bad to say about the founder of the nation. But in Brown's eyes, Washington's success had been incomplete. He had indeed created a nation based on the idea of freedom, but had not gone all the way to eradicating slavery. Therefore, one reason Brown specifically wanted Colonel Lewis Washington was for George Washington's sword. The idea was simple, but powerful. Brown would complete what Washington had left undone.

How successful was Brown on the night of October 16–17, 1859?

By any objective standard, Brown was sensationally successful that night. He and roughly twenty followers seized the arsenal at Harpers Ferry, cut the telegraph wires

39

north of that town, and took several hostages, the most important of whom was Colonel Lewis Washington. Brown and his followers accomplished all this without the loss of a single man. But just as everything went "right" that night, everything began to unravel.

Brown's biggest mistake was to allow the night train, of the Baltimore and Ohio Company, to pass through Harpers Ferry. There was a small gunfight as the train went through, and the conductor, thoroughly alarmed, used the telegraph further up the line to alert the authorities. Though Brown had done extremely well in his opening, he had not planned his follow-through very well.

The 1,500 pikes had been brought to the Kennedy farm, but not all of them could fit in the wagons that went to Harpers Ferry. Even so, Brown was all confidence on the morning of October 17, 1859. He did not know that large forces were being arrayed against him.

What was the response to Harpers Ferry in Washington, D.C.?

Thanks to the train conductor's swift telegraph message, the top officials in Washington, D.C., knew about the raid on Harpers Ferry by 9 A.M. Secretary of War John Floyd hurried to the White House for a discussion with President Buchanan; together, they decided that their action needed to be swift and furious. The only troops on hand, however, were a few companies of U.S. Marines. Then, too, they needed a leader.

The president and the secretary of war selected Lieutenant-Colonel Robert E. Lee (1807–1870) for the task and then went about their own, which included a good deal of damage control. One thing that they agreed on was that nerves and tempers in the North and the South were so jangled that the last thing anyone needed was news of a raid conducted by Northern abolitionists. Though the newspapers would surely obtain the story, Buchanan and Floyd did their best to downplay it.

Who was Robert E. Lee, and why was he chosen?

Born in Westmoreland County, Virginia, in 1807, Lee was fifty-two when he received the call to stamp out John Brown's rebellion. Lee came from one of the most distinguished families of the Virginia plantation aristocracy: the Lees had been active in Virginia politics for almost a century and a half. This does not necessarily mean that his road had been easy, however.

Robert E. Lee was one of the most admired of all Southern gentlemen when, in 1859, he was asked to quell the revolt at Harpers Ferry.

What was the Lee connection to George Washington?

Robert E. Lee came from the type of elegant Southern family that many of us sometimes daydream about. The lives of Lee and his relatives were filled with cocktail parties, long afternoon picnics, and lazy days of courtship. Of course, most of this idyllic scene was made possible by the possession of slaves who did all the heavy lifting.

Light Horse Harry Lee—the most famous Lee until the career of his son blossomed—was a friend of George Washington, and when the great Virginian died, Harry Lee gave the eulogy that remains famous in American consciousness even today. "First in war, first in peace, and first in the hearts of his countrymen," Lee said. The connection between the Lees and Washingtons was made stronger when Robert E. Lee married a step-granddaughter of the former president. Washington had no children, but his wife, Martha Custis Washington, had two from her previous marriage, and the line of Washington was therefore alive in Virginia. By marrying Mary Custis, Lee attached himself to the most famous name in America and obtained ownership of Arlington House, a magnificent plantation and its eighty-odd slaves. Throughout life, Robert E. Lee cherished the association with President Washington and did his best to emulate the great man.

Being the son of Henry "Light Horse Harry" Lee of Revolutionary fame had its benefits but also its hazards. Henry Lee had been important both during the Revolutionary War and as a friend and advisor to President George Washington, but Lee had fallen on hard times, financially and otherwise. He wasted most of the fortune he obtained through his second marriage, and he left the country in 1812, when his son Robert was only five years old. Though the family letters do not display it, one suspects that Robert E. Lee grew up with constant admonitions from his mother to the effect of: Don't be like your father!

When did Robert E. Lee arrive at Harpers Ferry?

Lee's home, Arlington House, was right across the Potomac from Washington, D.C. Even so, he had to make such haste that there was no time to change out of civilian clothing, and when he arrived at Harpers Ferry late that afternoon, Lee looked like any other middle-aged traveler, not the commander of a crack force of marines. Upon arriving, Lee expressed his desire to attack at once, but the local townspeople urged him to wait. They already had John Brown cornered, they said.

Since daybreak, there had been a number of slow-motion gunfights through the town. Alarmed and enraged, the people of Harpers Ferry rose up and engaged in rifle battles that they usually won, and by evening John Brown and his accomplices were cornered in the engine-house at the extreme east end of the federal arsenal. There was no

41

chance that Brown and his men could escape, Lee was told. Reluctantly, he agreed to wait until morning.

Who was J. E. B. Stuart, and what did he do with that handkerchief?

James Ewell Brown Stuart (1833–1864) later became the most famous of all Confederate cavalrymen, known for his magnificent reddish hair as well as his gallant cavalry charges and maneuvers. In 1859, however, Stuart was a twenty-six-year-old U.S. Army officer: he volunteered to serve as Robert E. Lee's aide. The two men knew each other from Stuart's West Point days, when Lee had been the superintendent of the academy.

J.E.B. Stuart was a U.S. Army lieutenant in 1859, but he soon rose to become the most flamboyant and beloved of Confederate generals. After many successes in reconnaissance and cavalry direction, he was killed at the Battle of Yellow Tavern in 1864.

Early on the morning of October 18, 1859, Lieutenant Stuart stepped out from the lines of the U.S. Marines carrying a white handkerchief, which he kept aloft as a sign of truce. Approaching the engine-house, Stuart was met by John Brown, who kept inside, and a short conversation took place. Stuart said that only an unconditional surrender would be accepted, to which Brown replied he was not ready to surrender under any terms. Seeing the futility of further talk, Stuart stepped back and away from the door, dropping his white handkerchief as he went. That was the sign for the attack.

What was the result of the attack on Harpers Ferry?

Six minutes later it was all over, and the wounded John Brown and several of his accomplices were dragged out onto the grass. Knocking down the double doors of the engine-house was hot work, but the marines accomplished it, and the local militia swarmed in. One officer met Brown and attacked him with his sword. The sword point broke, but Brown was wounded by a U.S. Marine who stabbed him twice with a bayonet.

Out on the grass, Brown and three or four survivors were interrogated by Colonel Lee, Lieutenant Stuart, and a group of civilian leaders. Time and again, the Virginians asked Brown why he would attempt such a bold, really insane, venture, and each time Brown either scorned to answer or gave a quick reply to the effect that the Almighty had directed him to do so. Lieutenant Stuart took Brown to task, saying that the Bible did not authorize this kind of violence, to which Brown replied that he had his own opinion on that score. The most significant part of the interrogation was when an anonymous person posed the following question:

"Brown," the questioner began, "suppose you had every [slave] in the United States, what would you do with them?"

"Set them free."

"Your intention was to carry them off and set them free?"

"Not at all."

"To set them free would sacrifice the life of every man in this community."

This was the heart of the matter. To Brown, setting the slaves free seemed like a wonderful thing, the culmination of a lifelong dream and the fulfillment of a biblical necessity. To the people who lived in and around Harpers Ferry, the idea of the slaves being freed was terrifying. They expected it would result in a massacre. By this point, the discussion had become moot, however. Practically no slaves had appeared at Harpers Ferry, and the 1,500 pikes had hardly been used.

Was there any chance that John Brown's raid could blow over and everyone forget about it?

Virtually none. The alarm went out so fast, and so many people were alerted, that it seemed—to the slaveholders of Virginia at least—that the day of judgment had come. When they learned that God's wrath was really represented by a rather old man and twenty-odd accomplices—many of whom were now dead—the desire for retribution made itself felt. Newspapers of the North and the South alike sensationalized the episode; the *New York Times* carried "Servile Insurrection" and "General Stampede of Slaves" on its title column. The nation was thoroughly alarmed.

Brown spent the next few days in a lock-up surrounded by dozens of Virginia militiamen. There was a general fear that a rescue attempt would be made, perhaps by some misguided abolitionists.

JOHN BROWN'S MARTYRDOM

What was the scene at John Brown's trial?

John Brown and five of his accomplices were tried in Charlestown, Virginia (today it is part of West Virginia). Under heavy guard, the defendants were brought to the courtroom and charged with treason against the Commonwealth of Virginia. There had been some question as to whether federal charges should be brought, but President Buchanan was pleased to have Virginia do the work.

The scene at the trial was intriguing and heart-rending at the same time. John Brown had never looked more "old" than when he appeared in court. The bayonet wounds he had received incapacitated him to the point that he spent much of the trial lying on a cot. One witness after another was produced to show Brown's guilt, but he showed little interest in the proceedings. At times, he appeared to nap.

What was the verdict in Brown's trial?

On the first of November, 1859, the judge sent the jury to consider the evidence. Less than forty-five minutes later, they returned with a verdict of guilty. Allowed some last words, Brown spoke eloquently about the need for social and racial justice in the United States. His mission was to free the slaves, he declared, and he would do it again if he had the chance. The Commonwealth of Virginia came off rather poorly during the trial; it looked as if all the power of the state and its officials was afraid of one old man.

Appeals for mercy began coming in from different parts of the country, but the Virginia judge, and those who advised him, were adamant. John Brown must die.

What was the next month like for Brown and his admirers?

Many people in the North expressed admiration for Brown's actions. Though some people still spoke of "Osawatomie" Brown and "Pottawatomie" Brown, the majority of voices were full of praise for this old man who had attempted to free the slaves. Southern newspapers responded in kind, blasting the abolitionists for granting praise to such a person.

For his part, Brown seemed to relish the attention, but not to need it. During the month between his trial and his execution, Brown often seemed like the coolest, most collected person in his situation. He befriended his jailer, received a visit from his wife, and seemed quite ready to die. This, plus the noble attitude during his trial, earned Brown the admiration of many people.

Was there, then, no scene with the black baby?

Millions of us have at one time or another heard the wonderful story of Brown kissing a black baby while being led from his jail. The story is almost certainly false. The state militia was drawn up tight as a drum, and virtually no civilians, much less black ones, were allowed anywhere near John Brown. For all that, however, the story remains with us.

How many people went to see Brown executed?

Something in the neighborhood of two thousand, but virtually none of them were casual onlookers. Fearing a rescue attempt would be made, the Commonwealth of Virginia had militia regiments from all over the state on the scene.

Brown was taken from his jail and led to a wagon on which there was a coffin (he rode on the coffin on the fifteen-minute ride). Arriving at the place for his execution, Brown exchanged heartfelt goodbyes with Captain John Avis, who had been his jailer. Brown handed Avis a note that read: "I, John Brown, am now quite certain that the crimes of this guilty land will never be purged away but with blood. I had, as I now think, vainly flattered myself that without very much blood shed, it might be done." Minutes later, Brown was led to the gallows and hanged.

The reason for the story's continuance is that John Brown would, very likely, have done that had the opportunity presented itself. It was very much in his character to do something that would confound his foes and astound his friends.

How did John Brown achieve immortality?

He had already done it by virtue of his heroic performance. But the legends surrounding John Brown had only begun to develop. Take, for example, the words that many of us sing: "John Brown's body lies a-mouldering in the grave, but his soul is marching on!" Yet how many of us know *where* his body lies?

Mary Day Brown, the widow, asked for her husband's body. She took it by train from Virginia to Manhattan and from there to Albany. Then the body was placed on a wagon and taken on a very difficult trip into the Adirondack Mountains, all the way to North Elba, New York. Brown was buried in a family plot in the community he had established a decade earlier. Then, too, there was the power of song.

When did "John Brown's Body" first appear?

People began singing songs about John Brown almost immediately after his death. There was something quite wonderful about this man's story, especially the way he courageously set out to accomplish what state and federal governments did not even attempt. To the best of our knowledge, the first time that the song or songs appeared in print was in the summer of 1861, when the New York *Tribune* published these words:

> John Brown's body lies a-mouldering in the grave;
> John Brown's body lies a-mouldering in the grave;
> John Brown's body lies a-mouldering in the grave;
> His soul's marching on!

Three other stanzas followed, with less edifying sentiments, such as hanging Jefferson Davis to a tree, but the fourth and last stanza says it all:

> Now, three rousing cheers for the Union;
> Now, three rousing cheers for the Union;
> Now, three rousing cheers for the Union;
> As we are marching on!

Was John Brown, then, really as important as we say in bringing on the war?

He certainly was. No one would claim that the Civil War would not have happened without him; there were plenty of other people and events that could have launched the war. But if John Brown had not carried out the raid on Harpers Ferry, and if he had not gone to his death in so noble a fashion, it is quite likely that the war would have been delayed. And the North—to be sure—would have lacked one of its best marching songs.

1860

What was the national scene like at the beginning of 1860?

There were prayer meetings in the North, with an emphasis on prayer for the Union. There were marches and protests in the South, with an emphasis on finding some way to cage the abolitionists. The *New York Times* used the expression "The Political Crisis" on Monday, January 2, the first time that newspaper used such words to describe the state of the nation.

Clearly, John Brown's raid had accomplished something. One might not applaud his action, but the nation felt like a rather different place than a year earlier.

What was the political scene in the winter of 1860?

As a new decade began, the American political scene was in the greatest disarray seen in many years. The Democrats had won the two previous national elections, but they were divided on many issues. The Whigs and the Know-Nothings were both spent forces, and the new Republican Party was seen as a strong contender. The difficulty for the Republicans was that they were not seen as a national party, but as a sectional one.

Perhaps unfairly, the Republicans were often called the "Black" Republicans, meaning they were favorable to the cause of abolition. This does not mean that Republicans always liked blacks, but rather suggests that they were against the institution of slavery. As 1860 dawned, it seemed likely that the career of William H. Seward (1801–1872) a U.S. senator and former New York State governor, would now hit its highest point. An outspoken opponent of slavery, Seward seemed like the right person to lead the Republicans. He was upstaged by Abraham Lincoln, however.

How did Lincoln make his first appearance in the East?

Many people knew the name of Abraham Lincoln because of the Lincoln–Douglas debates of 1858. Most people remembered that Lincoln lost that senatorial election, however, and some believed that his political career was over. Ever ambitious, always looking for the right moment and situation, Lincoln announced his candidacy for the Republican presidential nomination in 1860.

Lincoln faced numerous obstacles, but the single most difficult was to persuade men of the Republican Party establishment in the Eastern and Northern states to accept an essentially Western man for the nomination. Lincoln, therefore, accepted an invitation from Reverend Henry Ward Beecher—the brother of Harriet Beecher Stowe—to give a political speech at his church in Brooklyn, New York. When he arrived in Manhattan, Lincoln learned that the Republican Party leaders had changed the venue and that he was instead to speak at the Cooper Union Institute. Everything was made ready for the big speech, on February 22, 1860.

How important was photography to the Civil War?

During the actual conflict, the years 1861–1865, photography was seen as something of an add-on, an extra that was not completely necessary. There were, after all, plenty of watercolor and pen-and-ink artists, including the remarkable Winslow Homer, to record the war's events. But as time passed, the power of photography became more apparent.

There was something about an actual photograph of a young soldier—Confederate or Union—lying dead in a ditch that transcended even the powers of the greatest artist. The photographs of the dead and wounded at the Battle of Antietam turned many Northern viewers into die-hard Union men and abolitionists, but they also turned some viewers into die-hard pacifists. As the war progressed, more photos emerged, sometimes with heartbreaking scenes. In fact, it might be said that the cheerier and more optimistic views of the war usually came from the artists, and the drearier and more appalling looks from the photographers. This did not mean that all, or even most, of the great Civil War photographers became rich or famous, however. Many of them were anonymous, and some were hired "photo men" from firms like that of Mathew B. Brady. The great New York City photographer was not even immune from the economic downturn that followed the war; he died in obscurity and in relative poverty in 1896.

Why was the Brady photograph of Lincoln so important?

On the morning of February 22, Lincoln and a friend strolled to the Broadway offices of Mathew B. Brady (1823–1896), New York City's most successful commercial photographer. Photography was undergoing a big boom, and Lincoln did not wish to miss this opportunity for what we would today call "cheap publicity."

The photograph taken (or, more properly, "made") that afternoon is one of the many striking representations of Lincoln. The man's height and length are readily apparent, as is his awkwardness. The enormously strong hands are displayed, as is a rather tight expression in the mouth, indicating a firm will. As was the style, Lincoln was portrayed with his left hand resting on two large books, one of which may have been the Bible. The photograph was reproduced a great number of times, and copies of various kinds later appeared in thousands, if not millions, of homes, mostly in the Northern states. Lincoln did not exaggerate when he claimed "Brady and the Cooper Union made me President."

Who introduced Lincoln at the Cooper Union?

Born in western Massachusetts in 1794, William Cullen Bryant was only fifteen years older than Lincoln, but his flowing white beard made him seem much older. Through a lifetime of literary and commercial success, Bryant had become the grand old man of

47

New York literary society, yet he shared some things with the unpolished man from the West. Like Lincoln, Bryant had been born in a log cabin. He was an intensely physical person (his long walks were something of a legend) and like Lincoln, Bryant believed that the American future was brightest when one looked farther West.

"The great West my friends, is a potent auxiliary in the battle we are fighting, for Freedom against Slavery; in behalf of civilization against barbarism; for the occupation of some of the fairest region of our Continent on which the settlers are now building their cabins.... These children of the West, my friends, form a living bulwark against the advance of slavery, and from them is recruited the vanguard of the armies of liberty.... I have only, my friends, to announce the name of ABRAHAM LINCOLN of Illinois."

What did Lincoln say to the audience of 1,500 at the Cooper Union?

Like the Western lawyer he was, Lincoln moved slowly and deliberately; it was never his way to rush an argument or proposition. Without using the precise term "founding fathers," Lincoln spoke at length on the beliefs of the men who had written the Constitution in 1787. Working his way cautiously, and employing a selective use of the evidence, Lincoln pointed in the direction of freedom. The founding fathers had not been in favor of slavery, he declared, but had recognized its existence as a necessary evil in the young republic. And even though he might personally be opposed to slavery, Lincoln did not believe that he, the chief executive, the Congress, or even the Supreme Court could wipe out slavery where it currently existed. Nothing in the Constitution granted such powers to any of the three branches of government. Lincoln then addressed the Southern states directly:

"You consider yourselves a reasonable and a just people; and I consider that in the general qualities of reason and justice you are not inferior to any other people. Still, when you speak of us Republicans, you do so only to denounce us as reptiles, or, at the best, as no better than outlaws. You will grant a hearing to pirates or murderers, but nothing like it to 'Black Republicans.'"

What did Lincoln say about John Brown?

He disavowed him. John Brown's raid on Harpers Ferry was the act of one man and a handful of accomplices, Lincoln declared. The raid had nothing to do with the Republican Party or with his own goals.

How did Lincoln conclude, and how was the speech received?

"Wrong as we think Slavery is, we can yet afford to let it alone where it is, because that much is due to the necessity arising from its actual presence in the nation; but can we, while our votes will prevent it, allow it to spread in the National Territories, and to overrun us here in these Free States?" The obvious answer was no.

Lincoln received three rousing cheers, and when he walked among the large crowd to talk with various persons, it was apparent that he had succeeded. The Cooper Union speech made him seem rational, reasonable, and as polished as a man from the backwoods might be. He was not the equal of William Cullen Bryant, but those who listened to him that evening believed he might one day rise to that esteemed a level.

Where did Lincoln go after the Cooper Union speech?

He had already planned on a trip to Massachusetts to visit his eldest son, Robert Todd Lincoln (1843–1926), who was studying at Phillips Exeter Academy in Exeter, New Hampshire. The success of the Cooper Union speech broadened his possibilities, however, and before long Lincoln agreed to deliver eleven other speeches. All were given in New England, and all were well received.

The chair in which Lincoln sat and gave his Cooper Union speech is preserved at the Smithsonian Institute in Washington, D.C.

Where did Lincoln go after his New England tour?

Straight home to Springfield, Illinois. Lincoln had already decided he would be more effective at home than on the road. Lincoln was a good orator, but he gave so much time and energy to his speeches that they had the potential to drain him. By contrast, he could spend time in Springfield, Illinois, monitoring events by use of the telegraph. As it turned out, this was a much more effective use of his time.

Who were the leading contenders for the Democratic nomination?

James C. Buchanan, the sitting president, was so unpopular he did not even make an attempt to secure his party's nomination. John C. Breckinridge (1821–1875), of Kentucky, the sitting vice president, announced his candidacy, as did Stephen A. Douglas. When the Democratic party convened in Charleston, South Carolina, it was apparent that the party had split into two sections: Northern and Southern Democrats. The last thing that Northern Democrats wanted was another "dough-faced" Democrat who would be perceived as too favorable to the South; the last thing that Southern Democrats would accept was a Northern candidate perceived as too responsive to the calls for abolition.

After days of bickering, the convention ended. The Northern Democrats reconvened in Baltimore a few weeks later and eventually nominated Stephen A. Douglas of Illinois. The Southern Democrats nominated John C. Breckinridge. Anyone who paid careful attention could see that the road toward a Republican victory in November was being paved. The trick was to avoid any of the major potholes that might emerge.

Where did the Republicans hold their convention?

In the Windy City. Chicago had 109,260 residents in 1860, and prided itself on being the center of the Western states and territories. As a gesture, or nod, to the growing importance of the West, the Republicans held the convention—only the second in their history—in Chicago.

To play up the Western and frontier themes, the Republican Party organizers had an enormous, temporary building constructed; labeled the Wigwam, this tentlike structure was well remembered for many years. The two major candidates were William H. Seward of New York and Abraham Lincoln of Illinois, and as the convention began, on May 15, 1860, most well-regarded observers thought that Seward had the edge. He was still better known than Lincoln, and thanks to his outspokenness on the issue of slavery, he was more acceptable to the radical, or extreme abolitionist, wing of the Republican Party. As so often, the political men underestimated Lincoln and *his* political team.

What did Lincoln plan for the convention?

By 1860, Lincoln had become a rather skilled political operative, but he also needed the help of a team, and he had one that was growing in numbers and skill. These political "handlers" decided that Lincoln would remain in Springfield, while they would pack the convention hall with Lincoln supporters. This was not hard because Lincoln was the only Western man contending for the nomination.

As the balloting approached, Lincoln's handlers formulated their plan. They knew that Seward would "win" the first ballot in terms of a plurality, but they intended to prevent him from gaining an outright majority. With each successive ballot, they reasoned, Lincoln would gain strength. The reason for this was that Seward, with a longer track record, had earned more enemies. Lincoln would, by comparison, seem eminently inoffensive. But there was more to the magic than the planning. The handlers also developed the single most enduring image of Lincoln: that of the Rail-Splitter.

How close was the nomination fight?

Seward won the first ballot by a strong plurality, but he did not have the majority necessary. On each of the successive ballots, Lincoln's numbers grew, and on the fourth, the convention managers paced the floor, asking the delegates to make it unanimous. Lincoln, who had been little known just two years earlier, had won the nomination of the Republican Party.

Lincoln immediately began a campaign to win over those he had defeated (this type of conciliation became a hallmark of his political style). The delegation from Wisconsin had been almost unanimously in favor of Seward, for example, and Lincoln's campaign managers made a great effort to bring them into the new camp. By the end of June, they had largely succeeded.

Was Lincoln as truly "physical," as much of a "he-man," as the image suggests?

Lincoln was always composed of opposites, or contrasts. Blessed with outstanding physical strength, he was also notoriously cerebral and could fall into complete lassitude for hours at a time. In youth, he had indeed been an outstanding wrestler; given the length of his arms, he could hold off, then throw, almost any opponent. He had also split plenty of wood in his youth: nearly all Western boys did. Whether he actually split any true "rails" is debatable, but when a handful of middle-aged men brought rails to the convention and claimed Lincoln had split them thirty years earlier, it was irresistible, both to the political handlers and then the general public. No previous president—not even Andrew Jackson—ever built so much political capital based on one good story, and none would do so again until Theodore Roosevelt capitalized on his "charge up San Juan Hill" during the Spanish-American War.

Were there three parties in 1860?

Actually there were four. The Republicans nominated Lincoln; the Northern Democrats nominated Douglas; the Southern Democrats nominated John Breckinridge; and a brand-new group, named the Constitutional Union Party, nominated John Bell (1797–1869). One has to look back all the way to 1824—the year that Andrew Jackson and John Quincy Adams were the main contestants—to find a political year with so much activity and controversy.

John Bell was nominated for president, and Edward Everett (1794–1865), an orator who had previously served as chaplain to the U.S. Senate, was nominated for vice president. The Constitutional Union Party was formed out of a desperate effort to prevent the nation from disintegrating; everyone could see that Northern, Southern, and Western states were on the verge of a great separation.

When was the Eighth Census of the United States considered complete?

The eighth national census was considered complete on June 1, 1860, meaning that the population figures were considered accurate as of that day. Though the results were not immediately released to the public, we can examine them to see how the nation, and its various sections, were coming along in terms of population.

Which of the three major sections gained the most from the 1860 census?

This is easily answered. The North and the West far outpaced the South, but between those two it was a narrow race, with the West coming out on top. For example, Illinois increased from 851,000 to 1,711,000, the largest single increase of any state. Wisconsin

51

more than doubled, growing from 305,000 to 775,000. And Iowa had the most spectacular growth in relative terms: the Hawkeye State went from 192,000 to 674,000.

The industrial North did fine, too. The Empire State increased from 3,097,000 to 3,880,000, and Pennsylvania rose from 2,311,000 to 2,906,000. No state in the Union decreased in population, although Vermont was very close, increasing only from 314,000 to 315,000. When one examines the census results, the North and the West were the clear winners, but the Far West did well too. California rose from 92,000 to 379,000, and Oregon increased from an uncounted figure in 1850 to 52,000 in 1860.

How did the South look from the vantage point of the 1860 census?

No one would call the South the "loser" because it, too, gained in overall population. Both in relative and in absolute terms, the South was falling behind the North and the West, however.

The Old Dominion state increased from 1,421,000 to 1,596,000. This was more impressive than it seems because Virginia was losing population to other states in the South. South Carolina rose from 668,000 to 703,000, a rather small gain, all things considered. Only when one crossed the Appalachian Mountains into the wilder sections of the South did one see much population growth. Mississippi rose from 606,000 to 791,000, and Tennessee increased from 1,002,000 to 1,109,000. Alabama made a significant rise, from 771,000 to 964,000, and Texas rose from 212,000 to 604,000.

What was the African American population in 1860?

The number of black slaves rose from 3.3 million to 3.95 million, and those who extended this population growth forward declared that slaves would one day outnumber free persons throughout the South. The free black population, nationwide, increased to about 470,000 persons.

The census also revealed that the black population was moving steadily west and south. As recently as 1820, the great majority of slaves had been in the Tidewater states of Virginia, Maryland, and North and South Carolina, but Louisiana, Mississippi, and Texas were the places where the slave population was growing the most.

What about the numbers of horses and mules?

To people of the mid-nineteenth century, horses and mules were at least as important as automobiles and motorcycles are to us today. There were, according to the census, slightly more than six million horses and slightly more than one million asses and mules in the United States in 1860. That seems as if it would be plenty to mount all the Union and Confederate forces, but the majority was still needed at home to plow the fields. The states that were the most fortunate in having a surplus were Illinois (575,000 horses), Indiana (409,000 horses), and New York (503,000 horses). In terms of mules, the states that were the most flush were Alabama (108,000), Kentucky (117,000), Mississippi (112,000), and Tennessee (119,000).

Who were the Wide Awakes?

It is easier to say when and where they appeared: the spring and summer of 1860. At about the time that Lincoln commenced his short speaking tour in New England in February, small groups of men began nighttime marches in Northern cities. Their activities were so secretive that we might almost compare them—in some respects—to the Ku Klux Klan, which came after the Civil War.

One of the most famous rallies was on Boston Common. At something like 9 P.M. on a certain night, thousands of young men—dressed in semimilitary apparel—were assembled, and at a prearranged signal, thousands of them suddenly lit candles and pressed them upwards, chanting that they were wide awake! Most people who saw the Wide Awakes were both impressed and frightened. It was impossible to say exactly what being wide awake meant, but over time, the movement became associated with Lincoln's election campaign.

Was there a Southern equivalent to the Wide Awakes?

No. What was most apparent in the South was that Lincoln, and indeed the entire Republican Party, would be kept off the ballot! That was worse, in many respects. In ten states—almost all in the South—Lincoln's name did not appear on the ballot, and in the one Southern state where his name was permitted, Virginia, he would receive very few votes. This meant that if Lincoln did win, he could be accused of being the leader of a sectional, rather than a national, party.

There were plenty of Southerners who viewed Lincoln and the Republicans as sinister, even evil, however. Labels and descriptions of Lincoln as the great baboon, the silly ape, and the would-be liberator of the black slaves began to emerge. Had white Southerners actually read any of Lincoln's policy papers and speeches, they would have realized that he was no radical or wide-eyed abolitionist. As long as they read only Southern newspapers and periodicals, white Southerners continued to be deluded.

Was there any chance Lincoln could have lost the general election?

Not in an absolute sense. Given that there were four parties involved, and that the once-mighty Democrats were split in two, it was almost inevitable that the Republicans would win in November. But the margin of the victory would be very important in the effort to assert that Lincoln was the legitimate chief executive.

Did Lincoln campaign during the autumn of 1860?

Hardly at all. A much better use of his time—as he perceived it—was to monitor events from Springfield. The telegraph assisted him greatly.

Springfield did throw one large party for its most famous resident. In the heat of the late summer, thousands of people came to the Lincoln home, practically taking it over for the afternoon. A photograph taken that day shows Lincoln in a white suit, dominating the scene—as usual—by virtue of his height.

What happened on Election Day?

Election Day fell on November 6 in 1860. Lincoln and his political group were in Springfield, Illinois, receiving and monitoring the results by telegraph. That he would win was almost certain, but the margin mattered, both to the candidate and to thirty-two million Americans who awaited the results.

Lincoln lost New York City (it was not yet divided into separate boroughs) by 33,290 to 62,293 for Stephen Douglas, but he won the all-important Empire State by 362,646 to 312,510. Months later, when he visited Manhattan, Lincoln joked that he was not the first choice of its people. Lincoln won the Keystone State of Pennsylvania by 270,170 to 176,435 for the so-called Fusion Ticket. Douglas won only 17,350 votes, and the Constitutional Union Party picked up 12,755. Lincoln took all the New England states and all the Western ones, save Indiana. On the West Coast, he took California by the relatively narrow margin of 38,646 to 37,349 for Douglas. John Breckinridge and the Southern Democrats did much better than anticipated in the Golden State, coming in third with 33,357. The story was quite different in the South, however.

How did the election map look in the Southern states?

It was almost as if there was no Lincoln and no Republican Party. Ten Southern states kept Lincoln and the Republicans entirely off the ballot, and Virginia granted Lincoln a

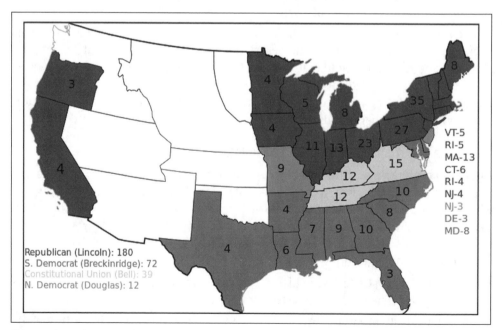

Republican (Lincoln): 180
S. Democrat (Breckinridge): 72
Constitutional Union (Bell): 39
N. Democrat (Douglas): 12

VT-5
RI-5
MA-13
CT-6
RI-4
NJ-4
NJ-3
DE-3
MD-8

This map shows the results of the 1860 presidential election and the electoral votes received by the four candidates.

How does Lincoln's 1860 election stack up when compared to other major election races?

Ever since George Washington made a clean sweep of the electoral vote in 1789, Americans have looked for clear-cut winners. But once the popular votes were counted and made public, there have been a whole number of close and contested elections.

Lincoln did not have a majority election decision, as did Andrew Jackson in 1828 and 1832, and he did not clean up on his opponents as Franklin Roosevelt did in 1932, 1936, 1940, and 1944. But his margin of victory was far larger than that of John F. Kennedy in 1960, and his Electoral College victory was better than that of Bill Clinton in 1992. Then, too, those who criticized Lincoln for being a minority president ignored the simple fact that Lincoln did more with his slender margin of victory than almost any other president of any century.

total of 1,929 votes (for comparison, John Bell won with 74,584 and John Breckinridge came in a close second with 74,335). The candidate who suffered the most was Stephen A. Douglas. Nationwide, he came in second with over a million votes, but in state after state and section after section, he was squeezed out. Douglas won only the state of Missouri (by a narrow margin) and the Garden State of New Jersey, where he split the electoral vote with Lincoln.

To those who claim—then and now—that Lincoln was a minority president, with only thirty-nine percent of the popular vote, the answer is that Lincoln did exceptionally well, when one considers the number of states that kept him off the ballot. In any case, it did not matter. John Quincy Adams had been a minority president, winning in the Electoral College in 1824.

How long did Lincoln have to celebrate?

About three days. When he first learned of his election, Lincoln went into the first state of relaxation he had felt in months. An enormous obstacle had been faced and crossed, and all seemed well till the first news of South Carolina arrived in the North.

South Carolina had long been the most obstreperous of all the thirty-three states. As early as 1832, she had nullified one federal law and practically threatened to depart the federal union. South Carolina, the Palmetto State, did not have popular vote results for 1860 because both the presidential electors and the governor were chosen by the state legislature. But the sentiment of white South Carolinians was soon demonstrated. Two days after Lincoln's election, a new flag appeared on the battlements of Charleston, the Palmetto flag, with a single star. The action was not completely unanticipated, but it still came as a jolt to many Northerners to learn that even one state was truly leaning toward secession.

SECESSION

What is nullification? What is secession? How closely are they linked?

Both ideas are American in content and ideology. Both came from ideas and concepts expressed by Thomas Jefferson and James Madison in the Virginia and Kentucky Resolutions.

Nullification involves the difference between state and federal law. A nullifier, and there were many in South Carolina in 1860, believed that the government of a state can nullify the effects of a federal law within the boundaries of that state. This was attempted by South Carolina in 1832, but on that occasion the firm response of President Andrew Jackson led to a swift pullback. *Secession,* on the other hand, is a true severance of relations between the government of a state and the federal government. Nullification is clearly a major, and dangerous step, but secession ups the ante considerably. In both cases, the belief proceeds from the idea that the thirteen original states—those that won independence from Great Britain—did not yield any of their sovereignty when they entered the federal union in 1787. The doctrine of states' rights was more strongly held in the South than the North or West.

What was the first step for South Carolina?

The governor of South Carolina called for a special convention to be held in mid-December. Meanwhile, the state militia began seizing federal properties in and around the state. Things began to look rather like 1832, except that on this occasion there was no sign of the Palmetto State backing down.

The only federal garrison in South Carolina was an eighty-odd man group of soldiers, officers, and musicians at Fort Moultrie. Located on the northeast side of Charleston Harbor, Fort Moultrie was a strong place, except if imperiled by forces from the land. Major Robert Anderson (1805–1871), the garrison commander, therefore began looking about for alternatives. His first messages to the War Department were either rebuffed or ignored, leading Major Anderson to believe he would have to act on his own. He did not have the first move, however: that went to South Carolina.

How did the Palmetto State depart the federal union?

On December 16, 1860, 150-plus delegates from the towns and counties assembled at Columbia to discuss and debate the idea of secession. Not only were the quarters cramped, but there was an outbreak of

Major Robert Anderson was the garrison commander at Fort Sumter at the time of the attack.

smallpox in the vicinity: these two circumstances persuaded the delegated to adjourn and to reconvene in Charleston a few days later. On December 20, 1860, 167 delegates to the special state convention signed the Ordinance of Secession, which declared that South Carolina now resumed her position as one of the free and independent nations of the world. All connections with the association known as the United States of America were dissolved.

The final vote, which was unanimous, was taken around 1 P.M., and less than one hour later a special was issued by the *Charleston Mercury* announcing that the federal union was dissolved. The real shock would, of course, take some time to sink in.

How did Major Anderson rescue, or evacuate, his garrison?

As South Carolina resumed its position as one of the free and independent states of the world (the expression employed in many state records), the militia of the state began to press against Fort Moultrie. Major Robert Anderson was deeply concerned, and when there was no reply to his telegrams to the War Department, he took action on his own. On the night of December 26–27, 1860, Anderson evacuated his entire garrison, under cover of night, from Fort Moultrie to Fort Sumter (both forts were named for South Carolina heroes of the Revolutionary War).

The movement was masterfully executed, and the people of Charleston were outraged to learn that Anderson had taken his men to a more defensible location. Telegrams practically flew between Charleston and Washington, D.C. When he was confronted about the action, President James C. Buchanan complained that he had not ordered it. This was confirmation, if any was needed, that the president of the United States was not up to his job.

How did 1861 begin?

President Buchanan held his annual afternoon reception at the White House, but newsmen and correspondents thought it a rather sad affair. The president seemed preoccupied, and almost everyone present was more interested in scanning the headlines of the major newspapers than listening to the pious requests for God's protection of the nation.

Suddenly there were thirty-two states and several territories instead of thirty-three. The very idea required considerable adjustment. It was around this time that men and women of the North and the West began speaking of the Union in new, almost sacred, terms. The expression had been around for some time, of course, but people had previously used lowercase letters to begin the two words *federal union*. Sometime in 1861, people in the North and the West began to drop the word federal and simply say "Union."

Where was Lincoln in early 1861?

The president-elect was in Springfield, Illinois, and he showed no hurry to get to Washington, D.C. If relations between the Republicans and outgoing Democrats had been bad before the election, they now became much worse. Lincoln did not wish to be conflated, or equated, with President James C. Buchanan.

As he examined his options, Lincoln decided on a simple rule: no more speeches or policy announcements. As late as January 1861, he still believed the questions of freedom and slavery could eventually be solved without a civil war, and he did not wish to add fuel to the flames. He, therefore, made no public speeches in January. When newspaper editors pressed him, declaring that the country was in crisis, Lincoln replied that he had long since said all he had to and that repetition would do no good. Lincoln was usually a keen observer of public sentiment, but this time he was mistaken. Had he spoken vigorously of his belief that slavery—while abhorrent—was protected by the Constitution, war *might* have been prevented.

Whom did Lincoln choose as members of his Cabinet?

The historian Doris Kearns Goodwin has aptly described Lincoln's Cabinet as a "team of rivals." As a minority president, Lincoln wanted to embrace as much of the country as possible in his Cabinet: he was even ready to have Southerners. The single most important choice was that which came first: secretary of state.

William H. Seward had been one of the standouts of the Republican Party for half a dozen years, and a national figure for five years before that. A fine speaker possessed of strong convictions, Seward had positioned himself too far to the left (in our modern parlance) to win the Republican nomination in 1860. Lincoln needed Seward, however; in fact, they both needed each other. Lincoln offered the post of secretary of state and Seward accepted, believing he would be well positioned to guide the inexperienced president-elect. For secretary of war, Lincoln chose Simon Cameron of Pennsylvania, another of his former political rivals, and for secretary of the treasury he chose Salmon P. Chase. All the Cabinet members did not meet until Lincoln reached Washington, D.C.

What was the second state to depart the Union?

Mississippi departed the Union on January 9, 1861. The convention in Jackson adopted the Ordinance of Secession by a vote of 84–15.

> The people of the State of Mississippi, in convention assembled, do ordain and declare, and it is hereby ordained and declared, as follows, to wit:
>
> … That all the laws and ordinances by which the said State of Mississippi became a member of the Federal Union of the United States of America be, and the same are hereby, repealed, and that all obligations on the part of the said State or the people thereof to observe the same be withdrawn, and that the said State doth hereby resume all the rights, functions, and powers which by any of said laws or ordinances were conveyed to the Government of the said United States, and is absolved from all the obligations, restraints, and duties incurred to the said Federal Union, and shall from henceforth be a free, sovereign, and independent State.

What was the reaction or response to South Carolina's secession?

Only three weeks had passed since South Carolina's secession, but those weeks had been a painful, anxious time for South Carolina's leaders. Once they learned that Mississippi would join them, hopes rose for an eventual Confederacy of the Southern states.

The delegates to the Mississippi convention voted overwhelmingly in favor of secession, but there were gaps and separations between them on some issues. Did secession automatically mean the perpetuation of slavery, for example? In Mississippi's case, the answer was yes, but it would not be as easy or clear-cut for those that followed. The language of the Mississippi Ordinance of Secession closely followed that of South Carolina. The federal union had served its purpose and was now disbanded, so far as the people of Mississippi were concerned.

What was the third state to leave the Union?

Florida had already called for a convention, and on January 10, 1861, its delegates approved the Ordinance of Secession by 62 to 7.

> We, the people of the State of Florida, in convention assembled, do solemnly ordain, publish, and declare, That the State of Florida hereby withdraws herself from the confederacy of States existing under the name of the United States of America and from the existing Government of the said States; and that all political connection between her and the Government of said States ought to be, and the same is hereby, totally annulled, and said Union of States dissolved; and the State of Florida is hereby declared a sovereign and independent nation; and that all ordinances heretofore adopted, in so far as they create or recognize said Union, are rescinded; and all laws or parts of laws in force in this State, in so far as they recognize or assent to said Union, be, and they are hereby, repealed.

Given Florida's tiny population (140,424 in 1860) and great dependence on the federal government, it was strange that Florida would depart the Union so early. Slavery was an important aspect of Florida's economic life, but she was not a true "Cotton State" like Louisiana. Even so, her delegates voted Florida out of the Union by 67–11.

All eyes turned to the White House, but all eyes were confounded by what they saw. President Buchanan was fully aware of the situation, along with its dire possibilities, but he did not see any constitutional remedy, or political response, to secession. The White House, meanwhile, was losing some of its last political figures. Buchanan's secretary of war, John Floyd, and Vice President John C. Breckinridge made no secret of their support for Southern secession.

What was the fourth state to depart the Union?

Alabama's delegates convened on January 7, and adopted the following ordinance on January 11, 1861:

> Whereas, the election of Abraham Lincoln and Hannibal Hamlin to the offices
> of president and vice-president of the United States of America, by a sectional

party, avowedly hostile to the domestic institutions and to the peace and security of the people of the State of Alabama, preceded by many and dangerous infractions of the constitution of the United States by many of the States and people of the Northern section, is a political wrong of so insulting and menacing a character as to justify the people of the State of Alabama in the adoption of prompt and decided measures for their future peace and security, therefore:

Be it declared and ordained by the people of the State of Alabama, in Convention assembled, That the State of Alabama now withdraws, and is hereby withdrawn from the Union known as "the United States of America," and henceforth ceases to be one of said United States, and is, and of right ought to be a Sovereign and Independent State.

What was the fifth state to leave the Union?

The fact that Georgia was relatively slow to secession is more important than it seems. The Peachtree State had more Unionists, especially in the northern part, than any other of the Deep Southern states. Even among its ardent partisans, there was some dissension, with some arguing for a slower process. The "immediatists" prevailed, however, and on January 19, 1861, the Georgia convention approved the following ordinance by 208 to 89.

We the people of the State of Georgia in Convention assembled do declare and ordain and it is hereby declared and ordained that the ordinance adopted by the State of Georgia in convention on the 2nd day of Jany. in the year of our Lord seventeen hundred and eighty-eight, whereby the constitution of the United States of America was assented to, ratified and adopted, and also all acts and parts of acts of the general assembly of this State, ratifying and adopting amendments to said constitution, are hereby repealed, rescinded and abrogated. We do further declare and ordain that the union now existing between the State of Georgia and other States under the name of the United States of America is hereby dissolved, and that the State of Georgia is in full possession and exercise of all those rights of sovereignty which belong and appertain to a free and independent State.

What was the sixth state to depart the Union?

On January 25, 1861, the Pelican State left the Union. The delegates to the convention, held at Baton Rouge, adopted the following measure by a vote of 113 to 17:

We, the people of the State of Louisiana, in convention assembled, do declare and ordain, and it is hereby declared and ordained, That the ordinance passed by us in convention on the 22d day of November, in the year eighteen hundred and eleven, whereby the Constitution of the United States of America and the amendments of the said Constitution were adopted, and all laws and ordinances by which the State of Louisiana became a member of the Federal Union, be, and the same are hereby, repealed and abrogated; and that the union now subsisting between Louisiana and other States under the name of "The United States of America" is hereby dissolved.

The convention then adopted a second measure, recognizing the importance of navigation on the Mississippi River and offering to enter into stipulations with any friendly states or nations for that right.

Did any states choose *not* to secede?

Virginia and Arkansas both held state conventions, but the delegates chose to back away from the dread possibility of secession. The trend continued to accelerate, however, with Alabama, Georgia, and Texas voting to secede. One of the few places that showed any resistance was Texas, where the venerable Sam Houston (1793–1863) the hero of the Texas Revolution of 1836—prophesied to his countrymen about the dangers of civil war.

His fellow Texans prided themselves on a military spirit and willingness to sacrifice, Houston said, but they did not realize the enormous willpower of the men of the North and the West. These men—from the states ranging from Maine to Minnesota—were slow to anger and action, but when they launched upon a cause, they seldom turned away from it. Houston's warning was not heeded, and the special state convention in Texas voted to secede. At least the convention agreed to put the matter to the voters.

Was there anything President Buchanan could have done to stop the states from seceding?

Buchanan has been thoroughly vilified over the decades, and no doubt exists that he was a rather poor chief executive. Andrew Jackson had faced down the South Carolina nullifiers in 1832, but Jackson was essentially a military man in civilian clothing while Buchanan was a civilian who had become "the Old Public Functionary." Then, too, Buchanan had the disadvantage of knowing he would soon leave office. Only if he and Lincoln, the president-elect, had gotten together to make joint statements would action have been possible. And where holding off, or standing back, was concerned, Lincoln was just as bad as Buchanan.

Lincoln's predecessor, James C. Buchanan, is justly regarded as among the poorest of all American presidents.

LINCOLN'S JOURNEY, DAVIS' SPEECH

When did Lincoln finally depart from Springfield, Illinois?

On February 11, 1861, a special train had been rented for the occasion. Just before he boarded, Lincoln spoke to the crowd. "My friends," he began, "I cannot sufficiently express to you the sadness I feel at this parting. To you I owe all that I am. Here I have lived more than a quarter of a century; here my children were born, here one of them lies buried. I know not how soon I shall see you again. A duty devolves upon me perhaps greater than that which has devolved upon any man since the days of Washington. He never could have succeeded except for the aid of Divine Providence, upon which he at all times relied. I feel that I can do nothing without the same divine aid which sustained him … that divine assistance without which I can not succeed, but with which success is certain.… I bid you all an affectionate farewell."

Aboard the train were Lincoln's two personal secretaries—John Hay and John Nicolay—and most, but not all, of the Lincoln family. An important person in the group was Colonel Elmer Ellsworth, a young man of twenty-four who was about as close to the president as any one person could be.

When did Jefferson Davis leave Brierfield?

On the same day that Lincoln left Springfield, February 11, 1861. The six states in secession had called a provisional congress that met in Montgomery, Alabama, at the beginning of February. Of the fifty delegates, forty-nine were slaveholders, and almost twenty of these belonged to the class called "planter," meaning that they owned more than twenty persons. Because of the great need for speed, the provisional government elected Jefferson Davis of Mississippi the provisional president of the Confederate States of America without even asking him beforehand. When he received the news, Davis was thunderstruck. It was not that he lacked ambition, but he had hoped to be awarded a military, not a political, command. Duty called, however, and on February 11, Davis bade farewell to his household staff and the 113 slaves on his plantation. He and his wife Varina were soon on a five-day journey, by water and by rail, to Montgomery.

Where did Lincoln's train stop?

One can almost ask the opposite: where did the train *not* stop. Lincoln had sequestered himself all through the winter; he now exposed himself to the public in all sorts of cities and towns. The train took a meandering route through Illinois, Indiana, and Ohio, then headed for New York State. Lincoln spent some time in Albany—the center of William H. Seward's political base—and then went down the Hudson to Manhattan.

Lincoln delivered numerous speeches along the way: some well planned and some right off the cuff. He generally combined folksy sayings with learned ones, and at no point during the rail journey could he be said to have reached a high point of eloquence.

Most of his listeners liked what they heard, however. In Pittsburgh, for example, he won cheers by playing down the situation rather than magnifying it:

> Notwithstanding the troubles across the river [Lincoln gestured to the Monongahela River and the land southward], there is no crisis but an artificial one. What is there now to warrant the condition of affairs presented by our friends over the river? Take even their own views of the questions involved, and there is nothing to justify the course they are pursuing. I repeat, there is no crisis excepting such a one as may be gotten up at any time by turbulent men, aided by designing politicians. My advice to them under such circumstances is "Keep cool." If the great American people only keep their temper both sides of the line, the troubles will come to an end.

What did Lincoln say in Manhattan?

Lincoln understood the importance of New York City, the nation's largest and most prosperous city. Manhattan had voted for Stephen Douglas in the 1860 election, but Lincoln, typically, let bygones be bygones. He gave solid, if not sparkling, speeches, and to those who met him, the president-elect seemed optimistic. Where many other persons were lamenting the states in secession, Lincoln acted as if it were a temporary matter that would soon be overcome. Whether this light confidence was real or feigned cannot be known: he was not the type of person to reveal his full hand.

Where did Jefferson Davis stop along the way to Montgomery?

Davis had only known he had been elected for a few days; it was not possible to have a special train for him. The president-elect of the Confederacy, therefore, traveled much like any other passenger. But as he came closer to Alabama, he was met at a variety of train stops, and the level of oratory rose. Davis was a good, though not a great, speaker, and he rose to the occasion, promising that the new Confederacy meant peace, but that if resisted, she would show her opponents "Southern steel."

On the evening that he arrived in Montgomery, Davis was escorted to the Exchange Hotel by the flamboyant fire-eater William Yancey (1814–1863), who introduced him with the thrilling words: "The man and the hour have met." Davis gave a much more subdued speech, alluding to the fact that he had given no fewer than

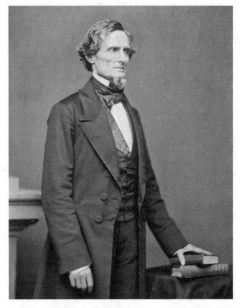

President Jefferson Davis, the one and only leader of the Confederate States of America.

twenty-five during the last week. When he went to bed that evening, Davis knew that he was the leader, and that the hopes of the Confederacy rested upon him.

What was the first Confederate inaugural like?

Montgomery was a small place with a population of 10,000, but the number had perhaps been doubled by the visitors who wanted to see and hear Jefferson Davis. February 18, 1861, dawned fair and mild, meaning that the observers could wear their light, rather than heavy, clothing.

Precisely at noon, a carriage pulled by four white horses took President-elect Davis and Vice President-elect Alexander H. Stephens up the street from the Exchange Hotel to the Alabama Capitol building; the band played "I Wish I Was in Dixie's Land" as they ascended. Coming out of the carriage, Jefferson Davis and Alexander Stephens both made brief addresses to the provisional Congress of the Confederate States of America and then went out of the building to a stage erected on the front portico.

What did Jefferson Davis say at his inaugural?

Davis made a strange but compelling presence that day. Worn out from years of political and administrative work, he had suffered a severe attack of the shingles three years earlier, and he was far from well. He covered his weakness well, however, and his tone struck many of his listeners as melodious.

The Confederacy was a political experiment unequaled in the memory of man, Davis declared. Never had a people risen so suddenly to make a separation from their former countrymen, and never had a government been so swiftly created (if not wholly true, this was at least true in parts). Between an agrarian nation such as the Confederate States of America and a commercial and industrial one such as the United States of America, there need be little contact and no friction, he asserted. But if the Northern and Western men should perceive his kindness as soft or weak, then "we must prepare to meet the emergency and maintain, by the final arbitrament of the sword, the position which we have assumed among the nations of the earth."

How did Davis conclude? What was the reaction?

Davis' face broke into a warm smile as he drew to his conclusion. "It is joyous in the midst of perilous times," he said, "to look around upon a people united in heart, where one purpose of high resolve animates and actuates the whole; where the sacrifices to be made are not weighed in the balance against honor and right and liberty and equality." There was no mistaking his sincerity, even though we today might question his use of the word "equality."

The speech was well received in Montgomery, but it drew mixed reviews in other parts of the new Confederacy. Many fire-eaters, particularly in South Carolina, felt that Davis had not gone far enough, and quite a few other Southerners, especially in the mountain sections of Georgia and Alabama, felt he had gone too far. What has to be admitted—then and today—is that Davis did very well, considering he had only learned of his election one week earlier.

Where, meanwhile, was Lincoln?

Lincoln was still traveling to the capital: his rail journey from Illinois to Washington, D.C., took twelve days. Lincoln generally won higher applause for his homespun jokes and simple manner than for his policy speeches. One speech he labored over was given while he helped raise a new flag at Philadelphia's Independence Hall. It was a federal flag with thirty-four stars.

Clearly, neither Lincoln nor the flag's maker wished to credit the seven states in secession with any acknowledgement of their actions. In that thirty-fourth star, however, was a particular success, because Kansas had just shed its territorial status and become the thirty-fourth state in the Union. Lincoln knew the importance of symbols, particularly where the flag was concerned, and he was all too pleased to be the first to raise the new flag over Independence Hall.

What did Lincoln say that morning?

He had been criticized in the newspapers for his hasty, ill-delivered remarks in Cleveland and Buffalo, and by the time he reached Philadelphia, the president-elect was more cautious. There was something quite wonderful about raising the flag that day, however, and Lincoln consented to say a few words.

"I have never had a feeling politically," Lincoln said, "that did not spring from the sentiments embodied in the Declaration of Independence. I have often pondered over the dangers which were incurred by the men who assembled here, and framed and adopted that Declaration of Independence.... Now, my friends, can this country be saved upon this basis? If it can, I will consider myself one of the happiest men in the world, if I can help to save it. If it cannot be saved upon that principle it will be truly awful. But if this country cannot be saved without giving up that principle, I was about to say I would rather be assassinated on this spot than surrender it." This was the first time Lincoln had ever employed the word "assassination" in public; very likely, it sprang from the warnings he had received over the possibility of an assassination attempt in Baltimore.

Why did Lincoln break from his itinerary and go to Harrisburg, Pennsylvania?

Harrisburg was not on the original itinerary, but Lincoln was advised that there might be an assassination attempt in Baltimore. It made sense, to his chief of security, to reroute the train so that Lincoln would have an extra day to prepare, *and* so that the presidential train would arrive in Baltimore at a different time.

Baltimore was deeply hostile to the president-elect. In November 1860, Lincoln managed just 1,083 votes, compared to 1,503 for Douglas, 14,958 for Breckinridge, and 12,605 for John Bell. Lincoln knew perfectly well that Baltimore was dangerous terrain. He allowed his security chief—who was assisted by Allan Pinkerton of Chicago—to sneak him off the train and get him onto another while in disguise. For years afterward, political foes would lampoon Lincoln for what they considered his cowardice in 1861. Anyone examining the evidence is more likely to conclude that Lincoln did the smart thing.

What did Lincoln find upon arriving in Washington, D.C.?

Lincoln went straight to Willard's, the most famous hotel in the nation's capital, and he largely remained there for the next week. There were unofficial meetings with the members of his Cabinet, and there were social courtesies, but there was also an underlying feeling of tension. Washington, D.C., was sandwiched between the South and the North, and if Maryland—Baltimore especially—continued to be hostile, the nation's capital would be in a very tight spot.

Lincoln paid court to many of the longstanding members of Washington society. First Lady Dolley Payne Madison was no longer the doyen of the group: she had died fifteen years earlier. The longest-serving person in Washington was Winfield Scott (1786–1866), general of the U.S. Regular Army. Nearly seventy-five, the overweight Scott was the butt of jokes while still retaining an immense reputation. He had been a brigadier-general in the War of 1812, and he was still around in 1861. Lincoln sounded Scott out as to the situation of the federal forts in the Southern states, but he received little satisfaction. Scott was an ardent Union man, but he was a Southerner by birth, from Virginia, and he believed it would be better to let the secession forces seize all the Southern forts, rather than initiate the conflict.

What was Lincoln's inauguration like?

On March 4, 1861, President James C. Buchanan's carriage pulled up to the the Willard Hotel at 1 P.M. Washington had almost 100,000 people, but the number had perhaps doubled thanks to a great number of visitors for the occasion.

What Lincoln and Buchanan said to each other in the carriage is difficult to imagine. Their policies could not have been more different; their personal styles, too, were diametrically opposed. The Old Public Functionary was giving way to the Rail-Splitter. When the carriage arrived at the Capitol, Lincoln found the place jammed with onlookers. General Winfield Scott had posted men throughout the city, but if anyone were to attempt an assassination, this would be the moment. Lincoln displayed no fear as he walked through the Capitol, greeting persons from all walks of life (this was part of his personal style). At 2 P.M., he went outside to stand among a great crowd of dignitaries and to have the oath of office administered by Chief Justice Roger Taney. Again, the irony was evident to all that looked on. Taney had affirmed the rights of slaveholders in the infamous *Dred Scott* decision.

What did Lincoln say during his inaugural address?

It was a lengthy inaugural address, delivered in a slow but effective fashion. Lincoln began by stating the obvious, that the republic was in the greatest peril it had ever seen. Then he transited to the past, marveling at how the nation had met and overcome all sorts of obstacles. Lincoln then turned to the advent of secession.

The Rotunda at the Capitol was still being built at the time of Abraham Lincoln's first inaugural address.

It was wrong in all sorts of ways, he said. Secession was a betrayal of the principles of the founding fathers, but it also was completely mistaken on a geographical basis. If things had been otherwise, if the Mississippi ran from west to east instead of from north to south, then some sort of division of the real estate might be possible. "Physically speaking, we cannot separate," Lincoln declared. "A husband and wife may divorce, and go out of each other's presence, but this the different sections of our country cannot do." In five short, clean words, Lincoln put his stamp on the heart of the matter. The United States was an all-or-nothing proposition.

How did Lincoln conclude his address to the nation?

Lincoln was very careful to leave the onus, or potential blame, with the South. "In *your* hands, my dissatisfied fellow citizens, and not in *mine,* is the momentous question of civil war," he declared. But as he drove to the conclusion, Lincoln held out an olive branch.

67

"I am loath to close," he said. "We are not enemies but friends. We must not be enemies. Though passion may have strained, it must not break our bonds of affection." This was classic Lincoln, giving something away in order to attain a desirable result. But, like practically everything he had said a year earlier at the Cooper Union, it fell on deaf ears. The South believed what it wanted to believe.

Was Lincoln truly in charge right from the first day of his administration?

No. Lincoln lacked Washington experience, and he needed to find his feet in that truly complicated arena. In the first two, or even three, weeks of his presidency, Lincoln frequently turned to William H. Seward, the secretary of state, for advice. Because of Lincoln's excessively humble and deferential attitude, Seward began to think that he would become the real force of the Lincoln government, with Lincoln as its figurehead. This notion was dispelled when Lincoln sent a return letter to Seward, who had proposed all sorts of alterations in policy.

"I must do it" was the key phrase employed in Lincoln's letter. Though it would take some time for Seward to realize that Lincoln fully intended to exercise the powers of the presidency, he became—to his great credit—the president's right-hand man. As so often, Lincoln deftly turned what could have been a confrontation into an opportunity for cooperation.

Whom did Lincoln appoint as his most important ambassadors?

Although the expression used was "ministers," the meaning was the same: the highest-level diplomat to a foreign country. Lincoln was influenced by Secretary of State Seward, who wished Charles Francis Adams (1807–1886), the son and grandson of presidents (John Adams and John Quincy Adams), for the all-important post at the Court of St. James in London. Lincoln chose William L. Dayton of New Jersey to serve as minister to the court of the Emperor Napoleon III in Paris. And for the post to the court of Czar Alexander II, Lincoln chose Cassius M. Clay of Kentucky.

As different as these men were, and as challenging their assignments, they all had one type of briefing from the president and the secretary of state: show no weakness. In all conversations with foreign dignitaries, the ambassadors were to act as if the United States remained one compact entity, which was undergoing a domestic disturbance.

How did the approach of the war register in the major newspapers?

The front page of the *New York Times* did not yet have those immortal words: "All the News That's Fit to Print." But the *Times* was developing a reputation for sound reporting, and it had a special, unnamed correspondent in Charleston. Receiving constant updates both from him and from its Washington, D.C., correspondent, the *Times* tracked the approach of war with the headlines of 1861 as follows:

"Anxiety relative to Fort Sumter" (April 2); "Cabinet Meeting on the Southern Policy of this Administration" (April 3); "The Crisis Approaching" (April 5); "The Impending Crisis" (April 6); "The War Cloud" (April 8); "The Impending War" (April 10); and "The War Imminent" (April 11).

None of these appeared at the top of the masthead, as news sometimes does today; instead, they were placed either at the top of the extreme left-hand column or the top of the extreme right. The reader could not possibly be confused as to what was the lead story of the day. Even so, there were some Americans who refused to believe it. Civil conflict had been threatened numerous times in the past, and it had always been averted.

Was there any chance that the war could—at this late moment—have been averted?

Virtually none. To make that happen, Lincoln and his Cabinet would have had to make concessions that might bring down the wrath of their Northern supporters. For Jefferson Davis and his Cabinet, too, the question of morale was all-important. The Southern people were keyed up, and this seemed like the propitious moment to strike. And so, after a decade of dissension and division, the thirty-four states of what had been the Union prepared to go to war, not with some foreign power but against each other.

THE FIRST BATTLES: APRIL 1861 TO FEBRUARY 1862

FORT SUMTER

When did the Civil War truly begin?

At 4:20 A.M. on April 12, 1861. The Confederate batteries surrounding Fort Sumter commenced a bombardment, inaugurating the Civil War.

Of course, some argue for other deadlines and commencements. Some say that the war was inevitable after the execution of John Brown, while others assert that Lincoln's election was the dividing line. Regardless of where one draws the line of inevitability, however, the war itself commenced with those guns firing early on the morning of April 12, 1861.

Where is Fort Sumter located?

Fort Sumter is a masonry fort located just off the coast of South Carolina in Charleston Harbor.

How much lead-up was there to the bombardment?

Almost thirty days. For all that time, the Confederates built up their batteries at different locations, with the guns all trained on Fort Sumter. That the Confederates could bombard and force the fort to surrender was beyond doubt; whether they would choose to do so was another matter. But on April 10, 1861, President Jefferson Davis telegraphed the commander in Charleston, giving him the go-ahead either to accept the fort's surrender or to compel it with cannon fire.

Brigadier General Pierre T. Beauregard (1818–1893) was a Louisianan, but he had been chosen for this assignment, partly because of his special knowledge in the use of artillery. An irony that escaped no one was that his opposite number, Major Robert Anderson, had been his instructor at West Point and was a specialist in artillery. The two men began by sending polite greetings, and even the occasional bottle of wine, but by the time Jefferson Davis' order arrived, the "game" had become deadly serious.

Was there any chance that Fort Sumter could hold out?

Not really. The single most immediate problem was a shortage of food, but even if that had been solved, a dozen other logistical problems stared Major Anderson in the face. Most unfair, he had little communication with Lincoln or other members of the administration. As they jostled with each other over the best way to proceed, members of the Lincoln administration left Major Anderson very much in the dark.

Nor was Fort Sumter truly necessary for the defense of the Union. It would be convenient, to be sure, to keep such a fort in that location, but the morale effect was far more important than the strategic one. Lincoln cleverly maneuvered so that it was the Confederates who fired the first shots of the war.

When did Major Anderson return fire?

The federal soldiers held their fire until about 7 A.M. The reason was twofold: they wished to preserve their ammunition, and they wanted to prevent running around in the dark. By 7:30 A.M., Fort Sumter was blazing back at the Confederates, however.

How soon did the rest of the country learn the news about Fort Sumter?

Much sooner than we might think. If the Civil War had started in 1841, rather than 1861, it might have taken three weeks for the news to reach all parts of the nation. Thanks to

The attack on Fort Sumter by Confederate ships on April 12, 1861, is what started the actual exchange of gunfire in the Civil War, though some historians feel the war was inevitable for quite some time before that.

the electric telegraph, however, the news reached all the major cities within twelve hours and most of the countryside areas within forty-eight. North and South, Union and Confederacy alike, there was a profound sense of relief. The tension had lifted, and action had begun. The *New York Times* put it succinctly: "The ball has opened. War is inaugurated."

How long did the siege, or bombardment, of the fort last?

By the morning of April 13, 1861, it was apparent that Fort Sumter was dying. The massive fort had been built with an eye to attack from the sea, not by land. The strongest casements and battlements were therefore on the seaward side, and those on the land side were being crushed by the Confederate guns. Even so, the manner in which Fort Sumter fell is rather comical.

Louis T. Wigfall was a former U.S. Senator from Texas and now a colonel in the Confederate army. A rather pompous, overbearing person, Wigfall wanted to seize the glory for capturing Fort Sumter. He, therefore, had himself rowed out to the fort, and the federal soldiers were astonished when he literally knocked on the gate. Once admitted, he attempted to persuade Major Anderson to surrender. While Anderson wavered, Wigfall took out a white handkerchief, stuck his hand through one of the gun openings, and waved. Almost at once, a Confederate cannon shot crashed into that very area. No one was hurt, but the combination of Wigfall's silly action and the realization of hopelessness persuaded Major Anderson to yield. Later that day, he accepted the same terms which had been offered him two days earlier, before the siege began. His garrison was accorded all the honors of war, including the right to fire a one-hundred-gun salute to its flag, before hauling it down.

Fort Sumter as it looks today. Tourists can visit the national park, and you can find out more at http://fortsumtertours.com/.

Who died during the Siege of Fort Sumter?

To the best of our knowledge, no persons died during the bombardment itself (one Confederate horse was killed). But in a tragedy, one federal man was killed and two others badly wounded when a gun burst during the firing of the one-hundred-gun salute. Even so, considering that so many shots had been fired, it was astonishing that there were not higher casualties. One European observer concluded that an American battle, or siege, was as harmless as a country fair.

On April 15, 1861, Major Anderson and his men were taken on a Confederate steamer. They landed at Manhattan two days later. Anderson became a national hero and was quickly promoted to brigadier-general. He and his men received heroes' welcomes in New York City.

Who moved next? Who held the initiative after Fort Sumter?

Lincoln had cleverly maneuvered the Confederates into a bad position. Even though he could summon three times as many soldiers, and perhaps ten times as much industrial power, the Confederates were seen as the aggressors. This allowed Lincoln to issue a proclamation, on April 15, 1861, asking the states of the Union for a total of 75,000 volunteers to serve for three months' time. The secretary of war sent the specific request to the governors of all the states: the total requested came to ninety-seven regiments with the largest requests being for New York, Ohio, and Pennsylvania.

Lincoln played his hand well. When he sent out the proclamation, it went to all the loyal states plus the Border States. By that simple action, Lincoln continued to refuse to admit any loss to the Union, which, in his mind, was perpetual. Nor did he dignify the actions at Fort Sumter with terms such as "war" or even "rebellion." Lincoln acted as if this would be a police action that would be over in three months' time.

FLAG FEVER

What was the response in the North?

It is hard to describe the speed and fervor with which young Americans flocked to the colors. Nothing like it had been seen before, and nothing like it would happen again until the Japanese attack on Pearl Harbor eighty years later. Young men and boys in Northern cities, towns, and hamlets came out to volunteer in amazing numbers. Several state governors telegraphed Washington, D.C., to say that their original regiments were already filled, asking permission to form new ones. These requests were, of course, granted.

Of all the demonstrations for the flag, the Star-Spangled Banner, the single greatest was held in New York City on Saturday, April 20, 1861. Roughly 100,000 persons jammed Union Square in the lower part of Manhattan to hear no fewer than thirteen speakers extol the Union. Those who watched could find no fault with the demonstration. It was not so much anti-Confederate or anti-South as pro-Union. Given that New York City enjoyed a profitable trade relationship with numerous Southern states, the Union Square demonstration was a powerful example of Union sentiment.

Were there any notable songs or poems that came as a result?

There were so many that we cannot list or describe them all. Let these poetic lines, published in the New York *Tribune*, stand as an example:

Ring out the tidings round the earth;
To all the families of men;
A nation hath been born again,
Regenerate by a second birth!

Rent are the bonds of gain and greed,
Once coiled around our common life,
Hushed are the hate of party strife,
And jealousies of race and creed....

Lord God of Hosts to whom we pray
In all times, favored or forlorn,
We thank thy name that thus is born
A nation in a single day!

Were there similar poetic outbursts in the South?

Again, there were many, far too many to count. On the whole, however, the North, or Union, had the better part of the poetic argument. The answer is not too far to seek. It is much easier to cheer *for* something, or to rally people around something, that already exists than to generate enthusiasm for something that is just coming into being. But when one looks for a counterpart to the Northern poems, one finds poetry such as follows, published in the *Richmond Dispatch* on May 23, 1861:

Now bring me out my buckskin suit!
My pouch and powder too!
We'll see if seventy-six can shoot
As sixteen used to do!

Old Bess! We've kept our barrels bright!
Our trigger quick and true!
As far, if not as fine a sight,
As, long ago, we drew!....

Give boys your brass percussion caps!
Old "shut-pan" suits as well!
There's something in the sparks; perhaps
There's something in the smell!

We've seen the red-coat Briton bleed!
The red-skin Indian too!
We've never thought to draw a bead
On Yankee-doodle-doo!

What about in the Southern states? Was there recruiting?

There certainly was. First, however, the Southern states had to show, in some way, that they were no longer part of the Union. The seven states already in secession could do this easily: they simply refused to answer Lincoln's call for volunteers. But the states that were on the brink of secession were in an awkward spot. Missouri, for example, was sharply divided between Union and Confederate sympathizers. Its governor sent a blistering letter to Lincoln, declaring that the call for volunteers was illegal, immoral, and would put the country on the road to damnation.

Because the South was profoundly rural and had fewer newspapers, we have little knowledge of what the recruiting was like. We know that many thousands of young men signed up quickly, but we are not certain whether they thought of themselves as Confederates, state militia men, or just volunteers brought together for a state of emergency. Throughout the war, this posed a great difficulty to the Confederate cause. How could a new nation, which had been founded on the demand for states' rights, *compel* men to serve in a national army?

What did Sam Houston have to say, and why was it so important?

When Texas moved to join the Confederacy in March 1861, it found its governor, Sam Houston, so dead-set against it that the legislature removed him. Many had expected

What was the original Confederate flag?

There were so many different ones, stitched together so quickly, that the question is nearly impossible to answer. The first one to appear was the Palmetto Flag, which showed up in the harbor at Charleston within days of Lincoln's election. But when the seven states in secession banded together to form the Confederate States of America, another race was on to see which flag would be best.

The most hopeful and optimistic flag was the one that proudly showed fifteen stars: South Carolina, Mississippi, Florida, Alabama, Louisiana, Georgia, Texas, Virginia, North Carolina, Tennessee, Arkansas, Maryland, Delaware, Kentucky, and Missouri. Had this collection actually joined the Confederacy, it is difficult to see how the Union could have prevailed. But, as we will see, only four of the other states joined the seven already in secession, and later Confederate flags acknowledged the fact by placing eleven stars rather than fifteen.

Houston, the greatest living hero of the Texas Revolution of 1836, to be on their side, but he had deep misgivings about the war. On May 1, 1861, he revealed the full extent of his concerns to a crowd at Independence, Texas.

"We have entered upon a conflict which will demand all the energies of the people," Houston declared. "The South, chivalric, brave, and impetuous as it is, must add to

Most people today think that the flag shown at top was the official flag of the Confederacy. Actually, that is the flag of the Army of Northern Virginia. The flag on the bottom, called the "Stars and Bars," was one of several official flags proposed for the Confederacy.

these attributes of success thorough discipline, or disaster will come upon the country. The Northern people by their nature and occupation are subordinate to orders. They are capable of great endurance and a high state of discipline. A good motto for a soldier is, Never underestimate the strength of your enemy. The South claims superiority over them in point of fearless courage. Equal them in point of discipline, and there will be no danger."

Which state was the first to secede after Fort Sumter's fall?

Virginia, the Old Dominion, had been teetering on the edge of secession for some time. The most populous of all the Southern states, Virginia had a longstanding commitment to slavery: its slaves were, perhaps, those who had lived in America the longest. Virginians rightly feared, however, that their lands would be the ones most torn up in a civil conflict; the Old Dominion, therefore, stayed its hand till after Fort Sumter.

A special state convention was held in Richmond, and the delegates voted to secede. The action would not become law until it was ratified by the people: the vote was scheduled for the third week in May. But as it became clear that Virginia would indeed depart the Union, something like panic seized the upper echelons of the U.S. Army. Where would the Northern armies find their leaders, their general officers? And, perhaps because Virginia was so clearly part of the problem, all eyes turned to the special case of Robert E. Lee.

Why did Robert E. Lee join the Confederacy rather than the Union?

In April 1861, General Winfield Scott offered Colonel Robert E. Lee field command of all the volunteer forces being raised in the North. The seventy-five-year-old Scott had witnessed Lee in action during the Mexican War and considered him the finest field officer he had ever seen.

Lee took two days to consider, then declined the offer. Whether he went across the Potomac River to speak in person or sent a letter is not known, but in either case he cut a very close tie. Scott was also a Virginian, but he had no doubt where his loyalties were. Lee was a U.S. Army officer, who had given thirty years to the service, but he decided, finally, that he could not serve against his home state. What makes this so important is the realization that it was loyalty to his state, not the Confederacy, or even to the institution of slavery, that made up Lee's mind.

Given that we associate the name of Lee with that of Stonewall Jackson, where was Jackson when Fort Sumter was attacked?

Born and raised in rural Virginia, Thomas Jonathan Jackson (1824–1863) came from very different circumstances than Robert E. Lee. There was blue-blooded aristocracy in his veins, but because of a variety of circumstances—including his father's early death— Jackson had a difficult time in early life. West Point saved his life in that it provided a focus, and Jackson served as a lieutenant in the Mexican War. The spring of 1861 found

Jackson where he had been for nearly a decade, at the Virginia Military Institute, where he was a professor of mathematics.

Jackson was not meant, or cut out, for teaching. He did his best, but his students found him eccentric, gloomy, and overly attentive to detail. When he learned of the attack on Fort Sumter, and that Virginia was about to secede, Jackson assembled his cadets and brought them, by forced march, to Richmond. This was his first action, and it was emblematic in that he would always be known for the speed of his march.

One can ask the same question about Union leaders. Where was Ulysses S. Grant?

Poor Ulysses Grant (1822–1885)—his birth name was Hiram Simpson Ulysses Grant—had endured a miserable decade. After graduating West Point, in 1845, he served with distinction in the Mexican War. Subsequent assignments to lonely barracks on the West Coast had nearly been the death of him: Grant succumbed to depression and heavy drinking. He resigned from the U.S. Regular Army in 1854.

The start of the Civil War brought Grant back to life. Though he was working as a clerk in his father's leather tannery in Galena, Illinois, Grant joined the local militia and was soon elected colonel of his regiment. His friend, neighbor, and confidante—to the extent that anyone filled that role—John Rawlins later declared that Grant took on a new look and attitude in a matter of weeks. Where previously he had slouched, he now stood erect. Grant had divided feelings on the subject of slavery—his wife Julia's family had long been slaveholders—but on the question of union or secession, he had not the slightest doubt.

We associate the name of Sherman with that of Grant. Where was Sherman in 1861?

Like Grant, William T. Sherman (1820–1891) had resigned from the U.S. Regular Army. In most other respects, their lives over the previous decade had been quite different.

Sherman had married the daughter of a well-to-do merchant, but the marriage had created stresses and strains (his in-laws were always trying to get him to leave the military and join their family business). Sherman and his wife had moved to San Francisco for a time, and, like Grant, Sherman had hated life on the West Coast. The spring of 1861 found him in Washing-

General William T. Sherman would form a close working relationship with General Grant. Sherman is often remembered—and criticized—for his "scorched earth" tactics in utterly defeating the South.

ton, D.C., and he quickly entered a volunteer regiment, then was transferred to the Regular Army. For a time he outranked Grant, but throughout their long partnership, Grant would usually be the heavyweight.

What about George B. McClellan?

When the war began, George Brinton McClellan (1826–1885) was the brightest of the young and rising stars. A graduate of West Point, he had served in the Mexican War, specializing in artillery. This concentration only increased when he served as an unofficial observer of British and

General George McClellan.

French forces in the Crimean War. The son of a prominent Philadelphia physician, married to wealth, McClellan was both prosperous and successful when the war began. Unlike Grant or Sherman, he did not "need" the war.

When McClellan first presented for duty in the summer of 1861, very few people saw or detected the weakness that lay underneath. McClellan had many things going for him, including a fine physical presentation. Attentive to detail, absorbed in the well-being of his troops, McClellan had one great flaw: he was indecisive.

ONE SPECIAL YOUNG MAN

Was there anyone else of whom special notice was made? Any young rising star?

There were many. But out of all of them, one stands out. His name was Elmer Ellsworth.

Born in upstate New York in 1837, Ellsworth was a dreamy, introspective boy who nursed delusions of grandeur. His workaday parents did not know what to make of their son, who knitted uniforms and spoke of far-off places, and he seems to have made his way almost entirely on his own. By 1859, he was clerking in a law office in Chicago, eating porridge or whatever else came to hand and forming a group of Zouaves. Ellsworth's Zouave group toured the northern part of the nation in 1859; a year later, he came to the attention of Abraham Lincoln. Ellsworth rode to Washington, D.C., aboard Lincoln's presidential train, and when the war began he went to New York City, announcing his desire to recruit and form the New York Fire Zouaves.

What was it about the b'hoys?

B'hoy was an imitation of the Irish speech in New York City, and Ellsworth wanted to create a Zouave Brigade composed entirely of New York City firemen. By imitating their

What was Zouave Fever?

It was a fad, a craze, something that had almost never been seen before. In the late 1850s and early 1860s, thousands, perhaps even hundreds of thousands, of Americans caught the fever for the Zouaves.

Dressed more like acrobats than soldiers, and performing drills that elicited deep-throated cheers, the Zouaves were paramilitary groups that formed all across the nation: North and South, East and West. All Zouave groups took their name and part of their identity from the French Foreign Legion, which had used special tactics to fight a group of Algerian tribesmen of that name. By 1859, the year Elmer Ellsworth's group toured, Americans were thrilled, even bowled over by the athletic young men who delighted in showing their tricks to audiences. One imagines that Ellsworth was completing a dream he had nursed in youth: a dream of glory, beauty, and above all, fun.

No one expected that Zouave Fever would lead to, or help along, the Civil War. That is precisely what happened, however. When the recruiters—North and South—went into different cities and towns, they spoke of the glories of the military life, and thousands of boys and young men—many of whom had seen the Zouaves on parade—were quick to sign the rosters.

speech—at least on occasion—and by inspiring them to join the Union cause, Ellsworth performed a great service for the North. He made military service fashionable.

On arriving in New York City, Ellsworth declared his intention to enlist 1,000 men. He had that number within a single day. The New York firemen were volunteers, aggressive men, and natural brawlers. Some people criticized the Zouaves on first sight, and quite a few historians single them out for negative treatment: their poor fighting at the Battle of Bull Run earned them a lot of disparaging comments. But in the early days and weeks of the war, there was nothing more exciting than a Zouave, and of them, the New York Fire Zouaves were the best of all.

What did the British government have to say about secession and war?

Queen Victoria (1819–1901) issued a statement in April 1861 declaring that England was happily at peace with all "Sovereigns, Powers, and States" and given that she was at peace with the United States, she enjoined her subjects to observe a "strict and impartial neutrality" in the American Civil War.

It is difficult to say precisely what the feeling was on the part of the English people. Historians, generally, believe that the upper class of England was somewhat favorable to the Confederacy, while its working class was distinctly favorable to the Union. It should be pointed out that the British laborer, whether in Manchester, Liverpool, or Leeds, had more to gain from an alliance with the Confederacy than he had to lose with an alliance with the Union. Even so, the British working class generally remained sympathetic to the North throughout the war, a powerful testimony to the importance of *Uncle Tom's Cabin*.

When did the *New York Times* go to a Sunday printing?

On Sunday, April 21, 1861. One day after the amazing Union flag day, on April 20, the *Times* became a seven-day-a-week newspaper and never looked back.

What was the Baltimore riot of 1861?

Baltimore was known as one of the most contentious cities in the nation. Back in 1812, there had been a mob attack on a newspaper headquarters: one of the persons badly injured that day was Light Horse Harry Lee, father of Robert E. But things were much worse in 1861, thanks to Baltimore's position as the northernmost of all southern places and the southernmost of all northern ones.

On April 19, 1861, which just happened to be the anniversary of the Battles of Lexington and Concord, the Massachusetts Sixth Regiment of volunteers was attacked by a crowd as it changed trains in Baltimore. Three soldiers were killed, as were several civilians, and there was an undetermined number of wounded. The Massachusetts Sixth made it through to Washington, D.C., to Abraham Lincoln's great relief, but it was more apparent than ever that the national capital was imperiled by the proximity of Maryland, in general, and Baltimore, in specific.

Citizens of Baltimore attacked federal troops on April 19, 1861, in what is now called the Baltimore Riot. The attacks were particularly troubling because of the anti-federal feelings they showed in a city so close to Capitol Hill.

When did the Old Dominion make its first move?

On April 17, 1861, the Virginia convention voted to secede from the Union, making Virginia the eighth state to join the Confederacy.

"We, the people of Virginia, in the ratification of the Constitution of the United States of America, adopted by them in Convention, on the 25th day of June in the year of our Lord 1788, having declared that the powers granted them under the said constitution, were derived from the people of the United States, and might be resumed whensoever the same should be perverted to their injury and oppression, and the federal government having perverted said powers, not only to the injury of the people of Virginia, but to the oppression of the Southern slaveholding States.

"Now, therefore, we, the people of Virginia do declare and ordain that the Ordinance adopted by the people of this state in Convention on the twenty-fifth day of June in the year of our Lord one thousand seven hundred and eighty-eight, whereby the Constitution of the United States of America was ratified … is hereby dissolved, and that the State of Virginia is in the full possession and exercise of all the rights of sovereignty which belong to a free and independent State. And they do further declare that the said Constitution of the United States of America is no longer binding on any of the citizens of this State."

What was the first military action undertaken by Virginia?

Just days later, Virginia militia leaders initiated a series of daring attacks on federal installations and properties.

The major intent was to prevent the Union from bottling up Confederate ships in the James River. To that end, Confederate—or rather Virginian—forces attacked and seized the U.S. naval base at Norfolk. Other forces rushed toward Fortress Monroe, the largest of all federal installations, but they were stopped by the sudden arrival of several Massachusetts regiments. Even so, the Virginians did amazing things in the first two weeks of their Civil War. The speed with which they moved appeared to justify the notion—promoted in many Southern newspapers—that Southern men were natural fighters and that their Yankee opponents were too slow.

What was the Anaconda Plan?

In late April 1861, General Winfield Scott submitted to Lincoln his proposal for the Union war strategy. Scott was so heavy and weary he could no longer ride a horse, but his mind was still sharp, as evidenced by his writing. First and foremost, Scott predicted that this would not be a short and easy conflict. It might take as long as three years, he declared.

A Virginian by birth, Scott predicted that the Old Dominion would be the toughest nut to crack. Rather than march straight south, various Union forces should move at and into the Confederacy from oblique angles, including the Tennessee and Cumberland River valleys. At the same time, the Union Navy would blockade the entire coastline, and eventually, by capturing New Orleans, accomplish a snakelike effect of strangling the Confederacy.

Scott's idea came in for much ridicule in 1861, but by 1865 many people saw that he had been correct in at least two-thirds, perhaps even three-quarters, of his predictions.

How long had General Winfield Scott been around? Why didn't he lead the armies?

Born in Virginia in 1786, Winfield Scott was commissioned a lieutenant of artillery in the U.S. Regular Army in 1808. Almost at once he ran into trouble with his superiors and was court-martialed out of the army, but his superior talent, as well as the beginning of the War of 1812, opened a new path for him. Scott rose to major-general during that war and was renowned for the discipline he brought to his army units. Right after the war ended, Scott sailed to Europe to observe the Allied armies that

One of the most distinguished soldiers in American history, General Winfield Scott, who had served in the military since the War of 1812, conceived of the Anaconda Plan to defeat the South.

had brought down the Emperor Napoleon. He returned with many valuable observations. This was only the beginning, however, of his long and distinguished career.

In 1847, Scott led the American forces that captured Vera Cruz on the coast of Mexico, then marched inland, all the way to capture Mexico City. His achievement was monumental; his skill was at that time unequalled, but he had few friends. In part this was due to an overwhelming ego that turned off many people. Scott ran for president in 1852 as a Whig, but was defeated by one of his former military subordinates, Franklin Pierce. When the Civil War began, Scott was obviously the sharpest mind left in the War Department, but he was, physically speaking, a wreck. Overweight and weary, he kept up with his duties until the end of October, when Lincoln removed him.

Was the Union up to the job? Could it carry out the Anaconda Plan?

Not in 1861. The Regular U.S. Army was still small, and the U.S. Navy was almost puny. But in terms of sheer, raw potential, the Union could field all the men and build all the ships it would ever need. By contrast, the Confederacy could throw men into the fight more quickly, and perhaps gain some early victories, but it could never match the industrial power of the North.

Jefferson Davis and his number-one military adviser Robert E. Lee knew this quite well. Both men knew that the Confederacy had to act with lightning speed if it were to have any chance. Therefore, the provisional Confederate government decided to move the capital of the Confederate States from Montgomery, Alabama, to Richmond, Virginia. This had the effect of making Richmond a "forward" capital, aimed at the heart of its foes. It also meant that the two opposing capitals would be 110 miles apart.

What was Lincoln most concerned about?

It took Lincoln weeks to adjust to the fact that the Southern states truly were in earnest, that the war was real. Even after he issued the call for 75,000 volunteers, there was some hesitation in his movements. Once he fully realized the extent of the danger, however, Lincoln proved himself a strategist of no mean ability (one confidante claimed that the president spent more time with the war maps than all of his generals combined). As a Western man, hailing from Kentucky, Indiana, and Illinois—in that order—Lincoln saw the trans-Ohio battlefields as the most important. As long as the Confederates could be contained, or fought to a draw, in the East, the Union would eventually prevail in the West. On the other hand, if the Confederates gained some of the Border States, the whole war might be turned on its head.

Was the importance of the Border States fully appreciated in Washington?

Lincoln, in that inimitable fashion which was beginning to appear, wrote a letter to a friend back home in Illinois, saying this on the Border States:

> I think to lose Kentucky is nearly the same as to lose the whole game. Kentucky gone, we cannot hold Missouri, nor, I think, Maryland. These all against us, and the job in our hands is too large for us. We would as well consent to separation at once, including the surrender of this capital.

What were the Border States? How important were they?

Delaware, with 112,216 people, was the smallest and least consequential of the Border States, but if it combined with Maryland (687,049), the federal capital would be both cut off and in danger of being captured. Kentucky, with 1,115,684 persons, was vital to the Union cause. So long as it possessed Kentucky, the Union would be on the offense in the West; if it lost Kentucky, all sorts of terrible trouble might emerge. But as important as Kentucky was, Lincoln may have misjudged, because Missouri was even more important.

The 1,182,012 persons of Missouri represented a fascinating mixture of the North, South, and West, as well as the old and the new. Until about 1845, Missouri had been an unrepentant slave state, whose politics were guided by Virginians and North Carolinians who had emigrated west a generation earlier. But by 1861, the German and Irish immigrants of St. Louis outnumbered the "old" immigrants from the Southern states, and their sentiments were strongly for the Union and against slavery. This did not mean that Missouri was a pushover, however; it meant that the Show-Me State would remain divided throughout the war.

What were the key points or places on the map, the "must-haves" for both sides?

The Union established its single biggest must-have when it held on to Fortress Monroe, at the end of Old Point Comfort, Virginia. So long as the North held this position, it dominated shipping traffic in and out of Chesapeake Bay as well as the entrance to the James River. The second all-important spot for the Union was Cairo, Illinois, a sandy spit of land at the confluence of the Ohio and Mississippi Rivers. Colonel Ulysses S. Grant was there by the summer of 1861, holding on to a vital piece of real estate.

The trouble for the Confederacy was that, given the naval strength of the Union, it had so much more real estate to defend. There were thousands of miles of Atlantic and Gulf Coast shoreline where the Yankees could attack. But to Confederate planners, it was evident that New Orleans, because of its commercial wealth, and Richmond, because it was the national capital, were the most important places. There was also a long-shot chance that the Confederacy could go on the offensive in the Far West, and to that end, a major effort was made to enter the Arizona Territory.

What about the link between East and West Coasts?

No one ever described it better than Adam Goodheart in *1861: The Civil War Awakening*:

"They must have glimpsed one another sometime during that week, at some unrecorded point along the Central Overland Trail. Perhaps it was here, at a bend in the sluggish stream. Perhaps the mule drivers paused in their labor and watched the thing coming toward them: a shimmer against the dull, flat sky that resolved itself, quickly, into a horseman."

The Pony Express had been established just eighteen months earlier, and it was still the fastest way to get news from the East to the Pacific Coast, but it would soon be upended by the new transcontinental telegraph. Men of the Central Overland company were stringing up telegraph poles to connect Sacramento, California, with St. Louis, Missouri. Once that was complete, the telegraph would "flash" messages between East and West.

What was Lincoln's first military move in the East?

During the night of May 23 to 24, 1861, several thousand Union soldiers crossed from Washington, D.C., to Arlington, Virginia. They quickly occupied the empty mansion of Robert E. Lee, who was in Richmond, then moved against Alexandria, a few miles south.

Colonel Elmer Ellsworth and the New York Fire Zouaves were part of the Union effort, and when he entered Alexandria, Colonel Ellsworth expressed a desire to bring down the large Confederate flag he saw flying over the top of a three-story boarding house. The Confederate flag was so large that President Lincoln could see it from the top floor of the White House, several miles distant. Ellsworth and three of his soldiers entered the Marshall House, proceeded to the top story, and cut down the Confederate flag (whether it was the Stars and Bars or some other concoction is not known). As they reached the second-floor landing, they were confronted by James W. Jackson, the proprietor, who swiftly shot and killed Colonel Ellsworth. Seconds later, Jackson was bayoneted and killed by one of the New York Fire Zouaves. Ellsworth's body was wrapped in the flag he had brought down and taken to Washington, D.C.

How did Lincoln, and others, respond to Ellsworth's death?

There was profound mourning. Ellsworth had, among all the early Union commanders, exhibited something very special: a charming mixture of innocence and devotion. Lincoln was clearly distraught: this was when the reality of the war truly hit him. Ellsworth's body lay in the East Room of the White House for several days and was seen by thousands. There were commemorations in other cities and towns. In New York City, the diarist George Templeton Strong commented that the lamented Colonel Ellsworth had done more for the Union cause in death than he could ever have accomplished in life.

This Currier & Ives illustration indicates the power of Colonel Elmer Ellsworth, of whom it can rightly be said that he was more important to the Union in his death than in life.

Confederates, naturally, pointed to James Jackson as their hero, the man who courageously resisted the first federal incursion to Virginia. But the fifty-something-year-old Jackson could not compare to Ellsworth in youth or appeal. Therefore, the first armed clash between Federals and rebels along the Potomac was a clear moral victory for the Union.

When and where was the first controversy over black slaves in the Union forces?

In May 1861, a Confederate colonel called at the gates of Fortress Monroe, asking for the return of three of his slaves. They had escaped his nearby plantation and made their way to the federal fortress. Just a few days earlier, Brigadier General Benjamin Butler (1818–1893), of the Massachusetts volunteers, had arrived to take the command. Butler took a few minutes, then responded that he would not return the escaped slaves. When the Confederate colonel persisted, saying that the Fugitive Slave Law of 1850 remained on the books, Butler neatly returned that Virginia had seceded from the Union and could therefore claim no special protections. But when the Confederate continued to argue, Butler answered with the simple and effective: "I mean to hold them."

It is possible that Butler did not realize the momentous step he had taken. By considering the escaped black slaves as "contraband" of war, Butler put them in an entirely different class, legally speaking. They were not "free" men and women, but they might well be on their way to achieving that status. Lincoln surely recognized the importance of Butler's action, and he did nothing to countermand it. In fact, for the first year and more, Lincoln preferred to have commanders on the ground navigate those difficult legal grounds.

When and where was the first gunfight in the West?

The federal arsenal in St. Louis, Missouri, was a prize desired by both sides. Given that Missouri was on the fence—it had neither seceded nor affirmed the Union— the arsenal was in danger of a Confederate takeover. Governor Claiborne Fox Jackson (1806–1862) pretended to be neutral, but those who knew him were quite certain he

Brigadier General Benjamin Butler set an important precedent in 1861 when he refused to return a number of slaves to a Confederate colonel, asserting that the Compromise of 1850 no longer applied since the South had seceded.

was angling for the right moment to declare for the Confederacy. During early June 1861, several hundred pro-slavery men gathered in St. Louis, naming their encampment for the governor.

Under ordinary circumstances, St. Louis might well have gone to the Confederacy. There was a very unusual Union commander on the scene, however, Captain Nathaniel Lyon. An eccentric—some even said deluded—person, Lyon was absolutely convinced of the need to act. Working with Frank P. Blair Jr. (1821–1875), brother of the very influential Postmaster General Montgomery Blair (1813–1883), Lyon gathered his men and entered Camp Jackson on June 15, 1861. He was completely successful in disarming the pro-slavery men, but as he marched them to a holding place, his men were attacked by a crowd. Who fired first and who shouted insults the loudest will forever remain mysterious, but Lyon and his men killed several people in the crowd, and a pro-slavery demonstration was made the following day. By then, Lyon had succeeded, however. Camp Jackson was broken up, and the federal arsenal was, for the moment at least, secure.

How many soldiers did the Union have at the capital?

By early July 1861, there were over 40,000 men in and around Washington, D.C., and another 25,000 in the Shenandoah River Valley. Many of them were scheduled to depart soon, however; practically all of them had volunteered for three months only.

Lincoln and his commanders—East and West—faced a continuing problem throughout 1861: how to integrate militia units into the Regular Army. In some cases it just was not possible. Lincoln, therefore, believed it necessary to strike a first blow at the Confederacy before these men's enlistments were up. He pressed General Winfield

Was Lincoln gay? Bisexual?

The short and simple answer is that he was not. Lincoln was a heterosexual who, for whatever reason, found it easier to express affection toward men than women. His often-remarked-upon friendship with his law partner was nothing out of the ordinary, and his extraordinary affection for Elmer Ellsworth was thoroughly conventional by the standards of the time. What was not so normal was Lincoln's ease at expressing affection toward men in public.

Both during his election campaign and then his presidency, Lincoln thought nothing of linking arms with other men and parading, usually to celebrate. On the day of his inauguration, Lincoln linked arms with James C. Buchanan, and the two—who had taken plenty of pot shots at one another earlier—walked into the Capitol arm in arm. In the fine movie *Lincoln*, released in 2012, one such moment occurs when Lincoln takes the arm of Secretary of War Edwin Stanton and folds it in his own as they await the news of the Siege of Fort Fisher.

Scott, who pressed General Irvin McDowell (1818-1885). When McDowell complained to Lincoln that his men were "green" (or untried), the president replied that the Confederates were green as well and that the time had come to strike a blow.

What about the federal arsenal at Harpers Ferry?

That was where John Brown had nearly started the war, two years earlier, and Harpers Ferry remained very important. Union men held it when the war began, but they were chased out by Virginia militia in the summer of 1861. Harpers Ferry would change hands so many times that it became, perhaps, the single most occupied place in the United States. It took the town, and its people, a long time to shake off the effects of the war.

What was so special about the Fourth of July in 1861?

For starters, it was the eighty-fifth anniversary of the signing of the Declaration of Independence: the young republic had lasted almost four generations. For a second, both the Union and the Confederacy claimed the founding fathers and the Revolution as a basis for their ideas and ideals. This Fourth of July was also different in that Lincoln had called for a special congressional session to begin, and that he now asked for four million men and four hundred million dollars. Lincoln expressed his views of the war in a special message to Congress:

"This is essentially a People's contest. On the side of the Union, it is a struggle for maintaining in the world, that form and substance of government, whose leading object is, to elevate the condition of men—to lift artificial weights from all shoulders—to clear the paths of laudable pursuit for all."

BULL RUN

What was the Confederate's military plan?

The Confederates wanted to hold on to what they had in the East; the Union wanted to press its advantage. In the second week of July 1861, General Irvin McDowell (1818–1885) prodded his men across the Potomac and into northern Virginia.

The landscape was quite different from what the men knew; the social and economic differences between the North and the South became readily apparent. Instead of towns and villages, they found plantations and hamlets, with more real living space than expected, but many people living in mild poverty. Another eye-opener had to do with the federal troops themselves: they were, for the most part, in poor physical condition. Americans of 1861 worked harder and longer than their descendants today, but even farm boys were not accustomed to long walks: they rode hay wagons whenever possible. Therefore, as the federal troops moved into the Virginia countryside, they experienced exhaustion and the occasional case of heat stroke.

Where were the Confederates?

Led by General P. G. T. Beauregard—the hero of Fort Sumter—the 30,000-odd Confederates were poised in a defensive position near the stream called Bull Run, which meandered through the fields to flow into the Potomac. Three miles behind them was Manassas Junction, the most important railroad connection in this part of the Southern states. Holding that railway link was vital to the Southern cause.

Another 20,000 or so Confederates were in the Shenandoah River Valley, about eighty miles away, but they were shadowing, and being shadowed by, a Union force of almost 30,000. Although we know a lot of the numerical strengths and weaknesses, they were not always apparent at the time, not even to the generals on the ground. This led to a lot of false numbers being circulated and a lot of false claims after the first battle was fought.

Was Bull Run the first battle of the war?

One can argue the point because there were events such as the capture of Camp Jackson in St. Louis, as well as the engagement at Big Bethel, on the Yorktown Peninsula, both of which came earlier. But in terms of a true battle, pitting true armies, Bull Run was certainly the first battle of the war.

Bull Run was also emblematic of the war in many respects. Men on the ground knew little, and their commanders knew only a little more. Smoke obscured parts of the battlefield, and it was nearly impossible for a commanding general to learn all that was happening. Much depended on guesswork, timing, and luck.

What was General McDowell's plan?

Irvin McDowell had been forced into this battle by the insistence of President Lincoln. McDowell drew up a very solid plan of attack, nevertheless. On the evening of July 20,

1861, he stood with his brigade and division commanders, going over the maps a number of times.

The right part of the federal army, which was stationed to the north, would drive another three miles north, come across the Bull Run at a high point, and come south against the Confederates. The center part of the federal army would attack slowly, waiting for pressure to be exerted from the right. And the left, or southern, side of the federal army would demonstrate but not make any attack until the other two sections had accomplished their work. If not Napoleonic, it was nevertheless a fine plan. One trouble emerged right away, however: General McDowell rolled up the maps and kept them. Not a single brigade or division commander walked away from the meeting with a first-rate map.

How did the battle begin?

The Battle of Bull Run began with a night march by a number of regiments from the federal right flank. They moved north-by-northwest and encountered more difficulty than expected. Not only were the men tired and foot-sore, but they collided with the equipment wagons, often jostling each other to see who could remain on the road. In the tiny hamlet of Centerville, thousands of federal men collided, with no one understanding who had priority in the advance. Even so, daylight found thousands of federal troops on the west side of the Bull Run, executing the flanking maneuver that McDowell had planned.

The first firing began just before dawn and increased rapidly from that moment. The Confederates, especially those on their left flank, were astonished to find the Federals so close, and a few artillery salvoes drove them into a dignified retreat. To this point, McDowell's plan was coming along nicely.

What did the Confederates do in response?

By now, there were two Confederate commanders. Beauregard had been the only one to this point, but he was now joined by General Joseph E. Johnston (1807–1891), who outranked him. To make matters easy, they agreed to share command on the battlefield.

Beauregard and Johnston were both surprised to hear cannon fire to their left: since the previous evening, they had been convinced that the Federals would attack against their right flank. Two hours passed before Beauregard and Johnston made the all-important decision to move regiments from their right to their center, and in that time the Federals might have won the battle. The Northern men were weary from the night march, however, and enough Confederates shifted position to hold them off for the time being.

What was the day itself like: the weather?

July 21, 1861, was just what one would expect: hot, humid, and muggy. The Confederates were definitely more accustomed to the heavy, damp air, but men on both sides suffered in the heat. The average infantryman at Bull Run carried thirty pounds of equipment, making his task all the more difficult.

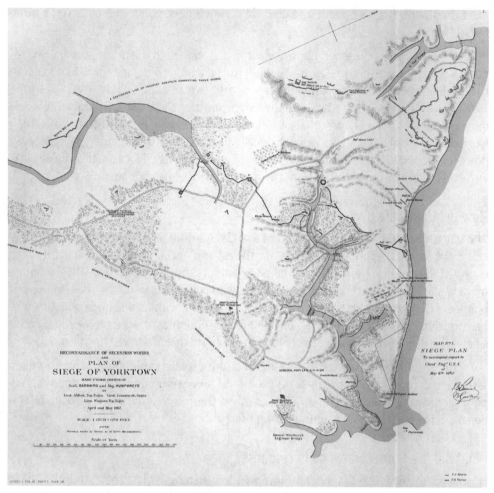

A map showing the siege of the Yorktown Peninsula in 1862, which might be said to be the earliest battle of the war, though it was more of a skirmish compared to Bull Run.

What was the critical point of the battle?

There were, in fact, several. At several different moments, the Confederates could have been pushed out of their defensive position and into a full-scale rout. Most of the heroes, the men who performed above and beyond the call of duty, are anonymous to us, but the single best-known case is that of Colonel Thomas Jonathan Jackson: it was here that he gained his famous nickname.

At around 2 P.M., the Federals were pressing hard against the Confederates on Henry Hill, the center part of their position. General Barnard Bee rode up the hill to its crown to find Colonel Jackson and his regiment of Virginians waiting orders. General Bee expressed great concern, saying that some of his men had run out of ammunition. Jackson, typically, replied: "Well then, we'll give them the bayonet." Encouraged, General Bee rode back to his own position and rallied his own men with these words: "Look yonder, there is Jackson and his Virginians, standing like a stone wall!"

Did General Bee mean his remarks about Jackson as a compliment?

This has long been debated. Did General Bee perhaps mean that Jackson and his men were too stationary, that they should come down the hill to assist him? Or did he mean, as we usually interpret, that Jackson and his Virginians were the exemplars for the rest of the army?

Most historians, perhaps even ninety percent, lean to the second of the two possibilities. We will never know for certain, however, because General Bee was killed about an hour later. What we do know beyond the shadow of a doubt is that this is where Thomas Jackson became Stonewall Jackson and that his reputation would only increase.

Could the Federals have won the day?

Absolutely. As late as 3 P.M., the battle was still a stalemate, but with the Federals enjoying a narrow advantage. At just about that time came a group of Confederate reinforcements, however, by train from the Shenandoah Valley. This was one of the few times in the war that the Confederates were able to use up-to-date technology to their advantage. As the Texas regiments debarked from the train, they rushed to the battlefield, and the fighting began to turn to the Southern advantage.

What was the turning point at Bull Run?

By 4 P.M., the Confederates had the initiative, or momentum, and by 5 P.M., the Federals had begun a slow, dignified retreat. No one knows precisely how it happened, but some of the retreating men, finding supply wagons in their way, tipped them over, and it was now that a full-scale rout commenced.

A British journalist, reporting for the London *Times*, came to the battlefield late, and was appalled by what he saw: regiments disbanded, men on the run, and a general feeling of complete defeat. Some men threw their muskets or rifles away and simply ran. That night and the next morning found most of McDowell's beaten force on or near the western side of the Potomac River, where they were safe, thanks to federal gunboats. Losses on the two sides were about equal, for a total of 6,000 men killed, wounded, and missing. This was much bloodier than had been expected.

Why did the Confederates not pursue?

President Jefferson Davis was, by nature and inclination, a military rather than political person. Davis arrived at the battlefield at 4 or 5 P.M., just as the tide turned in his favor. Exultant and exuberant, Davis sent a telegraph to Richmond, announcing a great victory (in his haste, he declared that 15,000 Confederates had beaten three times that number of Yankees). But even Davis, who often let enthusiasm get the better of him, had no thought of pursuing the enemy or of attacking Washington, D.C.

Even now, flushed with victory, the Confederates did not have the means to invade the North. Had they attempted to capture Washington, they might well have been cut up by the federal gunboats as well as artillery on the ground. And even if they had captured Washington, it is unlikely that the Confederates could have kept it. Now, as so often during the war, a limited system of supply and reinforcement dogged the Confederate cause.

How did Lincoln respond to the defeat?

Lincoln was, by now, beginning to assume the mantle of the presidency. While he still hesitated on some decisions—critics liked to say that he always preferred delay to action—Lincoln was now convinced of the righteousness of the Northern cause. Once that "why" was settled in his mind, the various answers to "how" became easier for him. Lincoln realized that he contributed to the defeat at Bull Run because of the

A staff and supply officer with little battlefield experience, General Irvin McDowell was ill prepared and consequently met defeat at the First Battle of Bull Run.

way he had hurried General McDowell: from that point on, Lincoln deferred to his commanders in terms of timing (sometimes he did so to a fault).

Within days of the defeat, McDowell was removed from command—he remained in the army—and was replaced by Major-General George B. McClellan. Handsome, dominant, and dashing all at once, the thirty-five-year-old McClellan seemed like just the man to whip the army into shape. Born into wealth and raised in prominent social circles, McClellan exemplified much of what was best in Northern culture. He had one great fault, however: he liked to delay.

MOVEMENTS IN THE WEST

What happened in the West during the summer of 1861?

There were times, in the summer of 1861, when it seemed as if the Confederacy would succeed in greatly extending its reach westward. As early as June, there were Texans crossing into the New Mexico Territory, and by August they raised Confederate flags over Flagstaff, Arizona. This operation was undertaken with the slenderest of means, but for once, the Union could be said to experience the same difficulty.

Jefferson Davis and his Cabinet were keen on expanding to the New Mexico Territory, but they neglected something closer to hand: the state of Missouri. Ever since a small federal force kept the federal arsenal at St. Louis, the North had the upper hand. But former Governor Claiborne Jackson and Texas Ranger Ben McCulloch put together an army of about 11,000 and reclaimed the western part of Missouri. Their big clash with the Federals took place at Wilson's Creek on August 10, 1861.

Why do we know so much less about the fighting in the West?

In part this is because there were so many more reporters, newspapers, and telegraphs in the East. News traveled more quickly there, and, over time, the seekers of news came to listen more to what happened in Virginia than in Missouri or Kentucky. But if one examines the situation from a modern-day perspective, it is apparent that Missouri and Kentucky were extremely important: if the Confederates had won both of those states, it is unlikely that the Union could have prevailed.

Operating under that belief, Nathaniel Lyon, who had recently been promoted to brigadier general,, led about six thousand federal men into central Missouri, where they battled almost twice as many Confederates at the Battle of Wilson's Creek. Lyon fought with the same crazed ferocity that marked his conduct in St. Louis, and he died that afternoon, the first person of general rank to die on the Union side. The battle was a bloody standoff, but in its wake, the Federals withdrew across the state, leaving much of Missouri in Confederate hands.

Where was Ulysses S. Grant during this time?

Recently appointed a brigadier-general of volunteers, Grant was ordered to take possession of Cairo, Illinois, the spit of land at the confluence of the Ohio and Mississippi Rivers. This was one of the most important, strategic locations in all the West, and Grant managed to keep it without having to fight. From his vantage point, the situation was ripe for an attack on the Confederates, and in October he led his men to attack them at Belmont, Missouri. The Battle of Belmont was not a big affair as military events go, but it showed Grant's determination, letting the Confederates know they were going to have to fight for their section of the West.

What was the action like on the East Coast?

Lincoln declared a federal blockade of all southern ports as early as May 1861, but the Union Navy took some time getting ready for that task. By August, the Union Navy made attacks against the Confederate forts at Cape Hatteras, and by the early autumn, it was in command of that vital sea-link. Here, too, the importance of Fort Monroe was again evidenced. If the Confederacy had been able to take Monroe, it would have had a clear path to the Atlantic Ocean. Lacking that, the Confederates had to ship materials down to the North Carolina coast and out the outlets there.

The North had a major, even a huge, advantage at sea, with hundreds of vessels compared to just a few for the Confederacy. Lincoln and his advisers had one great, gnaw-

Why did the Pathfinder stumble so badly in the Civil War?

During the late 1840s, no person stood higher in the public estimation than John Charles Frémont. He led several federal exploratory expeditions into the Rocky Mountains, and the maps and charts made by the expedition members became the standard for those who followed the Oregon and California trails. When the Civil War began, Frémont was also fortunate in that his wife, Jessie Benton Frémont, was extremely well connected to the East Coast establishment. There were those, in 1861, who believed Frémont would become the outstanding military hero of the war.

Frémont had a dictatorial style, however, and he stumbled badly when he declared martial law in Missouri. Not only did he assume all sorts of powers in St. Louis, but Frémont declared—without asking Lincoln or anyone else—that all slaves used by the Confederacy in fighting or building fortifications were now and forever free. To our modern ears, this sounds quite wonderful, but Frémont clearly exceeded his authority, and Lincoln—who was ever conscious of the delicacy of the Border States—had to step in to countermand Frémont's order. Abolitionists, naturally, hailed Frémont, but by the end of 1861 he was in very bad shape politically and militarily.

ing concern, however: what if either Britain or France threw its weight behind the Confederacy? It was conceivable that the Northern blockade would be smashed and that Confederate cotton would flow to Europe, earning the Confederacy both dollars and an increased reputation.

Which side deployed the first balloons in war?

It might be more accurate to ask which side deployed the first *successful* balloons: those that went up and stayed there for a time. When the war began, Thaddeus Lowe of New Hampshire offered his services to the Union. Labeling himself Professor Lowe, he claimed that the balloon offered superior types of reconnaissance. General Winfield Scott was quite dim on the prospect, and it took some pushing from Lincoln to make this a reality.

Lowe had a balloon ready by the Battle of Bull Run, but the weather was against him that day. Two weeks later, he brought General George B. McClellan aloft, probably the first time a commanding general had ever made an ascent. Unfortunately, that aerial reconnaissance reinforced McClellan's natural disposition to believe that his foe was stronger than was truly the case. Believing that the Confederates had large artillery batteries in and around Manassas, Virginia, McClellan continued to delay. For their part, the Confederates quickly recognized the value of balloon reconnaissance, but they had neither the materials nor a person as dedicated to the task. Control of the "air" usually went to the North, which made little use of its advantage.

When did the federal forces become known as "the Army of the Potomac"?

The federal forces in and around Washington, D.C., were reorganized after the Battle of Bull Run. There was still a division between Regular Army and volunteers, but the former was gaining in size and strength. General George B. McClellan proved a masterful organizer, separating the army into brigades and divisions, and by October 1861 people were calling it the "Army of the Potomac."

That name was actually coveted by the other side. For a time, the Confederates called their men in that vicinity by the same title. But in the spring of 1862, they carried out a reorganization and were thereafter called the "Army of Northern Virginia."

What was the situation like in California in 1861?

Throughout 1861, California manifested a strong desire to remain within the Union. In part this was thanks to the tireless efforts of a Massachusetts Unitarian minister, Thomas Starr King, who traveled the state, giving speeches on behalf of the North. There were economic reasons too, however.

Just as New York City and Washington, D.C., were dependent on California gold for the U.S. Treasury, so was California dependent on emigrants from and trade with the East Coast. Many people did not venture around Cape Horn but took the Panama Isthmus route, then caught another steamer up to New York City. By the fall of 1861, there were regular shipments of gold from the West and a constant flow of persons and news

Gold miners dredging the bottom of a California river in the 1850s. Gold from the state became a critical source of income for Washington, D.C., while California needed trade and labor with the East. The result was that California chose the North over the South.

With one lone exception, the answer is no. Roughly ninety-nine percent of the time the North held a major, and sometimes an overwhelming, advantage.

Not only did the North have more economic and technical resources, it also had a commander-in-chief who was fascinated by many aspects of the work. Lincoln spent a good deal of time at the Washington Navy yard conversing with Commandant John Dahlgren, for whom the famous artillery piece was named. As the war progressed, Lincoln showed interest in practically every military innovation: he tested the new rifles when they appeared and borrowed books from the Library of Congress to inform himself on the newest developments. How Lincoln ever found the time to do this remains one of the puzzles of his life.

to the West. All that remained to make a complete link was the completion of the transcontinental telegraph, and that happened late in October 1861.

What was the first message sent across the continent?

On October 24, 1861, the governor of California wired the mayor of New York City. "May the Union be perpetual," the telegraph message began.

In a sense, that was it so far as the Confederate cause in the Far West was concerned. Once the East and West coasts were connected by a telegraph in Union hands, Northern troops, ships, and money could be sent back and forth with relative ease. The Confederates, by contrast, could only guess as to what was happening in the Far West. For the second time—balloons had come first—the Union demonstrated its technological edge, a superiority that would only increase.

Who held the initiative in the autumn of 1861?

Because of the Confederate victory at Bull Run, the Confederacy looked like it was in a strong position, but it had no resources or reserves with which to press its advantage. The Union, therefore, was able to act after a pause.

In October 1861, nearly one hundred Union vessels, with 15,000 troops aboard, sailed down Chesapeake Bay and into the Atlantic. Many of the ships were scattered in a major storm, but they regrouped and by the beginning of November were attacking the Confederate defenses in and around Port Royal, South Carolina. The defenders wired Richmond frantically, but Jefferson Davis had no troops to spare. First the seacoast forts fell, then the town itself. This was the first solid, incontestable Union victory of the war.

INTERNATIONAL EVENTS

What about the diplomatic front? What was the *Trent* affair?

In October 1861, President Davis sent three commissioners overseas to negotiate with Britain, France, and Spain. He knew, as did all of his advisers, that the Confederacy had to have outside help in order to win.

Two of the commissioners, James Mason and John Slidell, were captured when the USS *San Jacinto* stopped and boarded the British mail steamer *Trent*. Union Captain James Wilkes (1798–1877) had a fine reputation as a naval explorer—he had sailed much of the Pacific in the 1840s—but he overstepped diplomatic boundaries in seizing the two Confederate commissioners, whom he brought as prisoners to Boston. The people of that city were delighted, and the nation rejoiced to hear of the matter until it was learned that Great Britain might bring on a war against the United States.

What was the reaction in Great Britain?

Victoria was the queen of England and the empress of a vast overseas empire, but her government was run by Lord John Palmerston. Tradition has it that on learning of the *Trent*'s seizure, he flung down his hat on the table and shouted to his Cabinet: "You may stand for this, but damned if I will!" Recognizing the vulnerability of British Canada, Palmerston rushed 8,000 veteran soldiers there, and he sent blustering diplomatic messages to the United States. The implication was clear: return the commissioners, or face a war.

What Palmerston overlooked, however, was that many workaday English men and women were strongly for the Union. There was a marked separation between the British upper class, which favored the Confederacy, and the industrial workers, who were dead-set against slavery. Even if Palmerston had forced a war, it is unlikely that he could have led a united nation.

What was the reaction in the United States to the *Trent* affair?

At first there was jubilation because the Confederates had been caught red-handed. As the war signs from Britain approached,

In England, the aristocrats favored the South, while most British citizens were with the North, so when Prime Minister Lord John Palmerston threated war on the Union after the USS *San Jacinto* stopped a British ship and seized the two Confederate diplomats on board, he had no support from his countrymen.

many Americans tended to favor a bellicose response, saying they could handle England and the Confederacy at the same time. One high-placed person who felt this way was William H. Seward, the secretary of state. Writing a friend, Seward predicted that the world would be "wrapped with fire" if Britain attempted to intervene.

Lincoln, as usual, was more realistic. While he loved the idea of twisting the tail of the British Lion, he recognized the danger of fighting two wars at the same time. His comments to his Cabinet were strictly off-record, but the suggestion is that he told them the day would come when Britain could be chastised, but it had not yet arrived. On Lincoln's decision, the two Confederate commissioners were released and the United States sent a letter of apology to Lord Palmerston. The *Trent* Affair fizzled out as 1861 came to an end.

What was the public mood on New Year's Day of 1862?

It had long been the fashion for presidents to open the White House to the public, and Lincoln decided this would be a good occasion to meet and greet his fellow Americans. Dignitaries arrived as early as 10 A.M., but the doors were opened at noon, and Lincoln commenced his talks and jokes, at which he was a true master.

The Marine Band played all afternoon, and there was an appearance of celebration, but in fact Lincoln and his Cabinet were deeply concerned. The *Trent* Affair was fading rapidly, but it had excited fears of a second war, and the news from the various battlefields was not at all encouraging. About the only place where Lincoln felt much security was with his beloved family and his Cabinet, which had increasingly become like a second family to him. In the Confederate capital, things were even gloomier. The Confederacy had almost nothing to celebrate; all its efforts were expended merely in keeping the situation together.

ARMY OF NORTHERN VIRGINIA: FEBRUARY TO SEPTEMBER 1862

UNCONDITIONAL SURRENDER U. S. GRANT

Why had the Army of the Potomac remained in place?

This was, and remains, one of the most perplexing of questions. Was George B. McClellan something of a chicken, or was he merely a good father to his troops, wishing to see them perfectly ready before commencing a campaign? McClellan fell ill in the last part of 1861: typhoid fever nearly claimed his life. But even when he regained his health, he showed no signs of moving, and Lincoln, therefore, prodded him with Executive Order number 1.

On January 22, 1862, Lincoln directed that all sections of the various Union armies were to commence actions against the Confederate foe on or before February 22, 1862, which just happened to be Washington's birthday. Privately, Lincoln expressed concerns that even this would not persuade McClellan, with whom he was increasingly exasperated, to move.

What was the low point for Lincoln and the Northern cause during the winter of 1862?

On or around January 10, 1862, Lincoln fell into a deep gloom. Not only was the Army of the Potomac still in place, but the western forces were under attack, with the Confederates penetrating central Kentucky. The news from the Far West was equally bad, with the Confederates in possession of most of the New Mexico Territory. On one occasion, Lincoln was heard to say that perhaps he had better prepare himself for two countries rather than one. But there was no corresponding high point for the Confederacy. Everything—from the supply system to the men in army camp—was under strain.

101

When did things begin to pick up for the Union?

The latter part of January revealed some encouraging signs, but it was not until early February that Lincoln received anything that could truly be called "good" news. The word was that the Army of the Cumberland was moving in Tennessee and that Brigadier-General Ulysses S. Grant was demonstrating some marked initiative.

Grant was a brigadier-general of volunteers, under the command of Major-General Henry Halleck (1815–1872) of the Regular U.S. Army. In the winter of 1862, Grant persuaded Halleck to allow him to test the Confederate defenses along the Cumberland River, and he quickly found them wanting. Along with Grant's bulldoglike tenacity was the Union superiority on the waterways: there were ten Union ironclads in the vicinity of Cairo, Illinois (thanks to their slowness, they were called the River Turtles). By contrast, the Confederates had not a single ironclad in those waters.

Where did Grant make his first move?

On February 7, 1862, Grant moved down the Cumberland River with several several River Turtles and about 10,000 men. The Confederate commander at Fort Henry tried to fight off the Turtles with cannon shots, but he was quickly defeated. Seeing the impossibility of holding his position, the Confederate sent most of his men away, overland, to Fort Donelson, and with the rest he surrendered on February 10.

This, the first clear-cut Union victory in the West, raised Northern spirits beyond anything yet seen. Grant had seldom been heard of to this point, but he now became a Northern hero. Lincoln, for his part, quickly perceived the importance of the Cumberland and Tennessee River Valleys. Even better news was about to arrive, however.

How did Grant move so quickly against Fort Donelson?

Those who had known Grant in the Mexican War thought him a fine fellow, a good man, and a decent soldier. None of them had any sense of the speed with which he could move, however. This short, cigar-smoking man had an eagle's eye where his opponents' weaknesses were concerned.

Within days of capturing Fort Henry, Grant moved his men fourteen miles overland to besiege Fort Donelson. Located on the western side of the Tennessee River, Donelson was much stronger and more strongly defended than Fort Henry: in fact, there were almost 15,000 Confederates there. When the ironclads approached, the cannon at Fort Donelson drove them off with significant losses. Showing no discouragement, Grant settled down to a siege.

When did Ulysses S. Grant become known as "Unconditional Surrender" Grant?

The Confederate defenders of Fort Donelson made a huge effort to break out on February 15, 1862. The battle was touch-and-go, but Grant was on the scene, judiciously throwing in enough men to hold them, and when the effort failed, the Confederate leaders lost all heart. General John Floyd—who had previously been President Buchanan's

Fort Donelson (shown here in a modern photo) had a strategic position overlooking the Tennessee River, so Ulysses Grant made it a target for his next attack after capturing Fort Henry.

secretary of war—and General Nathan Bedford Forrest decided to escape. The former crossed the river, and the latter broke out with his cavalry. Command of Fort Donelson therefore devolved upon Brigadier-General Simon Bolivar Buckner (1823–1914), a West Point graduate of 1845.

Remembering Grant as a friend from his West Point days, Buckner sent a letter asking to meet in order to discuss terms. Grant fired back with the words that became immortal: "Nothing but an immediate and unconditional surrender will be considered. I propose to move immediately on your works." Saying that his former friend acted in an unchivalrous manner, Buckner yielded, surrendering almost 14,000 men and equipment that might have equipped an entire Confederate army. It was by far the largest Union victory to this point and the greatest Confederate disaster.

How did the Confederacy react to the news?

The news of Fort Donelson's fall arrived in Richmond just in time to spoil Jefferson Davis' second inauguration as president of the Confederacy. He had been, till now, the provisional president. The weather, too, failed to cooperate. It was a wintry day in Richmond when Davis rose to deliver his inaugural address. The mood was gloomy, to say the least.

In the North, all was jubilation. In Grant, the Union had a military hero, a man who would not take no for an answer. Lincoln, too, was in fine spirits over Donelson's surrender, but, as so often, he had to handle a domestic tragedy.

What happened to Willie Lincoln?

Named for the Scottish hero William Wallace, William Lincoln was the apple of his father's eye. For reasons that remain mysterious, Lincoln had a cool relationship with his eldest son, Robert, and a very affectionate one with Willie. Just as General George B. McClellan recovered from typhoid fever, Willie Lincoln came down with it.

Abraham and Mary Lincoln were many things, and they had a rather difficult marriage, but one thing they agreed on was abundant love for their children. The couple was devastated by Willie's death, which took place on February 20, 1862. His was the first death of a child in the White House.

How did the Lincolns recover from the loss of Willie?

In some ways they never did. Mary Lincoln was consumed by grief. Even months later, during the summer of 1862, she sharply insisted that the Marine Band not play anywhere near the White House lawn because the music reminded her of how much her son had loved it. Lincoln, typically, handled the loss with a more balanced approach, but his aides knew not to disturb him when he spent time in his deceased son's room.

As the 2012 film *Lincoln* showed, the loss of Willie created a powerful rift between the first couple. The president thought his wife went too far in her grief; she claimed that he did not seem to care. As a result, Mary Lincoln was adamant that their eldest son, Robert, not be exposed to the war. Over time, this became something of a scandal, because so many young men—from all walks of life—were participating in the conflict.

Where did the conduct of the war stand in February 1862?

The superiority in men and materiel, on the part of the North, was much more in evidence than before. Lincoln had asked Congress for 400,000 men and 400 million dollars the year before, and the legislature had largely granted his request.

The fighting quality of the Southern soldiers remained in high regard, but the spirit of the Confederate leaders lagged after the surrender of Fort Donelson. How could Generals John Floyd and Nathan Forrest have snuck away in such a cowardly fashion? The former was deprived of his command.

McCLELLAN'S COMMAND

Who held the initiative in February 1862?

The North, in almost every respect. McClellan's Army of the Potomac seemed ready, at last, to move. Grant and the Army of the Cumberland now occupied much of the river valley of that name. The Confederate defenders in the West had to pull back, almost 300 miles, to a line that was weakly defended. At sea, the disparity was even greater.

The Union Navy was at one hundred vessels of all sizes and climbing almost every week. The South had nothing other than privateer vessels with which to contest mastery of the ocean. And every week that passed showed yet another weak spot along the coast that the Union might assault.

What measures did the Confederate leaders take to remedy the situation?

There was only one thing they could do, and they knew it would be very unpopular. In February 1862, President Davis proposed a general conscription law, which was soon passed by the Confederate Congress. Under its provisions, all able-bodied white males between the ages of eighteen and thirty-five were liable for military service. Very few exemptions were proposed.

The men already in uniform had a profound distaste for the conscription law; they said it would cheapen their efforts. The men who had previously avoided military service now found themselves in a tight spot. Women of the Confederacy, too, expressed discontent. The conscription law was easily the most unpopular measure undertaken by the Confederate government.

Was there any bright spot for the Confederacy?

There was one, and one only. In March 1862, the ironclad CSS *Virginia* was launched. The *Virginia* was built on the hull of the USS *Merrimack,* a Northern ship that the Union had deliberately sunk in the Norfolk Navy Yard to prevent it from being captured. The Confederacy salvaged the hull and converted it to an ironclad using metal from the Tredegar Ironworks at Richmond. By the late winter of 1862, the CSS *Virginia* was ready, and when she sallied from port on March 7, she inaugurated an entire new phase in naval warfare.

What was the reaction in Washington, D.C., to the *Virginia*?

No single action during the entire war frightened Northern leaders as badly as the one-day sally of the CSS *Virginia*. The secretary of war was nearly beside himself with fear that the *Virginia* would sink all vessels in the area, then attack Union vessels on the Potomac River. The secretary of the navy was, naturally, somewhat calmer, indicating that the shore batteries could at least prevent the latter possibility. On the whole, however, one is inclined to agree with the fears of the Union commanders. In the single presence of the CSS *Virginia*, nearly all the Northern plans could, potentially, be thwarted. Lincoln, typically, was more intrigued than dismayed. How had the South chanced upon this new possibility, he asked? And what did the Union Navy intend to do about it?

What was that first day like for the CSS *Virginia*?

Equipped with heavy cannon and a fifteen-foot battering ram, the CSS *Virginia* came out and immediately met two Union warships. Both were larger, and carried heavier ordnance, but their cannon shots literally bounced off the heavy metal of the *Virginia*'s sides. One Union warship was sunk by cannon fire, and the other went down to an attack by the battering ram. The battle was over in less than two hours.

Critics—then and now—have long asserted that the *Virginia* should have completed her task that day, annihilating all Union Navy warships in the vicinity. The captain and crew of the *Virginia* were astonished by their own success, however, and not a little weary from the endeavor. The *Virginia* returned to port that afternoon, having demonstrated that the days of the sailing navies were nearly over.

What was the *Monitor*?

The development of ironclad vessels had been under way for some time; the first steam frigate had been designed by Robert Fulton and built in New York Harbor in 1815. But manufacturers and governments alike continued to believe in the power of the sailing navies, and development was therefore slower than might be expected.

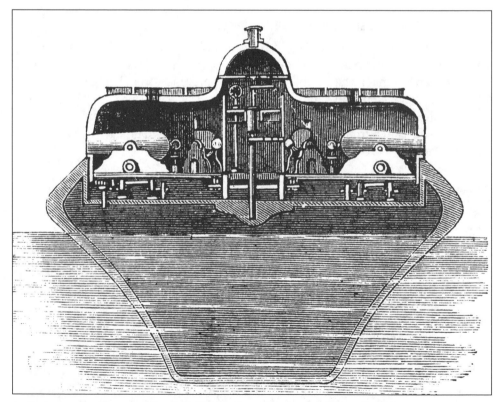

An illustration shows a cross-section of the USS *Monitor* and the inner workings of its turret.

Under a rush contract, a firm in Brooklyn turned out the USS *Monitor*, which many observers likened to a cheesebox resting atop a raft. Extremely low to the water, the *Monitor* had a turret rather than traditional gun placements: its two cannons could therefore be rotated. This novel device was thanks to the Swedish inventor John Ericsson. When one first viewed the *Monitor*, the sight provoked laughs, giggles, and expressions of disbelief. But the little cheesebox was about to demonstrate its worth.

What was the naval battle like between the *Monitor* and the *Virginia*?

The CSS *Virginia* edged her way out of port on the morning of March 9, 1862, and encountered the USS *Monitor*. The Confederate crew was amazed by the smallness of this enemy ship and believed at first they could pound it into submission. Time and again, however, the *Monitor*'s diminutive size proved an asset rather than a liability.

The naval battle lasted for four hours, with the rotating cannons aboard the *Monitor* proving at least a match for the *Virginia*. The crews of both ships were thoroughly exhausted when the action broke off, and the captain of the *Monitor* was temporarily blinded when a shell made a direct hit on the rotating tower. As the two ships moved apart, signaling the end of combat, it marked the end of the Confederacy's brief threat to naval supremacy. Simply by holding off the *Virginia*, the *Monitor* ensured that the North would have the time to build more ironclad vessels, and that was a race that the Union could not lose.

The first battle between ironclad naval ships in world history occurred during the Civil War, when the CSS *Virginia* (left; formerly the Merrimack) fought the USS *Monitor* (right) to a draw.

What was the next move for the Army of the Potomac?

General McClellan had been putting off action for months, but Lincoln finally used one more stick to prod him into action. By another presidential war order, Lincoln removed McClellan as general of the Union armies while keeping him in charge of the Army of the Potomac. Lincoln made it plain, however, that the time had come.

McClellan had spent much time designing his plan, and as he revealed it, Lincoln felt that it was both too complicated and unwieldy. Rather than march against the Confederate forces at Manassas, McClellan intended to ship most of the Army of the Potomac to the James Peninsula, situated between the James and Chickahominy Rivers. Doing so would put the Army of the Potomac within sixty miles of Richmond without incurring any danger other than those faced by a voyage. Lincoln was skeptical, but any action was better than none.

When did the loading begin?

Toward the end of March 1862. Over 100,000 men were loaded onto something in the neighborhood of 300 vessels and brought down the Potomac to Old Point Comfort. This was, almost certainly, the largest amphibious movement in nineteenth-century America, and it would not be exceeded in size till the First World War.

McClellan was involved in each and every aspect. He had won the hearts of his men by his obvious concern for their welfare. Whether they called him "Little Mac" or "Mighty Mac," he was clearly the man, so far as they were concerned. Lincoln, observing from a distance, believed that a major move was at last under way. One foreign observer reported that the Army of the Potomac had made a giant stride, and that it acted like a giant.

What was the number of the defending Confederates?

To the best of our knowledge, Major-General John Magruder (1807–1871) who had the intriguing nickname of "Prince John"—had only 15,000 men to defend against more than 100,000. At the moment, the Confederacy had no other men, and it would not until General Joseph E. Johnston brought his men back from Manassas. Never had the Confederacy been in such danger.

Magruder—who was a colorful character—played his part to the maximum, however. Knowing that McClellan tended to err on the side of caution, Magruder did everything possible to make it seem that he had more men. The Confederates marched and then remarched, and they set up dummy fortifications with wooden guns. Here was where balloon reconnaissance should have done the trick, but McClellan did not even believe the reports that came from "Professor" Thaddeus Lowe. When he sent up one of his best friends, General Fitz-John Porter, to investigate, Porter was nearly lost when the air carried the balloon in the direction of the Confederates. From that moment, McClellan placed even less confidence, or credence, in reports from the balloon men.

Could McClellan have pushed right through to victory?

One hesitates to give a categorical "yes." Something unexpected could have occurred. Still, when one examines the numbers and the terrain, it seems as if the chances were 90–10 in McClellan's favor.

For the Confederates, it was fortunate that McClellan took their "fake" numbers at face value. Before long, McClellan settled into a siege of the Confederate fortifications around Yorktown. Many persons—including foreign observers—remarked on the irony. This was the very place where George Washington and his French allies had compelled the British to surrender in 1781.

BATTLE OF SHILOH

Meanwhile, what was happening on the Western front?

The Southern efforts in the West had come to grief in so many places that the leaders were on the verge of despair. As recently as the first of January 1862, there had been a strong-looking Confederate line, extending from Columbus, Mississippi, to Bowling Green, Kentucky: that line was now in fragments, because of Ulysses Grant's successes at Fort Henry and Fort Donelson. Realzing that the defensive line could not be reconstituted, General Albert Sidney Johnston (1803–1862)—not to be confused with Joseph E. Johnston—assembled all the men he could at Corinth, Mississippi, just a few miles south of the border with Tennessee. By the end of April, Johnston had roughly 40,000 men and Pierre Beauregard as his second in command.

Neither Ulysses Grant nor Major-General Henry Halleck suspected the size of the Confederate force at Corinth. Thinking it was perhaps half that number, Grant brought his men down the Cumberland River to a place called Pittsburg Landing. Dropping 35,000 men off, Grant positioned his forces in a two-mile perimeter with its outward sec-

Why did the Confederates take so long to make their attack?

Johnston and Beauregard set out from Corinth on April 3, 1862. They did not know, but they had achieved complete surprise: the Federals had no idea they were about to be attacked. The spring rains held up the Confederate movement, however. Had they been able to make the march in one day instead of two, the Confederates might have achieved a knockout blow.

Even so, the Confederates managed to preserve the element of surprise. On the evening of April 5, 1862, the Confederate and federal pickets were within a few hundred yards of each other, and the latter did not suspect the former's presence. Had the Confederates not been so weary from their two-day march, they might have attacked that night: it was decided, instead, to save all their energies for the next day.

tion facing a place called Shiloh, a tiny church. It was here that the greatest battle to date would be fought.

When did the Battle of Shiloh begin?

At 4:30 A.M. on April 6, 1862, federal pickets reported noises to the south and southwest of their encampment. An enterprising federal colonel had his men investigate, and the first musket and rifle shots probably went off around 5 A.M. Even so, the woods muffled the sounds, and many Federals slept on for another half hour before learning they were under attack.

General Albert Sidney Johnston had planned his attack well. The Confederates swarmed from the woods and overran the first line of Union defenses. In an unusual oversight, General Ulysses Grant had not ordered his men to entrench their positions. As a result, the Confederates succeeded beyond expectation in the first hour of the battle. As they neared the little church, from which the battle takes its name, sections of the federal line stiffened their defenses. Here is where General William T. Sherman made his stand, using the church as his headquarters.

Where was Grant?

He had taken a fall from his horse the day before and gone to a nearby plantation, about seven miles upriver, to recuperate (for this he would receive much criticism). As soon as he heard the cannon fire, Grant was on a steamer, headed for the battle site, but in the precious two hours it took, the battle could well have been lost. Grant was fortunate that General John McClernand and his brigade fought like lions in the Union center, holding their position for hours.

When he arrived, Grant found the situation difficult but far from hopeless. The Confederates were attacking in an arc or semicircle that ran from south to southwest, attempting to drive the Union men straight into the Tennessee River. Grant had his gunboats there, and very likely could have made a desperate last stand on the waterfront, but he did not have to. Thanks to Sherman's adroit defense, and the heroics of McClernand's brigade, the situation was holding.

How far had the Confederates come?

They had advanced perhaps two miles, and there were times when it seemed they would punch through the federal line and do what General Johnston insisted was their mission: to water their horses in the Tennessee River. But they ran into a defensive position so tough that they labeled it the Hornet's Nest.

For more than three hours, roughly 4,000 Northern men held the center part of their line against at least three times their number of Confederates. The numbers are misleading in that the position was so narrow that the Confederates could not bring all their forces to bear. The Union men in the Hornet's Nest fought with great courage and skill, employing fast-loading rifles. They very likely saved the day for the Northern side.

In one of the more important battles of the war, Ulysses S. Grant faced a surprise attack by Southern forces but managed to reverse their advantage and win the 1862 Battle of Shiloh.

Who fought better that day at Shiloh?

This is a tough one to answer because there were plenty of heroes on both sides. It is safe to say, however, that Shiloh represented the appearance of the rebel yell and the fury of the Confederates on the attack; it also demonstrated the solid, cool spirit of the Northern men on defense. In a sense, one can say that both armies fought very well.

On the Confederate side, the worst loss was experienced around 2:30 P.M. General Johnston was impressed by the federal defense, and, intending to break its center, he rallied his men and led a charge. He took a relatively small bullet wound to his foot, but quickly bled to death. Johnston's death was a serious blow to the Confederate effort. General Beauregard, who replaced him as commanding general, attempted to disguise the fact that Johnston had fallen.

When was the crisis?

The whole day was a crisis, so far as the Union defenders were concerned. For the Confederates, however, the crisis came at around 4 P.M. They could feel that it was now or never: they must push the Yankees to the river, or be pushed back themselves.

One area, near the Union center, was attacked fourteen times. The Confederates made major successes, including receiving the surrender of General McClernand and almost 3,000 of his men, but they never pushed the Northern men off their last row of defenses. As the sun went down, men on both sides were horrified by the loss of life, which far exceeded anything they had previously seen. The rain that evening turned to hail, and some men who lay on the ground wounded may well have died from exposure.

What did Grant say to Sherman?

Throughout the war, Grant was known more for what he did than what he said. There were some rare occasions, however, when his words seemed almost like poetry.

Sherman found Grant under a tree, nursing the wound he had suffered from falling from his horse. Sherman intended to ask about a retreat from Shiloh, but something in Grant's demeanor prevented him. He, therefore, simply commented that it had been a terrible day, full of losses and difficulty. Grant nodded, adjusted the cigar in his mouth, and replied: "Lick 'em tomorrow, though." This was, beyond doubt, the finest moment in Grant's career. He had already shown himself a fantastic offensive fighter, capturing Forts Henry and Donelson. Now he had been pushed almost to the limit of what his men could stand, and all he could think was how he would thrash the rebels the next morning. This was why Grant's men came to admire him, and why his armchair critics would come to detest him. Grant confounded expectations.

What was that night like?

It was—with one exception—the worst night of the war (see page 277). The cold made the men's wounds more difficult to bear, and the pelting rain turned the battlefield into one great site of misery. The screams of the wounded kept most men up all night, and the adrenaline created by their heroics made it nearly impossible to rest (one can compare this to the raised adrenaline that we experience after an automobile accident).

The morning of April 7, 1862, revealed a battlefield soaked in blood. Some of the Confederates believed they were close to victory and wanted to resume the fight, but General Beauregard refused. Then Grant struck, with all his force.

What was the second day's battle at Shiloh like?

Reinforced by General Don Carlos Buell, whose men came off of steamers all morning long, Grant struck at the Confederates. There was hard fighting for about two hours; the Confederates then withdrew, leaving the field to the Union. Beauregard put the best face on a bad situation, telegraphing Jefferson Davis that he had fought the enemy to a draw, but the casualty lists revealed something different. Each side had slightly more than 10,000 men killed, wounded, or missing in slightly more than twenty-four hours. That was a bad casualty list for the North, but for the South, with its limited manpower supply, it was simply disastrous.

How did the Confederate rank-and-file respond to the retreat?

Private Sam Watkins, in his memoir *Co. Aytch*, had this to say:

Now, those Yankees were whipped, fairly whipped, and according to all the rules of war they ought to have retreated. But they didn't. Flushed with their victories at Fort Henry and Fort Donelson and the capture of Nashville, and the whole State of Tennessee having fallen into their hands, victory was again to perch upon their banners, for Buell's army, by forced marches, had come to Grant's assistance at the eleventh hour. (Watkins, p. 28)

Grant did not follow up on his victory. He did not need to. Having retreated from Shiloh, the Confederates virtually abandoned northern and central Tennessee, leaving the way open for Union invasions from all sorts of angles. Grant also had to fend off his many critics, who blasted him for not entrenching prior to the battle. When a good friend approached Lincoln, asking if Grant should be removed from command, the president replied: "I can't spare this man. He fights."

Was there any good news for the Confederacy in April 1862?

Only in the negative sense. The Confederates could claim to have restricted George B. McClellan and the Army of the Potomac to the lower part of the James Peninsula. In terms of positive news, there was virtually nothing to report. And as bad as things were, they were about to get worse, from the Confederate point of view.

BATTLE FOR NEW ORLEANS

Who was David Glasgow Farragut?

Born in Tennessee in 1801, Farragut was the son of a Spanish immigrant—from the Island of Majorca—who had arrived in time to serve as a privateer captain during the American Revolution. Farragut also had a second, foster family in the Dixon family, one of the most renowned members being naval officer Admiral David Dixon Porter. Even so, few people expected the dramatic rise of Farragut, which took place in 1862.

Promoted to Commodore, Farragut was made commander of the flotilla preparing to attack New Orleans. According to the federal census of 1860, the Crescent City had about 168,676 people, of whom 13,385 were slaves, making it by far the most populous, as well as the most prosperous, place in the Confederate States. The Confederates knew an attack was coming. They had sig-

Admiral David Farragut led the flotilla of Union ships against the city of New Orleans.

nificantly reinforced Fort Jackson and Fort St. Philip, sitting on opposite sides of the Mississippi River, and a fleet of gunboats was under construction. Even so, New Orleans was significantly undermanned because so many soldiers had been siphoned off to join Johnston's army before the Battle of Shiloh.

How large was Farragut's fleet?

Farragut had more than twenty sloops and schooners and almost as many bomb ketches (the bomb vessels were commanded by his foster brother, Captain David Dixon Porter). In addition, there were transport vessels carrying 15,000 soldiers led by Major-General Benjamin Butler of Massachusetts. If not the largest American armada, it certainly came close.

Farragut was well aware of the difficulties he would encounter. The Confederates had reinforced the forts seventy miles below New Orleans and collected a veritable fleet of steamboats, swiftly turned into vessels of war. On the land side, however, the Union enjoyed an advantage of almost five-to-one because many of New Orleans' defenders had been siphoned off to assist with the effort made at Shiloh.

Was the lower part of the Mississippi different from what we know today?

Thanks to Hurricane Katrina in 2005, Americans are more familiar with the lowness of the land and the possibility of high water striking the area south of New Orleans. The land was higher in those days (the Mississippi deposits millions of tons of cubic feet of sediment into the Gulf each year), but the hazards of navigation were quite severe. The Union vessels had to climb over the various bars that blocked the mouth(s) of the Mississippi, then carefully thread their way upstream against a current of five knots. Here, if anywhere, is where the Confederates should have based their defense, but they had yielded the lowest part of the river several months earlier.

Moving upstream, Farragut came within striking distance of the Confederate forts. Now was the time for David Dixon Porter and the mortar gunboats. Employing camouflage as well as hiding under sections of trees, the mortar boats commenced a twenty-four-hour-a-day bombardment from the west side of the river. They directed their stronger fire at Fort Jackson, also on the right, or west, bank.

How much damage was done by the bombardment?

Each day, Farragut demanded a report from his foster brother, Porter, and each day the answer was the same: just a little more time would result in complete success. Farragut was both skeptical and impatient, however: he believed that the Confederates, given time, would make their defenses even stronger. Farragut, therefore, convened a council of war, at which he heard largely negative opinions. The current was too strong, the Confederates had the advantage; it would be better to let the mortar boats do their work.

Farragut was well within his rights to overrule the council of war and order the attack. In so doing, he took two major risks, however. There was always the chance that the forts had not been badly damaged in the bombardment and that his men would suffer the consequences. Then, too, his own career would be finished if he failed. Farragut was an intrepid person, however. He had seen too many years of peacetime and slow advancement. This was his opportunity, and he would make the most of it.

How was the chain broken?

On the night of April 22, 1862, a federal steamboat went right up to the chain rigged between the different sunken wrecks. Even as the two forts commenced firing, an intrepid Yankee got off his boat and onto one of the hulks, where he unwrapped the chain, allowing his steamboat through. The vessel came through, went upstream a few hundred yards, then turned, and—with the current of five knots behind it—rammed the chain, breaking it. The way had been cleared.

Union ships surround New Orleans in 1862 in this illustration from the 1894 book *Campfires and Battlefields*.

How many hazards were faced and overcome?

On the night of April 23, 1862, roughly fifteen federal gunboats were lined up, with Farragut's flag aboard the USS *Hartford*. Knowing that the chain was broken helped to lift the spirits of the men: even so, many of the officers wrote farewell letters to their families and sweethearts. The attack commenced at around 1 A.M.

The Confederates knew the attack was coming and had done all in their power to prevent it. As the federal steamboats passed through the former chain, they came under heavy fire, which was returned in kind. That was nothing compared to the flotilla of Confederate steamboats that descended upon them, however, and for the next two or three hours, something akin to hell enveloped the area. There were numerous barrages and salvoes, but there were also many attempts to ram: only one of the federal vessels was sunk in this manner, however. Farragut, who believed in leading from the vanguard, nearly perished when he swung amid the ropes and lines, trying to get a better glimpse of his foes. But with each passing minute, it became clearer that the Confederates were outmatched. As the hapless Confederate commander of New Orleans admitted, the Mississippi riverboat men were a poor choice as defenders: they were ill disciplined and disorganized. The Confederates had pinned their hopes on the construction of the CSS *Manassas*, a powerful ironclad, but it exploded after a particularly destructive barrage. By morning, the federal victory was complete.

Where did Farragut go next?

He could have spent his time reducing the two Confederate forts, but Farragut was concerned that the defenders upstream would use the time to accomplish something else. He, therefore, steamed straight for New Orleans on April 24 and came close the next morning.

Only one last set of defenses remained: a handful of Confederate guns ashore, located rather close to where the Battle of New Orleans had been fought forty-seven years earlier. Not only did the federal guns reduce this battery in short order, an entire Confederate regiment yielded when it found no exit and shells breaking over the men's heads. If not the absolute first, it was certainly one of the first times that troops ashore ever yielded to a fleet on a river. With these last obstructions removed, Farragut steamed straight into the port at New Orleans, where he and his sailors beheld something like an inferno. Knowing that Farragut was on his way, the Confederates set 30,000 bales of cotton afire and pushed them onto rafts drifting south. Equally destructive were the hands that set fire to practically all the shipping of the port.

Who received the surrender of the Crescent City?

In a sense, no one did. Upon his arrival in the port, Farragut sent in a group of marines to hoist the Stars and Stripes, but they were soon hauled down. The city was on the verge of complete disintegration for the next three days, with the mayor saying he had no authority to yield while anarchy threatened. There were some terrible stories, some too terrible to credit, the most notable of them being that a group of Confederate cavalry fired into a group of unarmed civilians that had the nerve to applaud the raising of the federal flag. Though Farragut was master of the city in a military sense—his big guns saw to it—he did not really gain control of the area until April 30, 1862. One day later, thousands of federal troops—led by General Benjamin Butler—arrived.

How significant was the capture of New Orleans?

It was, perhaps, the single most underestimated action of the Civil War. Men and women of the Confederate states, including Jefferson Davis, fully comprehended the magnitude of the disaster, but histories written over the next few decades tended to bury the event because of the relatively low number of casualties. In exchange for fewer than 250 men killed, wounded, and gone missing, Farragut brought about the surrender of the largest of all Southern cities and the collapse of the linchpin of the Confederate economy.

For many Confederates, the loss of New Orleans was the most poignant, even searing, event of the year 1862. First had come the terrible news of Forts Henry and Donelson, then the near-victory at Shiloh that cost so many lives. Then came the news that the Federals had penetrated the inner part of Cape Hatteras, then the surrender of New Orleans. No less a fire-eater than Edmund Ruffin, the man who claimed to have fired the first cannon shot against Fort Sumter, expressed consternation and dismay at the loss of New Orleans. And yet, with all this bad news, the Confederacy was actually menaced even more spectacularly, right at its heart.

Where were McClellan and the Army of the Potomac?

Given the practical flood of victories for the Union cause in the spring of 1862, it seemed as if McClellan would succeed and thereby end the war in that season. But McClellan was a foot-dragger.

It took McClellan until the first week of May even to attack the Confederate defenses in and around Yorktown, Virginia. The Confederates, wisely, got out just before the full weight of McClellan's two hundred pieces of artillery were brought to bear. As the Confederates moved up the James Peninsula, McClellan followed at a snail's pace. Those observers who remembered the British person who claimed the movement of the Army of the Potomac was akin to a giant now said it had become like that of an ant.

Could the Union Navy have captured Richmond as it had already done to New Orleans?

There was an excellent chance of this happening. In May 1862, the Union Navy was practically unopposed on the lower James River. But on May 15, a federal squadron attacked Drewry's Bluff and ran into the first real setback in some time.

The USS *Monitor*, which had won such applause in its battle against the CSS *Virginia*, was accompanied by the USS *Galena*. Technically, these two ships had the firepower necessary to reduce the Confederate battery at Drewry's Bluff, but the guns on the *Monitor* were unable to be elevated properly. In a three-and-a-half-hour battle, the USS *Galena* was hit no fewer than forty-four times. The Federals gave up the attack by noon, having suffered fourteen men killed and another ten injured. The casualty figures were small, but the moral effect for the Confederacy was very great. Clearly, the Union Navy could not subdue Richmond. The Army of the Potomac would have to do its work.

Were McClellan's follies equaled on the Confederate side?

Very nearly. General Joseph Johnston was perplexed by the situation. General John Magruder had fallen into bad order as a result of the fall of Yorktown. General Robert E. Lee, acting as military adviser to President Jefferson Davis, appeared out of sorts. His men had recently given him the title of "King of Spades," referring to his constant commands to them to entrench their positions.

Jefferson Davis, perhaps, kept the clearest and coolest head. He had sent Joseph Johnston and his men down the Peninsula in March, and he now saw them coming back. To Davis, this was a moral victory in that the Union advance had been slowed for nearly two months.

Where were Lincoln and Secretary of War Edwin Stanton in all of this?

Both men were perplexed by McClellan's slow progress. When McClellan asked them for reinforcements, Lincoln promptly telegraphed that by his reckoning, McClellan had

Edwin Stanton was secretary of war under Abraham Lincoln. He and the president were both puzzled by how slowly General McClellan moved his troops instead of taking advantage of Confederate errors.

104,000 men fit and ready for duty, but that McClellan claimed, or owned up to, only 80,000 of them.

Secretary of War Stanton was at his wits' end with McClellan, who seemed to misjudge his opponents' strength at every turn. But Lincoln and Stanton made some mistakes of their own, thinking that Confederate General Stonewall Jackson might attempt an assault on Washington, D.C. An entire federal corps of nearly 40,000 men was held back at Fredericksburg; had this force gone to meet McClellan, it is difficult to see how anything could have saved the Confederate capital.

When did Joseph Johnston make his first attack?

On the last day of May 1862, Johnston sent out nearly 50,000 men to attack the Federals in the area that the Confederates called Seven Pines and the Union labeled Fair Oaks. As noted historian Stephen W. Sears claimed, "Few battles ever go entirely as their generals plan them, but seldom does a battle stray so far from plan as Seven Pines." Johnston planned for twenty-two infantry brigades to attack the Federals that day: instead, thanks to poor planning and confusion, only nine brigades got into action. Those that did arrive fought with a passionate fury, but the results were about what one would expect. The Confederates had 5,002 men killed, wounded, and missing in a day and a half of fighting. Joe Johnston was one of the wounded, struck first by a rifle bullet, then by a fragment from a shell.

APPEARANCE OF ROBERT E. LEE

Who replaced General Joseph Johnston?

For roughly one day, he was replaced by General Charles Smith. President Jefferson Davis overrode that decision, however, and by June 3, 1862, Robert E. Lee was commander of the Army of Northern Virginia.

Lee did not yet have the sparkling reputation with which he is today associated. He had performed in a mediocre fashion when commander in the Shenandoah Valley in 1861. But those who knew Lee well dismissed these criticisms. Captain Joseph C. Ives—

a Northern man who had joined the Confederacy and become one of President Davis' special aides—retorted that "General Lee's name might as well be audacity."

How close were the Federals to Richmond?

They were so close that some of them could distinctly hear the clock bells of Richmond tolling the hours and that fashionable society persons in the city could see the federal entrenchments in the distance. Never had the capital been in such danger, and never had it been closer to disaster from within. The author of *The Beleaguered City* described the scenes after the Battle of Seven Pines:

"The ambulance corps was swamped by [the wounded]. People loaded the great vans of the Southern Express Company and went out to help bring them in. The hospitals, in spite of the dreadful lesson of Manassas, proved to be altogether inadequate. Wounded men—most of them shot above the waist on account of the abattis and thick brush through which the attack had been made—filled tobacco warehouses, warerooms, even stores on Main Street." This kind of messy aftermath attended most Civil War battles, but it was the first time that Richmond—or any other major city, North or South—received so many of the wounded in its hospitals.

What were Robert E. Lee's first plans?

From the day he assumed command of the Army of Northern Virginia, Lee seems to have always thought in terms of the attack, or offensive. His Mexican War training showed him that a small, highly disciplined number of men could achieve miracles when opposed to larger, less organized bodies of troops. This actually was not the case here—the Army of the Potomac was very well organized—but Lee believed the only answer was to go on the attack.

To that end, he ordered General Stonewall Jackson to bring a section of his army from the Shenandoah Valley to Richmond (this proved much more difficult and trying than anyone anticipated). At the same time, Lee planned a series of audacious attacks, all designed to drive the Federals away from the gates of Richmond. What Lee had going for him was the nearly unlimited confidence of Jefferson Davis.

What was the famous "ride 'round McClellan"?

Colonel J. E. B. Stuart was only twenty-eight, but he had already come quite a way since he delivered a demand to John Brown to surrender (see page 42). Stuart had established himself as the most successful and flamboyant of all Confederate cavalrymen, partly through his richly eccentric clothing, which made him look rather like an English cavalier of the seventeenth century. When Lee asked Stuart for more specific intelligence concerning the enemy, Stuart asked permission to make a daring semicircular ride around the federal positions. Without giving an unqualified "yes," Lee also did not say "no." Stuart took that as his marching, or riding, order.

How did that action go?

On June 13, 1862, Stuart brought 1,200 Confederate troopers around McClellan's far-flung right flank. There were a few short gun fights, but on each occasion, the outnumbered Federals pulled back. By evening, Stuart was actually at the back, or southeast, side of McClellan, and he had yet to lose a single man. For his part, McClellan was not concerned. He believed that cavalry were an outdated military arm and that his artillery would soon tear holes in whatever Confederate defenses remained.

Stuart resumed his ride the next morning, and by that evening, he was completely around the southwest part of the federal lines. Leaving his men to rest, Stuart rode ahead to deliver the news to Robert E. Lee in person. Stuart lost precisely one man on his daring ride and he brought back much-needed intelligence, but the effect of the ride was primarily morale. Confederate spirits lifted when they learned that their cavalry could swing all the way around with the Yankees, too slow to do anything in reply.

Why did McClellan not press his advantage?

The answer remains the same as before: he constantly overestimated the numbers of his foes. But by this point there was also a real defeatism that had crept into McClellan's mind. He began firing telegraph messages that claimed the Confederates had 150,000, even 200,000, men and that his army might soon perish.

Why did Lincoln not sack McClellan?

This one is more difficult to answer. Lincoln had seen and witnessed enough to know that McClellan was no fighter, but he did not wish to repeat his mistake of 1861. In that summer, he urged General Irvin McDowell to fight too quickly, with the defeat at Bull Run as the result. Then, too, Lincoln and Secretary of War Stanton did not really believe that McClellan could fail. He had the largest army ever seen on the North American continent, along with the heaviest artillery train ever seen in the Western Hemisphere. He was less than six miles from downtown Richmond. Surely, they reasoned, McClellan would succeed in spite of himself.

Was McClellan the worst of the best? Or was he the best of the worst?

As a fighting man, McClellan ranks at or near the bottom of all Civil War generals. Time and again during the Peninsula Campaign battles, he was either distant from the battlefront or else riding back and forth and accomplishing very little. Nothing in his previous military career had suggested he would be such a dismal failure as a battlefield commander. And yet....

As a military organizer, McClellan ranks at or near the top. No other Union general ever kept so many men constantly in a good state of order or so well supplied.

When did the Seven Days' Battles begin?

It began on June 26, 1862. Robert E. Lee, naturally, did not expect that this would be a set of battles lasting for seven days. His plan was to attack McClellan's exposed right flank which "hung" to the north and drive him away from Richmond.

The Battle of Mechanicsville, the first of the Seven Days' Battles, began poorly for the Confederates because Stonewall Jackson did not get into position to attack until almost 1 P.M. (a 7 A.M. start had been anticipated). This failure of alacrity was so atypical of Jackson that many historians have given him a pass for his performance that day. What can be said is that Jackson, who had marched and ridden with great speed from the Shenandoah Valley, was exhausted. The battle began late, but went on with fury into the early evening. The Confederates suffered 6,134 men killed, wounded, or missing: the Union suffered 5,031.

This portrait depicts the grimness and tenacity of Stonewall Jackson, the legendary leader of the Stonewall Brigade, but he and his forces were so exhausted by the time they got to Mechanicsville that they were not prepared for the battle until the afternoon.

Could the Confederacy sustain casualties of that magnitude?

Absolutely not. If Joseph Johnston had still been in command—he was out with a wound for the next six months—the daring set of attacks on the Union positions would have been halted after that very first day. But Robert E. Lee was adamant. He had to attack.

The second great battle was at and around Gaines' Mill, about eight miles due east of Richmond. The Confederate attacks were better coordinated on this occasion, but Stonewall Jackson was still not at his best. Again, a fight over a long afternoon resulted in thousands of casualties for both sides. By now, General McClellan had become thoroughly alarmed. Believing that there were 200,000 Confederates in the field, he made accusations of treason against Secretary of War Stanton, alleging that he intended to destroy the Army of the Potomac. By this point, Lincoln and Stanton had given up attempting to persuade McClellan of anything. "Save your army by all means," the president telegraphed.

Could McClellan have disengaged and headed straight down the James Peninsula?

Not with so many Confederates at his back. The Army of the Potomac had to stand and fight, and thanks to numerous heroics on the part of individual soldiers and regiments, it played its part quite well.

The Seven Days' Battles resumed on June 29, 1862, with furious Confederate attacks in and around Savage's Station. A pattern had now developed. When the Confederates unleashed their attacks, usually at midday, they often made significant progress, pushing the Federals back. But by midafternoon, the federal defenses had usually stiffened, and when the Confederates came for one last charge, in the early evening, they were usually repulsed. Nowhere was this more true than at the Battle of Malvern Hill on July 1, 1862.

How many Confederates fell on the first of July 1862?

The precise number may never be known, but somewhere in the neighborhood of 6,000 Confederates went killed, wounded, or missing that day, with the worst losses coming in the desperate, late afternoon attacks on Malvern Hill. The Northern men had clearly gained much—in courage and stamina—over the past few weeks, and they gave the Southerners hell as they attempted to capture fortified positions. Not many men on either side possessed repeating rifles, but they hardly needed them in the turkey shoots that ensued. There were Confederate regiments that lost half their men on the afternoon of July 1, and when the complete fighting of the Seven Days' Battles was reckoned, it was clear that Lee and the Army of Northern Virginia had lost in the neighborhood of 21,000 men.

Did anyone criticize Lee for this series of attacks?

Many people did. Southern newspapers, especially those in other states, lambasted the Confederate general for his constant attacks and the enormous losses. But the *Richmond Enquirer*, the mouthpiece of Jefferson Davis' administration, was fiercely loyal to Lee, and as it became apparent that McClellan would retreat all the way down the James Peninsula, Lee took on the appearance of a major hero.

Those who examine the Peninsula Campaign in detail tend to concur with Stephen W. Sears, who concluded that it was an enormous lost opportunity for the Northern cause. Had McClellan pressed all the way and captured Richmond, it is quite likely that the war would have ended thirty-one months sooner. No one can say just how many lives might have been saved by such a drastic attempt; given that the war went on so long, it is plausible to say that 400,000 lives—North and South combined—might have been preserved.

Where was McClellan on the Fourth of July?

He and the Army of the Potomac were back where they had started the campaign, in and around Fort Monroe at the bottom of the James Peninsula. Richmond was safe for the moment, and the initiative had passed to the Confederates.

Could the Confederates have attacked McClellan in his new position and perhaps ended the war on their terms?

From our modern-day vantage point, it seems possible. But the Confederacy struggled under a heavy burden throughout the war: the burden of getting the right number of men into place at the right time.

Lee had perhaps 50,000 men ready for battle, but just one serious defeat could have turned the entire equation upside down. Conferring with President Jefferson Davis, Lee reluctantly came to the conclusion that it was better to leave McClellan alone and press the advantage in other parts of Virginia. Stonewall Jackson and his brigade had already been sent back to the Shenandoah Valley, and it was possible that a turn of events there would allow the Confederates to menace Washington, D.C.

Who replaced McClellan?

General McClellan had been on the downward slope for some time. In October 1861, he was general-in-chief of all the Union armies and leader of the Army of the Potomac. In April 1862, Lincoln removed him as general-in-chief, but kept him as general of the Army of the Potomac. Now, in July 1862, Lincoln brought Major-General Henry Halleck from the West, making him general-in-chief. McClellan temporarily was replaced by Major-General John Pope, also brought from the Western theater.

Pope had an unfortunate personal style. On first arriving to take the command, he issued a blustering address to the troops, declaring that he came from the Western department, which had only known victories. This was far from the case, and some men may have laughed, but others took offense. For the moment, Pope assembled the new Army of Virginia, protecting Washington, D.C., while McClellan continued to command the Army of the Potomac.

What persuaded the Southern leaders to go on the offensive in the summer of 1862?

At one level, it was a case of "now or never." The Confederates had taken so many losses—of men and materiel—in the first half of 1862 that if they did not take the offensive now, there might never be another opportunity. At the same time, however, there was a shrewd calculation that the Western European powers might recognize the Confederate States of America.

Everyone involved—from Jefferson Davis to his lowest private—knew that it was a quixotic undertaking. Britain and France had a record of nearly eighty years of diplomatic association with the Union: they had only known the Confederacy for a year and a half. But if an opportunity existed, it lay in the chance of winning a major battle on Northern soil. That *might* persuade the European powers to recognize the Confederacy and perhaps even intervene on its behalf. Therefore, when Robert E. Lee proposed an invasion of the North, Jefferson Davis agreed.

Where was Stonewall Jackson in the summer of 1862?

In the place that he knew best, doing the thing at which he was most accomplished. A native of the mountains of Virginia, Jackson had a field day with the Union forces in the Shenandoah Valley, out-marching, out-thinking, and out-guessing them. Those who study the campaigns of "Old Jack," as the men called him, marvel at the speed with which Jackson marched, but they do not realize the weariness it brought to his soldiers.

No section of the armies—Confederate or Union—marched as many miles, or made do with such poor rations, as the Stonewall Jackson Brigade.

By mid-August of 1862, Jackson's reputation stood sky-high. Even some Yankees admitted a grudging admiration for his military style. But Jackson's men were practically dead on their feet, when he called on them to make yet another heroic effort, to come around the right—or western—flank of General John Pope (1822–1892) and the Army of Virginia.

How could two big battles be fought at the same place?

Most of us are more familiar with the "Battle of Bull Run" than with the "Second Battle of Bull Run." The Confederates, typically, labeled them "First Manassas" and "Second Manassas." All of the names and titles aside, however, the stark and intriguing fact is that the two big contests were fought on almost precisely the same ground.

Robert E. Lee brought about this battle. He brought the Army of Northern Virginia from Richmond and wished to strike General John Pope before General McClellan could bring the Army of the Potomac over to join him. As it turned out, McClellan's anger over having been removed from top command played right into Lee's hands.

How hard was the Second Battle of Bull Run?

In terms of a slogging match, it was as eventful and full of chance as any of the Peninsula Campaign battles. General John Pope was forced into the battle in that he had to protect the western approaches to Washington, D.C., but once the battle was joined, the Northern and Southern men fought with equal vim.

The key to Lee's victory lay in the positioning of his forces. By now, Lee had become a master at the art of dividing his forces, even when in the presence of a foe with superior numbers. Because the Confederates generally mobilized faster—even on a daily basis—than the Union men, Lee could have his outriders go around his enemy's flanks with great success. Stonewall Jackson was, of course, the exemplar of this method of maneuver, while James "Old Pete" Longstreet was Lee's "Old War Horse," the solid and steady man in the center. The Second Battle of Bull Run lasted for a day and a half, and the outcome was often in doubt, but once the Northern men began to retreat, it turned into a major Confederate victory. Some historians label it Lee's masterpiece, but the Union defeat is more readily explained by a failure of McClellan, and others, to come to Pope's assistance.

How did Lincoln view this infighting between his generals?

There were times when he could scarcely believe it. Practically all day on the Second Battle of Bull Run, Lincoln telegraphed McClellan, urging him to move to Pope's assistance. One of McClellan's replies, to the effect that Pope had to cut his own way out of the situation he had created, was especially revealing. But these personal animosities cost the North a major defeat.

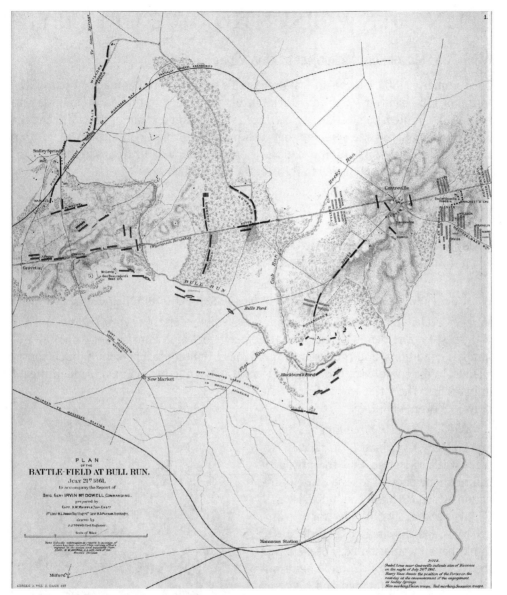

The area surrounding Bull Run where Confederate and Union troops faced off in two significant battles during the Civil War.

When he learned the extent of the loss—10,000 men killed, wounded, or missing—Lincoln collapsed into a chair, exclaiming, "What will the country say?" Typically, he was quicker to recover than some of his generals. Within hours, a plan was established for a defensive perimeter of Washington, D.C. There were plenty of men available to serve, but the difficulty lay in their low morale, brought about by a series of missed opportunities and striking defeats.

LINCOLN VERSUS HORACE GREELEY

Where was Lincoln on the subject of emancipation?

The summer of 1862 was the critical time for his thoughts on that matter. Up until the spring of 1862, perhaps even until July, Lincoln continued to think a limited war was possible. By limited, he meant that a Northern victory would result in the North and the South shaking hands and agreeing that it all had been a mistake. Lincoln was far from alone in this. The letters of some of his advisers, and many of his troops in the field, indicate that a majority preferred to think of the war in this way.

Lincoln never revealed the full workings of his mind to a diary, but July 1862 seems to have been the critical month. The more that he examined the conflict, the more Lincoln became convinced that a limited war was impossible: this was a life-or-death struggle between two societies and two ways of life. One would have to prevail, and in so doing it would naturally alter the lifestyles of the other.

What did Horace Greeley say to Lincoln on the subject of emancipation?

Horace Greeley (1811–1872) was the influential editor of the *New York Tribune* and one of the best-known men in the nation. Like Lincoln, he came from humble, almost hardscrabble conditions, and had risen through merit to become a person of much consequence. In the summer of 1862, Greeley wrote an open letter to Lincoln and printed it in his paper. The letter was entitled "The Prayer of Twenty Millions."

Without declaring that Lincoln should immediately emancipate all the slaves, Horace Greeley asserted that the president had not done enough for the cause of the nation: white and black combined. He was, Greeley declared, fighting the war on a limited basis, and allowing the Confederates to think that all would someday be well: that the North and the South would be reconciled. To that end, Lincoln and his army men had gone too softly on the Southern slaveholders. "I close as I began, with the statement that what an immense majority of the loyal millions of your countrymen require of you is a frank, declared, unqualified, ungrudging execution of the laws of the land, more especially of the Confiscation Act. This act gives freedom to the slaves of rebels coming within our lines."

Horace Greeley, the founding editor of the *New York Tribune* as well as founder of the Liberal Republican Party, was a critic of Lincoln, saying that, in essence, the president was being too soft on the South.

How did Lincoln reply to Greeley's request (which sometimes seems like a demand)?

Lincoln's reply has been quoted many times because it is so revealing of the workings of his mind, especially on the question of slavery. It deserves a short quotation here as well.

"Dear Sir," Lincoln began. Though there may have been missteps or mistakes of fact, his policy was not in any way doubtful. "I would save the Union. I would save it in the shortest way under the Constitution. The sooner the national authority can be restored, the nearer the Union will be 'the Union as it was.' If there be those who would not save the Union unless they could at the same time *save* Slavery, I do not agree with them. If there be those who would not save the Union unless they could at the same time *destroy* Slavery, I do not agree with them. My paramount object in this struggle is to save the Union, and is *not* either to save or destroy Slavery."

Was this the truth, the whole truth, and nothing but the truth?

Not quite. Lincoln was, in his reply to Greeley, as candid as he could be, but there were, in fact, entangling webs that he did not admit to.

Very few historians would argue with the plain fact that Lincoln and the Union men of 1861 fought primarily to save the Union. The flag-waving of April 1861 as well as the letters of hundreds of Northern men clearly show this to be the case. But by the summer of 1862, that initial enthusiasm had waned and was nearly exhausted. Lincoln, who had an unerring eye where popular sentiment was concerned, knew that the war had to be enlarged in some respect, or else he would get no more volunteers. Therefore, although preservation of the Union was clearly his number-one goal, Lincoln had, by the summer of 1862, come around to the idea of some sort of emancipation. Whether this meant compensation for the former slaveholders or some sort of colonization scheme, under which African Americans would be returned to Africa, remained to be seen.

How did the Confederates get the jump on the Union?

By crossing the Potomac and invading Maryland. On September 4, 1862, the Army of Northern Virginia crossed at Leesburg and headed toward Frederick.. This movement had long been desired by Confederate leaders, who believed Maryland would rise to become the twelfth Confederate state. There was a popular song, "Maryland, My Maryland!" that had been composed with this in mind, and the Confederate bands played it as the men crossed the Potomac. Many observers claimed this was the high point of the war for the Confederacy.

Their sight was good, but their knowledge was incomplete. Aside from the desire to win a major battle on Northern soil, Robert E. Lee was practically forced to invade because his army was close to starvation. The lands of Northern Virginia, especially in the vicinity of Bull Run, had been picked over and devastated by crossing armies so many times there was no food, milk, or well water to be had. Maryland, by comparison, offered large expanses of land and fields and farms which had not yet felt the hand of war.

What song did the Confederates sing?

"Dixie" is of course the best-known of all Civil War songs, but to the Confederate soldier, "Maryland, My Maryland!" was almost equally compelling:

> The despot's heel is on thy shore,
> Maryland!
> His touch is at thy temple door,
> Maryland!
> Avenge the patriotic gore
> That flocked the streets of Baltimore
> And be the battle queen of yore,
> Maryland! My Maryland!

The Confederate bands played the song as the army forded the Potomac, and there were high hopes that Marylanders would arise, just as the song predicted.

Did Marylanders rise to the Southern cause?

The response was disappointing, to put it mildly. Over the next ten days, Lee and the Army of Northern Virginia received roughly two hundred recruits while losing roughly five times that number of men to desertion. Marylanders did, by and large, favor the Confederate cause, but they did so from a distance. Once they saw the war brought to their doorsteps, they were much cooler toward the Southern men in gray uniforms.

Lee recognized his mistake early on, but he had committed himself and could not turn back. He still harbored the hope of drawing out and destroying one of the various

What did McClellan write to his wife?

Their relationship was exceptionally close, and McClellan revealed many things in his letters that should probably have never been committed to paper. McClellan's views of Lincoln varied, for example. At times, McClellan believed that he practically had Lincoln in his pocket; at others, he railed at "the baboon" or "gorilla." McClellan also had very strong feelings about Secretary of War Stanton, whom he practically accused of treason. When reading McClellan's letters, at times one wonders if he is an imbecile, but then one realizes he is, rather, a messianic type of religious zealot.

Time and again, McClellan referred to the divine hand of Providence, saying it had chosen him to save the Union. Time after time, McClellan thanked God for allowing him to be the deliverer of the nation. Significantly, McClellan almost never spoke of African Americans, and when he did it was always in disparaging terms. Though he had some fine qualities, McClellan was a quiet racist, one who wanted to ensure that the Civil War ended soon so that the question of black emancipation would *not* become the leading element.

Union armies, and that alone would make the invasion of Maryland worthwhile. For the moment, however, Lee was content to have his men forage in Maryland for supplies, and for his cavalry arm, led by General J. E. B. Stuart, to keep a watchful eye on the Federals.

What did the Union do in response to the invasion?

Lincoln had already made a difficult decision: to place McClellan at the head of the Army of the Potomac once more. Those who watched—and those who today read—marveled at Lincoln's incredible patience with McClellan, the man who so often let the rebels off the hook. There were good reasons for restoring McClellan to high command, however, and the main one was the incredible confidence he instilled in the men.

There were so many people involved, so who was in charge?

Major-General Henry Halleck, in Washington, was general-in-chief. Lincoln was commander-in-chief. McClellan was general of the Army of the Potomac. It was indeed a complicated scene.

The telegraph allowed for more rapid communication than we might imagine, but there were times when the fighting was in areas that had no telegraph wires. At such times, Lincoln and Halleck were in the dark, and McClellan had full authority to do as he wished. The trouble was that McClellan sometimes acted in that way even when he was in full communication with his superiors.

How did Lee position his forces?

In the second week of September 1862, Lee broke his Army of Northern Virginia into four different sections. He and James Longstreet led the main body, which continued to forage, while three other sections, one of them led by Stonewall Jackson, moved against Harpers Ferry.

This move was something of a comedown for Lee; he had already accepted the truth that Maryland would not rise for the Southern cause. So long as his main force was not threatened, it made perfect sense to attack Harpers Ferry, which had many muskets, rifles, and cannon, all of which could be employed for the Confederate cause. Lee took a major risk dividing his army into so many sections, however; the

General James Longstreet, whom Lee called "Old War Horse," performed admirably in the early part of the war, but would later be criticized and partly blamed for the defeat at Gettysburg.

very fact of his doing so indicates the level of contempt he had for McClellan. All might have been well had two Union soldiers not found a message from Lee.

What was Order 191?

On September 10, 1862, Lee wrote orders for all his commanders, not only telling them their tasks, but indicating where the other sections of the Army of Northern Virginia were positioned. One extra copy was made, by Lee's personal secretary, and this *may* be the one that was found by two Northern soldiers.

Among the Union soldiers at Frederick, Maryland, were Sergeant John Bloss and Corporal Barton Mitchell. Seeing an envelope in the grass near their encampment, they opened it to find a set of orders wrapped around three cigars. For the first few minutes, the soldiers were more interested in the cigars, but on examination they found that the orders were from Lee and concerned every part and section of the Army of Northern Virginia. The men rushed to their commanding officer, who then rushed to his, and just a few hours later, McClellan held in his hand something of inestimable worth. Observers claimed that he shouted: "Here is a paper with which if I cannot whip Bobbie Lee, I will be willing to go home."

With McClellan, the first enthusiasm was never the whole story, however.

FROM ANTIETAM TO CHANCELLORSVILLE: SEPTEMBER 1862 TO MAY 1863

McCLELLAN IN CHARGE

What is the significance of the words "How does it look now?"

These five words were the ones most frequently used by Lincoln as he sent telegraph messages to General McClellan. There were days in which McClellan did not respond for hours, and the president continued to send the same message. If McClellan or Robert E. Lee had been able to see the Maryland campaign from the air, this is what either one would have reported.

The Confederate Army of Northern Virginia was entirely on the Maryland side of the Potomac, but it was split into three sections, two of which were besieging Harpers Ferry. Smoke was rising from the Ferry, which had already changed hands twice in the war, and was about to do so a third time. Six corps of the Army of the Potomac were converging on two mountain passes: Crampton's Gap and Turner's Gap. Beyond them lay the central part of the Army of Northern Virginia, at this point only 25,000 strong. A foot race had commenced the day before. The Army of the Potomac was attempting to catch and destroy the Army of Northern Virginia in pieces; Lee, for his part, recognized the danger and was calling in his outposts.

What happened at Harpers Ferry?

The garrison, under the command of Colonel White, held out longer than anticipated, but by the evening of September 14, 1862, Stonewall Jackson had twice as many men, as well as enough guns to commence a fierce artillery bombardment. Had the Federals managed to secure the nearby hills, they might have been able to hold out. Lacking this, they readied themselves to surrender.

The cavalry section of the garrison refused to yield and made a daring escape from Harpers Ferry that night. Their courage prevented the Confederates from gaining over

1,000 horses and saddles, both of which were badly needed. Even so, Stonewall Jackson recorded an impressive victory. Over 11,000 Union men laid down their arms and were soon set free on parole, with the understanding that they would not serve again in the war. Almost as soon as he succeeded in reducing Harpers Ferry, Stonewall Jackson redirected his men, saying they had to go to the assistance of General Lee.

How did McClellan excuse his slowness?

McClellan's telegraphs to Washington, D.C., are a masterpiece of subterfuge. Everything he describes—from the weather to the condition of his men's shoes—suggest that circumstances delayed him.

In fact, McClellan was simply not the person to respond with alacrity. Had Robert E. Lee obtained a confidential dispatch, revealing the disposition of the enemy forces, he would have had every man on the move within an hour: Stonewall Jackson would have been even quicker. But McClellan, the master organizer, was not one for rapid movements. He did have the Army of the Potomac on the move, but it was not until the morning of September 15 that they battled the Confederates for the two mountain passes.

What was the lay of the land just prior to the Battle of Antietam?

Up to September 14, 1862, the Confederates had felt safe on the western side of a ridge of mountains running from north to south through Maryland. J. E. B. Stuart's cavalry provided a much-desired screen, keeping the Federals out. But on September 14, McClellan's forces began to attack through Turner's Gap—which separates two sections of South Mountain—and Crampton's Gap, which separates South Mountain from Maryland Heights. Parts of the area still look a good deal as they did in 1862, and even the most casual tourist remarks on both the beauty and the difficulty of the terrain.

The battle for the two mountain passes raged all day, with reinforcements for both sides arriving at various times. The battle was touch-and-go, but the superior federal numbers eventually held, and both gaps were in Union hands by nightfall. The Confederate leaders still did not realize the extent to which McClellan understood their dispositions, and there was some wonder expressed at their headquarters. Why had McClellan suddenly become so aggressive? Lee did not believe the situation was lost, however. He had new sets of orders out that evening, with the plan for all sections of the Army of Northern Virginia to converge on the little town of Sharpsburg.

What kind of shape were the Confederates in?

On the most important level—that of morale—they were doing quite well, but in terms of supplies and materiel, they were at their lowest ebb. Perhaps two thousand pairs of shoes had been found during the marches through southern Maryland: these were not nearly enough. The Confederate supply system, always suspect, was completely unable to keep up with events. The only bright spot was Stonewall Jackson's capture of Harpers Ferry.

Northern observers frequently remarked on the trials of their opponents. The *New York Times* outdid itself in this regard. "The [Confederate] men are found with rags around their feet instead of shoes; they are seen eating ears of green corn, cob and all; they search for, pick up and eat the bits of hard bread that our troops throw away; while for clothing and tents a set of vagabonds would excel them." (*New York Times*, September 10, 1862)

That the Confederates were dirty, weary, and hungry was beyond dispute, but they continued to move, and to do so like a pack of wolves. The Army of the Potomac, by contrast, was well fed, but its men appeared like slackers in comparison.

How far is it from the two mountain passes to Antietam?

Roughly eight miles. McClellan's men began their pursuit on the morning of September 15 and got into position late that afternoon. They found, however, that the Army of Northern Virginia had turned and established a strong defensive position in and around the town of Sharpsburg.

Lee's men had Antietam Creek to their front and the town in their midst. They had the Potomac River two miles to their back, making retreat unlikely if not impossible. Had McClellan known that Lee had only 30,000 men, he might have ordered an all-out assault, but the Confederate positions—and the placement of their artillery—suggested a much larger number. McClellan paused, therefore, and waited not only that evening but all of the next day. The Battle of Antietam—or Sharpsburg as the Confederates called it—had to wait until Monday, September 17.

What was McClellan's plan?

Like General Irvin McDowell on the night before the Battle of Bull Run, McClellan did not reveal his full hand to anyone. It was his intention to attack the next morning, but all that his different corps commanders received was the order in which they would enter the battle. Examining the battle plans, one is almost forced to conclude that McClellan did not wish to shed too much blood. Perhaps he believed that a sharp early morning contest would persuade Lee's Confederates to surrender.

The honor of beginning the battle went to General Joseph Hooker (1814–1879), commander of the First Federal Corps. A native of Massachusetts and a West Point graduate, Hooker was one of the more stubborn of McClellan's subordinate generals: he had gained a fine reputation during the Peninsula Campaign, and his men called him "Fighting Joe." To make certain his men would recognize their commander, Hooker rode out on a magnificent white horse on the morning of September 17, 1862, which just happened to be the seventy-fifth anniversary of the signing of the U.S. Constitution.

BATTLE OF ANTIETAM

How did the battle commence?

Hooker had his men in position by 5 A.M., and the attack was made at first light (accounts differ as to the precise clock time). Hooker made a splendid sight, and target, on his white bay, and he urged his men forward with an uncommon insistence.

The men of Hooker's corps were more than ready: they had been in pursuit of the rebels for days, and they made the most of their attack. Several times, between 7 and 9 A.M., Hooker's men were on the verge of punching right through the Confederate left wing, but on each occasion, heroics were performed. At one point it was a regiment of Mississippians, a second time it was the heroics of a group of men from Alabama. The men of General John B. Hood's Texas division were especially infuriated because they had just been given their first real rations in several days and were beginning to cook breakfast when the call came. For many of those men, perhaps as many as a third of them, they had missed their last meal.

What is meant by "The Cornfield"?

Those men, on either side, who fought in numerous battles became very used to the presence of corn fields. This was true whether they fought in Virginia, Maryland, Kentucky, or Tennessee. What they—and we—call "The Cornfield" is a very specific thirty-acre area that was contested throughout the morning of September 17, 1862. The fighting was so intense that Hooker's corps, as well as Stonewall Jackson's brigade, were practically ruined. Hooker later surveyed the area and declared that the bodies were heaped on top of one another.

Why did McClellan take so long to send in his second corps?

As ever, McClellan believed the Confederates to be stronger than was really the case. And he took too long to send in General Joseph Mansfield with the second corps. Once they were across the bridge, however, Mansfield's men made a terrific effort and came within a few minutes, or a few hundred yards, of piercing the Confederate defensive lines in two. But as so often happened on that day, Lee brought some men from his right flank, which had not yet been assaulted, and managed to hold the Union men off. By this time, General Mansfield was mortally wounded, and General Joseph Hooker was out of combat, having suffered a bullet wound to his foot.

Was there no sense of urgency among the top Union commanders?

Hooker had initiated the day's battle with tremendous intensity, but he was now off the field. Mansfield was dead, and McClellan, counting the wounds to his regiments and divisions, was becoming terribly cau-

General Ambrose Burnside faltered during the Battle of Antietam, failing to take an important bridge quickly enough and then holding back instead of attacking vulnerable Confederate forces.

tious. Even so, McClellan cannot be blamed for the poor performance by General Ambrose Burnside.

Burnside had roughly twenty thousand men, leading the left flank of the Union force. He was in no possible danger—the fighting was all to his right (or to the north), and he was under orders to take the bridge that would bring his men into the battle. Why Burnside fumbled so badly on this occasion is not fully known, but he did not have his men in motion till 2 P.M., and the bridge was not taken until two hours later. The Confederates prudently withdrew, and Burnside was satisfied with occupying the ground on the west side of Antietam Creek. None of the top Union commanders seemed to realize that complete victory was within their grasp. One vigorous attack from the Union center would, very likely, have brought about a complete Confederate collapse.

What was the scene like toward the end of the day?

The day, in the opinion of most of the participants, had gone on far too long. There was something eerie, too, in the reddish quality to the last sunlight of September 17, 1862. Even those who had fought in the worst of it, however, did not fully recognize the awful toll until days later. The Battle of Antietam, or Sharpsburg, was the single bloodiest day in American history.

Can that be accounted for by the simple fact that Americans were fighting each other?

No. The total casualties on the Union side came to 2,010 killed, 9,416 wounded, and 1,043 missing, for a total of 12,469. Confederate losses are harder to be named with certainty, partly because there had been so many desertions, but it was at least equal to the Northern loss. Therefore, we can say, with little hesitation, that roughly 25,000 Americans were killed, wounded, or went missing in one day's battle. Let us compare that to other terrible days in American history.

On December 7, 1941, 2,386 Americans died when the Japanese bombed Pearl Harbor. That was indeed a black day in American history, but it did not come close, either in relative or in absolute terms, to the blood that flowed at Antietam. On September 11, 2001, 2,996 Americans were killed in the immediate aftermath of the terrorist attacks on the World Trade Center in New York City. While it was a horrific scene, and day, it does not approach the losses at Antietam. And even at the height of the Second World War, when the United States fought on two fronts—the battle-hardened Germans on one and the fanatical Japanese on the other—there was no day in which the casualty number or percentage came even close.

Antietam stands alone.

Did anyone manage to capture the scene at Antietam in all its awfulness?

Many people attempted to do so. The photography studio of Mathew B. Brady was on the scene, and pictures later emerged, especially marked by the dead and wounded lying in

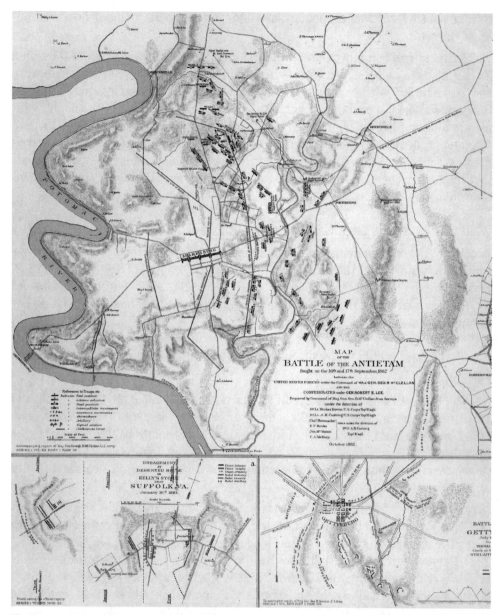

The Potomac River snakes past the village of Sharpsburg, where Robert E. Lee and the Army of Northern Virginia made their stand on September 17, 1862.

the so-called Sunken Lane. Pen-and-ink artists were there as well, but it was, truly, impossible for one camera shot or landscape painting to take it all in. One of the better attempts made by use of the written word comes from the pen of Captain George Noyes.

"Passing through this corn-field, with the dead lying all through its aisles, I saw bodies attired mainly in rebel gray, lying in ranks so regular that Death, the Reaper,

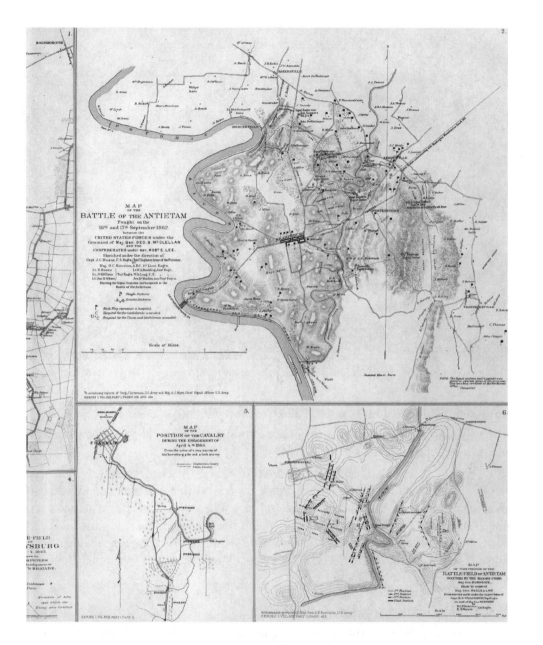

must have mowed them down in swaths. Our burying parties were already busily engaged, and had put away to rest many of our own men—still here, as everywhere, I saw
them scattered over the fields. The ground was strewn with muskets, knapsacks, car-
tridge-boxes, and articles of clothing; the carcasses of horses, and thousands of shot and
shell. And so it was on the other side of the turnpike, nay, in the turnpike itself. Ride
where we may, through corn-field, wood, or ravine, and our ride will be among the dead,
until the heart grows sick and faint with horror."

137

The Army of the Potomac charges Confederate soldiers during the Battle of Antietam in this lithograph from 1888.

What did McClellan do on September 18, 1862?

Virtually nothing. He, and the Army of the Potomac, were completely shocked by the bloodletting of the previous day.

Even so, if McClellan had given the order to attack, the chances are excellent that the Civil War would have been won that day. Lee had, at that moment, roughly 30,000 men who could still stand and fight, and not one of them was truly fresh: all had been engaged. McClellan, who received reinforcements the previous night, had close to 70,000 men fit for combat, of whom almost 30,000 were completely fresh: they had not yet been engaged. By standing where he was, McClellan allowed the single most golden opportunity of the war escape him.

How did McClellan justify his inaction?

By saving every scrap of paper or copy of telegrams sent, McClellan was able to build a case for his nonaction. Even now, over a distance of 150 years, it seems rather weak.

"After a night of anxious deliberation and a full and careful review of the situation and condition of our army, the strength and position of the enemy, I concluded that the success of an attack on the eighteenth was not certain. I am aware of that fact that, under ordinary circumstances a general is expected to risk a battle if he has a reasonable prospect of success; but at this critical juncture I should have had a narrow view of the condition of the country had I been willing to hazard another battle.... At that mo-

When did Clara Barton become well known as a nurse?

Born in Massachusetts in 1821, Clara Barton had struggled with issues of insecurity throughout life, but the beginning of the Civil War provided her with a new spirit and mission. She was often frustrated by army officials, who seemed not to comprehend the importance of providing medical supplies, but the Battle of Antietam was her breakthrough moment. As she later described, Barton followed the Army of the Potomac with three supply wagons, and she arrived at the battlefield early on the morning of September 17, 1862.

Never had the need been so obvious or immediate. Wounded men were brought into the army tent literally by the minute. Barton and a few assistants were there to assist in the terrible choices that army surgeons had to make. Probably two times out of three, the wounded soldier had to lose a limb in order to save his life. As the day wore on, Barton experienced war in all its terror. One wounded soldier was killed by a cannon shot, and the blood spurted all over her. She continued her work. The irony in all of this is that Barton—to the end of her days—never regarded nursing as her number-one priority. In a career that spanned the Civil War and the Spanish-American War, she always considered herself primarily as a deliverer of much-needed medical supplies.

ment—Virginia lost, Washington menaced, Maryland invaded—the National cause could afford no more risks of defeat."

What did Lee do in the aftermath of the Battle of Antietam?

Lee never confided his feelings about the battle to paper, but he had to have known that it was a disaster. The Confederacy could not afford battlefield casualties in the way that the Union could, and now he stood with the river to his back and McClellan's army in front of him. Very likely, Lee knew the full extent of his peril. But he bravely acted as if the situation was under control.

When another day passed without a federal assault, Lee took his chance to escape. On the night of September 19 to 20, the Army of Northern Virginia began passing over the Potomac, departing Virginia. Remarkably, there was no attack, or even any sorties by the Federals, and the Army of Northern Virginia successfully exited Maryland. The Confederates had taken a bad beating, but they were still in the field.

THE EMANCIPATION PROCLAMATION

What did Lincoln do in the aftermath of the Battle of Antietam?

Lincoln was infuriated that McClellan did not pursue Lee's army, but in another sense his moment had finally come. For months, Lincoln had been mulling the idea of eman-

This 1864 painting by artist Francis Bicknell Carpenter recreates the scene of the first reading of the Emancipation Proclamation. Shown are (left to right) Secretary of War Edwin M. Stanton, Secretary of the Treasury Salmon P. Chase, President Lincoln, Secretary of the Navy Gideon Welles, Secretary of the Interior Caleb Blood Smith, Secretary of State William H. Seward, U.S. Postmaster General Montgomery Blair, and U.S. Attorney General Edward Bates.

cipation, occasionally discussing it with his Cabinet and writing various drafts. Now, with a major Union victory in the field, he felt able to release it to the world. Therefore, on September 22, 1862, Lincoln took the step. He began with these words:

"I, Abraham Lincoln, President of the United States of America, and commander-in-chief of the army and navy thereof, do hereby proclaim and declare that hereafter, as heretofore, the war will be prosecuted for the object of practically restoring the constitutional relation between the United States and each of the states, and the people thereof." In other words, the issue of Union versus disunion continued, officially, to be the main reason for the war. But Lincoln did not stop there.

When did Lincoln get around to the slaves?

He got closer on the second paragraph. "That it is my purpose, upon the next meeting of Congress, to again recommend the adoption of a practical measure, tendering pecuniary aid to the free acceptance or rejection of all Slave States so called, the people whereof may not then be in rebellion against the United States, and which states may then have voluntarily adopted, or thereafter may voluntarily adopt, immediate or gradual abolishment of slavery within their respective limits...."

Lincoln still was acting cautiously. He wanted to coax some of the Confederate states back into the Union, and he wanted to keep the Border States. Therefore, he spoke of practical measures, including his long-cherished idea of colonization, meaning that black Africans would one day return to Africa. But he finally got to the heart of the matter in the third paragraph.

Who was actually freed by the Emancipation Proclamation?

Almost no one was freed on the spot. But the promise of freedom was very close, so close that some of the slaves who read—or heard—the Proclamation could taste it:

> That on the first day of January, in the year of our Lord one thousand eight hundred and sixty three, all persons held as slaves within any state, or designated part of a state, the people whereof shall then be in rebellion against the United States, shall be then, thenceforward, and forever, free; and the executive government of the United States, including the military and naval authority thereof, will recognize and maintain the freedom of such persons.

> It had finally happened. Thirty-four years after the first abolitionist groups were founded, eleven years after the publication of *Uncle Tom's Cabin*, and four years after John Brown's raid on Harpers Ferry, a bold, powerful step had been taken, and as of January 1, 1863, millions of black people *would* be free.

How was the Emancipation Proclamation received?

There were so many varying responses and reactions that it is difficult to list them all. Many people expressed wonderment and surprise, thinking that Lincoln had gone very far indeed; but there were plenty of others who said the president had not gone far enough. Many white Americans feared the possible ramifications, including how four million African Americans would someday be employed, housed, and fed. But in the North, there was a general feeling among the white population that the time for this step had come.

It was not well received among the men in the Union armies. Many soldiers had long argued that the war was primarily about Union versus disunion, and the slavery issue was a distraction from the main event. A few soldiers threw away their guns and deserted, but the great majority grudgingly accepted the Proclamation, saying that it now gave two great causes for which to fight.

On January 1, 1863, a number of persons—black and white—wrote comments on how the Proclamation was celebrated. One of the most articulate comes from the pen of a white Massachusetts surgeon, attending to black soldiers of Colonel Thomas Wentworth Higginson's (1823–1911) regiment. Dr. Seth Rogers, in the camp along the South Carolina coast, had this to say:

> "This is the evening of the most eventful day of my life. Our barbecue was a most wonderful success.... After the presentation speech had been made, and just as Col. Higginson advanced to take the flag and respond, a negro woman standing near began to sing 'America,' and soon many voices of freedmen and women joined in the beautiful hymn, and sang it so touchingly that every one was thrilled beyond measure." Just five days later, the same surgeon wrote, "I

am steadily becoming acquainted with very remarkable men whose lived in slavery and whose heroism in getting out of it, deepens my faith in negro character and intellect."

How was the Proclamation received by the African American community?

This is more difficult to gauge, both because of a lack of literacy and a lack of persons to record the reactions. We have to rely on the anecdotal record, which comes to us primarily through the diaries and letters of slaveholders in the Confederate states. They tell us that the slaveholders were very concerned that the black slaves were becoming uppity, believing that Father Abraham—the expression began around this time—had set them free.

Among the free persons of color in the Northern states, there was some dissension, with people saying that the president had not gone far enough, but the single most powerful voice was that of Frederick Douglass. He had been on the abolitionist trail for thirty years, and now, he finally saw the light. To Douglass, it did not matter that the Proclamation was conditional, or that the slaves had to wait until January 1, 1863. The great, overwhelming matter was that Lincoln had made the cause public, and that the power of the federal government was now behind the cause of abolition.

How was the Proclamation received in other nations, European ones especially?

Many Europeans disliked the piecemeal approach under which Lincoln specified that only the slaves living in states that were then in rebellion would be freed. But it was difficult to argue against the Proclamation as a whole because the major European nations, with the exception of Portugal, had long since outlawed slavery and the slave trade. Lincoln had clearly put this in mind when he wrote the Proclamation.

Had Lee and the Army of Northern Virginia won the Battle of Antietam, the chances are that one or more of the European powers would have recognized the Confederacy as an independent nation. But because Lee lost the Battle of Antietam, and because of Lincoln's Proclamation, the prospect for European intervention was dramatically reduced.

Where were some of the most famous photographs of Lincoln taken? The ones where he appears in an army camp and towers over everyone else.

On October 1, 1862, Lincoln took the train from Washington and reached McClellan's camp on the banks of the Potomac River. This was his most determined effort to date to persuade McClellan to take action. During the three days Lincoln spent in the army camp, he was photographed numerous times, with the most famous ones showing him with McClellan and his staff.

In part, it is because of his stovepipe hat that Lincoln towers so dramatically. But there was something else, too, something noted by many observers. Lincoln had come more fully into his own: he looked and acted like the commander-in-chief. He still relished jokes of all kinds, and could be very merry, but there was a gravity about him as well,

One of the most famous photographs ever taken of President Lincoln is this one of him at Antietam meeting with General McClellan. A young George A. Custer is seen at the far right.

one imposed by the rigors of the war. No previous president—not even Washington—had shouldered such immense responsibilities or seen so many young Americans perish.

What did Lincoln mean by "McClellan's bodyguard"?

One morning while in army camp, Lincoln rose early to take a walk with a friend from Illinois. The two walked to the highest ridge, or point, taking in the immensity of the Army of the Potomac, whose tents and fires seemed to stretch for miles. The two were silent for a time, then Lincoln suddenly asked his friend, "Do you know what this is?" Puzzled, his friend replied that of course he knew, it was the Army of the Potomac. "So it is called," Lincoln replied, "but that is a mistake. It is McClellan's bodyguard."

Like so many witty words from Lincoln, these could be construed in several ways. The obvious meaning, of course, was that McClellan was a fearful man who did not wish to risk his splendid army in combat, and there was much truth to the assertion. But a second, hidden meaning was that Lincoln, as commander-in-chief, did not feel able to get rid of McClellan, so long as the general was admired by his men. And at this point, he still was.

What was Lincoln waiting for?

He had to see what would happen during the off-year elections of 1862. By most reports, the Democratic Party was gaining strength in most areas, and Lincoln and his Republicans were on the defensive. There was already talk, in New York City, of running McClellan for president in 1864.

The election returns came in piece by piece (there was no one single election day that year). Right from the start, it was obvious that the Democrats had gained ground, though perhaps not as much as they hoped. Lincoln's good friend Orville Browning lost his Senate seat from Illinois, and there were other "casualties," but the Republicans retained control of both Houses of Congress. That was what Lincoln needed to see, and he finally sacked McClellan on November 7, 1862.

How did McClellan respond?

In public, he was the model of acceptance. In typical McClellan style, he issued a proclamation to the troops, and he made quite a scene on the day of his departure, but there was no talk of a coup, or rising against the administration.

In private, McClellan also held true to form. He lambasted Lincoln, Stanton, and the rest of the administration in letters to his wife. Their concern for African Americans ran particularly against his grain, and McClellan very likely decided to run for president sometime that autumn. So far as the Army of the Potomac was concerned, he was out, and General Ambrose Burnside was in.

Why had Burnside not risen to the top prior to this?

Ambrose Burnside (1824–1881) is one of the most likable of all Civil War generals. Modest, friendly to all, and interested in the well-being of his men, Burnside was an ideal division commander, perhaps even corps commander, but he did not have the kind of killer instinct necessary to be commander of an entire army (the same could be said for McClellan). Lincoln had previously offered high command to Burnside, who had turned it down. On this occasion, he accepted, becoming the new commander of the Army of the Potomac.

Burnside at once began to reorganize the army. There were so many corps and divisions that the command chain had become unwieldy. He, therefore, divided it into three grand corps. Whatever other faults he might commit, Burnside would not demonstrate the "slows" as had McClellan.

What kind of shape were the Confederates in?

The worst they had yet experienced. 1862 was a heartbreak year for many Confederates. The tide of bad news began early, with Grant's victories in the West, and just accelerated as the year went on. The loss of New Orleans was keenly felt.

In Richmond, the price of just about everything had doubled since the war commenced, and this at a time when many people were out of work. The price of bread became so high that there would be a street riot by women of the city the following year.

The Army of Northern Virginia remained the pride and the hope of the Confederate cause. Despite his defeat at Antietam, Lee was practically revered for his tactical skill. Lee took this opportunity to reorganize his forces. Upon his recommendation, Stonewall Jackson and James Longstreet were both promoted to lieutenant-general with command of wings—or corps—of the army.

Where was Lee in the competition between Jackson and Longstreet?

Lee's feelings, or sentiments, are harder to discern because he kept his public persona up so constantly. He had recently lost an adult daughter to typhoid fever, and he seldom talked

Was there any competition between Longstreet and Jackson?

This has long been debated. The reason is that Longstreet lived longer than al-most any of the other top commanders, and his memoirs, published in the 1880s, produced a firestorm of criticism. Most observers at the time did not see any conflict between the two men, who represented such different aspects of the Confederate battle strategy.

Jackson, known to his men as "Old Jack," was a relentless fighter and perhaps marched his men even harder than he made them fight. A devout Presbyterian, Jackson believed that God was with the Confederates and that his arm would uphold them, even when all sorts of terrible sacrifices were demanded. Longstreet was dispassionate. He, too, harbored a deep religious faith, made stronger by the recent death of *three* of his daughters to scarlet fever. Longstreet did not put much hope in the Almighty, in foreign intervention, or any other external help. To him, it was self-evident that the Confederates would win or lose on their own.

of the Almighty or Divine Providence, but one suspects that he had a powerful inner faith. Lee may actually have enjoyed having Longstreet and Jackson—two such different men—on his staff because they presented such varying views of the same set of circumstances.

BATTLE OF FREDERICKSBURG

When did the Army of the Potomac begin to move?

On November 15, 1862. Burnside wanted to move quickly in order to avoid the type of criticism that had previously gone to McClellan. Burnside had a good plan, which was to cross the Rappahannock River at Fredericksburg and move quickly against Richmond. Lee and the Army of Northern Virginia would be forced to throw themselves in his way, and he would fight them at an advantage.

The trouble lay in execution of the plan. The roads were full of mud, and the heavily laden Army of the Potomac moved more slowly than anticipated. Even so, Burnside did get to the Rappahannock in time to make a quick move across, but the pontoon bridges were not ready. While he waited, the Army of Northern Virginia began to coalesce.

How important was the artillery arm at this point?

Disappointed by the performance of his artillery at Antietam, Lee promoted a new commander of ordnance. Edward Porter Alexander proved to be one of the best subordinate commanders on the Confederate side for the rest of the war. By now, the Confederates were roughly equal to the Union men in terms of guns of all sizes, and Porter made the most out of what he had, consolidating the Confederate artillery.

145

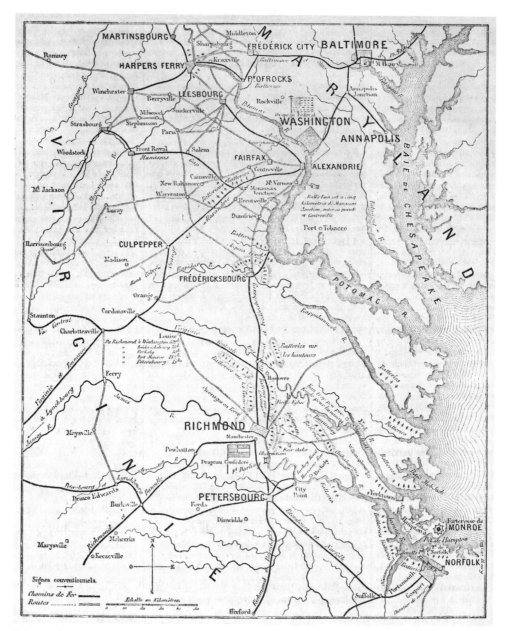

This map shows Fredericksburg as the key mid-point between Richmond and Washington, D.C.

The Federals had plenty of big guns and could always manufacture more, but there was a difficulty in getting them to the battlefield. Again, the November rains played an important role in slowing the federal advance. Still, by the end of November, most of the Army of the Potomac was on the northeast side of the Rappahannock River, and much of the Army of Northern Virginia was on its way south.

Why did Burnside wait so long before commencing his attack?

Burnside was unfortunate both in the weather and in his own uncertain command. An excellent commander of men, able to inspire as well as confide, he had many fine qualities, but was not the right person to command so large a force. Where McClellan erred on the side of caution, Burnside tended to err on the side of desperate action. Another trouble Burnside faced was that he had absolutely no benefit of surprise.

The Confederates, from their side, could detect every move that the Northern men made, and it was plainly obvious they meant to cross the river. Whether they would come directly at and through the town of Fredericksburg remained unknown, however.

How did Lee prepare his army for the coming battle?

Lee had not been thrilled when McClellan was removed from command; he feared that at some point, the Federals would find a commander whose aims he could not detect. This was not the case with Burnside, however, whose plans were readily detectable. Lee, therefore, had almost two weeks to bring up his entire force and deploy it in the most strategically defensible position.

No army is free from friction, however, and there was some discontent on the part of Stonewall Jackson, who believed that Lee had shown excessive favoritism to James Longstreet. The better clothing, materials, and food all seemed to go to Longstreet's wing of the army, and Jackson was in an unpleasant mood as the battle neared. One of his aides heard Jackson mutter something about resigning his commission, but nothing more came of it.

When did the federals begin to act?

On December 11, 1862, thousands of men of the Army of the Potomac crossed the pontoon bridges over the Rappahannock. They came under artillery fire that cost dozens of lives, but they kept coming.

Lee, from his vantage point on the southeastern Confederate flank, could do little because it was James Longstreet's position that was about to be attacked. One Confederate regiment held the town of Fredericksburg for hours, thereby allowing Lee and Longstreet to make their final arrangements. By the time the Federals took the town, the men were angry and exhausted; some of the worst rape and pillage of the entire war followed. That some of the townspeople had aided in the Confederate defense was given as the excuse, but in reality the men on both sides of the conflict had nearly reached their breaking points.

When did the federal attack commence?

On the morning of December 13, 1862, thousands of men from three different corps of the Army of the Potomac began to ascend from the village of Fredericksburg, moving toward the heights. There were many in the Union ranks who sensed the hopelessness of the endeavor, but no one turned back.

An illustration from the Parisien *Journal Universel* shows Confederate soldiers preparing themselves for battle near the Rappahannock River.

The Confederates waited till the Federals were within three hundred yards, then unleashed the most ferocious artillery bombardment yet seen in the war. Colonel Porter, commanding the artillery, had assured General Longstreet a week earlier that once his guns opened up, a chicken could not survive on that open field. Lee and Longstreet were at the former's headquarters, more than a mile away, but they could see all that transpired. It was sometime that morning that Lee made one of his most famous statements. "It is well that war is so terrible," he said, "otherwise we should grow too fond of it."

How bad was the slaughter?

It was, and is, difficult to describe. There were sections of Union infantry that were practically blown from one side to another by the force of the artillery blasts, which created something like temporary gusts of wind. There were men down in all locations, and there were regiments without commanders. The Confederates, meanwhile, continued to pour in more powder and shot.

No order from General Burnside brought the men back. They returned because there was no alternative. Examining the field and the losses, some men proclaimed that it was nothing short of hell on earth. A calmer, but still accurate, portrait was provided by a Massachusetts sergeant. "Our forces were trying to carry Marye's Heights, forming line after line of battle and sending them in all day long, but of no avail as they were cut down by the enemy posted behind stone walls on the heights, as fast as the lines could form and advance." (*War Diary*, p. 9)

What did Burnside do the next day?

Burnside actually contemplated a second attempt, but his brigadier generals talked him out of it. Burnside did not lose his head during the Battle of Fredericksburg; the kind-

Union forces camp near Fredericksburg in this illstration published in the Parisien *Journal Universel* in 1863.

est thing that can be said is that he was impervious to the disaster being created. A few days later, the federal troops backed off a few miles, leaving the Confederates in possession of the field. Roughly 12,500 Northern men were killed, wounded, or missing. Confederate losses came to about 5,500.

How did Lee regard the Battle of Fredericksburg?

Lee, surprisingly, was not elated by his success. He seems to have gauged Burnside accurately and believed that the Union general would make another attempt, in which the destruction would have been even greater. Lee later admitted to confidantes that he had hoped for a greater slaughter of the Union army. Even the capture of a great deal of federal equipment did not thrill him; he commented that it only meant more money for the Northern manufacturers and profiteers.

The rest of the South did not share Lee's apprehensions, however. The news of Fredericksburg cheered up thousands, perhaps even millions, of white Southerners who had received a multitude of bad news during 1862. For the South, it was appropriate to close the year with a defensive victory.

What was the situation on New Year's Day of 1863?

Given the sea of blood that had issued during 1862, one might expect the public mood in Washington to be somber, but this was not the case. Like the previous New Year's Day, Lincoln received callers for hours and shook so many hands that his own felt

How could any experienced general—North or South—have made such a calamitous error as Burnside at the Battle of Fredericksburg?

The answer is not as difficult or complicated as we might think. The men and women of Civil War times lived right on the cusp of great technological changes, but they did not always recognize them. Sometimes it was younger men who recognized the importance of the new equipment and technologies. General Burnside clearly did not.

Just fifteen years earlier, during the Mexican War, many Mexican positions had been carried by daring United States assaults: Lee had been one of the instrumental scouts in the campaign that resulted in the capture of Mexico City. The Mexican army had been well behind the technological curve, however, and that curve had greatly accelerated in the fifteen years since. Therefore, by 1862 it was nearly suicidal to make a frontal assault against men strongly entrenched, but there were still commanders who would take the risk, mistakenly believing that the valor of their men would prevail. Something very similar would happen in the First World War, when the generals of numerous armies simply would not believe that the machine gun had outdated their style of warfare.

arthritic later in the day. Official Washington turned out in all its regalia; even Chief Justice Roger Taney came to the White House on this occasion. There were, of course, personal losses that tinged the day with sorrow.

Gideon Welles, secretary of the navy, had recently lost his nine-year-old son to illness. Of the eight children born to his wife, only two still lived. The president, of course, was now reduced to two sons out of the four born to Mary Todd Lincoln. And there were many other losses to members of the Washington community, men and boys who had died during 1862. The overall mood was upbeat, however, thanks to the numerous crises that Lincoln and his administration had weathered. Just a year ago, it had been doubtful as to who would prevail in the West: at this point, only Vicksburg and a stretch of land ten miles long remained to the Confederates along the Mississippi. A year earlier, the Federals had entertained hopes for a quick capture of Richmond, but they were now more realistic. And for all of these losses and difficulties, the men of Lincoln's administration knew they were in better shape than their opposite numbers in Richmond.

When did the Emancipation Proclamation take full effect?

After the White House doors closed at 2 P.M., Lincoln and his Cabinet members met to witness the signing. Lincoln had in his hands the official copy of the full Proclamation, which specifically outlined those areas "in rebellion," in which the slaves would be freed.

As he went to sign, Lincoln experienced a stiffness in his right hand, and he joked that the momentous occasion had unnerved him. Actually this was the effect of shaking so

An illustration from *Harper's Weekly* celebrates the emancipation of black slaves.

many hands earlier in the day. When he made his careful signature at the bottom, Lincoln handed the Proclamation to an aide, who swiftly took it off to be copied and printed. As of that moment, roughly four million slaves in the Southern states were officially free.

Does history record any event equal to this one in the number of persons set free?

Only one. We often forget that Russian and American events paralleled each other, at least in some ways, during the Civil War years. In March 1861, the same month that Lincoln delivered his first Inaugural Address, Czar Alexander II signed a special ukase (imperial order) that freed almost twenty-five million Russian serfs. Like the Emancipation Proclamation, the Czar's order had conditions. There were long periods during which the emancipated serfs had to work the farmlands of their former owners to recompense them for the financial loss. But if one puts the two events together, little doubt exists that the 1860s witnessed the largest liberation of persons yet seen in the Western world.

BATTLES FOR THE WEST

What was the scene in the West?

Humiliated by his repulse outside of Vicksburg, General Grant prepared for another means and method of attack. Clearly, Vicksburg was going to be a tough nut to crack, **151** and Grant began devising a plan that would take his army entirely around the natural defenses so that his superior numbers could be brought to bear.

The rest of the lower Mississippi Valley was rather quiet at the beginning of 1863. The federal occupation of New Orleans continued with more complaints of Union abuses of the civilian population. Natchez, Baton Rouge, and other points were firmly under federal control. One had to look farther west, beyond the Mississippi, to see evidence of Confederate strength, which in Texas remained large.

What was the scene in the East?

New York City was in the tumult of political discussions, while Baltimore was quieter than at any earlier point in the war. Washington, D.C., seemed secure for the moment, and the Northern states were breathing a sigh of relief that Lee's autumn invasion of Maryland had failed.

Ambrose Burnside was still commander of the Army of the Potomac, but this would not last long. Most people in the know expected that he would be replaced by General "Fighting Joe" Hooker, who had roundly criticized Burnside for the failure at Fredericksburg. On the Confederate side, the three-part combination of Lee, Jackson, and Longstreet was now so strong that these men carried the hopes and expectations of the South on their backs.

How did the New Year begin?

In Washington, D.C., the New Year commenced with a time-honored ceremony: that of the public shaking the president's hand. Official dignitaries came first, at 10 A.M., but the doors were opened to all at noon, and Lincoln spent the next two hours shaking hands. He was an accomplished master of the art, sizing up whether the recipient needed a bear shake or a gentle meeting of the fingers. Observers continued to criticize the president's personal appearance, but they marveled over his skill with the average American.

What was the military situation at the beginning of the year?

Downcast by his failure outside of Vicksburg, General William T. Sherman and his army were in a state of quiet and rest. Upbeat, believing he had found an answer to the riddle of Vicksburg, Ulysses Grant was preparing to have a canal dug. Pessimistic and humiliated by his defeat at Fredericksburg, Ambrose Burnside was willing to consider almost any possibility to retrieve the situation.

Even these generals and the forces they commanded were not the sum of the whole, however. There were Union troops in Texas, and naval vessels blockading much of the Confederate coast. There were regiments being disbanded almost by the day and new ones being formed. Any fair-minded observer had to admit that the Union had created a military juggernaut, an immense combination of forces on land and sea. There was no official British military presence in the North, but English merchants commented on the tremendous power of the Union, which, day by day, was being demonstrated for all the world to see.

What was the military situation from the Confederate point of view?

The only leading general who was truly upbeat was Robert E. Lee. Despite the defeat at Antietam four months earlier, Lee believed that the Army of Northern Virginia was in excellent shape and could defeat the Army of the Potomac any day, so long as circumstances were equal. His subordinates—James Longstreet and Stonewall Jackson—followed his lead in their opinion of the situation.

The Confederate garrison at Vicksburg, Mississippi, knew that it was the key to maintaining a true Confederacy, one that commenced in Virginia and ran all the way to Texas. If Vicksburg fell, the Confederate cause would be on very shaky ground. But the garrison was not confident in its commander, General John Pemberton, in part because he was Northern born. Raised in Philadelphia, Pemberton was thoroughly devoted to the Confederate cause, but both his accent and his appearance made him seem something of a foreigner to his men. In between the Army of Northern Virginia and the men who held Vicksburg was the Army of Tennessee, led by General Braxton Bragg.

Why does General Bragg have such a gloomy, almost dismal reputation?

Sad to say, he truly earned it. Born in North Carolina in 1817, Bragg graduated from West Point in 1837. Just a year later, serving against the Seminoles in Florida, he came down with a debilitating combination of fever, dyspepsia, and boils, and these would resurface to attack him many times over the years (especially when he was under stress). Bragg had a volatile temper, which often brought him into conflict with his subordinates, and that he rose in the Confederate Army is largely a result of his friendship with Jefferson Davis.

Bragg performed very well at the Battle of Shiloh in April 1862, and this accelerated his rise. By the summer of 1862, he was overall commander of the Western Department, but from that point on his fortunes declined. Not only did Bragg lack the tact necessary to deal with generals and colonels, but the Army of Tennessee had never—before and after him—enjoyed any substantial victories. There was, therefore, no core of optimism on which to build a positive future. To be sure, Bragg cannot be blamed for all the errors that were committed, but they took place under his watch.

Although he had success at the Battle of Chicka-mauga, Confederate General Braxton Bragg did not have the best of reputations, especially in his treatment of subordinates.

Where was Bragg's first major invasion?

Bragg had gone north, into Tennessee, in August 1862, his invasion paralleling that of Lee and the Army of Northern Virginia into Maryland. Bragg's invasion had, in some sense, been more successful, but the Federals mustered large numbers to bear on him, and by December 1862, the Army of the Cumberland, headed by William S. Rosecrans (1819–1898), was in a position to push Bragg out of the state altogether.

What was General Rosecrans like as a military leader?

No general—North or South—cared more about his men. No military leader—Union or Confederate—was so devoted to his faith (Roman Catholicism). He was the only commanding general on either side to have a priest with him at all times, so that he need never miss the Mass.

Born in Ohio in 1819, Rosecrans was a self-made man whose graduation from West Point, in 1842, was the launch of his career. He taught at West Point for a time, but resigned from the U.S. Regular Army in 1854 in order to begin a business career. He now had eight children to support. He rose quickly after the war began and at the end of October 1862 was made commander of the Army of the Ohio, which he quickly renamed the Army of the Cumberland. More than merely designating its name, Rosecrans brought a new, vigorous spirit to that force: he was an expert in supply and logistics, and the men were well prepared when the storm burst upon them on the last day of 1862.

What was Braxton Bragg's plan?

Rosecrans had the greater numbers and the initiative, but Bragg had the better plan. Late in December 1862, as Rosecrans advanced into central Tennessee, Bragg planned to meet him at Murfreesboro.

The Federals had about 55,000 men, the Confederates about 40,000. The Union men were also much better fed and supplied, leading to a higher level of morale. Numbers never reveal the entire story, but regarding December 31, 1862, two numbers, or digits, reveal the difference between victory and defeat. Rosecrans had the Army of the Cumberland scheduled to attack at 7 A.M. Bragg had the Army of Tennessee ready and scheduled to attack at first light. As a result, the Confederates attacked at 6:22 A.M.

They came with thundering force, the kind of massive endeavor that is fueled by a feeling of despair. They overran the first few regiments they encountered, then drove a massive wedge between the left and center of the federal position. For an hour or two, it seemed as if the Confederates would reach the river and utterly thrash the Union force.

Who held the Union position and prevented a complete disaster?

George H. Thomas was born in Southampton County, Virginia, in 1816. Neither of the planter (plantation) class nor a true hardship case, Thomas went to West Point, where he graduated in 1840. He saw much service in the U.S. Regular Army in Mexico, against the Seminoles in Florida, and against the Comanches in Texas. When the Civil War began, Thomas was on leave from the army, in New York City. Virtually all of his relatives sided with the Confederacy, and his ties to his family of origin were severed by his decision to stay with the Union.

At the Battle of Murfreesboro—or Stones River—Thomas held the center part of the Union line. Seeing the crisis straight ahead, he drew his men into a semicircle and held off repeated Confederate attacks. It remains in dispute as to whether Thomas persuaded General Rosecrans to continue the fight.

Union General George H. Thomas was a leading commander in the Western Theater and held off the Confederate forces at Murfreesboro.

Why did Bragg fail to press his advantage?

For once the answer is swift and short. Bragg was a notorious pessimist, always given to thinking that the worst would happen. He could not believe his own good luck on the morning of December 31, 1862, and by late afternoon too much time had passed. The battle was renewed on January 2, 1863, but Bragg soon commenced a retreat, giving up all the ground he had previously gained in Tennessee.

Did Rosecrans pursue?

No. Both sides had been badly mauled. Total casualties came to about ten thousand on each side, for a total of twenty thousand in all. Rosecrans waited and allowed his men to rest, while Bragg and his men fled all the way to Chattanooga. The first significant battle of 1863 was a tense one and could have gone either way, but General Thomas' holding the center had proven vital.

Where was Jefferson Davis?

The Confederate president had completed an exhausting four-week railroad trip to various parts of the Confederacy. There had been uplifting moments, as when he addressed the Mississippi legislature, but there had also been the feeling that the Confederate States were pressed on all sides. Arriving at Richmond on January 5, 1863, Davis received a number of good tidings, including a message sent from Braxton Bragg on December 31, 1862.

Elated over what seemed to be a major victory in the West, Davis prepared a celebration only to learn, on January 6, that it was all a mistake and that Bragg and the Army of Tennessee were on the retreat. The Richmond newspapers lambasted Bragg, putting him in the same category as General Beauregard, who had exulted too much in

Who were the first black soldiers in the Civil War?

The Massachusetts 54th regiment is always given the distinction, but there may have been individual African Americans accepted into federal units even prior to that. In the recruiting for the Mass 54th, it was agreed that the soldiers would be black, but that the officers would be white.

When the recruiting proceeded, it was found that the population of free men of color in Massachusetts was too small, so men from other states were allowed to enlist. Frederick Douglass, in Rochester, New York, was able to send many young men to Massachusetts. There they were trained and drilled by Colonel Robert Gould Shaw and Colonel Thomas Wentworth Higginson. Both men were true Boston Brahmins, belonging to the upper class of the city. Both initially had some doubts about the men they were called upon to lead, and both dismissed those doubts after just a few weeks. The black men made fine soldiers, they declared.

One naturally wonders if the recruitment of black soldiers for the Confederate side would have made any difference. But the logic was too strained. A nation built on the idea that there were two races—one superior and the other hopelessly inferior—could not arm black men to fight. No one would seriously raise the prospect until the war was nearly over.

his telegram after the Battle of Shiloh. There were many calls for Bragg to be replaced, but Davis stuck with his old friend.

What did Davis say in his twenty-page message to the Confederate Congress?

In a sense, there was little that he could say. Bragg's defeat at Murfreesboro was a crushing comedown, and the memory of Antietam was still fresh in people's minds. Worst of all, however, was the Emancipation Proclamation, with which Lincoln and the North had gained the moral high ground.

Davis, therefore, made his message to the Confederate Congress one of defiance. All sorts of measures that would have previously been unthinkable were now proposed. Conscription was already in place: Davis pledged to increase it. Taxation was already part of the Confederate nation: Davis planned to increase the taxes. Even farm equipment would be seized by the Confederate government, if necessary, to defend the Confederacy itself. Davis was all too aware that these desperate measures risked his being labeled a hypocrite. The Confederacy had broken from the Union because of states' rights; soon, it seemed, there would be no states' rights left.

What was the first action of 1863 in the East?

Ambrose Burnside was still commander of the Army of the Potomac. Lincoln contemplated removing him, but no better alternative had yet presented itself. Knowing that he was the laughingstock of many of his generals, and that the men of the army had lost their friendly feeling for him, Burnside made one last attempt. On January 21, 1863, he had a large section of the Army of the Potomac march upriver from Fredericksburg, planning to cross the Rappahannock with five pontoon bridges.

Lee had only the dimmest idea of what was in process, but the weather came to his aid. The morning of January 21 was fine, and the afternoon was not too bad, but a thunderous rainstorm set in that evening and just did not quit. When the federal troops set fires the next morning, the green wood they used turned smoldering fires into thick banks of smoke. Under normal conditions, these setbacks would have been considered par for the course. But the Army of the Potomac was not in a normal frame of mind. The Battle of Fredericksburg had unhinged it.

How did the "Mud March" conclude?

Burnside and his staff galloped to the river bank on January 22, finding the men they passed in sorry condition. On arrival, they found that the material for only one pontoon bridge—not five—was in place. A measure of whiskey had been given to each soldier that morning. The measure was given in the belief that the alcohol would raise the men's spirits; instead it nearly created a set of mutinies. Surveying the situation, Burnside did the only thing he could: he ordered the army to return to its previous camp by the same mud-soaked roads by which it had come.

That evening, Burnside wrote out a set of orders. He cashiered General Joseph Hooker, who, he declared, had acted with conduct unbecoming of an officer. He marked five other generals out for dismissal and decided to bring all the papers to the White House. Everything went wrong on his trip, however. The ambulance in which he rode overturned, and the commanding general had to "hitch" rides throughout the night. When Burnside finally arrived at the White House, he was a sorry sight, and Lincoln—while sparing his feelings—made his decision. A few hours later, Burnside was relieved of command, and Joe Hooker—who had created such turmoil for his commanding officer—was made commander of the Army of the Potomac.

"FIGHTING JOE" HOOKER

Where did "Fighting Joe" get his nickname?

Joseph Hooker was born in Hadley, Massachusetts, in 1814. He graduated from West Point in 1837 and entered the U.S. Regular Army as a lieutenant of artillery. He was an outstanding staff officer during the Mexican War, but, like so many other veterans of that conflict, he found peacetime advancement too slow, and he resigned his commission in 1853. The beginning of the Civil War found him in California, but he quickly made his way east and became a brigade commander under General McClellan.

When Lincoln looked for a replacement for Ambrose Burnside, he expressed concerns about "Fighting Joe" Hooker, whose nickname came as the result of a newspaper misprint. The column was intended to read "Fighting: Joe Hooker." But the colon was inadvertently dropped and thousands of readers simply saw "Fighting Joe." The name stuck, and his star rose. Lincoln was aware that Hooker had a drinking problem and that he had mouthed off about the need for a "dictator" to ensure that the Northern side prevailed. In a letter to Hooker, the president confessed his concerns, but said that victory was all-important. "Give me victory, and I will risk the dictatorship," he wrote.

General Joseph "Fighting Joe" Hooker had a reputation as a drunkard and a dictator over his men, but Lincoln chose him to replace General Burnside.

Did Hooker move out at once?

This kind of rash, precipitate action was what his reputation suggested, but Hooker proved to be—like General McClellan—an excellent organizer of men and materiel. Rather than taking rash action, Hooker showed great foresight in drilling and reorganizing the Army of the Potomac, the morale of which rapidly improved.

Lee and the Army of Northern Virginia were, meanwhile, very much on the defensive. Their numbers had not recovered since the Battle of Antietam, and given the rickety Confederate supply system, it was all they could do to maintain their position. There was no question of Lee going after "Fighting Joe" Hooker: he had to remain where he was.

What was the situation in the West?

The Western Theater was entirely dependent on Vicksburg. As long as the Confederates held that town, they prevented the Federals from removing the last section of the Mississippi Valley from Confederate control. The Confederate commander, Major-General John Pemberton, was not popular, however. He was a Philadelphia-born Yankee who had chosen the Southern cause when the war began. Many Confederates, civilian and military alike, considered his loyalty suspect.

Braxton Bragg and the Army of Tennessee were, likewise, very much on the defensive. They had not recovered from the disaster at Murfreesboro in January. When one examines the different armies and commanders, the only one that was in truly good shape was Grant's, and he was still stymied by Vicksburg.

What did Lincoln and Stanton think of Grant?

They were, in truth, rather puzzled. When Grant moved, he obtained results faster than any other Union leader, but when he remained in camp, he often seemed bogged down. Lincoln had never met Grant, and he wished to know more, so he and Secretary of War Stanton sent a "spy" into Grant's midst. This was Charles Henry Dana.

Born in New Hampshire in 1819, Dana had been the managing editor of the *New York Tribune* for fifteen years till Horace Greeley fired him (the reason for their falling out was the Tribune's call for "On to Richmond" prior to the Battle of Bull Run). Dana was sent to spy on General Grant, who clearly understood what was happening. Whether because of Dana's presence or in spite of it, Grant acted very much in charge of events, and Dana reported favorably. Had he not done so, Grant might have been relieved of command. Impressed with Dana's reporting, Stanton made him assistant secretary of war.

When was Joe Hooker ready to move?

By the beginning of April 1863, Hooker had his battle plans read and approved by Lincoln, and by the third week of April, the Army of the Potomac was on the move. It made a glorious sight.

Despite the unfulfilled promise of Antietam, and despite the bitter failure at Fredericksburg, the Army of the Potomac was a robust and confident unit in the spring of 1863. Hooker had made all the difference in the world, and as the men began moving from the posts they had occupied for three months, there was a clear optimism.

What was Hooker's plan?

Hooker had a complicated but nevertheless brilliant plan. Given his numerical superiority—roughly 120,000 to fewer than 80,000—he left Major-General John Sedgwick and almost 50,000 men at Fredericksburg to menace the Confederate right, while he led roughly 70,000 to go around Lee's left. This was a complicated maneuver and would require crossing the Rappahannock River, but unlike what happened on the infamous Mud March of January, most aspects worked according to plan. By April 30, 1863, Hooker had 70,000 men on the south side of the Rappahannock, ready to move against the Confederates, who were still perplexed by what they saw from Sedgwick's force on their right.

What was "the Wilderness"?

It was the trickiest ground to cover and the diciest part of Hooker's plan. The Wilderness was a virtually uninhabited area, perhaps thirty square miles of forest that lay between Hooker's section of his army and General Lee. If Hooker got through the Wilderness, his men would have the room to maneuver that would make all the difference. In the open countryside, the federal superiority in artillery and foot soldiers made it very likely they would gain the victory. But *in* the Wilderness, everything was open to chance.

Did Lee take advantage of this situation?

For once, he did not. As alert as he was—constantly receiving updates on the federal movements—Lee did not attempt to fight in the Wilderness. With 50,000 Federals to his right and 70,000 coming against his left, Lee had to be very circumspect. If a neutral observer had examined the situation—and there were very few real neutrals at that point—he or she would have noted the likelihood of a federal victory. But, as so often occurred, something unexpected intervened. Hooker's vanguard had actually reached the southeastern part of the Wilderness when it received an order to pull back and assume a defensive position.

What happened to Hooker?

At this point, no one knew. Everything was moving according to plan when the most exposed Union troops met their first Confederates. That first skirmish was a Union victory, but Hooker then made the command to fall back.

Those who examine the situation today believe that one of two possibilities exist. The first is that Hooker lost his nerve, plain and simple. But given the confidence he had exuded to this point, it seems unlikely. The second, and more plausible, possibility is that Hooker—a confirmed alcoholic—had dried out too quickly. An army physician was alarmed at the way in which Hooker went "cold turkey" on the bottle in the months prior to Chancellorsville; he remained convinced that had Hooker weaned himself more

How much more or less important were the general officers of that time compared to our world today?

They were infinitely more important. In the U.S. military today, five members make up the Joint Chiefs of Staff, but they are followed up by hundreds, perhaps even thousands, of persons of general rank. In other words, barring the possibility of a nuclear exchange with some enemy, in a situation of conventional military combat, many, if not most, of those thousands of generals could step into the shoes of their commander, if he or she fell. This was not the case in the Civil War.

To begin with, there was no Joint Chiefs of Staff. There was the president and the secretary of war, and once one stepped from that lofty platform, leadership and command devolved upon a few individuals. Hooker, for example, as leader of the Army of the Potomac, had to account to no one except Lincoln and Stanton. In some ways that was a good, even a preferable, thing because he could therefore make swift decisions. But if something happened to Joe Hooker, the Army of the Potomac was leaderless. If something happened to Ulysses Grant, the forces converging on Vicksburg had to fall back. As true as this was for the Union, it was even more the case with the Confederates. Lee to some extent *was* the Army of Northern Virginia, just as Braxton Bragg was the Army of Tennessee.

steadily, all would have been well. This, of course, begs yet another question: How could the good or bad performance of one man make such a difference?

Who now possessed the initiative?

By every logical rule of war, the Army of the Potomac still held the initiative. But it was up against a commander of great tactical gifts and a certain kind of arrogance. Lee believed his men could pull off the impossible and that he had the man to lead them.

On the evening of May 2, 1863, Lee and Stonewall Jackson conferred on a fallen tree, just a few hundred yards from the federal lines. They had already taken the measure of Joe Hooker and decided that he would tamely spend the next day observing their situation. Lee was all too aware of the danger posed by the fifty thousand Federals to his rear, but he had made his career in the taking of chances, and he was ready for one more. When he asked Stonewall Jackson for advice, "Old Jack" paused a moment, and he drew lines in the ground with a wooden stick. He proposed to take his entire division on a circuitous, twenty-mile march through the woods, bringing them all the way around to the federal right flank. Impressed by the audacity of the plan, Lee asked how many men he would leave. Jackson replied that he would leave only two divisions. That meant Lee would have to hold his position, and bluff extremely well, with only 14,000 men. Typically, Lee replied, "Well, go on then."

"The Wilderness" in Orange County, Virginia saw fierce battles in 1863 and 1864.

What happened on the next day?

On May 3, 1863, Hooker and the Army of the Potomac remained in a defensive posture. On Hooker's staff, no one perceived any danger except that of remaining too long in one position. There were grumbles and complaints about the general, who was acting out of form, however.

Lee and 14,000 men held their position and were delighted when nothing happened. Outnumbered approximately five to one, they would have been completely crushed if Hooker moved. He did not, however, and as midafternoon came, Lee and his staff began to breathe sighs of relief. They did not know exactly where Stonewall Jackson was, but they had heard nothing—cannon or rifle shot—to indicate that his extreme flanking maneuver had been discovered.

What was that march like?

It was, in many ways, the most audacious march any commander made during the war. Had the weather gone sour, it might have been ruined, but the sunshine remained bright all day, allowing Jackson and 28,000 Confederates to make their twenty-mile march. "Old Jack" was observed everywhere along the line, making his men close up, march more quietly, and sing no songs. He wanted no dramatics along the march: he wanted the men to save everything they had for the great contest that afternoon.

The men had to have some rest, so Jackson allowed them ten minutes out of every hour. The rest of the time he pushed them as no other commander—North or South— could do, and by 5:45 they were so close to the federal right flank that they could smell the campfires and even hear bits and pieces of conversation. To this point, everything had gone extremely well, and Jackson—after giving his men a thirty-minute rest—made the signal for the charge.

What was that afternoon charge like?

Those who received it claimed it was like no other—that the Confederate attack at 6:15 achieved complete, stunning surprise. The Union right flank was not well anchored, and it did not have large numbers, but if it had even one hour's warning, all might have been different. Instead, the first sign the Union men had was a group of deer leaping through the clearing, getting just ahead of the Confederates who chose that moment to deliver a full-throated rebel yell.

What followed was nothing short of pandemonium. Several federal units made brave stands, but were quickly swept aside. Other groups, even whole regiments, practically disappeared as men took to their heels. Nothing previous in the War in the East—neither the Battles of Bull Run nor the Seven Days' Battles—witnessed any collapse as complete as that of the Union on May 3, 1863.

Could the war have been won—or lost, depending on the point of view—that day?

No. Historians are fond of using expressions like "the federal army could have been annihilated," but nothing like annihilation ever took place. What could have transpired is that half the federal army might have been cut off and forced to surrender. Would this have forced the Union to sue for peace? Probably not.

How important was Stonewall Jackson at this amazing moment?

He had already demonstrated his worth a dozen times, but on that afternoon, he soared into a nearly mythical place in the annals of the Confederacy. Those who laud Jackson do not exaggerate his skill: no one could get men to march longer and fight harder than Stonewall Jackson. Within thirty minutes of launching the attack, Jackson and his aides were halfway to the Rappahannock River, and they believed they might get there by night-fall, driving an enormous wedge between the Northern forces. But fate then intervened.

As Jackson and several aides pressed forward, they encountered a group of their own men, who had taken shelter for a few moments. Very likely Jackson greeted them as he did all his troops, with an admonition to move forward. But they mistook Jackson and his aides for Northern men and fired upon them. Less than a minute was required for those sharpshooters to realize their error, but it was too late. Jackson was down, bleeding from three different wounds. Removed to the rear, he lost his left arm that night.

Where was Lee at that moment?

About five miles away, listening to the sound of gunfire. Because of the time at which it began, Lee correctly surmised that Jackson's march had been successful and the attack was going according to plan. Even though he still had only 14,000 men at his disposal, Lee lost all or any fear he might have previously entertained. On the morrow, he would strike from the east and Jackson from the southwest, and they would drive Hooker's remaining forces into the Rappahannock.

What did the next morning bring?

On May 4, 1863, Hooker examined his situation and found it difficult but far from terrible. The Confederate surprise attack had dented his right flank, but he still had plenty of men, many of whom had yet to fire a shot. As he prepared for battle, Hooker moved with his staff to the Chancellor House, for which Chancellorsville is named, then—much like the evening before—fate intervened. This time it was in the shape of a cannonball that hit the chimney of the Chancellor House.

Hit by the recoil from the chimney, rather than the actual cannonball, Hooker was stunned, even knocked out, for as much as half an hour. When he came to, he was groggy and ill-tempered, but he refused to allow anyone else to take over command of the Army of the Potomac. At that moment the battle began in earnest.

Who attacked whom on May 4, 1863?

It was a rather curious mess of backward and forward motion. The Confederates had the initiative, and the enthusiasm, but they did not have Stonewall Jackson. The Union men had plenty of fight left in them, but their commanding general did not.

General Joseph Hooker set up headquarters here at Chancellor House during the 1863 Battle of Chancellorsville

Lee, by now, knew that Stonewall Jackson was seriously wounded, and he worried that the attack from the southwest would not be strong. He should not have worried. The Confederates attacked with a will, but the element of surprise was gone, and they tussled on equal terms with the Yankees. On his side of the battle, Lee fought well, but there was no room for maneuver, no way to employ his marvelous tactical gifts. Then, too, he was deeply concerned that Major-General Sedgwick would cross the Rappahannock eight miles below. Sedgwick did cross, but he was bluffed by the Confederates at that location and soon went back to the north side of the river.

Who lost the Battle of Chancellorsville?

"Fighting Joe" Hooker did not live up to his nickname. He devised a fine plan and executed it very well up to two-thirds of the way; then, inexplicably, he fell apart.

The Army of the Potomac was not destroyed, however. Hooker and his staff got the large majority of their men safely across the river, and the battle petered out by May 5, 1863. The losses were immense, however. All told, the North lost slightly more than 18,000 men killed, wounded, or missing, while the South lost in excess of 12,500. Though Lee was the clear winner of the Battle of Chancellorsville, he was not satisfied. In letters to President Davis and others, he confided that he had hoped to inflict far greater losses on the Union. And though no one wanted to say it, the South could not afford 12,500 casualties, while the North could—in strict numerical terms—afford to lose 18,000. The single greatest loss was that of Stonewall Jackson.

How did Stonewall Jackson die?

He died slowly, over the better part of a week. The surgeons, having taken off his left arm, believed there was a good chance he would recover, but "Old Jack" began to fade about four days into his convalescence. His numerous fatiguing marches may have contributed to his demise: he may have had very little in the way of physical reserves by that point. Jackson died on May 11, 1863. Just minutes before his death, in a state of delirium, he was repeating orders he may have given in the past, such as "Send A.P. Hill's division...." But just before he died, Jackson's face took on an unmistakable look of peace, and his last words were, "Let us cross over the river and rest in the shade of the trees."

How significant was his loss to the Confederate cause?

Thanks to the last actions he undertook—the brilliant flanking maneuver at Chancellorsville—Jackson had acquired an incredible Civil War reputation. Some say the Confederacy would have lived if he had and that his death was the beginning of the end. Our task is not to praise him to the skies or to denigrate him, but to calmly assess: How important was Jackson to the Confederate cause?

In that he was not a slaveholder and that he made no public pronouncements about the institution of slavery, Jackson was not a help to the Confederate cause so far as slavery or secession were concerned. His incredible, almost inestimable, value was as a military commander who inspired his men to do more … and more again. Would the Confederacy have won the war if Stonewall Jackson lived another two years? Almost certainly not. But those two years might have been a lot more interesting.

How badly were the Federals whipped? How did they feel after Chancellorsville?

Oddly enough, the Army of the Potomac was in decent shape. There were regiments and even divisions in bad shape ("[It] was the first to break on May 2nd and is in a most disgusting condition as to discipline and morale," a Massachusetts colonel wrote with regard to the 24th Regiment, but the army as a whole was ready to stand on the defensive and protect Washington, D.C. President Lincoln, on the other hand, was truly beside himself. A good friend visited him the day he received the news. All Lincoln could say, time and again, was "My God! What will the country say!"

Why was the crisis not more severe?

Very likely Lincoln did not realize the extent to which he, and the average fighting man in the federal armies, had bolstered the cause of the Union. Had the Battle of Chancellorsville occurred a year earlier, there might have been need for despair. But in those twelve months, Lincoln had issued the Emancipation Proclamation, broadening the basis for the war, and reported a number of significant Union victories in the West. Chancellorsville was a terrible, painful defeat, but it did not dishearten those who believed in the Northern cause.

THE HOME FRONT: 1861 TO 1865

What was the home front? Where was it?

The home front was everywhere the war was not. In other words, if roughly three million men served at some point in the war, twenty-eight million persons did not. And their lives at home—some quite good, others quite awful—make up the sum total of the home front.

Did people on the home front know there was a war going on?

Everyone—from the president to his coach driver, and from the most recent immigrant to a person who claimed Mayflower descent—knew there was a war going on. There was simply no avoiding the fact. Of course some people were able to live relatively normal lives, but many did not.

The reason that the war intruded on so many lives is that Americans were avid readers of newspapers and magazines. Literacy, in the highest sense of the word, may have been stronger in some parts of the United States in 1861 than it is in our world today. Lacking the distractions of television, computer, and radio, Americans were keen to know the news, and those who read three newspapers probably related their contents to two other persons.

WOMEN'S ROLES

Why are so many of the names associated with the war male names? Did women play any significant roles?

In the 1860s, and for perhaps a few decades after, America was very much a man's country. Women were allowed to play roles behind the scenes, but practically all of the big decisions—at least those made in public—were decided on by men.

This was not unusual in the world of that time. Whether one traveled to China, to Australia, or toured Western Europe, he or she would usually see societies that practiced the same type of male domination in public matters. In answer to the second part of the question, women certainly played significant roles during the Civil War. It can be argued, in fact, that the war effort on both sides would have collapsed long before 1865 if not for the heroic actions of millions of women.

What did foreigners say about the condition of American women?

Some, to be sure, were scornful of American women as they were of the young republic as a whole. Others, however, saw that American women had it reasonably well in many ways. One in the latter group was Alexis de Tocqueville, the Frenchman who spent eight months in the United States from 1831 to 1832. His commentary on many aspects of American life is refreshing, and sometimes brilliant, but he is perhaps at his best, or most sympathetic, when describing the condition of American women. Here are some of his most flattering words:

> In no country has such constant care been taken as in America to trace two clearly distinct lines of action for the two sexes, and to make them keep pace one with the other, but in two pathways which are always different. American women never manage the outward concerns of the family, or conduct a business, or take a part in political life; nor are they, on the other hand, ever compelled to perform the rough labor of the fields, or to make any of those laborious exertions which demand the exertion of physical strength. No families are so poor as to form an exception to this rule.

Is there any way to verify what de Tocqueville wrote about American women?

One of the most intriguing kinds of verification comes from the pages of *The Atlantic Monthly*, which, in June 1862, lamented over the health, or lack thereof, in the current generation.

"Every [Northern] woman must have a best-parlor with hair-cloth furniture," the essay began, and "she must have a piano, or some cheaper substitute; her little girls must have embroidered skirts and much mathematical knowledge: her husband must have two or even three hot meals every day of his life; and yet her home must be in perfect order early in the afternoon, and she prepared to go out and pay calls with a black-silk dress and a card-case.... All this every 'capable' New-England woman will do, or die. She does it, and dies; and then we are astounded when her vital energy gives out sooner than that of an Irishwoman in a shanty, with no needs on earth but to supply her young Patricks with adequate potatoes."

What was the U.S. Sanitary Commission?

In 1861, almost as soon as the war began, President Lincoln approved the creation of the Sanitary Commission to have oversight of all nursing and medical supplies.

What was the First Family of the Union like?

Abraham and Mary Todd Lincoln had a strange, and sometimes strained, relationship. Nine years younger than her husband, Mary Todd came from a much more distinguished lineage, and in the early years of their marriage she may well have been the "boss," prompting her husband to become even more ambitious than he was by nature. Because of his long string of successes in the outer world, Abraham Lincoln eventually came to look like the "boss" in his family life as well, but one suspects that his wife could back him into a corner on occasion.

The Lincolns had four children—all boys—one of whom died while they lived in Springfield, Illinois. The second son, "Willie," died at the Executive Mansion—

First Lady Mary Todd Lincoln in a photo taken sometime during the war.

as the White House was then called—of typhoid fever in February 1862, throwing a pall of despair over the First Family. Mary Todd Lincoln suffered from intense, almost life-threatening grief, while Abraham Lincoln spent long, secluded hours in his former son's bedroom. In some ways, they were never the same again. Historians often wrestle with the question of how nineteenth-century American couples coped with the loss of a child, which was all too frequent. If the Lincolns are in some measure "typical," then the losses were deeply and keenly felt. The Lincolns were not alone in this experience. The first couple of the Confederacy also lost a child while in the Richmond White House.

What was Lincoln's relationship with his son Tad?

Lincoln was, by most accounts, an extremely indulgent father. Quite possibly, he attempted to give his children the type of affection he lacked in his relationship with his own father (their relations were

President Lincoln is shown with his youngest son, Tad, in this 1864 photo.

169

so difficult that Lincoln did not attend his father's funeral). Tad had the run of the Executive Mansion to such an extent that he was the only person who could stop his father from conducting business. Many evenings, Lincoln concluded a long day's work by playing on the rug with Tad. His relationship with his eldest son, Robert Lincoln, was much more formal, however. No one knows the reason.

What was the First Family of the Confederacy like?

Jefferson Davis and Varina Banks Howell married in February 1845. The groom was eighteen years older than the bride. This was Jefferson Davis' second marriage. His first, to the daughter of General Zachary Taylor, had ended with her death from malaria only three months after the wedding.

The Davis couple had five children, but only four came to the Confederate White House (the eldest had died at the age of two). Jefferson and Varina made an attractive couple, and visitors labeled their children the "rambunctious offspring," but all was not well. Mrs. Davis suffered from doubts about the wisdom of the war. She had very much enjoyed life as a U.S. senator's wife in Washington, D.C., and was not pleased with being the wife of the Confederate president. This was nothing compared to the loss that the couple endured following the accidental death of five-year-old Joseph. On April 30, 1864, he fell over a balcony, sustained severe head injuries, and died forty-five minutes later.

How did the Davis couple handle the loss of their child?

Their grief was similar to the Lincoln family's in that the wife took on the lion's share of expressing it. Mrs. Davis was practically prostrate, but she was also pregnant, so she had to force herself to make it through the next few months. Their daughter, Varina Anna Davis—later known as the Princess of the Confederacy—was born in July 1864.

Jefferson Davis was already a workaholic, but the death of his son made him more so. It was during the summer of 1864, three months after his son's death, that Davis received two peace visitors from the North (see pages 294–295) and his grief may have caused him, at times, to be even tougher and grimmer than one expected.

Is there a parallel that can be drawn with the leaders of some other nation?

Yes. In December 1861—when the Civil War was only eight months old—Prince Albert, the beloved consort of Queen Victoria, died of typhoid fever. Prince Albert

This photo was taken of Jefferson Davis and his bride, Varina, on their wedding day in 1845.

had, just a few days before his death, been involved in the diplomatic fracas known as the *Trent* Affair (see page 99). He amended a diplomatic note from London to Washington, D.C., and the tone of his missive allowed Lincoln and Secretary of State Seward to make a more conciliatory reply.

Queen Victoria wore mourning clothes for the rest of her life (she died in 1901). The mention of her husband's name would usually bring her to tears, and she frequently refused to meet with her prime minister, saying she was under the burden of too much grief. Victoria and Albert had eleven children, nine of whom lived to adulthood, but though her life was filled with family and fun, as well as affairs of state, she remained a "widow" in the fullest, deepest sense of the word.

What do these examples—the First Family, the Confederate First Family, and the British royal family tell us?

They suggest—but do not prove—that familial ties were extremely strong. To be sure, there were distractions from, and irritations with, matters of family, but nineteenth-century Americans deeply felt the loss of family members.

Did anyone claim that they didn't care about the war?

Very few. It was such an unpopular stance to take that most people shied well away from it. There may have been many people who privately said that the North and the South were two devils that could hang each other, but such words were not bandied about.

Was there any person, or symbol, on which virtually all Americans agreed?

George Washington—the man, the legend, and the symbol—was about the only person acknowledged by all sides in the conflict. Unlike Americans of our time, who can choose between Washington, Lincoln, and Franklin Roosevelt as to who was the greatest of leaders, the men and women of 1861 had only one: the man from Mount Vernon. Given that he was from Virginia, the South could proudly claim him. Given that he was the first chief executive of a united nation, the North could do so as well. Everyone wanted to claim Washington and to assert that he was on their side. This, of course, begs the corollary question: Was there a prominent woman on whom all sides could agree?

There was not. Women were gaining, throughout the land and the nation, in terms of social and economic importance, but those women who were well known tended to have their fame restricted to a certain area. Therefore, although women were becoming more noticeable in certain fields, there was no equivalent to George Washington in terms of a unifying figure.

The poetry submitted to newspapers and magazines had an unabashedly patriotic feel, and this is true whether one lived in Maine, Iowa, or Texas. There was no shame in calling oneself an ardent patriot; indeed, Americans from all sections tended to believe they were fulfilling the mandates of an earlier generation. What George Washington and the founding fathers had failed to accomplish, the men and women of 1861 would fulfill.

Were all mothers and fathers, then, patriotic?

They all appeared to be. We cannot know what they thought in the recesses of their hearts, but in public virtually everyone appeared committed to the cause. In New York City, it was the cause of commerce and of Union; in New Orleans it was the cause of freedom (from the Yankees) and commerce. To be sure, the initial patriotism waned when the first soldiers lacking limbs came home, or did not return at all.

Just as virtually everyone asserted his or her patriotism at the war's beginning, almost everyone expressed shock when the casualty lists appeared. No one had warned the general public of the dangers of this war, or the ways in which the instruments of destruction had increased in power.

PARENTS' ROLES

What were mothers and fathers like in 1861?

The first part of the answer is to flip the order that you see above. Put it as "fathers and mothers," and the sequence will be more accurate.

In 1861, the American father was not only the head of the household, but the moral and spiritual center of it. This is immediately surprising to us because in the twenty-first century it is almost axiomatic that a home lives or dies according to the condition of the mother. But that social condition that we know so well is largely the product of two centuries of the Industrial Revolution, which took the father *out* of the home and made the mother all-important *in* the home. Does this mean women were devalued in the mid-nineteenth century? Not at all. Rather, it means that most observers, including the children, saw the father as the pillar of the family.

How did this change?

The poet Robert Bly illustrated it beautifully in *The Sibling Society*. Published in 1996, *The Sibling Society* convincingly demonstrates that Americans of the nineteenth century attempted to look older than they were and to emphasize the "old-fashioned" virtues of home, hearth, and thrift. Perhaps by the 1920s, the trend completely flipped, and Americans—from then until now—have attempted to look younger than they actually are and to portray the "new-fangled" excitements of travel, expensive living, and fun. Does this mean that our great-great-grandparents were better, or more worthy, individuals than we are? No, but their values were different from ours.

What was so important about the Homestead Act?

Passed by Congress in April 1862, the Homestead Act opened up millions of acres of federal land for sale to individuals and families. The sale of federal lands had been going on for some time previous to the war, but the Homestead Act confirmed most of what was good about the system of land sales.

For $160 a person could obtain 160 acres of land, usually in the Far West. He or she had to "hold" or possess the land for five years and demonstrate that it was being put to good use; at the end of that probationary period, the land belonged to him or her in perpetuity. Just how many lives were altered and improved remains unknown, but one suspects that it runs into the millions. Of course, the Homestead Act did not open easily ploughed lands in the East; it offered opportunity to the person willing to brave the dangers and hazards of the West. Another way to look at the situation is to inquire what might have happened had there been no Homestead Act. One suspects it would have taken much longer to populate the Far Western states.

What was the great threat to the father as the center of the American family?

Three things, or dangers, presented themselves. The first was the presence of ever-abundant land in the West. A shiftless or unsuccessful father could always pick up and move, abandoning his family. The second was the growing industrial revolution that took the father out of the home, transforming him from a parent on the spot to a distant figure who won the daily bread. And the third was the Civil War itself.

If three million men served at one time or another, that means that *one-fifth, or twenty percent,* of the entire male population of the United States was absent from home at some point during the war. Even in our times, with additional mobility and with challenges such as the wars in Iraq and Afghanistan, we have never seen anything like the temporary removal of twenty percent of the men. In some cases, the absence was only for a few months, but in other cases it ran to several years, and in many cases the father never came home. Though few people were able to describe this as it happened, a social and familial revolution—however subtle—was the result.

What were mothers like?

The short answer is that they were quite different in 1865 from what they had been in 1861. When the war began, there was an upwelling of patriotism—North and South— a rush of adrenaline if one likes, that lasted for almost a year. When that was exhausted, the people at home had to make adjustments.

Some Northern women entered factories. Thousands upon thousands of Southern women knitted socks and caps for the soldiers. Some women dropped everything to become army nurses, and others actually dressed as men to serve in battle. Just how the children at home coped remains one of the mysteries of the time.

Who was the most famous woman of the war?

Clara Barton was, almost certainly, that person. Born in rural Massachusetts in 1821, she was the daughter of a Revolutionary War officer, and, like so many of her generation, she treasured the connection to 1776. Clara Barton was certainly eligible and attractive, and why she remained unmarried at the age of forty is somewhat mysterious: perhaps she never could find a man to equal her idealized image of her father. But in any event, in the first and second years of the war, Clara Barton transformed herself into a deliverer of medical supplies and a nurse's assistant.

Clara Barton, the founder of the American Red Cross, was a nurse and deliverer of medical supplies during the Civil War and did much to advance nursing.

Many other women did similar things, but Clara Barton had a gift for self-promotion and her tireless efforts, sometimes badgering, of men in high rank paid dividends. The U.S. Sanitary Commission already existed with a corps of army nurses, but Clara Barton brought a volunteer spirit to her enterprise. By the time the war ended, she was the best-known woman in America, and her later services in the Franco-Prussian War of 1870–1871 and even the Spanish-American War of 1898 solidified her reputation. She was the founder of the American Red Cross.

Who was the most accomplished woman of the war?

This, of course, is somewhat subjective, but it seems to be a tie between "Mother" Ann Bickerdyke and Mary Edwards Walker.

Born in 1817, "Mother" Ann Bickerdyke was living in Illinois when the war began. She was a member of the church of Edward Beecher, the younger brother of Harriet Beecher Stowe, and when the pastor learned there was a severe need for medical supplies at the front, some of the congregants went to Cairo, Illinois, where Ulysses Grant was then colonel of Illinois volunteers. Without holding any official position or title, "Mother" Ann commenced a revolution in the treatment of ill soldiers. A great believer in hygiene and sanitation, she brought the sick and wounded men outside, bathed them, and applied all sorts of relatively new medical knowledge to the situation. Within a year, she had become indispensable to the efficient running of the hospitals in the Cairo area. No one knows whether it was Ulysses Grant or William Sherman who first said "She ranks me," but the expression took hold.

Who was Mary Edwards Walker?

She was, quite possibly, the most eccentric person of a time that embraced eccentricity on many levels. Born on a farm in upstate New York in 1832, Mary Walker was the first female to earn a medical degree from Syracuse Medical College, in 1855. Though she soon married a classmate, she omitted the words "to honor and obey" from the ceremony, and she wore clothing that was an interesting mixture of male and female for the rest of her life (they divorced after fourteen years of marriage, including nine years of separation). When the war began, Mary Walker applied to the surgeon general for a medical commission; when this was refused, she acted in an unofficial capacity. She did heroic surgical work after the Battles of Fredericksburg and Chickamauga and finally won a civilian surgeon contract, issued by Major-General George Thomas. She may have performed other services, such as acting as a spy for Thomas, but no confirmation is available.

How could the government take away her Medal of Honor?

In November 1865, President Andrew Johnson issued the Medal of Honor to Dr. Walker; the citation clearly stated that it was for acts of meritorious service, not acts of valor. In 1917, perhaps under pressure from the beginning of the First World War, Congress reviewed all Medal of Honor winners and declared that they should only be issued for acts of valor and gallantry in battle. For this reason, the Medal of Honor was taken from Dr. Walker. Furious and eccentric as ever, she made numerous appearances at Capitol Hill, always attempting to badger or persuade members of Congress. She died after a severe fall in the Capitol Building in 1919. Her Medal of Honor was posthumously restored by President Jimmy Carter.

What was the most sympathetic, or important, treatment of women in fiction?

Little Women; or, Meg, Jo, Beth and Amy was published in 1868. Its author was Louisa May Alcott (1832–1888), the thirty-six-year-old daughter of Amos Bronson Alcott, a leading member of the Transcendentalist community in Concord, Massachusetts. Miss Alcott, upon receiving high praise, responded that she had written the novel in a hurry and had not anticipated its major effect on readers. *Little Women* has remained in print ever since, however, and we have to examine something about the author and the title to understand its importance.

Little Women portrays the lives of four sisters, three of whom are teenagers and the youngest of whom is nine. Meg is the quiet and together type; Jo is anxious and headstrong; Beth is the insightful but physically fragile daughter; and Amy is the spoiled, indulged child. Their father is away at war and their mother is the new center of the home, but the girls are growing up, in ways that are sometimes unexpected. *Little Women* definitely portrays a family that is better off than many, but scraping by with many frugal practices, and with the girls both lamenting their poverty and showing generosity to others. The girls know how to do almost anything, and the reader guesses that they will turn into strong, well-developed people.

Was that the story of the author herself?

Half and half. Born on November 29, 1832 (the importance of the date will soon become apparent), Louisa May Alcott was the second of four daughters. She grew up in an articulate, almost hyperintellectual family that believed in discussion of the day's events, but also in reflection and the writing of poems, essays, and diaries. When the war began, Louisa May was twenty-eight.

"All the young men & boys drill with all their might," she wrote, adding that "the women & girls sew & purpose for nurses. The old folks settle the fate of the Nation in groves of newspapers, & the children make the streets hideous with distracted drums & fifes." Many, many people observed this phenomenon—the turning of a quiet village into a beehive of activity—

Louisa May Alcott wrote *Little Women* (1868), a novel widely considered to be the most important and significant treatment of women in that time period.

but few ever expressed it as well as Louisa May Alcott. Her own feelings about the war seldom appear, even in her diary, and she may have pined for a lack of action. Therefore, as her thirtieth birthday approached, she applied to become a nurse in Washington, D.C.

What was her experience in the field hospital like?

It was overwhelming. Even so articulate a person as Louisa May could not fully express it to her diary; she saved it for later, when her book *Hospital Sketches* was published. Even in that book, however, she never fully got out of her system the horrors of the war. It was one thing to observe the people of Concord at work and play, another to see men's arms and legs come off with the agonizing strokes of the surgeon's saw. The experience was so daunting that Louisa May contracted typhoid fever and had to be sent home as an invalid herself.

It is one of the great coincidences of the war that Louisa May Alcott and Walt Whitman (about whom more is related in another question) were in Washington, D.C., at the same time. She went, perhaps, in response to an inner call to do something with her life; he went to answer a specific outer call, to tend to the wounds of his younger brother. For both of these great literary geniuses, the end of 1862—they arrived in December—was a turning point in their lives.

What happened to Louisa May Alcott in later life?

She was born on November 29, 1832, which just happened to be her father's thirty-third birthday. Coincidences like this happen all the time, to be sure, but in this case we are

> ## We all know that there was a battle at Lexington and a second one at Concord. But why was Concord still so important in 1861?
>
> The Revolutionary War commenced when British soldiers marched out of Boston, intending to seize the powder and ball stored at Concord, Massachusetts. By the end of that day the first battles had been fought, and the Americans had proven that they could face the British in the field. Seventy-five years later, in 1861, Concord was a village of several thousand people, but it was also the home of many of the leading poets, novelists, and philosophers of the period.
>
> Henry David Thoreau, Ralph Waldo Emerson, and Amos Bronson Alcott all lived there, as did at least a score of lesser-known literary figures. The quality of lectures and discussions in Concord was unsurpassed anywhere in the nation, and many people looked on the "Concord sages" as the cornerstone of the nation's morals. The leaders did not always enjoy this role—Thoreau, for one, much preferred his freedom to any fame—but they saw that they held a great responsibility, and, for the most part, lived up to it. Very likely, the Revolutionary War background served as inspiration to the intellectual leaders of this later generation.

confident that she formed a strong identification with her father and felt responsible for him. Not only did she care for him throughout his later years, but when he died in March 1888, she followed just two days later.

By the time of her death, Louisa May was the most famous of all female American writers. She had written many poems, pamphlets, and books, some of which she thought superior to *Little Women*, but there was—and is—not the slightest doubt of what the reading public favored. *Little Women* was, and remains, the best depiction of a Northern family holding down the home front during the Civil War.

Is there a Southern, or a Western, counterpart to *Little Women*?

Sadly, no. Perhaps it took a very special combination of experiences to produce Louisa May Alcott and her literary success. Then again, quite a few Southern women were so struck by the need for physical duties—including the sewing of clothing—that they had no time to write. But while we do not have a great novel from this time period from the Southern side, we have a number of letters and diaries.

SOUTHERN DIARISTS

Who is the best known of all Southern diarists?

Mary Boykin Chesnut, born in 1823, was married to one of the richest and most powerful of all South Carolina plantation owners, James C. Chesnut. Her husband served as a

U.S. senator prior to the war, and he became an important adviser to Jefferson Davis thereafter. Through his wife's diary, we have an unequaled look at the life of the major slaveholder, complicated, as one might expect, by the beginning of the Civil War. Mary B. Chesnut's diary was not discovered till the twentieth century; upon its publication, readers from around the nation had a new appreciation of what it was like for a true Southern lady—one who had the carriage, the plantation, and the slaves.

There were other Confederate diarists, however, including a teenage girl who recounted the events at the war's end. Richmond, Virginia, had more than its share of diarists, and, because Louisa May Alcott and Walt Whitman were both serving in army hospitals in December 1862, it is at this point that we turn to the diary of Mrs. Judith Brockenbrough McGuire.

The diary of Mary Boykin Chesnut provides readers with a good understanding of what it was like to be a rich landowner in the South during the war.

What did Mrs. Judith McGuire report in December 1862, the month that the Battle of Fredericksburg was fought?

Here is her diary entry:

> December 15th—An exciting day. Trains have been constantly passing with the wounded for the Richmond hospitals. Every lady, every child, every servant in the village, has been engaged in preparing and carrying food to the wounded as the cars stopped at the depot—coffee, tea, soup, milk, and everything we could obtain. With eager eyes and beating hearts we watched for those most dear to us. Sometimes they were so slightly injured as to sit at the windows and answer our questions, which they were eager to do. They exult in the victory. I saw several poor fellows shot through the mouth—they only wanted milk; it was soothing and cooling to their lacerated flesh. One, whom I did not see, had both eyes shot out. But I cannot write of the horrors of this day.

Was this kind of graphic description common?

It was. Southern women may have been delicate and refined, at least in the eyes of those who wrote about them, but they faced the war with unflinching resolve. Of course, not all comments about Southern women were so complimentary. Here is what a Union soldier had to say about female bushwhackers in February 1864:

"The women of the South," the Union soldier began, "are the goads that prick the men to action. I should have said first that there are female as well as male bushwhackers. When a woman takes one of these filthy creatures to her home or heart, as the case may be, she becomes a partner to his guilt, according to the common law.... She is the receiver, and the receiver is as bad as the thief. All the country [in Tennessee] is infested with these guerillas and bushwhackers; they have certain haunts, where they make their headquarters and store away their plunder."

This was not the only kind of prejudice, however.

Were there other Southern diaries by women?

One that really takes the reader into the Confederate hospitals is a record, rather than a diary, written some years after the events. Phoebe Yates Pember was the fourth of seven children born to a prosperous Jewish family in Charleston. She married a Northerner, but he died of tuberculosis shortly before the war began. Much like her Northern counterpart—Louisa May Alcott—Phoebe Yates Pember felt life was passing her by, and she volunteered for service in the medical hospitals. Somewhat to her surprise, she was named "matron" of one of the divisions at Chimborazo Hospital in Richmond. Thus commenced an adventure that is recorded in *A Southern Woman's Story*.

What kind of obstacles did Phoebe Yates Pember face?

She encountered any number of difficulties, many of which can be traced to the shortage of supplies, but some of which can be laid at the feet of her male colleagues. In her record, Mrs. Pember claimed that immediately upon her appearance at the hospital a story ran through the wards that "one of them had come," meaning that a woman had dared to stick her face where only men belonged. There were serious difficulties in gaining the right to administer whiskey to the patients—the Confederate medical teams used whiskey for all manner of things—and in persuading male colleagues not to dose the patients with too much alcohol. There were also all sorts of occasions on which she was either propositioned or insulted by male colleagues, but none of this seems to have daunted her. Very conscious of her status as an aristocrat, Mrs. Pember slowly came to like and sometimes admire the common folk she ministered to more than the grandees of Richmond society. She did make appearances among the latter group, however; given her upbringing, it was only natural.

Phoebe Yates Pember was a Southern aristocrat from a Jewish family whose telling accounts of working in a Richmond hospital are recorded in *A Southern Woman's Story*.

What is the most affecting story Mrs. Pember tells?

Several reach a grand level. The one that lasts the longest in most people's memories goes as follows:

> After the battle of Fredericksburg, while giving small doses of brandy to a dying man, a low, pleasant voice said "Madam." It came from a youth not over eighteen years of age, seeming very ill, but so placid, with that earnest, far-away gaze, so common to the eyes of those who are looking their last on this world. Does God in his mercy give a glimpse of coming peace, past understanding, that we see reflected in the dying eyes into which we look with such strong yearning to fathom what they see? He shook his head in negative to all offers of food or drink or suggestions of softer pillows and lighter covering.
>
> "I want Perry," was his only wish.

This must have happened dozens, perhaps hundreds, of times in the war. Why do we pay such attention to this one vignette?

Because it is seldom that we encounter this kind of story, especially when written by a person who was not concerned with the outcome. But Phoebe Yates Pember believed in ministering to the dying, regardless of what was involved. Making inquiries, she found that Perry was the dying soldier's best friend, his fellow soldier with whom he had spent most of the past year. They marched together and slept by each other's side. Before long, Mrs. Pember located Perry at another hospital—Camp Jackson—put him in her ambulance, and brought him to Chimborazo. Her own patient had, meanwhile, fallen asleep:

> A bed was brought, and placed at his side, and Perry, only slightly wounded, laid upon it. Just then the sick boy awoke wearily, turned over, and the half-unconscious eye fixed itself. He must have been dreaming of the meeting, for he still distrusted the reality. Illness had spiritualized the youthful face; the transparent forehead, the delicate brow so clearly defined, belonged more to heaven than earth. As he recognized his comrade the wan and expressionless lips curved into the happiest smile—the angel of death had brought the light of summer skies to that pale face. "Perry," he cried, "Perry," and not another word, but with one last effort he threw himself into his friend's arms, the radiant eyes closed, but the smile still remained—he was dead.

Why don't we hear more stories like this one? Are they unique to the Civil War?

No. Millions of men, as well as some unknown number of women, have died in circumstances like these from the beginning of human history to our current time. But there was something quite special, nearly unique, about the experiences in the Civil War hospitals. First, there were more volunteers caring for more wounded soldiers than at any previous time in our history. Second, the camera, or use of the daguerreotype, had emerged just in time so that some of these faces and moments could be caught for the future. And third, perhaps most important, the Civil War hospitals, as well as the battle-fields themselves, were filled with people of an unusual level of literary skill. Public schooling had caught on, at least in the North, twenty years before the war began, and many people who might have been rendered mute by their circumstances instead arose—with their pens, pencils, and artists' paper—to leave poignant records for us today.

Was there a standard for how men endured their suffering while in military hospitals?

The North and the South were different in many ways, but when it came to the endurance of pain, their attitude was strikingly similar. Nurses and doctors in Northern hospitals echoed what Mrs. Pember wrote about the Southern soldier:

> No words can do justice to the uncomplaining nature of the Southern soldier. Whether it arose from resignation or merely passive submission, yet when shown in the aggregate in a hospital, it was sublime. Day after day, whether lying wasted by disease or burning up with fever, torn with wounds or sinking from debility, a groan was seldom heard. The wounded wards would be noisily gay with singing, laughing, fighting battles o'er and o'er again, and playfully chafing each other by decrying the troops from different states, each man applauding his own.

Is this possible? How could people endure such pain?

Today, with our knowledge of modern medicine and our knowledge that suffering can be prevented or ameliorated, we might not be able to withstand the pain the way these men did. But to them, having grown up in a world full of dangers, having seen kith, kin, or neighbors die from any number of illnesses, men and women of the 1860s were hardened to handle pain. When we first encounter a vignette like that presented by Mrs. Pember, we tend to doubt, but when we read many others, by nurses and doctors from all parts of the country, we realize that this was the social code.

Does Mrs. Pember tell us anything else that we could not learn without her record?

Yes, She is quite explicit that in the early stages of the war, the wounded Confederate soldier had nothing bad whatsoever to say about his Yankee counterpart. The wounded Confederate might curse the loss of this battle or the results of that skirmish, but there was, in 1862 and 1863, nothing personal in his statements or recounting. This changed in the summer of 1864. When the Confederate wounded were brought from the Battle of the Crater (see page 289), they expressed great anger toward the Northern men.

Perhaps it was the explosions caused by dynamite that led the Confederates to say this was "unfair" and a violation of the rules of war, but equally they were infuriated by the use of black soldiers. Many Confederates claimed they had shot down numerous blacks, but took little pride or pleasure in it, saying this had been a waste of their energies.

Did Union soldiers feel men or women were worse in the South?

More than a trace of misogyny emerges in the letters of Northern soldiers. They tend to give Johnny Reb his due, saying he fought well for a bad cause, but they tend to be very hard on any Southern woman who assisted her menfolk. Such attitudes crop up in the letters of soldiers, but they also appear in the pages of the *Atlantic Monthly* and *Harper's Weekly*.

Very likely, an element of truth can be found in what is expressed. Southern women did, perhaps, make the war last longer by helping their husbands, brothers, and cousins. But the question that we—the modern-day reader—wish to ask is: What else were they supposed to do? If the men of the North and the South could not come to political compromise, why was it the responsibility of the women?

Do Mrs. Pember's letters tell us anything about the prices of commodities?

As a true Southern lady—and therefore interested in her wardrobe and appearance—Mrs. Pember lamented both the high prices in Richmond and the difficulty of getting anything, even if one was able to pay. She therefore sent a number of letters to her sister in New Orleans.

"Eugene says you mentioned something about black and white gingham at 4.50 a yard, but that I do not intend to give. I am going on a shopping expedition next week. I had to give fifty dollars a pair for leather shoes and what is worse wear them, with the thermometer at ninety-six. I think prices are better for the purchaser here than anywhere else. I had made a black cravat for Eugene and it was lying upon my table when Major Mason of the Army came in and took it, saying he needed one. I let him keep it and a few hours afterwards he sent me five new novels and twenty pounds of coffee, telling me he knew I was too honest and scrupulous to drink the Hospital [*sic*] coffee."

WALT AND THE OTHER WHITMANS

Do we have other family stories that indicate the strain and stress of the war?

We have so many that one can easily be overwhelmed by the sheer mass of data. One that really strikes the modern reader, however, is the story of the Whitman family of Brooklyn, New York.

Walter Whitman Sr. and Louisa Van Velsor had nine children, eight of whom lived to maturity. He was a master carpenter in Brooklyn, and she was—by all accounts—the steady rock of the family. When the Civil War began, the Whitmans were already under a good deal of strain because the eldest son, Jesse, had been injured while at sea, and the youngest son, Edward, had been born a cripple. As difficult as this sounds to us today, it was by no means uncommon in the nineteenth century, and the Whitmans did not consider themselves a "troubled" group.

Isn't Walt Whitman the most famous member of the family?

Yes. A journalist, poet, and wanderer—in the best sense of the word—Walt Whitman (1819–1892) self-published *Leaves of Grass* in 1855. It received some applause at the time, but has garnered much more since then. Whitman is considered one of the most original of all American poets. Whitman's younger brother, George, enlisted in the New York Volunteers and eventually rose to the rank of colonel. The Whitman family crisis, however, took place when George was wounded at the Battle of Fredericksburg in December 1862.

Walt Whitman was a famous poet best known for his collection *Leaves of Grass*. He also notably wrote about the death of Lincoln in his poem "Oh Captain! My Captain!"

Walt Whitman raced to the army hospital where his brother lay and spent eight days with him. Once assured that George would recover, Walt moved to Washington, D.C., where he became one of the most unusual characters in a city filled with all types of persons. Working a dull day job to pay his rent, Whitman visited army hospitals almost every night for the next two years. He saw the horrors of the war up close and personal, but he believed something magnificent was going on at the same time.

What did Whitman say about the soldiers? Was he gay?

Walt Whitman definitely loved men. Whether he had any interest in women as well is a matter of lively debate. But his wartime journals and record books show an intense interest in men of all types, sizes, and physiques. Some deride or downplay Walt Whitman's actions on behalf of the soldiers, saying that he was merely a gay man who used his vocation for the vicarious thrills of mingling with the men. If any truth can be found in this, it certainly is not the whole truth. As Whitman expressed it in *Leaves of Grass*:

> Do I contradict myself?
> Very well then I contradict myself,
> I am large, I contain multitudes.

What happened to the Whitman family after the war?

George Whitman survived the war and lived for another decade. He remained, to the end of his life, deeply proud of what he had done for the cause of the Union. Walt Whitman suffered a serious stroke in 1864, and was never the same—physically—afterward, but he continued to turn out marvelous poetry, including the most famous of all poems having to do with Lincoln's assassination (see page 336). Jesse Whitman, the eldest son who had suffered an accident at sea, was placed in an asylum by his brother Walt; he died there a few years afterward. The youngest son, Edward, was cared for by family members till the end of his days. Perhaps the saddest story is that of Hannah Whitman, the bright, vivacious, well-educated daughter who ended up in a childless and loveless marriage. Perhaps the most surprising story of all is that of Jeff Whitman, a brilliant, self-taught engineer who designed, among other things, the waterworks in St. Louis, Missouri.

How usual or unusual were the Whitmans?

They displayed one of the greatest ranges and assemblages of talent that one could find, but they also had more than their share of tragedy and sorrow. Perhaps they were truly just a family that came from the moon, figuratively speaking; more likely, they were a highly talented group who represented much of the best of what mid-nineteenth century America had to offer.

How long had the Anglos and the Irish been at war, culturally speaking?

The animosity between descendants of English and Scottish immigrants, and the more recently arrived Irish, had been under way for a full generation, but its roots went back even further. Throughout the colonial period, Anglo-Americans had looked on the French Catholics in Canada as their foe, and because the Catholic Irish sometimes fought as their allies, they received a similar kind of brand. And when the Irish came "off the boat" in the wake of Ireland's terrible potato famine, they came as Catholics *and* as speakers of Gaelic, not English.

Culture, religion, and linguistics all played their part in creating a gulf between the English speakers who had been around for a long time and the Gaelic speakers who had just arrived. Of course, the children of these Irish immigrants would soon learn English, but the prejudices against them remained strong, as is shown in the following story reported in *The Atlantic Monthly*.

What did the author mean by "only an Irish girl"?

In January 1863, *The Atlantic Monthly* ran an article written by a sympathetic member of the Anglo-American upper class. Whether she lived in Boston, New York, or Baltimore is unknown, but the story has an almost universal feel. This fortunate woman, well aware that she was blessed in her circumstances, had chosen to hire an Irish girl as her personal servant. Friends and relatives warned her against this, and they seemed to be vindicated when the girl died at the home in which she served. The police, on first entering, exclaimed that it was "only an Irish girl."

"She was such a maiden as her mother must have been, one of Nature's own ladies, but more refined in type, texture, and form, as the American atmosphere and food and life always refine the children of European stock—slenderer, more delicate, finer of complexion, and with a soft, exquisite sweetness of voice, more thrilling than her mother's, larger and more robust heartfeltness of tone—and with the same, but shyer ways, and swift blushes and smiles." Is this really how Bridget O'Reilly looked? What matters is that the upper-class Anglo-American is expressing an idea, very likely a current one, of what feminine beauty should be.

How and why did Bridget O'Reilly die?

She was the youngest of fourteen children, and when she came to this upper-class house she seemed quite happy. Over time, however, some suspicion of stealing developed, and someone may have accused her directly. Bridget O'Reilly began to weaken visibly, and in a few weeks she was dead. Can we really say that grief or anguish killed her? We cannot, and even her employer admitted that it was a tough case to know the truth. The longer she thought about it, though, the more the upper-class lady became convinced that the Irish servants did steal, it was simply self-preservation, and one should not marvel at it any more than if the black slaves in the South stole from their masters.

The clash between Anglo and Irish cultures would find its fullest expression in the New York City draft riots of 1863 (see page 190).

FATHERS AND SONS: OLIVER WENDELL HOLMES

Do we learn anything about relationships between fathers and sons during the war?

We have to admit that our evidence is almost entirely anecdotal, that is to say, based on word of mouth rather than numbers or statistics. However, both in the prose and the poetry of the time, it is suggested that there were deep feelings between fathers and sons and that these sentiments often went unexpressed.

One of our best anecdotes comes from the pen of a person in whom we can place a good deal of trust, the poet Oliver Wendell Holmes. A prominent physician and man of letters, he lived in Boston and had the joy of seeing his eldest son graduate from Harvard College in 1862. Oliver Wendell Holmes Jr. joined the Union Army and was badly wounded at the Battle of Antietam. Immediately upon receiving the news, Oliver Wendell Holmes Sr. and a friend were on a train, headed south.

What was the train trip like?

Oliver Wendell Holmes Sr. tells the reader about the train trip and his constant eager search for his son: the article is entitled "My hunt after 'The Captain.'" Numerous times he could have bumped into his son, but time and again circumstances thwart a meeting. First the son is released from the camp hospital at Antietam and sent to Philadelphia; on chasing thither, Oliver Wendell Holmes finds that his son has been sent

185

Oliver Wendell Holmes Sr. (left) was a physician and author, and his son, Oliver Wendell Holmes Jr., was a noted U.S. Supreme Court associate justice.

elsewhere. Finally, however, comes the magical moment when, as if it had all been planned, magically or otherwise, they meet on a train.

"How are you, Boy?"

"How are you, Dad?"

Oliver Wendell Holmes Sr. mused at length. How could such an atmosphere of distance emerge between them? Why had they not sprung to each other, full of rejoicing? The answer, quite likely, is that they came from an upper-class group, the so-called Boston Brahmins, who did not go in for that kind of emotional display. The son not only recovered from his wound, he lived to be ninety-three and served for many years on the bench of the Supreme Court.

What else did Oliver Wendell Holmes observe?

He had a keen eye for human nature, but sometimes went overboard in his interpretation of people's looks. When he encountered several Confederate prisoners, Oliver Wendell Holmes questioned them at length, asking why they fought against the nation that had given them birth. He received conflicting answers, none truly satisfactory, then noticed another prisoner, who he decided was the "true Southern type."

"A fine fellow, a little over twenty, rather tall, slight, with a perfectly smooth, boyish cheek, delicate, somewhat high features, and a fine, almost feminine mouth." When the Northern man asked the Southern one why he fought, the answer came soft but deliberate: "Because I like the excitement of it." Holmes went on to write that he knew those men with soft, delicate features and mouths who looked as if they belonged to women: men such as these were natural-born killers.

Given that this is so anecdotal, why do we pay attention to it?

We do so because the numerical and statistical evidence is so scanty and because a man like Oliver Wendell Holmes tends (not always!) to write better descriptions and make more informed decisions about the people of his time. If Edgar Allan Poe, who in some ways resembles the very kind of young man Holmes described, had been alive to witness the Civil War, we would surely pay attention to what he said.

Holmes was a very intelligent person, but he may have been influenced by the pseudoscience of phrenology, which was much practiced in America at the time. Introduced in the 1830s, phrenology claimed to ascertain character traits as well as defects from the shape of a person's skull; there were skull readers on the streets of New York in the 1830s. Holmes seems to have been more interested in the skin and muscles of the face than the bones of the head, but his manner of "reading" or interpreting a person was much in vogue at that time.

What would the phrenologists have said about Lincoln?

To the best of our knowledge, the president did not ever subject himself to a phrenological exam. Had he done so, chances are the reader would have marveled that someone with such thick bones—and consequent thickheadedness—was able to survive, much less become the chief executive of his nation. We do know that person after person—educated ones most especially—were repulsed when they first gazed on Lincoln, describing him as ugly and ill-shaped. But Lincoln was a child of his times in some respects. He was not immune from the kind of magical thinking that was prevalent at the time, and in April 1863 he consented to a séance, held at the White House.

Knowing Lincoln as we do, knowing the rigorously logical person he was, this seems incredible. Very likely, he allowed the séance because of Mary Todd, who wished to make contact with their beloved son Willie, who died in February 1862. If so, the first lady was disappointed because the medium's messages were nearly all about the war and the conduct of the Union armies. News of the séance leaked out, leading many people in the capital to hold an even lower opinion of the first lady.

Were there any other oddities, or quirks, evident in the American character of the 1860s?

There were plenty. Writers of that time, and historians ever since, marveled at how the people—common, middle class, and upper—exposed themselves to the public in letters to the editor, songs, and poems. One thing that the Civil War was *not* known for was the belief that the end of the world was near. Perhaps this is because people of the 1860s faced such dire and serious things right on their doorstep. In any case, the literature about the end of the world is very sparse in the Civil War period.

187

THE PRICE OF THINGS

Do we know how much people paid for commodities?

We know a great deal about the price of things. For example, on April 12, 1861, the very day the war began, the *New York Times* informs us of the following prices, commodities, and events.

Ashes, which were in demand that April, went for $5.31 per pot. Cotton, which was selling sluggishly ("dull and heavy," said the *Times*) went for 12.25 cents per bushel. Hay was selling for 75 cents per 100 pounds. Sugar was divided into three groups. Cuban sugar sold for between 4.5 cents and 5.5 cents per pound, while New Orleans sugar went for 4.75 cents per pound. Puerto Rican sugar, which seems to have held the highest demand, sold for 5.75 cents per pound. This is not all, however. Thanks to the *New York Times*, we know that the "Situations Wanted" advertised more for "coachman and gardener" than any other position for men and "waitress or chambermaid" for women. And we know that there were no fewer than eleven entertainments or amusements that day, ranging from the highbrow Academy of Music to Niblo's Saloon, which had a minstrel show.

Do we know of comparable prices for commodities in the South?

Our lists and figures are from a later date. When the war began, life in Richmond seemed normal for a few months, but as the new Confederate government printed money by fiat, the price of everything rose. In the spring of 1864, as things approached a crisis point, the *Richmond Enquirer* reported the following commodities and prices.

Oysters sold for $16 per gallon, and flour for $120 per barrel. Wheat sold for $16 to $20 per barrel, while coffee—the thing most missed by Richmonders—sold for $11.50 per pound. Brown sugar sold for $3.40 per pound, and crushed sugar for $5.50. Even a cursory examination of these prices suggests that either the Confederate government was, indeed, printing money like wildfire, or most people were simply going without.

Who were the "hucksters"?

The term was already around in 1861, but its use became much more frequent during the war. In the North, a huckster or a shyster was a person who squeezed profit out of people who might, on a good day, be able to afford it. In the South, a huckster was viewed about the same as an enemy. Whoever they were—most of their names have not survived—the hucksters attempted to corner the market on a certain commodity, sugar for example, and drive the price sky-high.

When did Richmond have its first bread riot?

There had already been riots over food prices in other Southern cities and towns, but people generally were shocked when a similar event took place in Richmond. On the first of April, 1863, as the price of bread rose out of control, a large group of women, accompanied by some men, agitated in downtown Richmond. Their leader was Nancy Walker, but she was superseded the following day by Nancy Johnson.

The rioters attacked several downtown stores, trashing the places and taking practically everything of value. Store owners who placed locks and wooden splints to keep out the rioters failed, as the infuriated people knocked down one door after another. An aide to the governor of Virginia arrived and threatened that the crowd would be fired upon, but he was hooted and jeered. That was when Jefferson Davis arrived.

What did Jefferson Davis look like? What did he do?

Anyone who claimed the rich and powerful lived too well only had to take one look at Jefferson Davis to see something different. He was the most powerful man in the Confederacy and at one time he had owned 120

The Confederate States of America created its own monetary system and printed paper money by fiat. As it did so, inflation became a problem for the Southern economy.

slaves, but by the midpoint of the war he was a haggard man, old before his time. Anyone could see the toll the war had taken on him; at the same time they could feel his resolve.

Standing on the top of a farmer's cart, Davis shouted, "I understand you need money. Here is all I have!" Taking out some coins, he flung them to the crowd. Davis then came to the bottom of his pocket and coolly picked out a fine gold watch. If the rioters believed he was about to throw that, too, they were mistaken. Holding it up, Davis announced that the crowd had five minutes to disperse, after which it would be fired upon. Though no militia or regular army units were in evidence, there was something about Davis' manner that was persuasive. Within five minutes, the city square was empty.

Were there subsequent riots?

There were. We suspect that the Confederacy was rather good at hushing up the details and that there were more than reported, but the Confederates—men and women— would have been less than human had they not protested, even rioted, at times. The food shortages continued and grew worse as the war progressed.

There was another form, or type, of rioting, however, and this one was concentrated much more in the North. This type had to do with conscription, or as we say in our time, "the draft."

THE MILITARY DRAFT

What was the first conscription—forced military service—in the United States?

Throughout its seventy-five-year history, the United States had relied on volunteers. This had its drawbacks, but very few nations had done so well with so little as had America till the Civil War began. The enormous demand for manpower made things more difficult, however, and in March 1862 the Confederacy enacted the first draft.

The Confederate conscription made all men between the ages of eighteen and thirty-five liable for service, with very few exemptions permitted. One important exception to the rule, and one that caused no end of headaches for the Confederacy as a whole, was the one man per twenty slaves rule. Any farm or plantation that had twenty slaves could have one man exempted from military service. While one can appreciate that the Confederacy did not want its slaves to escape, the exemptions seemed—to the average Southerner—to turn it into a "rich man's war and a poor man's fight."

When was the first conscription in the North?

The Enrollment Act passed Congress in March 1863. All men between the ages of eighteen and forty-five were liable for service, but a number of possible "outs" made their way into the final legislation. Flat feet—considered bad for marching—were one thing, but the idea that a person could hire a substitute (if he could find one) or pay a $300 commutation fee was entirely different. To make the act more palatable, Congress allowed that each state was to furnish a certain number of men and provided incentives to help the states do so. Only when a state fell short of its allotted number would the draft be employed. Lincoln and Congress made no bones about their power, however; provost marshals were assigned the duty of entering American homes to determine the number of men in the household. And then, there was the awful thing of the draft wheel itself.

Where did the draft produce disastrous results?

There was anger, and tension, in many parts of the North, but New York City filled its usual role as the catalyst. The Empire City had not voted for Lincoln in 1860 (and would not grant him a majority in 1864, either). New York City was deeply divided between its native-born and foreign-born populations, with the greatest strains being those between men and women of Anglo descent and those of Irish descent. Making matters much worse was the fact that $300 represented the average annual pay of an Irish laborer in Manhattan, while it was a modest sum for a well-to-do man of business. To many people in New York, this was evidence that the war was for the benefit of the rich.

When did the trouble begin?

On Saturday, July 11, 1863, one week after the conclusion of the Battle of Gettysburg, the first draft wheels were employed. Twelve hundred and fifty names were drawn that

What was the draft wheel?

The circular wooden wheel had brass plates and fixtures, but it was—from first glance—recognizably part of nineteenth-century American culture. A blindfolded man turned the draft wheel until a certain number of cards fell out. On the cards were the names and occupations of men who had been identified by the provost marshals.

day, and an equal number were scheduled for Monday, July 12. But on the morning of July 12, not hundreds but thousands of city people—many of them from the poorer ranks of society—turned out in protest. No one knows who fired the first shot, or who threw the first brick, but within two or three hours it was apparent that a genuine crisis was at hand.

The disaffected crowd attacked the homes of wealthy persons and threatened to burn the structures. The greatest anger was reserved for blacks, however. The idea that the war would be placed on the back of the poor white man in order to liberate the black man, who then might well take his place at the factory, was intolerable. Crowds chased black individuals, sometimes catching and killing them. But the nastiest and ugliest mob of all was that which attacked the Colored Orphan Asylum.

Where was the Colored Orphan Asylum?

It was in midtown Manhattan, very close to where the main branch of the New York Public Library stands today. The asylum housed 320 children, all of whom recognized that they were rather lucky to be cared for in such a fine place. There were organized games, books to read, and a staff that was trained under the best, most modern methods. The asylum was, quite likely, the best of its kind.

The mob was moving from midtown to downtown when shouts arose: "Kill the niggers! Burn their nest!" With that, hundreds of furious people began setting fire to the building. How and why people would turn against children was something of a mystery then, and it remains so today.

Did the children escape?

Several courageous employees of the asylum gathered the children and pointedly asked them if they believed the Almighty could save them from a moment such as this. They nodded. The leaders then brought the children out the doors and right into the worst section of the mob.

As terrible as their actions had been, most members of the mob stood by and did nothing as the children passed through. Just one or two persons started toward the children, whereupon other members of the mob interposed themselves. It was one thing to destroy a building, another to actually harm the children. They reached relative safety twenty minutes later, but as the violence in the city continued, they were taken to Governor's Island, on the East River, for safety. Although a new asylum was built, it was not in the wonderful location as before, and the second asylum was never the great success that the first had been.

Whose job was it to keep law and order?

One reason that the riots got so out of hand was that there were several people who could make that claim. Mayor George Opdyke and New York Governor Horatio Seymour (1810–1886) had conflicting

The draft riots in New York City from July 13 to 16 occurred as a reaction to anger from draft laws implemented to add soldiers to the Union army.

lines of authority, as did General John Wool and the leader of the Metropolitan Police. On the first day of the riots, it was noticeable that none of these leaders wished to call in the full power of the federal government to rectify the situation.

To do so would have been deeply embarrassing to the local authorities.

No American city had previously gone through anything like what happened on Monday, Tuesday, and Wednesday of that week. The rioters enjoyed control of most of the lower part of Manhattan, and they took vengeance wherever possible, burning the homes of prominent Manhattanites and attacking anyone connected with the draft law. The leader of the Metropolitan Police was beaten, stripped, and almost killed, but he was rescued and later recovered from his wounds.

What did Lincoln and Stanton do?

Secretary of War Stanton was convinced that the riots had to be stamped out, not only for New York City, but for the success of the draft in the nation. If New York managed to defy the conscription law and escape punishment, other cities might take heart. In fact, the mayor of Detroit telegraphed that his city had already seen a race riot—directed against the African Americans—and he feared much worse might soon occur. Boston, on the other hand, took a hard line; when the police office in the Old North End was attacked, the men there defended their position with pistols and rifles, and they beat the mob.

Stanton wanted to put New York City under martial law, but Lincoln demurred. He had never been at ease in New York, had lost the election in that city in 1860, and he wanted the Democrats—his political foes—to remain in control of the situation; otherwise he might be called a dictator. It was agreed to send regiments from Gettysburg, but that the local authorities should handle the crisis.

When did the first soldiers arrive?

They came on Thursday afternoon, July 15, and were greeted like saviors by the people of New York City. The mob had defied, and sometimes beaten, the Metropolitan Police and the local militia, but it could not confront men who had just come from the killing fields at Gettysburg. The crowds subsided on Friday, and the entire city started to breathe a little easier. To say that business returned as usual on Monday morning would be an enormous contraversion of the facts, however.

Dozens of buildings had been destroyed entirely. Dozens, perhaps scores, of others bore quiet testimony to the rioters' fury. The official death toll came to 117 persons, and almost twice as many wounded, but most scholars who have studied the event believe that it was considerably more, that as many as five hundred persons may have been killed during those terrible days in July 1863. It was, quite simply, the worst urban uprising in American history.

Did the draft resume?

It did. Just two weeks later, the draft wheels were brought forward and blindfolded persons began drawing names again, but with one very important difference. To prevent another or a similar uprising, a trust fund was established that would pay the $300 commutation fee for the poor in New York City. This was a clever sleight of hand, allowing the draft to continue with the locals not having to endure the results. It was completely necessary, however, because the city could not risk even a small repetition of the events of mid-July 1863.

The draft continued in other East Coast cities, and there were few dramatic events connected to it through the rest of the year. Lincoln and Stanton knew they had escaped by a hairsbreadth, however.

Were there other strong prejudices in the Northern cities or states?

The prejudice against the Irish was the most extreme, but almost any kind of Roman Catholic was seen as suspicious. Then, too, any immigrant who did not quickly rise in the world was seen as a laggard or sluggard. One way to make a more fitting comparison between the 1860s and our own time is simply to observe what did not exist at that time: unemployment compensation, welfare, life insurance for any but the wealthy. People from all walks of life were frequently injured or impaired while on the job, and almost no one thought it the duty of the employer to make them whole.

Were any communities abandoned because of labor shortages?

In the North and the West, virtually no communities were abandoned; on the contrary, quite a few new towns were chartered or incorporated. This was not the case in the South, however, where the needs of the agricultural population simply were not met.

Perhaps this was because of a preindustrial mindset; then again, it may have been sheer greed on the part of the cotton growers. In either case, the South continued to produce cot-

What was life like in the countryside during the war?

Let us first distinguish between the agricultural lands of New England, New York, and Pennsylvania—all of which fall under the "North"—and those of Ohio, Illinois, Indiana, and other states of what was then called the "West." In the former, the loss of so many field hands was sharply felt. New England was already experiencing a labor shortage when the war began, and the situation only became worse. New York and Pennsylvania held their own in terms of agricultural labor, while the Western states experienced a thorough boom during the war.

Farmers had long since discovered that the softer, more clayey soil of the Midwest was easier to work than that of the East Coast, and the advent of the McCormick reaper, two decades earlier, had made harvesting a good deal easier than before. There were lots of Western, or Midwestern, women who had to work in the fields, but the overall effect was clearly positive. The Western states produced enough corn and potatoes to feed the North and the West and still managed to sell some abroad.

ton—above all other crops—for the first year and a half of the war. Only in the spring of 1863 did the Confederate government finally attempt to persuade the big cotton growers to switch to foodstuffs, and by then it was almost too late. To name or number the Southern towns that became deserted is nearly impossible, but the federal census of 1870 would show that at least eighty percent of all counties of the former Confederacy had a surplus of females and a dearth of males. This is one reason why the "Southern widow" became a staple of literature and poetry: she was, in fact, representative of a very real situation.

CHILDREN IN WARTIME

How were children affected by the Civil War?

When they first learned of the war, many young boys wanted to go and serve. Of course, they knew little or nothing of what might happen to them; they simply yearned for adventure. But even when the casualty lists began to come in, and the newspapers printed long pages full of the dead and wounded, adolescent boys remained vulnerable to the shoddy recruiter and their own overactive imaginations. Nothing seemed so fine as being a soldier.

If they succeeded in concealing their age and being accepted into the lists, young boys often became the drummers for their units. A fair amount of touching poetry on the subject of drummer boys was written during the war, often with tragic endings. Many of these boys came from broken homes, or homes that had practically disappeared because of domestic quarrels (scenes like these existed long before the war began).

How were two young boys who later became presidents affected by the war?

Born in Manhattan on October 27, 1858, Theodore Roosevelt came from an old Dutch family on his father's side and a thoroughly Southern family on his mother's (his maternal grandfather had fought in the Texan War for Independence in 1836). Though he lived a life of privilege and pleasure, young Theodore Roosevelt was deeply affected by the war, not least because his father was away from home—working on behalf of the soldiers rather than serving in the Union Army—for a total of two years. The letters from Theodore's mother to his father indicate an increasing bitterness over his absence, as well as the painful fact that theirs was a

Though he was too young to fight in the war, President Theodore Roosevelt was profoundly affected by the conflict between North and South as a boy.

household divided between the North and the South. Young Roosevelt had his first attack of asthma—the illness that would, in some ways, define his life—at the age of three. Historians who accept psychological explanations tend to concur that Roosevelt's adult interest in war—he served in the Spanish-American War of 1898—stemmed both from his childhood memories of the Union soldiers and from the fact that his father did not serve an active role (according to the theory of compensation, Theodore Roosevelt attempted to do what his father had not). Equally affected was the man who served two terms as president in the second decade of the twentieth century.

Born in Staunton, Virginia, in December 1856, Woodrow Wilson was the son of a Presbyterian minister; the family moved to Augusta, Georgia, a year later. Like Theodore Roosevelt, Woodrow Wilson had lively memories of his Civil War boyhood; unlike Roosevelt, Wilson came from a united family, which believed in the Southern cause. As he matured, and became president of Princeton University and then governor of New Jersey, Wilson came to see the North's victory in the Civil War as a positive thing, in that slavery was destroyed. Like most Southerners of his age, however, Wilson had positive feelings for the Confederate leaders, Robert E. Lee most especially. Shortly before he entered the White House as the nation's twenty-third chief executive, Wilson wrote a stirring tribute to Lee: "He was a man who saw his duty, who conceived it in high terms, and who spent himself, not upon his own ambitions, but in the duty that lay before him." These words can almost serve as an unconscious model for Wilson's own behavior in the White House.

How was Helen Keller affected by her childhood in the rural South?

Born in June 1880, Helen Keller was not a Civil War child; the war was over fifteen years before she was born. In her youth she could not help but be affected, however, by the war's aftermath. Her father, who was the editor of the local newspaper, served as a captain in the Confederate Army. Her maternal grandfather was originally from New England, but he served as a Confederate, rising to the rank of colonel. And, perhaps most importantly, Helen grew up in the post-Civil War South, a place nearly defined by what had happened a generation earlier.

Her struggle with deafness and dumbness—which arrived after an attack of scarlet fever at the age of two—definitely helped Helen Keller to identify with the weak and underprivileged. It may also added to her knowledge, firsthand, of a society that was practically prostrate in the years that followed the Civil War. Throughout life, Helen Keller was willing to speak up for unpopular causes; in the First World War she became unpopular for speaking out against American involvement.

Where did the drums come from?

A majority of all the drums used in the Union armies came from one factory in rural Massachusetts. Noble & Cooley was formed in Granville, Massachusetts, in 1854, and by 1854 the small firm produced 631 drums. In the summer of 1860, its workers turned out a very special "Lincoln drum" for use in Lincoln's presidential campaign. But the real breakthrough came with the beginning of the Civil War. In 1863, when the conflict reached its height in terms of numbers, Noble & Cooley turned out 58,000 drums. If another industry exists that saw such rapid expansion, one is hard-pressed to find it.

How about the girls of the period? How did they see the Civil War?

Our evidence is scantier when it comes to the young females, but we can venture some guesses. Patriotism loomed large for the girls, as well as for the boys, and many wished to become nurses. Very few girls ran away from home, however, and those who did were not accepted into the U.S. nurses. Generally speaking, the war did not provide as many opportunities for young girls as for young boys, but this did not prevent the girls from daydreaming and thinking things were better, or that the grass was greener, on the other side of the fence.

When did Northern readers become acquainted with the people who are sometimes labeled "poor white trash"?

When the expression first appeared is not known, but it was current by the time the war began. In 1864, a Northern writer expounded eloquently on the theme in an article for *Harper's Magazine*.

In "The 'Poor Whites' of the South," this writer argued that the expression could be used to describe about 500,000 out of the Southern white population of roughly eight million. He went to great length to distinguish between the many white Southerners who struggled to get by and those who he claimed had given up the struggle to become vagrants, wanderers, and dangerous people (these are the ones he called "poor whites"). In the article, the author expanded on his theme that what most separated the poor peo-

What did the *Harper's Magazine* essay say about Southern women?

"**W**e may overrun the South," the essay declared, "we may make its fields a desolation, and its cities heaps of ruins, but until we reach the reason and the hearts of these men, we shall stand ever on the crater of a volcano." The answer was to educate the Southerners, with a gun in one hand and Yankee newspapers in the other, but to make a special effort where Southern women were concerned.

"If we convert *them,* the country is saved. Woman, in this century, is every where that 'power behind the throne' which is mightier than the throne itself, and the Southern women have been, and are, the mainspring of this rebellion." Just three years earlier, rather few Northerners would have subscribed to this view: they had seen Southern women as the mere tools of Southern men. But as the war continued and became more grim, quite a few Northerners came to the conclusion that Southern women were indeed at the heart of the rebellion. They did not raise guns; they did not have to. The mere fact that they endorsed the war, and told their husbands to go to the front, was evidence of their importance.

ples of the South from the poor peoples of the North was literacy: that there were practically no schools for the former. As long as this remained the case, the North would continue to have difficulties with its Southern brethren. As good as the writing was to this point, it became even better when the author addressed the subject of Southern women.

How does this account jibe, or not jibe, with our traditional view of the placid Southern woman?

Stereotypes such as that of the accepting, even downtrodden, Southern woman do not emerge out of thin air: usually some substance is behind the image. That particular stereotype comes to us, however, from the diaries and letters of "proper" Southern women, who usually did not have to fight to obtain their daily bread (even though some of them would later be reduced to a similar state). In order to obtain a fuller look at Southern women, we have to go beyond the "belle of the ball" image many of us have gained from films and novels.

The life that Scarlett O'Hara—the heroine of *Gone with the Wind*—lost when the federal army entered Atlanta was real, but it was only enjoyed by a few thousand women at the most. Far more common was the wife of a dirt farmer in Alabama, the woman who had lost her husband to a duel, or the aging spinster who could find no mate. Again, this does not mean we should "cancel" our view of the traditional Southern woman; rather, we should build upon and enlarge it.

Was there a typical or average Northern woman of that time?

She is even more difficult to describe than the Southern one, because a legend did not grow up around either her clothing or her mannerisms. We have far more diaries and

How did de Tocqueville know so much?

This remains one of the truly great questions, both in history and sociology. De Tocqueville and his friend Gustave de Beaumont spent only eight months in the United States, from 1831 to 1832, yet de Tocqueville's writings make it seem that he came to know every part of the young republic.

Some people have greater powers of observation than others and are able to extrapolate from masses of data to arrive at certain concepts which *may* reveal truths. That these philosophers and sociologists sometimes fail is beyond dispute; in their reach for great truths, they sometimes stumble. With the benefit of hindsight, we can point to several parts of de Tocqueville's writing—his chapter on race relations, for example—and declare that he was mistaken. But when we do so, we usually end up shaking our heads at the far greater number of things he got right!

letters from Northern men than women, and even the best-informed men of the time often leave us—the modern-day reader—in the dark. What we can say is that the Northern woman—whether of the city or the country—was no stranger to sacrifice. She had been sacrificing for her husband and children all her life. Here is what Alexis de Tocqueville, writing in 1835, had to say on the subject:

"The same strength of purpose which the young wives of America display, in bending themselves at once and without repining to the austere duties of their new condition is no less manifest in all the great trials of their lives. In no country in the world are private fortunes more precarious than in the United States. It is not uncommon for the same man, in the course of his life, to rise and sink again through all the grades which lead from opulence to poverty. American women support these vicissitudes with calm and unquenchable energy."

Do the lives of Abraham and Mary Lincoln bear out the "truths" or concepts to which de Tocqueville pointed?

We have to admit that the Lincoln couple defied his reason, and the statistics, time and again. They started out at opposite ends of the pole, with Mary being the more self-confident and possessed of the two and Abraham being the awkward stumbler. Because of her social connections, Mary Todd Lincoln did not subordinate either her will or her dark sense of humor to her husband in the early years of their marriage; somewhere along the line, he gained the upper hand, however.

De Tocqueville usually portrayed the American wife as the person who sacrificed the most, grimly but gently holding on till better days might arrive. In the relationship between Abraham and Mary Lincoln, however, we usually see the husband as the person tied to the pole, figuratively speaking. Lincoln often expressed ambivalence about marriage in general; after learning that one young soldier was about to be married, he commented that he would probably wish he was back in the army before long.

A BRITISH TRAVELER

Did things on the home front change over time?

Yes. In the autumn of 1864, a British travel writer arrived in Newfoundland, went to mainland Canada, then visited parts of the North and Midwest. His commentary, *A Short American Tramp in the Fall of 1864*, was published the following year. On first arriving in coastal Maine, he had this to say:

"The number of maimed men in the streets savored of war. Many strong young chaps, short of limbs, were walking or hopping about on crutches. With this exception there appeared to be no marked features in the Yankee population. All the names on the shops were familiar old-country names, the faces were familiar faces, the accent very like neighboring accents." If these people of Maine could be moved to Scotland, Ireland, Nova Scotia, or New Brunswick, they would fit in quite well, he declared.

What did John Francis Campbell say about the border crossings from Canada to the United States?

The British traveler was well aware that the Northerners dreaded a possible Confederate influence in Canada, but he said there was no way to prevent it. The Southerners looked too much like Northerners to be separated out. As he traveled in the northern part of New England, the British traveler was struck by the segregation, not between white and black, but between men and women. This was especially the case when traveling by railroad.

"Women have a car to themselves," he wrote, "and extra comforts. No man, unless he is accompanied by a lady, may enter the sacred car-ess, and even 'brutes' of husbands cannot smoke there. Elsewhere [on the train] there is a freedom and independence about the proceedings which has its charm. Everyone is at liberty to break his neck, or be left behind, if he thinks fit. Men jump off and on while the cars are moving, and no guard interferes. The engine stops and goes on again without the concert of station bells which proclaims the fact elsewhere. It does not whistle, but it tolls the big bell hung round its neck, and roars a strange variety of notes and tones."

What did this particular Englishman think about the Civil War?

His travel account speaks to social issues much more than military ones, and he makes the interesting comment that the war is good for American society. Until it began, he claims, the Americans were too parochial, with every man and family on a farm thinking they were the kings of the universe. Once thrown together in military association, the Americans started to see that there were other people in the world, people from whom they might, conceivably, learn things. As he expressed it: "One phase of this American war strikes a wanderer very forcibly; it is the change in the bearing of those who are engaged in it."

What were the prices for commodities at the end of the war?

April 12, 1865, marked the fourth anniversary of the war's commencement. It also fell within the week that saw the end of most hostilities: Lee had surrendered three days previous. That date, therefore, is useful for a comparison of prices, at least where the figures exist.

In New York City, ashes sold for $8 per pot. Coffee was divided into four groups: Java sold for 22 cents per pound; Rio sold for 18.25 cents; Laguayra sold for 18.5 cents; and Santo Domingo for 18 cents. Cotton sold for between 30 and 35 cents per bushel, and 3,000 bales of cotton were put up for sale on government account (this was specifically from General Sherman's recent capture of the city of Savannah). Hay sold for between $1.50 and $1.65 per 100 pounds. Petroleum, which had not been listed in the *New York Times* four years earlier, sold for 34.5 cents per gallon of crude. And the situations-wanted advertisements displayed mostly the same type of positions—waitress, nurse, gardener, and coachman—but with a decided new twist. Many of the situations-wanted advertisements proudly proclaimed "Protestant nurse," "Protestant gardener," and so forth. This religious addition was clearly in response to the draft riots of 1863, which had turned "Catholic" into a very bad name.

Can we say anything about the difference between the Americans of 1865 and those of 1861?

On an individual level, they had gone through all sorts of trials and torments. Very few Americans remained unaffected by the war. On a collective level, the people and the nation had become much more firmly entwined. Not until 1917, with the entrance to the First World War, would Americans experience such a searing set of events, and not until 1941, with the entrance to the Second World War, would there be such an emphasis on heroism and sacrifice. Along with these noble sentiments came an uglier side, however. Although some prejudices broke down under the pressure of the Civil War, others hardened and became more entrenched. The Irish would long be identified as the troublemakers in the Northern cities, and the African Americans would often be blamed, as if they had started all the trouble in the first place. On a familial level, the Civil War was instrumental in doing harm to the husband and father as the center of the family. The Industrial Revolution was under way when the war began in 1861, and by 1865 the trend toward iron, steel, and even the petroleum industry were well marked. But with each progressive improvement in the quality of the lives of the children back home, there was less exposure to the vital presence of their fathers in their lives.

MIDPOINT OF THE WAR: MAY TO JULY 1863

SMALL TOWNS IN A BIG WAR

What were Gettysburg and Vicksburg like before the Civil War began?

Nestled in the rolling hills of southern Pennsylvania, Gettysburg was, in 1860, home to 2,390 people, of whom 188 were free persons of color. The white population was divided into 1,099 males and 1,103 females.

Anchored hard by a bend in the Mississippi River, Vicksburg, Mississippi, was, in 1860, a place of about 5,000 population (we do not know the breakdown between white and black). Vicksburg was already well known to those who read the newspapers, first because it was the largest town close to Jefferson Davis' home plantation of Brierfield and because Admiral Farragut had attempted to force the place to surrender in 1862. He had failed.

Did the people of these two towns recognize the importance, or the name recognition, that was coming their way?

The people of Vicksburg certainly did. They were proud of having rebuffed the Union Navy the previous year, and they expected that the North would throw everything at them in 1863. The townspeople were generally confident because of the defenses which nature had provided and because of the manner in which the Confederate forces had augmented them.

The people of Gettysburg almost certainly did not anticipate that 1863 would be the year that their town would become famous. They knew that their town was at a cross-roads, that many important turnpikes ran through, but they had lived rather far from the scene of the war to this point.

When did the action begin to move toward Vicksburg?

During the winter of 1863, General Ulysses S. Grant directed the Army of Tennessee in a variety of operations, all directed toward the same goal. It was obvious to Grant, as well

An 1863 illustration from *Journal Universel* in Paris shows a view of the Gettysburg battlefield.

as to his immediate superior General Henry Halleck, that Vicksburg was the key to the Trans-Mississippi West: if that fortified town fell, the Union would enjoy unimpeded access to, as well as control of, the length of the great river. How to proceed was a mighty question, though.

Vicksburg enjoyed superb natural defenses. The fortified city sat atop a bluff that was 250 feet above the Mississippi water level and roughly 350 feet above sea level. Vicksburg was situated at a severe, almost 180-degree turn in the Mississippi, giving the Confederate garrison ample opportunity to employ its guns against any approaching flotilla. In 1862, the Union Navy had proven that it could, on occasion, pass by the Confederate batteries, but it had not solved the riddle of how to silence the guns.

How many men were in and around Vicksburg?

The Confederates knew that Grant intended to take the fortress, and they had almost 30,000 men either at Vicksburg or close enough that they could be summoned. When compared to the civilian population of about six thousand, this force seemed enormous.

General John Pemberton was commander at Vicksburg, but the forces deployed to the east and south were under the command of Joseph E. Johnston, who had by now recovered from the wound he suffered during the Seven Days' Battles. The negative, so far as the Confederacy was concerned, was that neither of these men specialized in seizing opportunity when it came: both of them were natural defensive fighters.

How many men did Grant have available to him?

The Army of Tennessee was about 55,000 men strong, but Grant could readily obtain reinforcements, if need be. He had the full backing of Lincoln, who—as a one-time Mississippi River keelboatman—believed Vicksburg was the central part to solving the Union problems on the Western front. Grant also had a tough, aggressive second in command in William T. Sherman.

There had been a time, roughly a year and a half earlier, when Sherman outranked Grant, but the latter had pushed well past the former. This did not prevent the two from being good friends and comrades-in-arms: one of their great attributes was that they saw many, if not most, military situations with similar eyes. Of course there were times when they disagreed, and Sherman—though outranked—was not shy in communicating his opinions.

General Ulysses S. Grant.

What was the first attempt made on Vicksburg's defenses?

On December 28, 1862, Sherman led thousands of men in an attack on the northeastern section of Vicksburg's natural defenses. His assault, in the area known as the Chickasaw Bayou, was a complete disaster. Fortunately for the Union, Sherman was able to extricate his men after suffering almost 3,000 killed, wounded, or gone missing. There was, surprisingly, some benefit to the Northern cause: the defenders of Vicksburg became overconfident, even complacent, that winter.

Seeing the failure of a major assault, Grant decided on something much less dramatic. In February and March 1863, he had thousands of men wielding pickaxes and shovels, attempting to dig a new canal. The plan was to divert part of the flow of the Mississippi River away from Vicksburg and thereby make the approaches easier to handle. Given the enormous size of the great river, it seems incredible that Grant would devote such resources, but he had the full backing of Lincoln and the War Department. If there was a cheaper and easier way to take Vicksburg, official Washington was all for it.

Was there any chance that the canal might have worked?

Just barely. Given the right kind of temperatures, and the right kind of snow melt coming down the Mississippi and Missouri Rivers, it was barely possible. But those natural circumstances did not "fall into line" and the harder Grant's men worked, the further behind they fell. Realizing this, Grant abandoned the attempt. March 28, 1863, appears to be the key day, the one on which Grant decided on an entirely different strategy. He

203

had, of course, considered it a few months earlier, but at that time it seemed even riskier, even more quixotic than digging the canal.

What was the new plan?

Given that Vicksburg commanded the water, and that it was practically impossible to come through the swamps and bayous that made up the Yazoo Delta, Grant decided to go down the other, meaning west, side of the Mississippi. He would then cross the big river and come at Vicksburg from its vulnerable, landward side. This sounded very good till one considered that there were practically no supplies on hand and that there was only one road running anywhere near the river on its western side. Moreover, how would Grant get his men from the western to the eastern side?

Admiral David Dixon Porter was confident, supremely so, about his ability to run past the Vicksburg batteries at night, but he warned Grant that it was a decision from which he could not reverse direction. The Mississippi current flowed at about six knots in that area, and to try to fight it, and the Confederate batteries on a return trip, would truly be hopeless. Therefore, it would be an all-or-nothing effort; Grant had always been a gambler, militarily speaking, and he decided to make the attempt.

Was anyone against the attempt?

Most of Grant's staff voted against it. General Sherman thought it was too ambitious an endeavor, especially because there was only one road on the western side of the river. Grant overruled them all and put them to work, however.

The toughest task, at least at first, was that of Admiral Porter. His men stuffed bales of cotton as well as other soft materials all along the sides of their vessels, preparing for the frightening and dangerous night run past Vicksburg. As luck would have it, the Confederates planned a ball for the evening of April 16, 1863. Most of the Confederate officers were taking their turns on the dance floor when a messenger burst in the door, exclaiming that the Yankee ships were close.

How many guns did the garrison have?

There were twenty smoothbore cannon and seventeen rifled cannon atop the heights at Vicksburg, more than enough to sink the entire Union flotilla. Knowing they needed to see their enemy better, the Confederates set fire to a number of houses near the turn, and as Admiral Porter and his vessels came on, things looked dire for the Northern flotilla. But Porter had laid his plans well, and just after making the turn, he surprised the Confederates by zigzagging from the Louisiana to the Mississippi side of the river. This actually brought his ships closer to the Confederate cannon, but it required the cannoneers to make sudden adjustments. Suddenly, the entire river bend was ablaze with the lights from cannon fire, with the Union ships giving as good as they got. The current favored the North that night: it carried the vessels quickly past, and an hour later the entire episode was over. Grant and his wife had observed the whole affair from the deck of a ship about a mile away.

What did Admiral Porter report? What did the Confederates tell their superiors?

Porter had the pleasure, and satisfaction, to report that he lost only one vessel, the *Henry Clay*, in making the passage of Vicksburg. Two other ships were damaged, but came safely through. Porter brought almost fifteen vessels past Vicksburg, making a mockery of the city's vaunted defenses.

The Confederates could scarcely believe it. For the past year they had taunted their Northern opponents with the knowledge that Vicksburg's guns commanded the river. Now that was revealed as an imaginary position. To be sure, the garrison could make mincemeat of almost any vessels passing upstream, but a daring commander could bring his ironclad or tinclad vessels past the town, employing both the current and his own cannon. In one stroke, Admiral Porter had altered the course of the Vicksburg campaign.

When did Grant have his men on the move?

Typically, Grant had his men moving out the very next day. He counted on the advantage of surprise, and the Confederate garrison seemed completely unaware of what he was doing. So, to some extent, were Lincoln and the War Department.

By this point, the War Department had decided to leave Grant pretty much alone. He had been so successful, in so many endeavors, that it seemed safe to count on him. One thing that neither Lincoln nor Secretary of War Stanton knew, however, was that Grant occasionally lost his footing where drink was concerned. Most of the time he was kept under the watchful eye of Brigadier-General John Rawlins (1831–1869), his good friend and his chief of staff. On the few occasions when Rawlins was not present, Grant sometimes fell off the wagon.

How hard was the army's march southward?

It was not nearly as bad as anticipated. Having spent most of the winter digging ditches in failed attempts to make canals, the men were eager for movement, and there was almost no Confederate opposition as they moved south. The men, too, had developed a great trust in their commander: as long as Grant was in charge, things would be well, they often said.

The rendezvous with Admiral Porter's flotilla took place in the last week of April. It was a heady moment as Grant and Porter got together, seeing the realization of so many of their plans. They both knew that a formidable hurdle still remained, however: they had to get Grant's men to the other side of the big river. The Confederates fully understood the danger, and Port Gibson, one of the most natural places to make a crossing, was strongly fortified. Even so, Grant and Porter decided to make the attempt.

Why did the attack on Port Gibson fail?

Given the success he had in running past Vicksburg's defenses, Admiral Porter expected to take Port Gibson if not with ease then with celerity. But on the morning of the first of May, when his gunboats and troop transports came within range, they found that the

Confederates had withstood the bombardment rather well. It turned out that earthworks resisted the Union bombardment better than wood, or even stone, would have done. Porter's losses were not heavy—only a few dozen men—but it was clear that another landing spot had to be found.

Where did Grant and his men come ashore?

Two days later, Porter and his flotilla brought Grant and his men ashore at Bruinsburg, Mississippi. There was some brief fighting as they waded ashore, but within an hour or two the beachhead was secure with hundreds of men coming ashore every hour. Grant had achieved one of the most successful amphibious operations of the war. Just how Grant managed this has been debated many times, but the answer is actually rather simple. As he did so many times, Grant dared, and his foe reacted too slowly.

Grant did not inform Washington, D.C., or even his generals, right away, but he had made up his mind to strike hard and fast. On May 2, he began to move east, with his men carrying only six days' rations in their knapsacks.

Why did the Confederate forces not combine to fight Grant?

The Confederates committed several errors in the Vicksburg campaign, but the top generals can be absolved from some of the worst of them. The single largest problem was that Jefferson Davis wanted to hold Vicksburg to the last, while General Joseph Johnston did not believe it possible. Johnston, therefore, sent conflicting messages to General Pemberton, who usually learned the most important intelligence a day or so too late. For example, if Pemberton had known that Grant's men had only six days' provision in their knapsacks, he might have marched quickly from Vicksburg to join Joseph Johnston. Lacking that information, Pemberton remained where he was.

DAILY CAMP RATION FOR ONE MAN

Pork/Bacon	12 oz.
or Salt/Fresh Beef	1 lb. 4 oz.
Soft Bread	1 lb. 6 oz.
or Flour	
Hard Bread	1 lb.
Corn Meal	1 lb. 4 oz.

DAILY CAMP RATION FOR 100 MEN

1 Peck of Beans
10 lb. Rice/Hominy
10 lbs. Green Coffee
or 8 lbs. Roasted
or 1 lb. 8 oz. Tea
15 lbs. Sugar
1 lb. 4 oz. of Candles
4 lbs. of Soap
2 qts. of Salt
4 qts. of Vinegar
4 oz. of Pepper
1/2 Bushel of Potatoes
1 qt. of Molasses

How did Grant come into possession of Jackson, Mississippi?

The capital of Mississippi had so far been spared the brunt of the war: its people had seen no Union troops throughout the conflict. But on May 16, 1863, Joseph Johnston was in Jackson, and on May 17, he was replaced by Grant.

The Union forces stole a march or two on the Confederates, and Johnston, having only six thousand men, escaped Jackson just in time. Grant occupied the city on

A sign displayed at a Civil War battle reenactment in Illinois shows what daily rations were like for soldiers at war.

May 17, but held it for only one day before setting fire to its main buildings. This was one of the first such destructions of a major Confederate city, and Grant came in for harsh denunciation from the Confederate newspapers. To Grant, however, it all made sense. He was engaged in the most desperate action of the war—at least the most desperate one faced by a Union general—and he would use everything at his resource to win. As Grant and his army marched out of Jackson, they headed west, ready to confront Pemberton.

What was the response in the East?

The Northern newspapers were looking for some good news, any good news, with which to counteract the terrible defeat at Chancellorsville. On May 16, the *New York Times* ran a special advertisement for newly published books, among which *The Conscript: A Tale of War* was heralded. This book was by Alexandre Dumas, the French novelist who had written *The Count of Monte Cristo, The Three Musketeers*, and many other well-loved books. *The Conscript* was a darker tale, based on the French Revolution, but, as the *Times* expressed it, this was a book with great relevance for contemporary Americans, who faced a coming conscription.

About the only good news from anywhere was that from Grant in Mississippi, and the *Times* as well as other Northern newspapers did the most with what they had. The *Times* reported, for example, that Grant's men had come upon the plantation of Jefferson Davis and found it in terrible condition. Much more important was the news that Grant was now marching on Vicksburg. Lincoln, in the executive mansion, did not usually read the newspapers, but in late May he scanned them eagerly because he had little other information to go on. Grant was feeding little information to the War Department, which had to go on faith that his campaign was proceeding in the right fashion.

What was the Battle of Champion Hill?

Even before he learned of the burning of Jackson, Mississippi, General Pemberton decided to fight Grant outside of Vicksburg. Leaving the fortified city, Pemberton brought about

The South's General Pemberton organized his army about twenty miles east of Vicksburg, where Ulysses S. Grant attacked and defeated him.

thirty thousand men to Champion Hill to await Grant's movements. Pemberton's men dug in, but they were not ready for the fierce assault that came their way on May 18.

Grant's men were, by now, so battle hardened and accustomed to difficulty that any force would have had a difficult time resisting them. The Battle of Champion Hill was exceptionally one-sided, with Pemberton losing two thousand men killed, wounded, or missing and Grant suffering less than half as many.

Champion Hill meant that Pemberton would not fight Grant again in the open, and it meant that the fight for Vicksburg would be a siege. How long that siege would be was partly up to Grant.

What did Vicksburg look like to the oncoming Yankees?

A Union officer described it thus:

> A long line of high, rugged, irregular bluffs, clearly cut against the sky; crowned with cannon which peered ominously from embrasures to the right and left as far as the eye could see. Lines of heavy rifle-pits, surmounted with head logs, ran along the bluffs, connecting fort with fort, and filled with veteran infantry.

Very likely, no Confederate position—of this campaign or even the entire war—presented quite so daunting an outward appearance as Vicksburg in May 1863. Had the Union Navy not commanded the waterways below the city, there would have been no possibility of taking the place. But Grant, as ever, believed his men could achieve the near-impossible. They had already done so by marching to take Jackson, winning the Battle of Champion Hill, and scattering their foes. Knowing that a long siege might be detrimental to morale, Grant decided on a frontal assault.

Was there any precedent for the Siege of Vicksburg?

Not in the Civil War. Never had so many men been positioned in such a strong place, and never had such a large army come to besiege it. Grant received reinforcements continually during the siege, bringing the total of his army to around 70,000, while Pemberton had about 32,000 men inside a city designed and built for a population of 6,000. For a precedent, one had to look back to the Napoleonic Wars, and even in them, there had never been such a large defending force. All this naturally begs the question: Why do most histories of the war give such large treatment to the Battle of Gettysburg and such small shrift to Vicksburg?

The answer is that the newspapers did it, even at the time. The *New York Times* gave Vicksburg (which it perennially spelled with an "h" at the end) front-page treatment until Lee and the Army of Northern Virginia invaded Maryland. Once that happened, events in Vicksburg were usually handled on page eight of the *Times*, with front pages devoted to Lee's invasion.

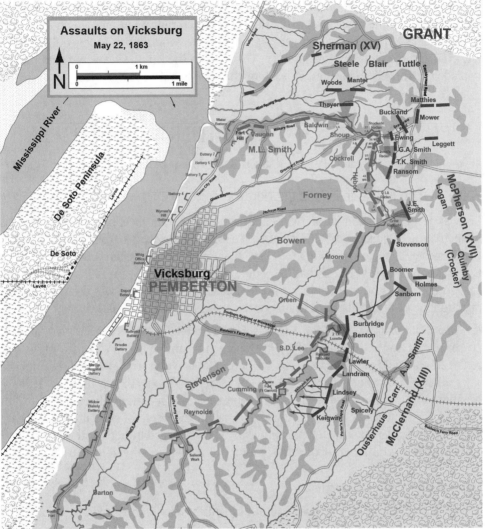

This map shows the positions of the Union and Confederate armies on May 22, 1863, during the siege of Vicksburg, Mississippi. The Confederate loss was a huge setback for the South and is generally considered a major turning point of the war.

How did the attack go?

Grant made rather few mistakes in the war, and he admitted to even fewer, but to the end of his days he regretted his decision to make a quick attack on Vicksburg. Grant's army lost over 1,000 men in the rash assault.

Even then, Grant did not give up entirely. He planned a second attack for May 23, and it failed as dismally as the first. From that moment, he knew he had to settle in for a long siege. The prospect was daunting. Vicksburg's defenses ran from Fort Hill on the north side to South Fort on the opposite, and the city had over 200 large cannon. The only way to take the place was with a slow, protracted movement of men and artillery. This was one of the few times in the war—to date—when either side would use the trenches and parallels of a formal siege. The men on the Union side would be more occupied with shovels than rifles, at least for the time being.

THE ARMY OF NORTHERN VIRGINIA MOVES NORTH

When did Lee decide to invade the North?

Lee was never one to confide all his feelings or beliefs to one sheet of paper, but it seems likely that he decided by the first of June. He was under pressure from many leaders of the Confederacy to do something to relieve the pressure on Vicksburg. Some, including General Longstreet, believed that Lee would do best to go west himself and do the job that Joseph Johnston seemed incapable of. Lee did not think this was the right course of action: he wanted to be with the men who trusted him so well and vice versa.

In a series of letters to Jefferson Davis, Lee indicated his desire to cross the Potomac and bring the war to the enemy. The North had, in his mind, tasted very little of the war so far, and it would please his men to live off the fat of Northern land. What Lee did not say explicitly, but what Jefferson Davis understood all too well, was that the Army of Northern Virginia could not safely remain where it was. Even in the aftermath of its glorious victory at Chancellorsville, the army was on the verge of starvation. The lands around the Rapidan and the Rappahannock had been foraged by both armies for so long that they simply could not support the presence of sixty to seventy thousand armed men.

What did Jefferson Davis say?

Earlier in the war, Jefferson Davis had put his fullest trust in one man, General Albert Sidney Johnston, who died at the Battle of Shiloh. Davis still had a tendency to play favorites with his generals—Joseph Johnston, for example, was *not* one of them, but Davis saw clearly when it came to Lee. There was only one person whom the Army of Northern Virginia would follow into any and all danger, and that was Lee.

Davis, therefore, gave his blessing to the invasion of the North, and, typically, he gave Lee a great deal of freedom in the design. Davis did not fear for the safety of Richmond because the Yankees would have to defend Washington. What he was concerned with was the situation at Vicksburg, but it had slipped beyond his control.

How ready was the Army of Northern Virginia?

It was, perhaps, at the best state it had ever been. The Confederate conscription had brought the regiments up to full strength, and the morale of the men had never been higher. They missed Stonewall Jackson badly, however, and they were in need of all sorts of supplies, shoes most especially. Though Lee did not say so outright, the need for equipment was one of the major reasons he desired to invade the North.

Lee knew that an invasion would be hazardous, but, much like in September 1862, he sensed that it was now or never.

A British observer noted that Lee's men were in excellent spirits and that they expected to beat the Union men, whom they had thrashed on several occasions. Of course it was one thing to fight the Yankees in Virginia and another to encounter them on their own soil.

What was a colonel of Her Majesty's Coldstream Guards doing in Virginia?

Colonel Arthur Fremantle was twenty-six and on a leave from official duty when he rather impulsively decided to observe the Southern rebellion for himself. As he described in *Three Months in the Southern States*, Fremantle was able to observe both the rebellion and many of its major leaders.

Landing near the mouth of the Rio Grande, Fremantle crossed Texas, meeting an aged Sam Houston along the way. Passing through Mississippi, he met General Joseph Johnston, whom he found very pessimistic about any attempt to relieve the garrison at Vicksburg. Much intrigued by the institution of slavery, Fremantle noted that in Texas a healthy male slave often sold for $2,500, but that a skilled seamstress would sell for as much as $3,500. Fremantle visited Mobile and Montgomery on his way to the Eastern front; he was one of the first to describe the Confederate battle flags, which he described as quite worn and tattered when compared to the captured Yankee ones. Fremantle arrived in Virginia in time to accompany the Army of Northern Virginia on its way north. At times when reading Fremantle's diary, one is led to ask: Can one person really have met so many people in so short a time? His record is backed by enough corroborative evidence, however, that the historian gives Fremantle full credit for most of his observations.

What was Lee's plan?

Lee was much better at improvising than at designing a grand strategy, but we cannot lay all the blame on this propensity. The need for food and supplies was so great that the entire Army of Northern Virginia could not march together; it had to march by separate army corps. Then, too, Lee did not often confide all his plans, even to his top generals. On the whole, however, his plan seems to have been simple. He intended to relieve Northern Virginia of the task of supplying his army, if just for a short time, and to march north in order to compel General Joseph Hooker to fight him. One major victory on Northern soil might do the trick, Lee thought.

If Lee's subordinates were concerned, they did not express those concerns, not yet. Everyone agreed that the time was more propitious than any other. The Federals were still reeling from their defeat at Chancellorsville, and the morale of the Confederates was correspondingly high.

What was the role of J. E. B. Stuart?

As ever, Stuart's role was to shadow the Confederate march and to keep the North in the dark, so far as Lee's movements were concerned. Lee had the utmost confidence in Stuart, a feeling shared by many, if not most, of the commanders. But a series of events, accidents almost, conspired to make Stuart less than his best on this occasion.

What was Stuart's standing at the beginning of June 1863?

It was at an all-time high. Over the past two years, Stuart had risen from lieutenant-colonel to major-general, and he was now the commander of all the cavalry on the Eastern front. There were those who criticized Stuart, on occasion, claiming he was too flamboyant, but everyone knew that Stuart had General Lee's trust, and that was enough for them. Stuart was feted on June 8, 1863, when hundreds of locals showed up to give parties for his men. At one point, a woman placed a laurel wreath around the neck of Stuart's horse, and Lee—who was standing nearby—jokingly warned Stuart, saying that Northern women had done the same for General Pope's horse just before the Second Battle of Bull Run.

Who was Stuart's number-one foe?

Thirty-eight-year-old Alfred Pleasonton was a cavalry officer who was much praised for his actions at the Battle of Chancellorsville. Joe Hooker even wrote to Lincoln, saying that Pleasonton had saved the Army of the Potomac during that battle. Promoted to major-general, Pleasonton was in command of most of the Army of the Potomac's cavalry arm, and he relished the opportunity to go after J. E. B. Stuart.

To this point in the war, Stuart's Confederate cavalry had gone unequalled. No other officer, North or South, it was said, could have ridden around an entire enemy army as Stuart had done during the Seven Days' Battles. Pleasonton wanted to take the starch out of Stuart's cavalry, and he resolved on a surprise attack. Stuart had no idea that the Federals were coming; they surprised him just one day after the locals feted him for earlier performances.

What was the Battle of Brandy Station?

Fought on June 9, 1863, it was the largest cavalry clash ever seen in North America. Pleasonton and about 11,000 federal cavalry completely surprised J. E. B. Stuart and a roughly equal number of Confederates. When the federal attack began, the Confederates were in disarray: some had no more than three minutes in which to mount up and ride off.

Though it was fought between cavalrymen, Brandy Station was an intriguing mix of fighting on horseback and fighting on foot. The Federals, most especially, were anxious to puncture Stuart's reputation, and they attacked time and again. Stuart recovered, but just barely, and the losses on both sides were about equal, in the neighborhood of six hundred men killed, wounded, or missing.

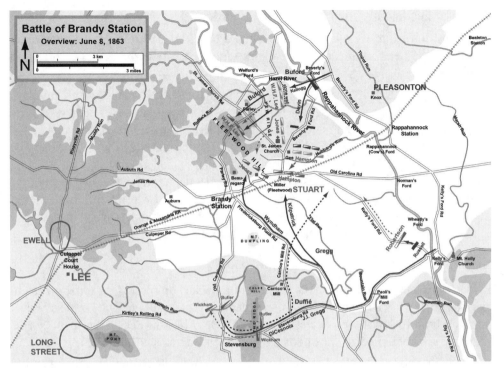

Troop positions during the Battle of Brandy Station on June 9, 1863. This was the single largest cavalry engagement ever seen on the North American continent.

In the short run, the attacks did not seem that important. Stuart was still ready to ride off as Lee's cavalry commander. But the Battle of Brandy Station did some harm to Stuart while doing great things for the Union cavalry arm. Up to that time, the Northern cavalry had been something of the joke of the Army of the Potomac. No more. Not only did Pleasonton do a number on J. E. B. Stuart, but the Battle of Brandy Station also saw the rise of a new, very young commander: George Armstrong Custer.

What had Custer achieved to this point in the war?

Born in Ohio in 1839, Custer was the son of farmers. He entered West Point in 1857 and graduated just as the Civil War began. Though he was outstanding at the military academy in terms of the combat arts, he graduated last, dead last, in the class of thirty-four cadets. He was commissioned in time to participate in the First Battle of Bull Run, and he then served as aide to General George McClellan. It was General Alfred Pleasonton, however, who really saw Custer's potential, and it was thanks to him that Custer became, in June 1863, the youngest brigadier-general in the Union Army.

Like J. E. B. Stuart—to whom he was naturally compared—George A. Custer was a natural leader of men. Handsome, fearless, and gifted with a marvelous tactical sense, he was a superb cavalry officer. By late June of 1863, Custer was on the rise, and woe to those who did not recognize the fact.

When did Lee and his army begin moving northward?

The Army of Northern Virginia began moving around June 18, 1863, but it did not all move at once. Lee had divided the army into four separate corps, each of which had tasks specific to it.

General Richard S. Ewell (1817–1872) commanded the Second Corps, much of which had previously been under the leadership of Stonewall Jackson. There were those who said no one could ever replace Stonewall, but Ewell came as close as anyone could. Known as "Old Bald Head" to his men, Ewell was missing a leg (he had been badly wounded at the Second Battle of Bull Run). Ewell had a wooden substitute, and he generally rode in a wagon, but he was as fierce a commander as any man could desire. The First Corps was commanded by James Longstreet, Lee's "Old War Horse." Ewell moved into Maryland, then Pennsylvania, well in advance of the rest of the army: his task was to forage, and, where possible, seize supplies from the enemy.

How did the North respond to Lee's invasion?

People were calm at first, but as the Confederates picked up speed, that spirit turned to alarm. The *New York Times*, for example, began with the headline "The Proposed Rebel Raid" on June 10, but it soon changed to "INVASION: The New Rebel Movement Northward," which contained an enormous map of Maryland and southern Pennsylvania.

Lee's invasion of Maryland, in September 1862, was well remembered, but he moved much more quickly this time. General Ewell's corps was in southern Pennsylvania by June 25. Because J. E. B. Stuart's men cut a telegraph line, official Washington, D.C., went more than twenty-four hours without any news, and by the last few days of June, the capital was in a state of near-panic.

How much food and supplies did the Confederates seize?

To the Confederates, almost anything was better than nothing. Lee issued very specific orders that everything was to be paid for, albeit in Confederate paper money, which was worthless in the Northern states. But there was one item that the Southern men seldom paid for: they were so desperate for hats that they would steal them from almost anyone's head.

The fierce summer sunlight beat down on the Confederate soldiers, making the need for hats more intense than usual, and the hard macadam turnpikes of southern Pennsylvania were murder on their bare feet. Just how many men of Lee's army were barefoot is not known, but it was certainly more than ten percent, and even those who possessed shoes saw that they were on the verge of giving out. Seldom has so successful an army gotten by with such tiny means.

What did Lincoln think of the rebel invasion?

Lincoln was, by now, the commander-in-chief in virtually all ways, but he still had never found a commanding general in whom he could rely. McDowell had been cashiered in

1861; McClellan had been a huge disappointment; Burnside had, in some ways, been even worse; and now Joe Hooker seemed unequal to the task.

Hooker proposed that while Lee went north, he could go south and seize Richmond practically unopposed, but Lincoln and Secretary of War Stanton would have none of that. Hooker therefore began pulling the Army of the Potomac over the river of that name, and in pursuit of Lee's force, but his heart was not in it, as almost anyone could tell. Therefore, on June 28, 1863, Lincoln accepted Hooker's offer to resign. But that begged the question: who would succeed him?

General George B. Meade successfully led the Army of the Potomac against General Robert E. Lee.

Who was General George B. Meade?

Meade was a little unusual in the Union Army in that he was born overseas. His father was serving as a merchant in Cádiz, Spain, when his son was born there in 1815. Meade was thoroughly American, however. He went to West Point, where he graduated in the middle of the class of 1838 and went on to a career in the Army Corps of Topographical Engineers (it was there that he met Robert E. Lee).

Meade had risen rapidly in the Army of the Potomac, but he had no outstanding success of which to boast; rather, one could say that he had not committed any untoward mistakes. Meade had been second or third in command for some time, and it came as a rude shock when he was awakened, on the night of June 28, and told that he was now the leader of the Army of the Potomac. His first response was that the command should go to Major-General John Reynolds, a good friend of his, and a man much loved by the soldiers. But there was nothing for it: he had suddenly become the commander.

What Confederate connections did George Meade possess?

That no one made a fuss over them indicates the extent to which the country was truly divided. George Meade's sister-in-law was married to none other than General Henry Wise, who, in 1859, had led the effort to have John Brown hanged. Even closer to home was that George Meade's younger sister had married a Confederate planter and moved with him to the Vicksburg area. In June 1863, perhaps before she was even aware that her brother had become commander of the Army of the Potomac, Elizabeth Meade wrote him a letter lamenting over what the Union men, led by General John McClernand, had done to her family home.

215

How important were shoes?

It is hard to overstate the importance of shoes to the Confederate soldiers, who suffered as their bare feet hit the macadam highways of the North. The Confederates, also, were impressed, even awed, by the relative prosperity of southern Pennsylvania. Here was a society that possessed no slaves, yet where all the work seemed to get done. Numerous Confederates admitted they had never seen such fine-looking houses and barns as those they passed.

The shoes reared their head on June 30, 1863, when Major-General Henry Heth, of the Confederate forces saw an advertisement for fine shoes and boots from a Gettysburg store. That afternoon, Brigadier-General James Johnston Pettigrew set out with a few hundred men to investigate; as they came close to Gettysburg, along the Chambersburg Pike, they saw their first Federals. These were just a few companies of blue-coated cavalry, but Pettigrew followed his instructions—which came from Lee—to the letter. No engagement was to be entered until the Army of Northern Virginia had consolidated. Pulling back to Cashtown General Pettigrew was scolded a little by General Heth for his timidity, whereupon Heth decided to take his division of Confederates to Gettysburg the following day.

Which side was more in doubt as to the other's location?

It was a tie. Never, at least on the Eastern front, had there been such confusion as to which army, or section of an army, was in which location. By the time Meade received his new orders, the Army of the Potomac was hastening northward from Maryland, attempting to converge to protect Baltimore from a possible attack. Lee and the Army of Northern Virginia, on the other hand, were scrambling to converge at a location in southern Pennsylvania. Part of this confusion was caused by the normal misfortunes of war, but if there was one person who could be blamed, it was J. E. B. Stuart.

Stuart had not recovered from the Battle of Brandy Station. Never before had he been surprised by the enemy to that degree, and never had one of his fights been so desperate. Given a nasty shock, Stuart took longer than expected to cross the Potomac, and when he did, he led his men on an overly ambitious ride toward Washington before making a sharp left-hand turn for the north. Stuart, clearly, wished to exorcise his near-defeat at Brandy Station, but the result was that he went so far as to deprive Lee of his eyes and ears.

Why was everyone—Union and Confederate—converging on the little town of Gettysburg?

The long and involved answer is "roads," but the short and simple one is "shoes." Both answers help to explain why Gettysburg would soon become a household name throughout America.

Gettysburg was a long-settled place, but it had never exceeded more than 3,000 souls. It had two institutes of higher learning—the Lutheran Theological Seminary and Pennsylvania College—but its main importance, even before the war, was the way different road systems converged on the town: the Chambersburg Turnpike came from the northwest, the Harrisburg Turnpike from the northeast, and the Emmitsburg Road from the southwest. Anyone examining a good map of the surrounding area could see that Gettysburg was bound to be important; even so, very few guessed just *how* important.

How close—or far—were the opposing armies?

As the sun went down on June 30, 1863, the opposing Confederates and Federals were all within a radius of forty miles: very close by our modern standards, but relatively far by theirs. J. E. B. Stuart's cavalry, for instance, was only fourteen miles off from Robert E. Lee, but given that neither man knew the other's whereabouts, it was almost as if one were in Virginia and the other in Maryland. In this muddled state of affairs, the Union leaders were generally better off because they knew the landscape better and because their forces were moving from south to north. The Confederates, on the other hand, were in areas they had seldom, if ever, seen before, and they were converging from three different points of the compass, headed toward their assemblage.

The Battle of Gettysburg is one of the most well-known conflicts in American history. A museum at Gettysburg is a popular tourist attraction, and hundreds of reenactors like those shown here relive those tragic days in remembrance of those who fell on both sides.

Did anyone really know that it would all unfold at Gettysburg?

No. There were members of Lee's staff who pointed to the place on the map, saying that it was one of great value, but virtually no one predicted that the two great armies would converge on one point. The geographic convergence began at around 7 A.M. on Wednesday, the first of July, 1863.

General Henry Heth's Confederates were on the road early, attempting to beat the heat of the noonday sun. They came to the outskirts of Gettysburg by 7 A.M. and ran straight into three thousand federal cavalrymen, led by Colonel John Buford. The first shots were exchanged shortly after the sun rose, and the Federals took cover behind a row of picket fences and low hills. Colonel Buford found the cupola of the Lutheran Theological Seminary an excellent observation point, and he noted with some satisfaction that the Confederates did not realize they were in for a real fight: the rebels were marching as if this were to be an easy skirmish, followed by an occupation of the town.

GETTYSBURG: THE FIRST DAY

What was different about Buford's men?

The Confederates had encountered plenty of Union cavalry in the past, but Buford's men were a little different. Their commander was a believer in the new style, which meant cavalrymen fighting on foot. Buford saw horses as a fine way to get from one point to another, but once a fight began, his men knew that every fourth one would become the holder of horses for the other three, who would fight dismounted, using their Spencer carbines. These seven-shot rifles were far superior to what the Confederates at Gettysburg possessed, and in the opening minutes of the day's battle, Buford's cavalrymen more than held their own. Buford realized this would not long remain the case, though, and he sent off urgent messages to Major-General John Reynolds, who promptly relayed them to other commanders. Within two hours of the first shots being fired, scores of thousands of men were on the march from all points of the compass, virtually all of them headed for Gettysburg.

Why did Buford not yield the town?

Buford had arrived the evening before and immediately perceived the great defensive potential of the area. The town itself did not interest him that much; rather, he was struck by the low range of hills that ran from its southern side. Like most other officers of the Army of the Potomac, Buford had been appalled—time and again—at the ease with which the Confederates had seized the high ground—the better location—and used it to their advantage. Here, he saw at once, was a possibility to turn the tables.

Buford's men fought fiercely, but they soon felt the pressure from Heth's entire division. Behind Heth were many other Confederates, their way temporarily blocked by the presence of their fellows. At about 9 A.M., Buford was joined in the cupola by Major-General John Reynolds, whose seasoned eye quickly took in the situation. Concurring with Buford, Reynolds told him to fight the Confederates as long as he could so that the Union forces on the march could occupy the hills south of the town. Minutes later, Reynolds was dead, killed by a Confederate sharpshooter (no one ever emerged to claim he was the man).

Where were Lee and his staff?

They were several miles to the northwest, but they heard the crack of rifle fire and galloped forward at once. Lee's plan was not to be pulled into any engagement on this day, and as he rode, the Confederate general lamented that some of his men—which, he was not certain—had been drawn into one. Lee did not yet realize that events were spinning out of his control, and that of his opponent George Meade as well. Subordinate commanders on both sides had chosen the battlefield, and the commanding generals would have to adjust.

John Reynolds was dead, but Buford's cavalrymen were still holding on, just barely, when the Iron Brigade arrived on the northwest side of the town. Composed of men from Minnesota and Wisconsin, the Iron Brigade was, quite possibly, the toughest unit in the Union Army. Its men wore their black hats in a distinctive style, and they were known for their absolute doggedness in a fight.

Who did the Iron Brigade run into?

General James Archer was leading a crack unit from Alabama, but his men recoiled from the first hit by the Iron Brigade. Tradition has it that the Confederates yelled to each other: "There's them black-hatted fellars again!"

Though logic dictated the Iron Brigade fight on the defensive, the opportunity was too good to pass up, and the Western men attacked the Confederates, capturing several hundred of them, including General Archer himself. This was a potential turning point in the battle, a moment when the Union might have seized and held all the ridges running to the west of the town, but just at that moment, the Northern men on the north side of town were hit by General Ewell's Confederates, coming south from the Harrisburg area. As the Union line recoiled, the Iron Brigade had to resume a defensive stance.

General James Archer commanded a unit from Alabama during the Battle of Gettysburg. He was captured by the Iron Brigade, the first general from Lee's army to be caught by Union forces.

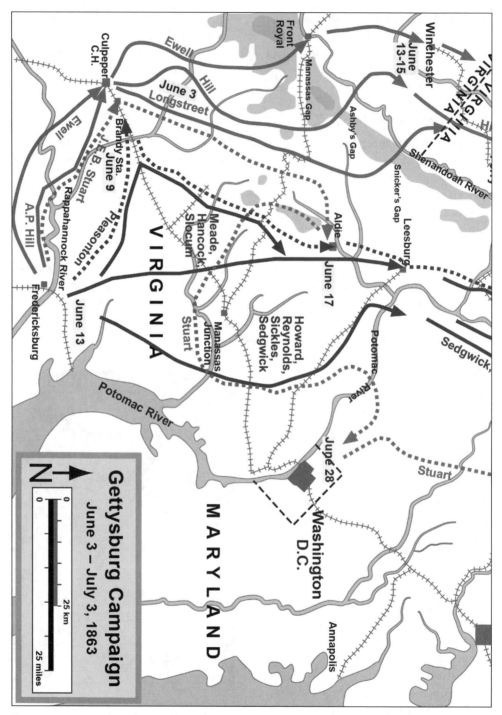

Troop movements are shown here as the North and South converged on Gettysburg, Pennsylvania.

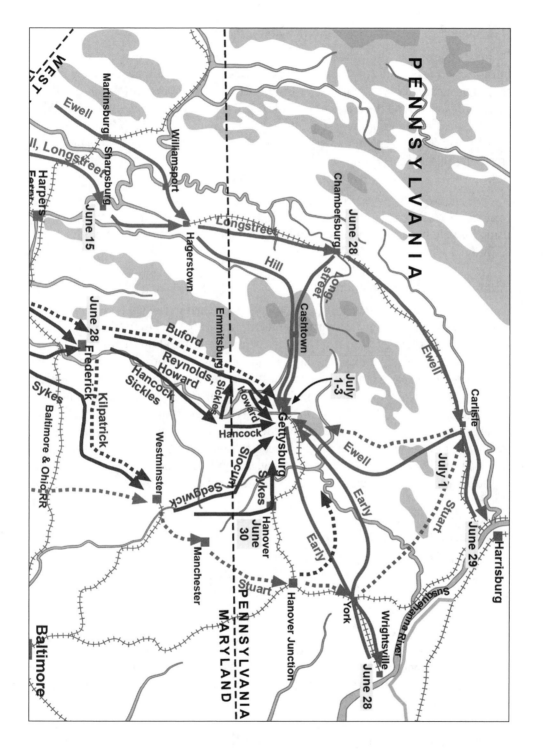

How many Confederates were in the neighborhood?

By noon, there were almost forty thousand Confederates within two miles of Gettysburg—all on the north, northeast, and northwest sides—and their numbers looked nothing short of overwhelming. At that moment, there were perhaps 25,000 Northern soldiers in and around the town, and it looked as if they would soon be pulverized. What this early calculation does not take into account was that the Union had more men, about thirty-five percent more, within a range of thirty miles, and that distance was shrinking all the time. Though the Confederates did not fully realize it, they had a very narrow "window" of time in which to take the town and surrounding location.

Lee and his staff arrived from the northwest at about 1 P.M. Snapping that he was not ready for a major battle on this day, Lee took ten minutes to examine the situation, using his field glasses. What he saw both appalled him and tantalized him with its possibilities.

What did Lee see? What did he decide?

As his field glasses swept the area, Lee saw his own men in ragged and disorganized fashion swarming over the northern and northwestern approaches to the town. He saw that the Federals were fighting with much greater determination than usual, and his perceptive eyes quickly took in the importance of the hills south of the town. Just for a moment—perhaps as long as two minutes—Lee considered breaking off the action. His men would take some convincing, he knew, but he could pull them back and fight on another day, when all his forces were "up." At that very moment, however, Lee saw something else. His eyes took in that the federal defenders north of the town, those facing General Ewell, were on the verge of breaking and that the entire Union line *might* soon cave in. These were the moments he had always seized, and Gettysburg was no exception. Overriding his own concerns, Lee ordered an all-out assault by every unit on the field.

Was Lee "right" to this point?

Yes. A commander who is perennially outnumbered, and who has to take long chances, becomes accustomed to doing so. Lee was technically correct, and the events of the next two hours appeared to verify his trust in his men.

What happened to the Iron Brigade?

When it finally fell back, in the direction of the town, the Iron Brigade had lost 1,200 men killed, wounded, or missing out of about 1,800 who entered the contest. As severe as this was, there were some Confederate units that suffered even more. One company of Confederates was completely wiped out: of the ninety-odd men who entered the fight, not one survived.

Practically everyone involved was shocked by the intensity of the fighting. This was not another Chancellorsville, still less another Fredericksburg. Men on both sides were

Artist Alfred Rudolph Waud created this depiction of the beloved General John Fulton Reynolds being shot to death as he leads the Iron Brigade during the Battle of Gettysburg.

fighting with everything they had, and there was hardly a unit that did not perform heroically in some capacity. Majors, colonels, and even brigadier-generals were falling at the same rate as enlisted men.

What was the situation at 5 P.M.?

It had been a desperate day, filled with all sorts of disasters, but by 5 p.m. the Confederates could justly claim a narrow victory. At the loss of many lives, they had caved in the Yankee defenses and were about to enter the town. On another battlefield, another type of terrain, this would have been sufficient. But given the range of low hills just south of the town, the logistics were turned on their head: the town mattered much less than did the hills. Realizing this, Lee sent an order to General Ewell, commanding the extreme Confederate left, to attack the Union defenders on Cemetery Hill (they had just gotten there and were pausing to catch their breath). Three hours of daylight remained, and one more push would ensure a major victory.

Why did Ewell fail to attack?

Almost an hour passed, during which chaos reigned in the town of Gettysburg, and the Confederates swarmed over the positions to its west. Nothing was happening to the east, however, and, worried, Lee rode over to see what was the matter.

Most accounts agree that Ewell and his division commanders had no more stomach for fight that day. This was unusual, given that the Second Corps had long been Lee's most important striking force. He found General Ewell resting in an armchair, apparently in a minor form of daze (it could have been brought about by sunstroke, as well as the possibility of what World War I and World War II soldiers called "shell shock"). Lee had committed one very large error: when sending his order to Ewell to attack, he had added the words "if practicable." Ewell clearly did not find it so, and Lee soon discovered that Ewell's men had no more punch left in them. Even so, he asked if they could attack at daylight. The disconcerting answer was that they had done all they could: the next day's attack should come at the other (southwestern) end of the line.

Who was now the federal commander on the field?

By 6 P.M., when Lee rode over to confer with Ewell, federal command had fallen to Major-General Winfield Scott Hancock (1824–1886). The thirty-nine-year-old West Point graduate was one of the most solid and underrated officers in the Union Army: he was also named for War of 1812 hero Winfield Scott. Hancock made the final arrangements before the sun went down on July 1, 1863, and he was satisfied that—all things considered—the Union had done quite well that day. The Confederates might have inflicted more casualties—actually it was almost a draw—and grabbed some territory, but the Union men were in by far the better position, topographically speaking.

Hancock remained in charge until General George Meade arrived late that night. Much like Robert E. Lee, George Meade had no choice: he had been pulled into a fight he had not chosen. The more he spoke with his aides and subordinates, however, the more Meade was persuaded that Gettysburg was as good a place to fight as the Union was likely to find.

What was that night like?

It was eerie. The moon was nearly full, and the Union men on Cemetery Hill had an excellent view into the fields where the Confederates were encamped. The cries of the wounded were heard by both sides, and there were men trapped in no man's land who could not be extricated. The town of Gettysburg was in shambles, with federal soldiers hiding in cellars, attics, and even pigsties while the Confederates had the run of the streets. There had been eerie nights before—one thinks of the night after the Battle of Shiloh—but the heat and humidity, which remained most of the night, added to the stillness and the sense of impending death. Quite a few men deserted that night. On the other hand, there was a hero who endured all the worst that that night could offer.

Who was John Burns?

His story is so incredible that we tend to doubt it on the first hearing, but it was verified enough times—by the man in question and his neighbors—that we have to take it as true. John Burns had lived in Gettysburg a long time—he was seventy—but he had grown up in New Jersey. After a short spell as a militiaman during the War of 1812—the only time he was ever properly measured, he claimed—Burns wandered for a number of years before settling in Gettysburg, where he married and raised a family. Even so, he had to win his fight with the bottle before winning respectability: once that was accomplished, he served for several years as a constable. Sometime on the afternoon of July 1, 1863, Burns saw a member of one of the Union regiments leave his musket, and seized by a sudden inspiration, he stole it and tagged along with the younger men. He must have made quite a sight, the old man with the youths, but his sharp shooting skills were soon made apparent, and the colonel of the regiment handed him a rifle and told him to make good use of it. Burns was in the midst of doing so when a panic seized the regiment, and in its quick retreat he was both wounded and cut off. He lay on the field that night, wounded in no fewer than four places!

What was the rest of Burns' life like?

On the morning of July 2, 1863, Burns crawled to the home of a neighbor, which was being used by the Confederates as a temporary hospital. His neighbor helped him get some medical attention but then brought him to his own home, which was also being used to treat the wounded. There John Burns lay, on his own bed, wounded in four places, but determined to get well. And so he did.

Disbelieving the story, a *Harper's Weekly* columnist went to Gettysburg a few months later and wound up being given a tour of the battlefield by none other than John Burns. He was, quite possibly, the only person to have served in both the War of 1812 and the Civil War; beyond that, his actions on the first of July 1863 seem almost superhuman. Many photographs were taken of the "old hero" in the months and years that followed; most of them showed him holding out his wounded leg, with his crutches by his side.

GETTYSBURG: THE SECOND DAY

When was Lee awake? What did he decide?

Lee was awake by 3:30, and he had his first view of the federal position by 5:00. What he saw should have dismayed him, but it did not.

Lee had, by this time in his career, trapped or enticed the Federals on several occasions. He had often seized the superior ground and lured his foe into attacking him, usually with disastrous results. This time, Lee did not fully recognize that it was he and the Confederates who were standing on the "low" ground, looking up at formidable natural defenses. He heard the clank of shovels and knew that the Union men were entrenching, but even this did not deter him. Therefore, when he met General Longstreet at breakfast, Lee declared his intention to hit the enemy hard.

How close were Lee and Longstreet? What did they decide on July 2, 1863?

Lee and Longstreet were never as close as Lee and Jackson had been; theirs was closer to a relationship between peers. The British observer Colonel Arthur Fremantle commented that the relationship between Lee and his "Old War Horse" Longstreet was touching, that they clearly enjoyed one another's presence. There was a difference between them where tactics were concerned, however, and it reared its head on July 2. Longstreet could practically feel his chief's impatience, but he felt he had to make an attempt to dissuade him. The previous day's fight had been brilliantly successful, Longstreet declared, and now the opportunity had presented itself for the Confederates to swing well around the federal left and take up a defensive position in their rear. Because they would be between the Federals and Washington, D.C., Meade would be forced to attack. On most occasions, Lee might have listened. His blood was clearly up, however, and he cut Longstreet off, saying that the enemy was "there" (he pointed to the ridge of hills) and he intended to strike them.

How many Federals were now in position?

They had been arriving all night, and there were at least seventy thousand men, drawn up in a defensive position that has often been likened to a fishhook. The barb of the fishhook was on Culp's Hill, at the southeast side of the town. From there, the fishhook made an extreme left-hand turn at Cemetery Hill and made a two-mile run through the range of hills, culminating at the two hills, Little Round Top and Big Round Top.

George Meade was clearly in charge, but the most experienced battlefield commander on the scene was Major-General Winfield Scott Hancock. The least experienced federal commander was Daniel Sickles (1819–1914), a former New York City congressman, who commanded the Third Corps. Sickles made one of the earliest, and potentially fatal, decisions of the day when he asked permission to move his corps from Seminary Ridge to another line, almost a mile to the east. Meade refused at first, but he did not make his order one hundred percent certain, and Sickles—like General Ewell the night before—made a decision on his own.

How far out did Sickles move his men?

Acting on the belief that he could, as corps commander, adjust his position, General Sickles moved his men a full mile farther out. Any experienced commander could see that this was a dangerous, and potentially disastrous, move because Sickles' left flank was hanging "in the air." Practically no one took notice of it, however, because the Confederate assault began at around this same time.

General John Bell Hood, whose Texans were part of Longstreet's corps, started their attack around 3 P.M. Longstreet dreaded the result, knowing that Hood's men were moving uphill against Union troops hidden behind boulders, but Hood showed no hesitation. Half an hour later, he was out of the battle, with a wound to his right arm. The Texans continued the attack, however, and the fight in front of Devil's Den became a true melee, with little to no command or control.

How on earth could the Federals have left no units on Big Round Top?

It is, truly, extraordinary. The only answer that can be guessed at is that in the confusion and haste, someone may have mislaid an order. But there was Big Round Top, with

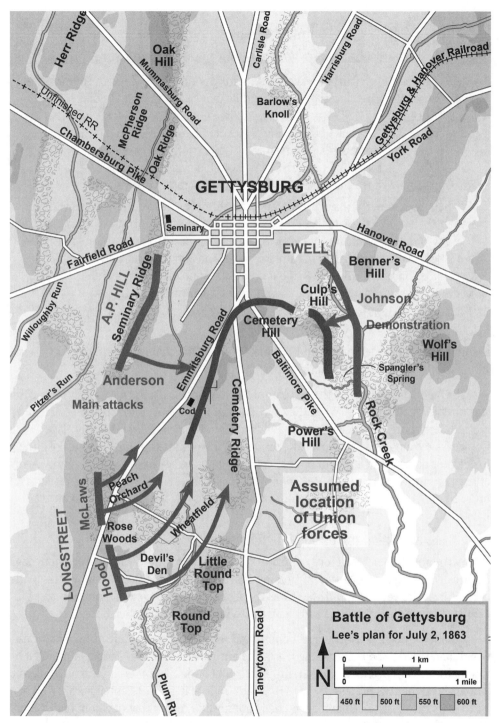

Herr Ridge

Oak
Hill

Carlisle Road

Harrisburg Road

Gettysburg & Hanover Railroad

Unfinished RR

Mummasburg Road

McPherson
Ridge

Barlow's
Knoll

Oak Ridge

Chambersburg Pike

York Road

GETTYSBURG

Seminary

Hanover Road

Fairfield Road

EWELL

Benner's
Hill

A.P. HILL
Seminary Ridge

Johnson

Willoughby Run

Culp's
Hill

Cemetery
Hill

Demonstration

Wolf's
Hill

Pitzer's Run

Emmitsburg Road

Anderson

Spangler's
Spring

Main attacks

Codori

Cemetery Ridge

Power's
Hill

Baltimore Pike

Rock Creek

**Assumed
location
of Union
forces**

Peach
Orchard

McLaws

Wheatfield

Rose
Woods

LONGSTREET

Hood

Devil's
Den

Little
Round
Top

Taneytown Road

Round
Top

Plum Run

Battle of Gettysburg
Lee's plan for July 2, 1863

0   1 km

N   0   1 mile

450 ft   500 ft   550 ft   600 ft

This map shows the various Confederate attacks made on the Union positions on July 2, 1863, a day when the
South came very close to success.

227

How could so many officers do more, or less, than what their commanding generals required?

No simple answer exists to this question: part of it has to do with the vagaries of human nature. One part of the trouble, however, lay with the difference between officers of the U.S. Regular Army—those commissioned before the war commenced—and the officers of the various volunteer regiments. Given that they were often elected by their men, volunteer army officers often showed an independent streak. This difference did not exist in the Confederate ranks, however, and cannot be used to excuse General Ewell's lack in following Lee's order.

There was something special about Gettysburg, however, and the answer to it lies in the speed with which events unraveled. If under normal circumstances there was some dissension between commanding and subordinate officers, that tendency was exacerbated by the smoke, noise, and confusion at Gettysburg. There were times on that battlefield when it seemed as if no one was really in command, as if it were every man, company, or regiment for himself.

absolutely no Union defenders, and Colonel William Oates' Alabamians, part of General John Hood's division, were practically there.

The Alabamians sprinted the last part of the way, and at around 4 P.M., they gained the summit of Big Round Top. What they saw amazed them. Not only was the entire valley around Gettysburg engulfed in smoke and flame, but they had found the only place where Confederate cannon could be placed. Admittedly, it would take a huge amount of energy to get guns atop that height, but once there, they could wreck havoc with the entire Army of the Potomac. Just minutes after coming to that realization, Colonel Oates received an order to move to Little Round Top, four hundred yards off. His protest was to no avail.

Were there any Union troops on Little Round Top?

At that moment there were only a group of signal-corps men, who waved their flags frantically, trying to create the impression there were more of them than was truly the case. But in the very nick of time, from the federal point of view, Colonel Strong Vincent rushed a group of his men from Maine to Little Round Top.

Colonel Vincent was in overall command, but the extreme left of his position—which happened to be the extreme left of the entire federal army—was commanded by Colonel Joshua Lawrence Chamberlain. Also from Maine, Chamberlain was an academic who had resigned his professorship at Bowdoin College in order to enter the army. When he took up his position, Chamberlain had roughly 260 men, most of whom had seventy rounds of ammunition. Given a five-minute respite, he prepared his men, explaining that the right wing of the rebel army was coming in their direction.

How many Chamberlain brothers were involved?

Joshua Lawrence Chamberlain commanded the regiment. His younger brother Thomas was a lieutenant, and still another brother, John Calhoun Chamberlain, was present as a volunteer for a Christian commission. There was a moment before the battle was completely joined when an artillery shell burst close by, and Colonel Chamberlain ordered his two brothers to stay far from him, adding that another shell like that could make it a "hard day for Mother."

Who were the men coming against Chamberlain and the 20th Maine?

Colonel William C. Oates led the 15th Alabama, which was coming straight for Chamberlain's men. The Alabamians were a crack outfit who had demonstrated their skill in numerous battles; they excelled at this kind of attack. But as they made their way up Little Round Top, they ran into rifle and musket fire that the oldest of veterans described as simply murderous.

What was the worst of it, from the Union point of view?

Chamberlain and his men had no way of knowing how the battle was going in other sectors. They only knew that they were the extreme left flank of Meade's entire army and that they had to hold Little Round Top. Given the many times the Confederates had succeeded in desperate attacks, over the previous two years, the Union men were shaky.

What was the worst of it, from the Confederate point of view?

They had already been fighting for two hours, and some of them were exhausted. They had taken Big Round Top with ease, then commands from above insisted they assault Little Round Top, which—in the overall scheme of things—was a tougher proposition. But the very worst thing was that as they charged up the hill, they were pounded by rifle fire from the sides. Colonel Oates remembered men being hit in the head by bullets from above, then in the stomach and legs by bullets from the side, or flank. But there was another factor involved: Oates, too, had a brother on the field.

John Oates had been sick for days before the battle, and no doubt he suffered even more than most of his fellows as they charged and attacked in the afternoon heat of July 3, 1863. After being wounded no fewer than five times, John Oates was captured by the Federals, and he died a few days later (his elder brother suffered from guilt for years afterward).

How many times did the Confederates charge?

To the best of our knowledge, Oates' Alabamians charged five times. Each attempt was more difficult and desperate than the preceding, partly because there were so many dead and wounded men in the way. Chamberlain's Maine soldiers, too, gained some confidence each time they repelled an assault. Even so, it would only have taken one success, one charge that carried the Confederates to the top, for the Union army to have been in severe straits.

229

Having repulsed five Confederate attempts, Chamberlain found that his men were out of ammunition. One more Confederate charge, and he would be overrun. Therefore, he drew up his men in an oblique column, and, pulling his sword, led them in a bayonet charge down the hill. The Confederates had been on the offensive all day long, and the sudden turnaround threw them into confusion. Exhaustion helped as well in repelling the last Confederate attempt.

The 1910 Pennsylvania Memorial is the largest of the many statues and other tributes erected at Gettysburg.

So the Union left held that afternoon? What about the Union center?

It had, by 6 P.M., been beaten to a pulp by Confederate attacks. General Sickles had been taken from the field with a wound that would cost him a leg. His men were in full retreat to Seminary Ridge. There was one moment when a group of Confederates appeared on the ridge, and—for once—had no opposition, but General Winfield Scott Hancock, who was the most ubiquitous person at Gettysburg, sent a regiment of Minnesota men in a desperate endeavor. The regiment lost seventy-five percent of its men, but they gained Hancock the five or ten minutes he needed to plug the gap.

How close had the Confederates come to success?

There were two, perhaps even three, times on July 2, 1863, when the Confederates were within view of complete success. The arrival of one or two of their regiments would have carried the day, and the Army of the Potomac would have suffered yet another injurious defeat. On each occasion, however, it was a Union regiment or brigade that appeared at just the right moment, and the federal positions held.

As night came on, Lee and his staff looked at the situation and found it painful. General Hood was out of combat; numerous other prominent leaders were down; and in the two days of battle the Confederates had already suffered twenty thousand men killed, wounded, or missing. This was the time, General Longstreet believed, that the Army of Northern Virginia must move away from Gettysburg to take up a defensive line. Lee would not hear of it, however.

What was that second night like?

It was much the same as the previous, though most observers claimed that it was noisier. The day's battle had removed some of the tension, among the Union men most notably, and there were many campfires burning that night. The Federals had gained in confidence simply by holding their positions, while the Confederates had lost something of their previous confidence.

No one—on either side—could be certain what the next day would bring. General Meade expected that the Confederates would attack, and he rightly guessed they would come for the Union center. General Lee could not be certain how many reinforcements the Army of the Potomac received overnight. Daylight of the third of July showed Lee as confident as ever, though.

GETTYSBURG: THE THIRD DAY

What was Lee's plan for the third day?

To Longstreet and a growing number of others, it was apparent that Lee should withdraw. To Lee, however, it was obvious that his men had failed only by the narrowest of margins, and that one more well-coordinated punch might well bring them to complete victory. Lee also had his eyes and ears back, because J. E. B. Stuart had returned on the previous afternoon.

When Stuart first came into Lee's presence, the latter raised his hand as if he might strike Stuart. Lee then upbraided Stuart, demanding to know how it was possible that he—the eyes and ears of the army—had been gone for a week. Stuart replied that he had enjoyed numerous successes and had brought 150 wagon loads of captured supplies, to which Lee replied, "Yes, but they are an impediment to me now." Within minutes, however, Lee brought back Stuart into the fold, saying, "Help me fight these people."

What did Lee and Stuart agree upon?

This is difficult to answer because Lee gave verbal orders that day, not written ones. Given the actions that Stuart undertook, however, we can surmise that Lee hoped for a double attack on the Union center, with Pickett's division attacking up the hill and Stuart's cavalry coming behind the federal defenders. If it worked, this would be a classic double envelopment, but it was riskier than those which Lee, Stuart, and others had studied while at West Point. Double envelopment—which dated to Classical times—was meant for one army to completely wrap itself around another, but given the disparity in numbers, there was no chance that could happen at Gettysburg.

What was the Union plan for the third day?

The previous evening, General George Meade had brought all his leading subordinates together and put the question to them. Every single person asked replied that it was best to stay where they were and let Lee make the next move. Meade went with this decision.

Who was most on the spot on July 3, 1863?

The honor has to go to Brigadier-General George Pickett (1825–1875), the leader of one of the divisions of Longstreet's First Corps. Like George A. Custer—whose star was rapidly ascending—George Pickett had graduated dead last in his West Point class. He was believed to be a very tough fighter, though, and, like Custer, he made the most of his physical appearance. Both men wore earrings, elegant hats, and wildly colored clothing.

By the morning of July 3, Pickett knew that General Lee expected him and his Virginians to attack the very center of the Union line and break it.

This assignment was a very tall order, not least because the Confederates would have to advance across slightly more than a mile of wide-open countryside. This was, in fact, the type of attack that Lee had so many times suckered his federal opponents into making, but on this day he was adamant.

What was Longstreet's reaction?

When Lee informed him, Longstreet replied that in his opinion, there was no body of 15,000 men—regardless of nation or ethnicity—that could cross that open field and take the center of the Union position. Lee answered that this was Longstreet's task, and he expected him to make it possible.

About the only thing that promised a ghost of a chance was the plan for all the Confederate artillery to unleash a massive bombardment before the infantry assault. All the Confederate field guns were in position by noon. The Union men, meanwhile, were hunkered down in their defensive positions, waiting for some sign as to where the attack would fall (that it would come was not doubted).

Who were Pickett's brigade commanders?

They were as interesting and diverse a group as one could expect. James Kemper was a Virginia politician, a former leader in the House of Delegates, who had left politics for the battlefield. Not as experienced as some of his fellows, he more than made up for this by his aggressive attitude. Richard Garnett was a dashing figure who chose to lead his men from the front. On July 3, he was mounted on a fine black horse. His fellow officers begged him to dismount, but he insisted on leading from the exposed position. The most colorful of all was Brigadier-General Lewis A. "Lo" Armistead. The nephew of the man who had commanded Fort McHenry, in the harbor at Baltimore, against the British, leading to the writing of the "Star-Spangled Banner," Armistead had attended West Point and was a very good friend of Winfield Scott Hancock. Armistead knew that Hancock was on the other side; perhaps he did not know that Hancock actually commanded the Union center, where the Confederate blow would fall.

Possibly the most tragic event of the already brutal Gettysburg battle was Pickett's Charge, in which Major-General George Pickett was ordered by Lee to charge the Union's line under Meade over an open field. Pickett's commander, General Longstreet, correctly predicted the futility of the charge, which decimated the army and marked the end of the South's drive northward.

When did the artillery bombardment commence?

At 1:04 P.M., Colonel Edward Porter Alexander had seventy-five pieces of artillery trained on the Union guns on the heights of Seminary Ridge, and he walked among his gunners for the next hour, exhorting them to give their all. What he could not do—and what was frustrating in the extreme—was to ascertain how successful the bombardment was. Years later, as he penned his memoirs, Alexander claimed that General Longstreet attempted to place the responsibility with him, asking Alexander not to send General Pickett unless there was a sign of success. This kind of "battle of the memoirs" is especially difficult to resolve; about all we can say for certain is that a colonel would never have been made responsible for determining what a lieutenant-general should have ascertained.

At about 2:15, Alexander noticed a slackening in the Union counterfire, and he saw a battery of federal guns departing the area. This was hardly sufficient evidence on which to base a major decision, but the heat, the smoke, and the confusion may have played their part. Alexander scribbled a note to General Pickett: "For God's sake come quick. The eighteen guns are gone. Come quick or my ammunition will not let me support you properly."

Was it not Longstreet's decision and responsibility?

Beyond any doubt. Most accounts agree that when Pickett received Alexander's note, he went straight to Longstreet to ask whether he should commence the attack. Most accounts concur that Longstreet would not say "yes" or "no," but only nodded.

Pickett then galloped along the mile and a quarter line of his men, who, till now, had been sheltered in the woods. Whether he shouted "Up men, and to your posts," or something to that effect, is not very important: what matters is they knew the moment had come. As they rose to begin their march, Pickett's men found many of their fellows unable to join them. Quite a few had been killed or wounded during the counterbombardment, but others were simply too terrified to rise. They knew this was a desperate venture.

How long was Pickett's line?

Ten brigades were assembled. Edward Porter Alexander sketched them as follows:

Brockenbrough, Davis, McGowan, Archer, Garnett, Kemper
Lane, Scales, Armistead,
Wilcox.

Whether another type of formation, more compact, would have been more effective is difficult to say. By spreading the ten brigades over a larger section of ground, there was, perhaps, less chance of the Union scoring direct hits.

Off they marched, roughly 14,000 Confederates engaged in the single most desperate military venture of the war, perhaps even of the century.

Was there any chance this magnificent undertaking could have succeeded?

Only if the federal defenders had lost courage and left their posts. As long as the Union men were in position, they had every chance to stop this juggernaut and perhaps to destroy it in the process.

Pickett's men moved at regulation march, 110 paces per minute. No quick-step was allowed. Who was more frightened, or awed, by the moment is difficult to say. Not until the advent of the moving camera, and the filming of movies such as *Gettysburg*, could anyone examine the moment from the perspective of each side. In the moment, one was either a Confederate, launched on the one-mile march, or one was a federal, gazing down on the sublime, but also terrible, scene.

When did the Federals open fire?

When Pickett's men had advanced about three hundred yards. Every yard counted, so far as Pickett and his men were concerned, but the Federals wanted to be sure that every shot counted. When the Union defenders opened fire, they began with rifles, but soon these were rendered almost silent compared to the roar of cannon. The Union artillery had not been shut down; in fact, far from it.

How many Confederates fell with each cannon blast is hard to say, but statisticians and engineers who experiment with the guns from that period believe that between ten and fifteen went down with each significant artillery "hit." Gaps soon appeared in the Confederate lines, but Pickett's men closed them. The major exception was a regiment on the extreme Confederate left, which broke under the terrible punishment. Most of its men ran away.

How far had the Confederates come?

They passed the halfway point with most of their regiments and brigades still in formation, but they had only entered the worst part. Two-thirds of the way up the hill was the lone rail fence, standing out like a sore thumb. It did not run the entire length of the Confederate front, but it represented an additional hurdle to at least half of Pickett's men, who were forced to leap over, climb over, or crawl under it. Given the extreme heat and the weight of their packs, each one of Pickett's men may have lost thirty precious seconds in getting under or over the fence. Then, to many of their eyes, the way seemed open. But the Federals had saved the worst for last.

The Union cannon now roared more furiously than before, and, seeing an extension of the Confederate lines, some of the Federals executed a flanking maneuver so as to create an enfilading fire. The miracle is that any of the Confederates continued their march, if that was still the appropriate word.

What was the high-water mark of the Confederate effort?

Perhaps fifteen minutes after leaving the shelter of the woods, a group of Confederates were close enough that the stone wall grew larger in front of their eyes. At that moment, Brigadier-General Armistead took off his black hat, stuck it at the top of his sword, and shouted, "Who will follow me!" And with that he moved—still not running—toward the stone wall.

In a sublime moment—almost impossible to believe—Armistead reached and climbed over the stone wall. There were perhaps twenty men with him, and they began at once to turn around one of the heavy pieces of artillery to fire on the Federals. Victory *seemed* possible.

How long did that high-water mark moment last?

Perhaps sixty seconds. Perhaps even ninety seconds. But once it disappeared, it was gone forever.

The Federals came streaming from a higher, defensive position. Armistead went down with a fatal wound. Hundreds, then thousands, of Union men came from all directions, converging on the 300 Confederates who reached the high-water mark. The battle on the heights lasted perhaps

Brigadier-General Lewis Armistead bravely led a charge over a stone wall to briefly overwhelm Union soldiers. Soon after, he was fatally shot and the Confederates were driven back.

235

five minutes, and when it was over all the Confederates who came that far were either killed or captured. Those who had been two hundred steps behind them were now either killed, wounded, or on the run. Pickett's Charge started as perhaps the grandest sight ever seen on the North American continent; forty-five minutes later, it presented nothing other than a sight of ruin.

Who is our best observer for the aftermath of Pickett's Charge?

Colonel Arthur Fremantle had been close to the action on the second day of battle, but he unaccountably missed the dramatic moment as Pickett's men began their ascent. Arriving perhaps an hour later, he beheld nothing but the wreck of regiments, men drifting almost aimlessly. Not realizing what had transpired, he went straight to General Longstreet to say that it was all sublime: he would not have missed this for the world.

"The devil you wouldn't!" Longstreet replied. "I would like to have missed it very much; we've attacked and been repulsed: look there!" Despite Longstreet's quick outburst, Fremantle went on to say that the Confederate general could not have been calmer or more composed. He was readying his men for an expected counterattack. If Longstreet's behavior was magnificent, then Lee's was truly sublime. Time and again, Lee went right up to returning officers, saying, "Never mind, gentlemen, all this has been my fault—it is I who have lost this fight, and you must help me out of it in the best way you can." Other accounts echo Colonel Fremantle; they differ only in the number of words. Several, for example, have Lee simply saying, "This is all my fault."

Could the Federals have counterattacked and won an even greater victory?

Of course, in the sense that hindsight always suggests the best move. But the Union men were accustomed to being beaten; this feeling of victory would take some time to adjust to. Then, too, there was always the danger that a counterattack would turn the retreating rebels into lions. It made far more sense to do what they did: to remain on Cemetery Ridge and see what Lee would do next.

Where, meanwhile, was the Confederate cavalry?

J. E. B. Stuart was roundly criticized by his peers for having ill-served Lee's army in the days leading up to the Battle of Gettysburg, and he was determined to reverse the situation. On the morning of July 3, 1863, Lee gave him verbal orders to the effect of swinging around the federal position and driving off their cavalry. Stuart, typically, wished to do even more; he planned to drive off the Union horsemen, then attack the rear of the federal lines on Seminary Ridge. Had he done so, there was a chance, however slim, that Pickett's Charge would have succeeded. But Stuart, like Pickett, was undone on July 3.

It was the newly minted brigadier-general, George A. Custer, who fought Stuart to a standstill, then saw the Confederate horsemen ride off in defeat. Custer made much

What was the oddest or strangest incident that Colonel Fremantle recalled?

There were many strange and wondrous scenes during the three days of the Battle of Gettysburg, but when one reads Colonel Fremantle's book, one is most struck by his encounter with a black civilian and a Northern prisoner. Fremantle records that the black man was dressed in a magnificent blue uniform, and that the Union man was dressed in civilian clothing: clearly, they had exchanged their clothes. The black man was driving the other as a prisoner to the back of the lines, and when he was questioned by some of the white Confederate officers, he replied that the white men assigned to guard this prisoner had been lax, and he had taken it upon himself to set matters right. Fremantle records that it was impossible to exaggerate the scorn and contempt which the African American showed toward his white prisoner and concluded that the Confederacy would do well to use the blacks as soldiers wherever they could.

of the success in his victory dispatch, and he perhaps exaggerated on some of the details, but the most important point was solid and could not be contested. The Union cavalry had attained a new level of success and were now fully on par with their Confederate foes.

When did Lee make the decision to retreat?

On the night of July 3 to 4, 1863, Lee decided to retreat. His army had been badly mauled, and it was imperative to get back to Southern soil. Lee realized, however, that to retreat in the face of the enemy would be perilous; he therefore scheduled the beginning of the retreat for the night of July 4 to 5. The Confederates saw the pounding rain of the next day as good fortune in that the Yankees did not know of their departure.

What, meanwhile, had happened at Vicksburg?

Beginning on May 23, 1863, Vicksburg had been subjected to a terrible siege. Not only did Grant's army have far more cannon, they also showed no desire to conserve ammunition. On the contrary, they threw everything they had at Vicksburg every day and through much of each night.

Grant was supremely confident of the ultimate result, but even he was at times frustrated by the stubborn defense of the Confederate defenders. Later he learned that General John Pemberton had believed that General Joseph Johnston would come to his aid. Every few days, Pemberton sent out messengers—many of whom got through—asking Johnston when the relief would come. For long periods there was no reply, but when it finally came, Johnston announced he would make a demonstration against Grant on July 8.

Would that be in time?

Pemberton and his men were on the edge of outright starvation. Thousands of civilians were living in caves cut along the riverbank. The endless noise from Grant's cannon and the mortars of Admiral David Dixon Porter's fleet were driving people crazy. No, July 8 was not in time.

Pemberton, who had a defeatist streak, had all along planned to ask for terms on the Fourth of July. Knowing the importance of the national holiday, he expected it would lead Grant to offer better terms. But when he sent his first, tentative letter on July 3, Grant replied with typical swiftness.

Completely cut off and isolated in Vicksburg, General John Pemberton's men were literally starving and he had little choice but to surrender to Grant.

Surrender would have to be unconditional, he wrote. Even so, he and Pemberton agreed to meet outside the city.

What was that meeting like?

Grant, Pemberton, and one general officer from each army met under a tree, within sight of the city. Pemberton asked for terms, whereupon Grant declared that the only ones he could offer were those he had named in his letter: unconditional surrender, to be followed by respect for those who had fought so valiantly in the city's defense. Irritated, nearly enraged, Pemberton said he would break off the conference, and Grant, typically, shrugged. The two general officers that accompanied these commanders asked to be allowed to speak to one another, and in the next hour or so, they sketched out the detail of what would be the surrender of Vicksburg.

The Confederate defenders could stack their arms in the city so they would not be watched while engaged in that humiliating exercise. They would then march out of Vicksburg, on the afternoon of the Fourth of July, and one Union regiment would enter. Over the next few days, lists would be made, and the Confederates would be sent home on parole. These terms were the best that could be pried from the victorious Grant. In a telegraph to Washington, D.C., Grant signaled his intention to commence a hundred-gun bombardment if Vicksburg did not yield by the morning.

Could Pemberton have fought on? Might it have made any difference?

Pemberton is often accused of cowardice, but the charge is unfair. He was a good general, who had been completely outmaneuvered and then overpowered by a much better one. Just as important, by July 3, 1863, Grant and his men had assumed a complete moral superiority over the Confederate defenders, who had known nothing but defeat. It is hard to say how much carnage would have resulted from a continuation of the siege, but one can state, categorically, that the men in blue were going to win this time.

What do we know of conditions in Vicksburg just before the end of the siege?

When the Union men entered the ruined city, they quickly compiled stories of how horrific the siege had been, but the better, firsthand accounts come from Vicksburg's several newspapers. The city had six newspapers when the siege began, and several were still operating when it ended. To continue to print required all sorts of sacrifices and odd compromises, however.

What was the surrender scene like?

Early in the afternoon on the Fourth of July, roughly thirty thousand Confederate defenders stacked their arms in the city, then marched between Union lines on their way to temporary camps outside of Vicksburg. Most observers commented that there was no jeering, no taunting, that Grant's men behaved themselves with aplomb. Soon after their departure, Grant and his officers began to assess the size of their victory. Not only had they captured a city and thirty thousand men, but they had taken nearly two hundred pieces of artillery and a vast amount of ammunition. They had achieved the single greatest Union success of the war to date.

VERDICT OF THE NEWSPAPERS

What did the newspapers have to say?

Almost as one, the Northern newspapers hailed the twin victories of Gettysburg and Vicksburg. The *New York Times* put it thus:

> Without any premeditation or arrangement—without any thought of, or striving for dramatic effect—for even Gettysburg was too serious, and issues too terrible to be thus paltered with, the late anniversary of American Independence has been consecrated afresh by victories of Liberty and Union that must render it more than ever the Sabbath-day of American freedom.

The Southern newspapers did their best to sugarcoat the twin defeats, but they did not have to persuade the soldiers of Lee's army. The men of the Army of Northern Virginia remained convinced that the defeat of Pickett's Charge was an unfortunate occurrence, a setback along the way to victory.

How did Lee make his escape?

On the night of July 4–5, 1863, the Confederates began to evacuate the battlefield. There was a little wind, which helped to disguise the sounds of their wagons, but it still seems incredible that the Army of the Potomac did not notice their departure. One possibility

239

Any person looking at the war from a neutral point of view could see that the North would win. It was only a matter of time. On the third day of battle at Gettysburg alone, the South had lost *one-tenth of one percent of its entire white population*. These casualty lists could not be supported for long. But in order to make doubly, perhaps triply, sure of its eventual victory, the North chose at this time to deploy black soldiers in growing numbers.

There had been movements toward this end as early as March 1863, but the first significant use of black troops in the field came at the attack on Battery Wagner in South Carolina.

is that the Northern men were so eager, and anxious, to see the end of this battle that they simply ignored the Confederates leaving.

Had Meade sent the Army of the Potomac, which still numbered roughly 52,000 effectives, in pursuit, the chances are good that the Army of Northern Virginia would have, after putting up a good fight, simply surrendered. Each day that passed without a federal pursuit, however, allowed the Confederates to stiffen their backbone.

How did the local newspaper comment on the Battle of Gettysburg?

The Adams Sentinel and General Advertiser had not published during the battle, but it was back in action by July 7, 1863, when the editorial page gave thanks and praise for the town's deliverance.

"The fortnight past has developed from it [from suspense] a terrible, and yet glorious reality," the editorial asserted. The terrible reality was, of course, shown in the vast number of dead, most of whom had yet to be counted. But the glorious reality was revealed, the newspaper declared, "in the vindication of truth, the triumph of right, the victory achieved for Liberty, Justice, the Union and good government." The editorial ended with these stirring words: "instead of mourning and repining at our misfortunes let us Thank God and take courage."

How long did it take for Lee to make good his escape?

Lee and the Army of Northern Virginia were in peril until July 17–18, when they slipped over the Potomac. From then on, they were reasonably safe.

Lee initially wrote Jefferson Davis that he was not the least bit discouraged, but a week later he wrote again, this time offering to resign. He was too old for his post, and the Confederacy needed a younger commander, he said. Jefferson Davis quickly wrote back with his refusal. The country could not spare Lee, he said.

Had the center of the war ever shifted back to the Palmetto State?

The center had been in Virginia and the Trans-Mississippi West for a long time, but in the summer of 1863 there was a strong movement from the Union to capture Charleston, South Carolina. That was where the first ordinance of secession had been approved, and Charleston had long been the place of the most virulent anti-federal sentiment. To capture Charleston, and avenge the loss of Fort Sumter, was therefore a major desire on the part of the Union leaders.

In the spring and early summer of 1863, the Union Navy commenced furious bombardments against the numerous forts that protected the harbor at Charleston. By mid-July, the guns of the fleet had softened up the defenses to the point at which the Army leaders were willing to risk a land assault on the forts on the southeast side of the harbor.

When was the first significant and well-reported use of African American soldiers?

Perhaps it is only coincidence that the first well-known use of black soldiers came in the same week as the New York City draft riots, but there were many ardent abolitionists who believed that the synchronicity was more like the hand of God. On July 18, 1863, as the riots just began to subdue, the federal forces outside of Charleston made a major attempt to capture Battery Wagner.

By chance and error it is often called Fort Wagner, but it was really a battery of Confederate cannon pointed directly out to sea and positioned very near the southern end

The all-black 54th Massachusetts Volunteer Infantry Regiment, shown here in a painting commissioned by the U.S. government, performed heroically at Battery Wagner, where they led the charge against the Confederates.

of Charleston Harbor. As long as the Confederates held this position, they could hold off the largest of federal ships, even the ironclads, from the harbor.

What was the buildup, the anticipation, like?

A captain in the regiment later recorded his memory of the event:

"To the survivors," he wrote, "those moments upon the sand will be ever present. A fresh breeze was blowing. Away over the sea to the eastward, the heavy sea fog was gathering. The western sky was bright with the reflected rays of the sun which had set. Far-away thunder reverberated through the air, and mingled with the occasional boom of cannon."

Who led the assault on Battery Wagner?

Lieutenant-Colonel Robert Gould Shaw (1837–1863) was a Boston blueblood who had somewhat reluctantly taken command of the first all-black regiment of Union soldiers. Shaw had been quite surprised, however, by the skill and energy of his men, and by the time he led them across the sandy beach to attack Battery Wagner, they had his respect and admiration. The men had reached a narrow spot of beach 600 yards from the battery the night before; Shaw now led them in a gallant charge across the sand. They covered about half the distance, and were just beginning to believe that the battery had been silenced the day before, when an awesome barrage of cannon, rifles, and muskets simply shattered their ranks.

Lieutenant-Colonel Shaw never hesitated; neither did his men. Some of them, including Shaw, actually reached the battery and stood, just for a moment, on its parapet, before falling to Confederate rifle fire. The color bearer of the regiment was killed, and Sergeant William Carney seized the U.S. colors (the Massachusetts state flag had been captured) and held them, kneeling on the parapet for what seemed like hours. On his return to where the attack began, Carney, who would receive the Medal of Honor for his actions, declared to his fellows that the colors had never touched the ground. Shaw died, as did 246 of his men. Another 880 were wounded, and another 389 went missing, in one of the bloodiest single encounters of the entire war. The Confederate defenders lost thirty-six killed and 133 wounded.

What enabled the Confederates to hold on to Battery Wagner and the forts around Charleston?

Sheer ornery desperation. Day after day, the forts were pounded by relentless barrages by federal artillery, but the defenders held on. Jefferson Davis made a special trip to Charleston in the autumn of 1863 and gave his view that the city and its defenders would never give up, but that if they someday had to let go of Charleston, they should leave it a smoking ruin.

Very likely, this courageous desperation derived from the fact that South Carolina had been the first state to secede, in 1861. Even so, when one counts the odds against the city's defenders, one can only marvel at their willpower to continue the fight.

How was the news received?

As bad as the human losses were, abolitionists, from Frederick Douglass to Harriet Beecher Stowe, took great heart at the heroic performance of the black soldiers. Never again could it be said that the African Americans were a childlike people, easily led. Never again could it be maintained that they did not know how to use weapons of war. The attack on Battery Wagner was a turning point in the war.

From that point on, it became relatively easy to fill the ranks of black regiments, and their numbers grew rapidly.

When did Battery Wagner finally fall?

It took weeks of men literally crawling through the sand, establishing slightly more forward positions each day, to finally take the battery. On August 26, federal troops captured the Confederate rifle pits in front of the battery, and two days later they found the place abandoned.

The defense of Battery Wagner had served its purpose, buying time for the defenders to increase the strength of their positions. The battery also became famous, in the North, as the place where African American troops proved their valor. In the South, the black assault on Battery Wagner had just the opposite result. Many white Southerners who had previously entertained rather low expectations of the blacks as soldiers now declared they would give no quarter to any that they encountered.

THE FIGHT FOR TENNESSEE: JULY 1863 TO JANUARY 1864

Had the West not already been won?

In a sense it had. Following the surrender of Vicksburg, there was no chance that the Confederacy could win the war in the West, but it could use battles and skirmishes there to delay its eventual defeat. In one way, things were a bit easier for the Confederates. No longer having Vicksburg to defend, they could concentrate their forces in Tennessee to await an expected hammer blow from the Army of the Cumberland, led by General William Rosecrans.

The Confederates now had a shorter line to defend, and they also were not divided between two generals, as had been the case in the Vicksburg debacle. General Braxton Bragg, one of Jefferson Davis' favorite generals, led the Army of Tennessee, which steadily received reinforcements during the late summer. Even so, Bragg retreated, losing the all-important railroad town of Chattanooga in early September.

Bragg seems to be among the worst of the Confederate generals. Why did he keep his position for so long?

Bragg had plenty of personal courage and a rather good tactical sense. His two greatest difficulties were physical infirmities and an overwhelming pessimism, which prevented him from seizing opportunities. Beset by skin disease, blinding headaches, and other maladies, Bragg was seldom at his best, and even on those rare occasions, he could see more problems than possibilities in a situation. In this way, he was just about the polar opposite of Robert E. Lee.

Bragg had one thing going for him, however: the personal friendship of Jefferson Davis. Like Abraham Lincoln, Jefferson Davis was an exceedingly loyal person who never forgot a friend; unlike Lincoln, Jefferson Davis also never forgot a slight or insult.

Thanks to Davis' friendship, Bragg kept his position as commander of the Army of Tennessee. But his opposite number, General William Rosecrans (1819–1898), had troubles of his own.

How important was Rosecrans' Catholicism?

Rosecrans was the most visible Roman Catholic to be found in the high command of the Union forces. Not only did he practice a faith that many of his soldiers found questionable, but he did so with an unabashed fervor.

Rosecrans always had a crucifix on his person, and he had a priest, Father Daley, constantly at his side. Rosecrans, who loved to talk, often sat up late into the evening, discussing theology either with Daley or members of his staff. None of this bothered the rank-and-file; they may have found Rosecrans' faith odd, but they liked, and sometimes adored, "Old Rosy," as they called him. The "trouble" surrounding Rosecrans' faith came at higher levels, in Washington, D.C., where some people questioned whether such an ardent "Papist," as Catholics were often called, should be a major-general of volunteers. After the Battle of Chickamauga, Rosecrans seemed to fall apart, and once again, both the man and his religion came in for scrutiny.

What did Stanton say to Rosecrans?

In the spring of 1863, Secretary of War Stanton had been encouraging to Rosecrans, suggesting that a major-generalship in the Regular Army might be his reward for good service. But by July, Stanton had become weary of Rosecrans' delays. The Army of the Cumberland was at full strength and receiving plenty of supplies, yet Rosecrans still held back. Three days after the Confederate defeat at Gettysburg, Stanton telegraphed Rosecrans: "Lee's army overthrown; Grant victorious. You and your noble army now have the chance to give the finishing blow to the rebellion. Will you neglect the chance?"

How did Rosecrans react to Stanton's prodding?

General Rosecrans had taken his sweet time arranging things, but once he went into action, he did so with great skill. Rather than force his way past the outnumbered Army of Tennessee, Rosecrans and his corps commanders executed some very clever and tricky maneuvers, continually going around Bragg's flanks. Given that this was Confederate territory, Bragg should have known the terrain better; instead, he looked like somewhat of a fool as the Federals continually outmaneuvered him. There were several skirmishes, but no battles, as the Army of the Cumberland made its way south.

Time and again, Bragg was caught off balance. Some of his errors were pardonable, but it was just plain stupid to yield the railroad town of Chattanooga. Three important Southern railroads ran through this locality, and its falling into federal hands brought about a crisis in Confederate supply systems and communications. A neutral observer—if such a person could be found—would have said this was the time to remove Bragg as commander, but Jefferson Davis kept him there and said that reinforcements were on their way.

246

Who was coming to assist Bragg?

General James Longstreet had fully recovered psychologically from the disastrous third day of the Battle of Gettysburg. He had not been wounded, but he had seen General Pickett's division torn to shreds. In September 1863, Longstreet was ordered to get 12,000 of the men of the First Corps of the Army of Northern Virginia onto railroad cars and on their way to northern Georgia. Because of the loss of Chattanooga, the Confederates had to go the long way around, but Longstreet's men enjoyed their train trip, and the locals in most villages and towns turned out to cheer them.

Longstreet brought his men, but he also brought a new theory about the launching of attacks. The failure of Pickett's Charge convinced him that attacks made on a broad front were hopeless, and that any future attempts would have to be short, swift, and compact. Longstreet arrived at the last train stop in northern Georgia during the night of September 19–20 and was taken to General Bragg's tent. The bleary-eyed Bragg told Longstreet he and his men would form an integral part of the assault, which was to begin about six hours hence.

BATTLE OF CHICKAMAUGA

What was Bragg's plan?

Thanks to his flanking maneuvers, General Rosecrans had brought the Army of the Cumberland right over the border of northern Georgia. He and his men had known nothing but success for the previous two months, and this perhaps led to some overconfidence. By the late afternoon of September 19, 1863, Rosecrans realized that Bragg now had the numerical advantage. Rosecrans, therefore, drew his men up on the west side of the creek called Chickamauga, which, in the language of some of the local Indians, may have meant "river of blood." (Native American linguistics are among the most difficult of studies because of the variety of tribal languages and pronunciations.)

Bragg had a solid, even inspired, plan for September 20, 1863. His men would attack all along the front, with Longstreet's corps threatening the federal center, but the main punch would come from his right against the federal left. By caving in that left flank, the Confederates would drive the Union men in a semicircle, counterclockwise, to slam them up against the banks of Chickamauga Creek. The plan had flair, even some brilliance, but it required excellent timing.

Were Rosecrans and his men ready for Bragg's attack?

They were, in the sense that they knew where the Confederates were placed, and could guess which corner, or flank would be attacked the hardest. They even knew that Longstreet and his men had arrived. But neither Rosecrans nor his corps commanders guessed how aggressively the Southern men would fight that day. It is not as if they did not warn him, however.

What was the conversation like?

Early during the Battle of Chickamauga, a Confederate captain from Texas, David K. Rice, was brought to Rosecrans as a prisoner. The Union general interrogated the Confederate officer, but on finding he would not succumb to rapid-fire questions, Rosecrans turned it into a conversation, which was later recorded in a Southern newspaper.

Rosecrans: Where are your lines?

Captain Rice: General, it has cost me a great deal of trouble to find your lines; if you take the same amount of trouble, you will find ours....

Rosecrans: How many of Longstreet's men got here?

Captain Rice: About forty-five thousand.

Rosecrans: Is Longstreet in command?

Captain Rice: O, no sir! General Bragg is in command.

Rosecrans: Captain, you don't seem to know much, for a man whose appearance seems to indicate so much intelligence.

Captain Rice: Well, General, if you are not satisfied with my information, I will volunteer some. We are going to whip you most tremendously in this fight.

How did the battle commence?

The Confederates had already pushed the night before, and on the morning of September 20, they practically swarmed across Chickamauga Creek. The Northern men were stunned by the violence of the attack, and they fell back.

General Longstreet, meanwhile, was asked only to make a demonstration on his section, but he probed and found a gap nearly a quarter of a mile long in the federal center. This was because of Rosecrans' rebuking an officer the night before, then sending an order for him to march to his left. That officer knew it might create havoc, but he decided to carry out the order to the letter rather than risk another verbal slap. Longstreet could hardly believe his good luck. Though he received no approval from Bragg, Longstreet went ahead, marching his 12,000 men in a tightly packed formation right into the gap, just to the left of the Union center.

General William Rosecrans had led successful campaigns at Tullahoma and Chattanooga, but a badly worded written order at the Battle of Chickamauga resulted in a line opening up that the South's Longstreet took advantage of, wiping out a third of Rosecrans' men.

This was the kind of opportunity field officers dreamed of: an opening that would split the enemy's force in two.

Where, meanwhile, was Rosecrans?

He had been at the center of his army, and in typical style was quite close to the action, but when the Confederate attack succeeded, he was nearly captured. Telling his staff to flee to save their lives, Rosecrans spurred his horse to the rear. He could have remained there and continued to give directions, but something overcame him (today, we might call it shell shock or posttraumatic stress disorder). Spurring his horse, Rosecrans galloped all the way to Chattanooga, and when he arrived there, he sat on a bench with his head in his hands. He could do no more.

Why didn't the entire Union army collapse?

Because of the energetic defiance of Major-General George Thomas. A Virginian by birth and a slaveholder at one time, Thomas was distrusted by the Union top command, and this may have slowed his promotion. At Chickamauga, however, he displayed the terrific fighting capacity that his men knew existed. Bringing his brigades into a semicircle of their own, Rosecrans held Snodgrass Hill and Horseshoe Ridge against repeated Confederate assaults: some of these were led by former Vice President John C. Breckinridge. Only toward evening did Thomas give up the fight and lead his men in an orderly withdrawal. By then, there was not the slightest doubt the Confederates had won: the only question concerned the magnitude of their victory.

What did the battle scene look like?

Not until dawn on September 21 would observers be able to take it in, but even during the night many Confederates sensed this would be the bloodiest ground they had ever seen. More men had been lost at Gettysburg, beyond doubt, but the fighting at Chickamauga was on a more narrow front, and the bodies were piled up by the dozen. Though it took some time to assess the damage, 16,000 Federals and 18,500 Confederates went killed, wounded, or missing in that terrible battle which seemed to justify the Native American name for the creek.

Had Bragg won?

Beyond any doubt. At a huge expense of life, he had shattered the Army of the Cumberland, and if he acted quickly, he might have recaptured Chattanooga. Indeed, his cavalry leader, General Nathan Bedford Forrest, urged him to take that action. Bragg was so stunned by the casualties, however, that his natural pessimism took hold. If he had won, it was at too great a cost. Several days passed before Bragg gave the order to advance, and that short window of time was enough for the Federals to keep hold of Chattanooga. Bragg and his men advanced unopposed almost to the town itself, but they had to be content with seizing Lookout Mountain to the southwest and Missionary Ridge, which ran from southwest to northeast in an angle that curved past Chattanooga. Bragg's tardy follow-up to his victory did not lessen the blow in official Washington, however. Lincoln and Secretary of War Stanton resolved to drop everything else, if need be, and make sure that Chattanooga remained in federal hands.

What did Lincoln and Stanton decide?

Just as Jefferson Davis had deprived his Eastern forces to send Longstreet to the West, so did the federal leaders divert all sorts of troops to Tennessee. General Joseph Hooker, who had seen little action since the Battle of Chancellorsville, was sent west with two divisions of the Army of the Potomac, and General William T. Sherman, who had recently captured Meridian, Mississippi, was ordered to march east. Most important was the choice of commanding general, however, and given his recent success at Vicksburg, Grant was the natural choice.

Some Union generals developed outsized egos and resented each new batch of orders. This was never the case with Grant: the moment he had his orders, he confirmed their arrival and said he would head to Tennessee. What he did not reveal, however, was that he had taken a bad fall from a horse, and that one leg was badly injured. It was a wounded, limping Grant who made his way to Tennessee.

Was alcohol involved?

We aren't certain. With Grant, this always seems to be a possibility, and he was a superb equestrian, who did not suffer many falls. To the best of our knowledge, however, Grant had fallen from his horse under normal circumstances, and the wound would take some time to heal. Lacking that time, he set out, first by steamboat, then by horse.

Where was John Rawlins?

We seldom hear his name these days, but Colonel—later Brigadier-General—John Rawlins (1831–1869) played an important role in the many successes of Ulysses S. Grant. The two men knew each other in Galena, Illinois, prior to the beginning of the war, and Grant made Rawlins his chief of staff as early as the autumn of 1861. By the time Vicksburg fell, Rawlins was nearly indispensable, not on a professional but rather a personal level.

Rawlins' father had been a serious alcoholic, and Rawlins detested liquor so much that he declared he would let a friend take poison before allowing him to

General John Rawlins was Grant's chief of staff, but even more importantly, according to some historians and Rawlins himself, were his efforts in keeping the leader of the Union forces away from alcohol as much as possible.

take alcohol. Rawlins acted as Grant's conscience on several occasions during the war, threatening to quit the post of chief of staff unless Grant kept away from the bottle. Grant could easily have found a successor to Rawlins—he was highly skilled in the drafting of orders himself—but he would not have found another person to act as his watchdog and guide. Some historians believe that Rawlins later overstated his own importance, but even if this is true, he filled a nearly unique role.

How did Grant get to Chattanooga?

First he went by train to Louisville to meet with Secretary of War Stanton. The secretary informed Grant that he could choose whom he wished to command the Army of the Cumberland, but that he was now in charge of all Union armies between the Appalachian Mountains and the Mississippi River. This was a huge change; Grant was the first person to be entrusted with such a variety of commands. Although Stanton made it seem like a choice, Grant knew he had to replace General Rosecrans because of his poor performance at the Battle of Chickamauga. The more he thought about it, the more he liked the idea of using Major-General Thomas who had been the "Rock of Chickamauga."

Departing Stanton, Grant again went by steamer, but there was a point where he could only go by horse. Accompanied only by a few aides, he made the difficult, dangerous journey on horseback, arriving at Chattanooga on October 23, 1863. He did it in typical style, which is to say there were no theatrics or calling attention to his recent injury.

What was so special about Grant?

This has been asked and pondered by many people: journalists, historians, and laypersons. Most of them have slowly come to the same conclusion: Grant was a very normal, even average, person in some ways, who was capable of truly heroic decision making and taking of action. Those who accuse him of merely being "lucky" are far off base. Those who claim he had only an average mind have not read his dispatches, which are a model of clarity.

When we compare Grant to the other great generals of his time, only Lee is in the same category. William T. Sherman liked to think he was on a par with these men, but Sherman never fought a campaign against the odds, as Lee so often did, nor did he have to interact with so many and varied individuals as did Grant. In American military history, we place Grant at the top of his time and the greatest U.S. commander from General Winfield Scott, whose active-duty career ended in 1861—to General John Pershing, whose fame came during the First World War.

SIEGE OF CHATTANOOGA

What was the situation that Grant found on arriving at Chattanooga?

The top commanders were in a state of depression and uncertainty. Major-General George Thomas already knew he had been appointed commander of the Army of the Cumberland, a force that was in a low state of morale. General Joseph Hooker was on

Why is it sometimes called Lookout Mountain and sometimes called Missionary Ridge?

The topography around Chattanooga was daunting to the soldiers and map-makers of both sides, but it also presented some of the most splendid sights of the war. For many years after, Union and Confederate soldiers alike would wax about the beauty of the area surrounding Chattanooga.

From the Confederate lines, atop Lookout Mountain and Missionary Ridge, there was an unparalleled view of the beauty of southern Tennessee. Gazing directly below, the Confederates saw the town of Chattanooga and almost the entirety of the federal forces. Looking to the horizon, they saw the mountains of central Tennessee, the area from which they had been chased by General Rosecrans four months earlier. From the Union point of view, standing in the town of Chattanooga, there was almost nowhere to gaze but "up." South and southwest of the town was forbidding Lookout Mountain, towering 1,300 feet above sea level. East and south of the town was Missionary Ridge, which, while not as high as Lookout Mountain, was even more formidable because of its length. There were other promontories, such as Orchard Knob, and the chances are that some of the soldiers got the names reversed at times. But for the journalists on hand, and there were quite a few, the fighting in and around Chattanooga provided, perhaps, the most sublime scenery of the entire war. In their dispatches to the newspapers, they made the most of it.

the way, as was General William T. Sherman. Between them, these forces would outnumber Braxton Bragg's Confederates; even so, Grant did not await their arrival. Assessing the situation in a matter of hours, he decided to force the Confederate hand.

Grant did not devise the plan himself; it was developed by one of the colonels of the Army of the Cumberland. But it was ambitious, even daring. One division of Federals would attack the Confederates around the base of Lookout Mountain, while another would float downstream on pontoons, to quickly establish a bridge across the Tennessee River. If all went well, a new supply line would be created that would cut the present time in half.

How did Grant's first action go?

He was no longer at the front, or even close. Grant had become too valuable for that. He was in Chattanooga, using his spy glass to observe, and things went well right from the beginning. The Confederates at the base of Lookout Mountain were surprised, then stunned, by the two-division attack that came on October 28, 1863. The only thing the Confederates had going their way that morning was that Colonel William C. Oates and his feisty Alabamian regiment—the same men who had attacked Little Round Top on

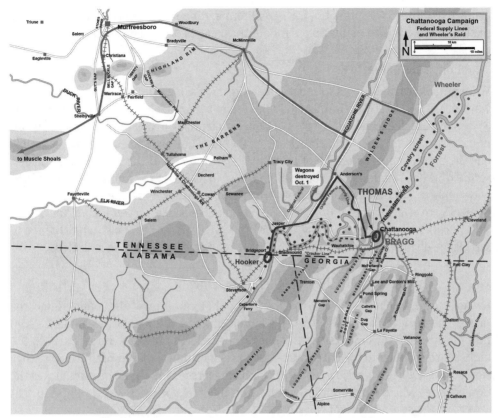

The battle at Chattanooga, Tennessee, marked the end of the last defensive position in Tennessee for the South. Grant successfully routed Bragg out of the state, and with this defeat, the South was ripe for an invsion deep into its territory.

July 2, 1863—were in the vicinity. Oates led a charge against the Federals, but when he went down with a wound that cost him a leg, the fight went out of his men. By later afternoon, the Federals had a pontoon bridge across the Tennessee River, and two days after that they had another, bridging the so-called Raccoon Peninsula. A new route for supplies was opened up, and Union men inside of Chattanooga cheered wildly, claiming that the "cracker line" had been established (this referred to the hunger which preceded the successful action and the men's desperate desire for any food, even crackers).

Why was Braxton Bragg *still* in charge of the Army of Tennessee?

To the modern-day observer, it is obvious that Bragg had to go. He had snatched an indecisive draw from the jaws of victory at the Battle of Chickamauga, and he had done little or nothing to prevent Grant's new offensive. To Jefferson Davis, however, Bragg still seemed like the right man. Not only did Davis like and trust Bragg, but there was no one on hand with whom to replace him. Davis traveled from Richmond to Marietta, Georgia, in October 1863, where he met with Bragg and all his subordinate officers. To a man, they claimed that Bragg was unfit, but Davis kept him in his position and sent a message to be read to the troops with pointed words about the dangers of insubordination and treason.

When did Sherman arrive?

William T. Sherman brought four battle-hardened divisions from Mississippi, arriving on November 15, 1863. Grant immediately showed more confidence and heartiness: he and Sherman were like a team in harness. Joseph Hooker had already brought four divisions of the Army of the Potomac, and Grant now enjoyed numerical superiority. Not only had the Union done a better job of coordinating its forces, but the Confederates made a serious, perhaps fatal, mistake of dividing theirs. Because of the animosity that existed between him and General Longstreet, Bragg sent Longstreet and almost ten thousand men away to attack General Burnside's garrison at Knoxville. Grant did not know all of this, of course, but if he had enjoyed a bird's-eye view, he would have been delighted to see his foe divide his forces at the very time when his were being concentrated.

What was the condition of the Confederate defenders?

It was terrible. When they first arrived at Lookout Mountain and Missionary Ridge, the men of the Army of Tennessee were on a high from their victory at Chickamauga. Even though they did not capture Chattanooga, they held the high ground—perhaps the highest ground seen in the entire war—and it seemed only a matter of time before they starved out the Federals. Now the situation had reversed, and in the interim, it was the Confederates who went hungry. Complicating their misfortunes was a cold snap that arrived in the second week of November.

When did Grant unleash his offensive?

The Federals went on the offensive on November 23, 1863, but things proceeded more slowly than Grant expected. Keeping Sherman's four divisions well out of sight of the Confederates, Grant sent them across yet another peninsula—this one north of the town—to arrive near the mouth of Chickamauga Creek. They did so very slowly because of the autumn rains, but did cross the pontoon bridge that had been constructed upriver, out of sight. Perhaps things were not proceeding smoothly, but one could see the general outlines of the plan.

BATTLE OF LOOKOUT MOUNTAIN

What was the first big success?

On November 24, 1863, General Thomas had ten thousand men of the Army of the Cumberland conduct a review on the plain below Missionary Ridge and in front of the town of Chattanooga. The Confederate artillerymen, three-quarters of a mile away, were taken by surprise when Thomas' men made a sudden charge at the rifle pits around Orchard

A lithograph by Kurz and Allison showing General Hooker's attack on the South's General Stevenson at Lookout Mountain.

Knob, one of the key points of the Confederate defense. Not only did they take the rifle pits, but they surged up Orchard Knob in record time, capturing the cannon. Thomas was thrilled. He sent a message to the effect that his men had taken too much ground to give any of it back: they would hold their new position.

Did Braxton Bragg recognize any of the danger he and his army faced?

Although we know that Bragg suffered from physical debility, we would truly like to know what the state of his mind, his thinking, was at this time. Here he was, atop a ridge that commanded the view for miles about, yet he was reacting to the Union moves, not sketching out any of his own. As bad as things were for Bragg and his men, they were soon to become even worse.

How do we know what Bragg's men thought of him?

Enough anecdotes entered the record that we are confident Bragg was the most disliked, sometimes despised, leader on either side during the war. There was the moment, for example, when Bragg was interrogating one of his men who claimed that the enemy were in full retreat after the Battle of Chickamauga. Bragg scowled at the soldier and demanded to know if he knew what a retreat looked like. "I should, General," he replied, "I've been with you throughout this whole campaign." The single best account of Bragg's misfortunes, however, comes from the pen of Sam R. Watkins, whose diary was later published as *Co. Aytch: A Confederate Memoir of Civil War*.

"In all the history of the war," Watkins wrote:

> I cannot remember of more privations and hardships than we went through at Missionary Ridge. And when in the very acme of our privations and hunger, when the army was most dissatisfied and unhappy, we were ordered into line of battle to be reviewed by Honorable Jefferson Davis. When he passed us, with his great retinue of staff officers and play-outs at full gallop, cheers greeted them, with the words, "Send us something to eat, Massa Jeff. Give us something to eat, Massa Jeff. I'm hungry! I'm hungry!"

Where did "Fighting Joe" Hooker get his new lease on life?

Hooker had been in a rather bad way ever since his monumental defeat at Chancellorsville in May of that same year. He was the same old "Fighting Joe," however, delighted to have a new opportunity. Therefore, though the orders of November 24 called for him to make a strong demonstration against Lookout Mountain, Hooker went for more.

By midafternoon, his men were scaling the 750-foot height that led to a large plateau. Just before Hooker's men reached the plateau, they disappeared from the view of the Federals on the plain below, leading the newspapermen to label this "The Battle above the Clouds." A heavy mist set in, and no communication was established between Grant on the ground and Hooker on the plateau. Many Union men in Chattanooga spent the night in uncertainty and some anxiety, but all that was dispelled when the first rays of morning sparkled on Lookout Mountain. A very large federal flag had been placed on top.

How close had Grant and Sherman become?

The relationship between the phlegmatic Grant and the tempestuous Sherman has been beautifully detailed in *Grant and Sherman: The Friendship That Won the Civil War*. Biographer Charles Bracelen Flood shows how these two men—from such different backgrounds—became such good commanders and friends.

Sherman was two years older, and, by most accounts, much brighter than Grant, who for his part was much steadier (except when he was drunk). The two knew each other, faintly, from West Point, and their acquaintance turned to friendship in the campaign that terminated at the Battle of Shiloh. Throughout the Vicksburg campaign, Grant considered Sherman his irreplaceable second-in-command, and by the time he went to Chattanooga, Sherman was convinced that Grant was the greatest general in the war. At times, Sherman attempted to bolster his self-opinion; he wrote in his diary and in letters to his wife that Grant possessed only an average mind, while admitting that he had an uncanny ability to seek and obtain victory. Their friendship blossomed by the autumn of 1863 and would only become stronger in 1864.

How did Hooker's men reach the top of Lookout Mountain?

The evening previous saw them establish themselves on the plateau, with a solid 500 feet more to go. No action was undertaken that night, but Hooker feared he and his men would advance under a withering fire in the morning. Instead, they moved up the side of Lookout Mountain to find that the Confederates had retreated in the night. Lookout Mountain was theirs.

There is no way to overstate the joy of the Federals in and around Chattanooga. The city was clearly relieved of any Confederate siege; the only question that remained was whether the Confederates would hold their ground or steal away to northern Georgia. General Bragg had, already, considered this alternative, and he decided it would be so bad for morale that he would hold on to Missionary Ridge.

Who was Patrick Cleburne?

Born in County Cork, Ireland, on St. Patrick's Day of 1828, Cleburne came from a Protestant family. His father was a physician and Cleburne was expected to follow in his footsteps, but he failed the entrance exam and joined the British Army instead. After a number of adventures, he and several siblings emigrated to the United States in 1851, arriving in New Orleans: he soon moved to Arkansas to become an attorney.

Cleburne adopted his new country fully, and when the Civil War broke out he had no difficulty in choosing the Confederate side. He rose quickly in the ranks and became a brigadier-general, serving under Braxton Bragg. Cleburne's unit performed the best of any of the Confederate forces during the fighting around Chattanooga, and it played a leading role in covering the retreat to northern Georgia. In January 1864, Cleburne advocated bringing the African American slaves into the Confederate army: he was the highest-ranking Confederate officer to make that motion until 1865.

Who was *scheduled* to make the big attack on November 25, 1863?

The honor went to William T. Sherman, who had done a fine job of bringing four divisions north of Chattanooga, over the Tennessee River, and into striking distance of the northernmost part of Missionary Ridge. The trouble was that Sherman was operating with a poor set of maps, and he was actually half a mile short of his true destination. When he, therefore, commenced his attack on November 25, Sherman ran into ferocious resistance from

Serving under General Bragg, Brigadier-General Patrick Cleburne effectively led his troops, protecting Confederate forces retreating from Chattanooga.

Patrick Cleburne's division. Sherman lost slightly more than 2,000 men killed, wounded, or missing, while Cleburne lost a quarter of that number. Another general might have been in trouble, with his commanding officer and the Washington brass, but Sherman, in his failure, was protected by Ulysses Grant.

BATTLE OF MISSIONARY RIDGE

Who *made* the really big move on November 25, 1863?

The Army of the Cumberland had performed well on November 23, but its members still smarted from their humiliation at Chickamauga two months earlier. They chafed under the supporting role they were supposed to play on November 25. While Sherman and his divisions were to take the northeastern end of Missionary Ridge, they were expected only to seize the Confederate rifle pits at the base of the ridge. While Grant and General Thomas could hear the cannon and rifle fire from Sherman's attack on Cleburne's position, the men of the Army of the Cumberland were itching to move. Acting on chief of staff John Rawlins' advice, Grant prodded General Thomas, who sent the first wave of Cumberland men forward at around 3 P.M.

How did that attack go?

It made for a magnificent sight. The Confederates atop Missionary Ridge had, perhaps, the best view, but the Union men atop Lookout Mountain had a good eyeball as well. The only people who could not see the scene very well were the Confederate defenders in their rifle pits. The Northern men opposed to them had been so quiet for so long that the Confederates did not expect a major attack, but when it came, they were not ready anyhow. They sprayed rifle and musket fire, but it seemed to make no difference. They looked above, anxiously, to see whether the Confederate cannon on the ridge were in action and were comforted to see that they were firing. The Confederate guns could not be properly depressed, however, and most of the cannonballs went far off target.

How soon were the rifle pits captured?

Between eight and ten minutes was all that was required. Shouting "Chickamauga!", the Union men crossed the field on the double-quick and jumped into the pits. The few remaining Confederate defenders surrendered on the spot, but the Federals could see that many of their comrades had gotten out in time and were now scaling the ridge, headed for safety. To the best of our knowledge, no one gave a command, nor even a suggestion. The Union men simply started to follow the Confederates up Missionary Ridge.

Was this planned?

Absolutely not. Grant's plan was for the men of the Army of the Cumberland to take the rifle pits and hold their position. When he saw them moving up the ridge, he barked to

After winning the Battle of Lookout Mountain, Grant continued to pursue Southern forces, who made a stand at Missionary Ridge near Chattanooga. The Confederate defeat there marked the beginning of an inevitable end for the South.

General Thomas, asking who had ordered this assault. Thomas replied, just as curtly, that he had not. Chomping on a cigar—he sometimes consumed twenty a day—Grant muttered that someone was going to be court-martialed if the attack failed. When he took a second look, Grant was transfixed. It was not only the few regiments that led the attack; it seemed as if the entire Army of the Cumberland was ascending Missionary Ridge.

What did it look like from the Confederate point of view?

The federal attack seemed like insanity, but when the Confederates atop the ridge used their rifles, they hit more of their own men, coming up, than Yankees. Panic seized the men atop the ridge, and the more they attempted to depress the muzzles of their cannon, the clearer it became that this was a hopeless endeavor. All of a sudden, the Confederates at the top began to run, and when their comrades from the rifle pits reached the top, they, too, took to their heels.

What did it look like from the Union point of view?

There was no plan, no coordination, just a group belief—gathered in the moment—that they had to capture that ridge. Climbing, sweating, and cursing, the men of Thomas' army kept rising, and the closer they came, the less resistance they encountered. One

Confederate sharpshooter did pick off the color-bearer of a Wisconsin regiment, whereupon an eighteen-year-old lieutenant and adjutant seized it, shouting, "On Wisconsin!" Minutes later, he and his fellows reached the top, gasped for breath, then realized they had, against all expectations, succeeded.

Eighteen-year-old Arthur MacArthur (1845–1912) was destined for great things. He later became a major-general in the Regular Army and military governor of the Philippines. But as great as his own success was, it paled in comparison to that of his son, Douglas MacArthur, who later became governor of the Philippines, Supreme Allied Commander in the Pacific, and Supreme Overlord of the Allied Occupation of Japan. Would the son's life and career have been so sparkling had the father not been a hero at such an early age? That is one of the questions that cannot be answered, but can only be pondered.

What did they find at the top?

As they cleared the last brow and stood atop Missionary Ridge, the Federals realized they had won. The few remaining Confederates surrendered on the spot; the others had fled. The moment was sublime: most of the men never forgot their feelings as they mounted that ridge.

Bragg's army was broken to pieces. They had not suffered great battle casualties, but their morale was completely gone. Nine weeks earlier, they had won a great battle. Eight weeks earlier, they had occupied a series of mountain positions too strong to be assailed. Now they were on the run. Sam Watkins expressed it thus: "I felt sorry for General Bragg. The army was routed, and Bragg looked so scared. Poor fellow, he looked so hacked and whipped and mortified and chagrined at defeat." Once on the run, the Confederates did not stop for almost two days.

Did any sections of Bragg's army fight well?

Several did. The one that did the best was Patrick Cleburne's division. An Irishman who had served in the British army before moving to Arkansas, Cleburne was a firm believer in the Confederate cause and a terrific fighter. His men had repelled Sherman's on November 23, 1863, and it was Cleburne's division that prevented the destruction of Bragg's army simply by making a stand.

Thanks to Cleburne's determination, the Army of Tennessee made it to the Georgia border more or less intact. That it still existed was beyond doubt; that it was finished as an offensive weapon also could not be questioned.

When was Bragg finally relieved of command?

Jefferson Davis finally removed Bragg in December, replacing him with General Joseph Johnston. He was the same person who had commanded the defense of the Peninsula in 1862 and at the Mississippi defense of Gettysburg in 1863. One of the first comments made about Johnston came from Private Sam R. Watkins:

> Allow me to introduce you to old Joe. Fancy, if you will, a man of about fifty years old, rather small of stature, but firmly and compactly built, an open and honest countenance, and a keen but restless black eye, that seemed to read your very inmost thoughts. In his dress he was a perfect dandy. He ever wore the finest clothes that could be obtained, carrying out to every point the dress and paraphernalia of the soldier, as adopted by the war department at Richmond.

All this sounds fine, if ornamental, but Private Watkins and many other men of the Army of Tennessee disliked Johnston's campaign style, which resembled one elegant retreat after another.

SIEGE OF KNOXVILLE

What happened to Longstreet?

The sending away of Longstreet's corps in early November had practically doomed Bragg's army. For his part, Longstreet enjoyed being away from the Army of the Cumberland, and—for one of the few times in the war—being in full command. His goal was to take Knoxville, which had been occupied by the Federals for several months.

Longstreet's reputation as one of the best offensive fighters on either side remained intact, and his men were confident as they took the railroad east to the outskirts of Knoxville. In a rather short time, however, everything began to go wrong. "Old Pete," as his men called him, did not seem disturbed by the fragility of the supply lines, or the difficulties of the terrain, but his men—who were much more accustomed to fighting in the Eastern theater—began to show signs of discontent.

Who was defending Knoxville?

Ambrose Burnside had experienced more than his share of defeats and humiliations. Once he took Knoxville in the late summer of 1863, he was determined to hold it. Knowing that Longstreet's corps was on the way to attack him, Burnside—who was a much better defensive than offensive fighter—shored up the defenses of the city.

Upon arriving, Longstreet probed the federal defenses and found them stronger than anticipated. Never one to hurry an attack, he settled into a quasi-siege and continued to look for the right place to strike. By the time he settled on Fort Loudon on the southeast side of town, he received alarming reports about what was happening back at Missionary Ridge.

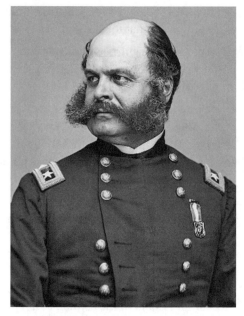

General Ambrose Burnside was in charge of defending Knoxville, Tennessee, from the Federals.

Was it Longstreet's job to save Bragg?

Technically it was not, but Longstreet's attitude was nothing short of callous. Knowing that Bragg was in a precarious position, and that the Army of Tennessee was all that stood between the Union men and northern Georgia, he stayed where he was, sending only occasional messages to Bragg.

Longstreet was definitely at fault—he did not seem to care whether Bragg and his men lived or died—but the largest measure of fault can be laid at the feet of Jefferson Davis. First he had insisted that Bragg remain in command, then he allowed Longstreet to detach his corps from the Army of Tennessee. But even as he learned of the dismal failure at Missionary Ridge, Jefferson Davis was also about to learn about Longstreet's mistake.

Why did the attack on Knoxville fail?

On November 29, 1863, after numerous delays, Longstreet sent his men forward. Longstreet often guessed "right," but on this occasion he was dead wrong. The federal defenders of Fort Loudon were awake when the first cannon roared at 6 A.M., and they were ready when the bayonet charge came ten minutes later. Hoping for surprise, Longstreet had his men attack without any rifle or musket fire: they came ready with the bayonet. The defenders poured in a heavy rifle fire, and the attackers were taken totally off-guard by telegraph wires, artfully strung between trees. In an attack such as this, the attackers needed every second to gain ground; that they lost as much as thirty seconds getting over and past the telegraph wires made all the difference.

The first attack was a total failure, and just as a second assault was in preparation, Longstreet called the whole thing off. He had just received an urgent message indicating that the Federals had won a great victory at Missionary Ridge and that he was needed to prevent a total collapse in the Western theater. His losses were 700 men, killed, wounded, or missing, and to add to his discomfort was the knowledge that the garrison of one well-placed fort, rather than the strength of Burnside's entire army, had repelled him.

Where did Longstreet move from there?

By rights, he should have brought his corps back to the Tennessee–Georgia border to assist Bragg and the Army of Tennessee. Longstreet really did not wish to return there, however, and for once the geographic circumstances argued in favor of his decision. Because it was too risky to move his corps back to the area around Chattanooga, Longstreet was allowed to

A Southern camp overlooking the Tennessee River near Knoxville during the siege of that city.

take his corps through the mountains back to Virginia. This, of course, begs another question: How much had Longstreet accomplished?

Longstreet and his men were a major disappointment to Bragg and the Army of Tennessee. Perhaps it was difficult integrating these "men from the East" with those of the Western theater; even so, the Union was able to do so much more effectively. That Longstreet was a good leader of men cannot be denied. He seems to have been best, however, when serving under Lee and in the Army of Northern Virginia.

GETTYSBURG ADDRESS

Who invited Lincoln to speak at Gettysburg?

The town had been overwhelmed by the necessity of burying the dead, and the state of Pennsylvania had to render assistance. The governor asked Lincoln to make some remarks at the dedication ceremony for the new cemetery, but Lincoln knew he would speak after the oration of Edward Everett.

Born in 1794, Everett was in some ways the most distinguished citizen of the nation. He had graduated from Harvard College in 1811, toured France and Italy, and, over the years, had served as an ambassador, a writer of political prose, and as chaplain to the United States Senate. A speaker of undeniable gifts, Everett was renowned for speaking without notes, and so it was on this occasion.

What was the scene at Gettysburg?

Almost twenty thousand people crowded the little town on November 19, 1863. Lincoln and his aides arrived by railroad car the night before and rose early to put their finishing touches on the speech. It is a measure of Lincoln's remarkable self-confidence that he wrote the words himself and showed them to no one that we know of. When the time for the dedication arrived, Lincoln walked over to the cemetery.

When did Thanksgiving—as we know it—become a national holiday?

Since Puritan times, Americans have been prone to selecting or designating certain days for thanksgiving as well as others for fasting, mourning, or prayer. But during the 1840s and 1850s, a social reformer named Sarah Josepha Hale urged that there be a national day for thanksgiving, and when she pressed, yet again, in 1863, Lincoln saw merit in the idea. Secretary of State William H. Seward drafted the proclamation, which was issued in October. He began:

> The year that is drawing to a close, has been filled with the blessings of fruitful fields and healthful skies. To these bounties, which are so constantly enjoyed that we are prone to forget the source from which they come, others have been added, which are of so extraordinary a nature, that they cannot fail to penetrate and soften even the heart which is habitually insensible to the ever watchful providence of Almighty God.

Newspapers printed the proclamation, but they also took up the cause, urging Americans to make the last Thursday in November 1863 a true day of thanksgiving.

Called upon to speak first, Edward Everett delivered a rousing speech that lasted two hours; he recited entirely from memory. It was a stunning vindication of the power of retention and served as an admonishment to those who claimed there was "too much" information in the world and that no one could master all of it. Perhaps it was not the single best performance of Everett's long career, but it ranks in the top three or four of all his speeches. Then came Lincoln's turn.

How did he look? How did he sound?

Lincoln looked much the same as ever. The preposterously long limbs were as prominent as when he had his photograph taken at Mathew Brady's studio in Manhattan. The earnest but pained expression was there, as had been the case for so many years. And, as ever, Lincoln looked as if he needed a good tailor: his clothes did not fit well.

Lincoln sounded a little different than usual. There was more twang and emotion in his voice, and he seemed at times to plead with the audience to stay with him. He need not have worried. The words, which came out during a speech of three minutes, had the power to reshape the people and the nation.

Why do we consider the Gettysburg Address so important?

Let us begin just as Lincoln did, and peruse the opening words:

"Four score and seven years ago our fathers brought forth on this continent a new nation, conceived in Liberty, and dedicated to the proposition that all men are created equal."

A reproduction of Lincoln's famous speech is shown here, giving a good idea at the brevity of the piece, which conveyed so much powerful emotions in a few words.

Of course someone else could have used that magical, almost Biblical, phrase "four score and seven years," but they had not done so. It was Lincoln, in his calm but fertile brain, who employed perhaps the most enticing words ever used in a major address to that point. The phrase "our fathers" triggered emotions in the audience. Eighty-seven years is a long time, but there were people in America whose fathers had fought in the Revolutionary War. Robert E. Lee was one; Joseph E. Johnston another. And then, to use that wonderful phrase "dedicated to the proposition." How very Lincoln. Right there he indicated to his audience that these things could not be taken for granted. One had to fight for the propositions one held.

Today we might say that Lincoln had "hooked" his audience. How did he proceed?

"Today we are engaged in a great civil war, testing whether that nation, or any nation so conceived and so dedicated, can long endure. We are met on a great battle field of that war."

Again, many other writers and orators could have come up with the same words. But they did not. It was left to Lincoln, with his special feel for history and the pulse of the nation, to question whether it could "long endure." Then, the next sentence seems so obvious, so without hidden meaning. Of course they had come to meet on a great battlefield, the greatest ever seen in North America. But Lincoln was playing his listener along, making it seem as if he might speak of the heroics of this action or that. Such was not his intent. He continued: "We have come to dedicate a portion of that field, as a final resting place for those who here gave their lives that that nation might live. It is all together fitting and proper that we should do this." If Lincoln had already employed the hook, he now came through with the justification. Implicit in his words was that there was no time, or space, to waste. While a nation was engaged in a great civil conflict, its leaders and its citizens must be able to justify their actions.

When we read slowly, we are overcome with the power of what Lincoln said. Was this the case for the people that day?

We just do not know. Very few of them left any detailed diary accounts of the speech. What we suspect is that people *felt* the power and importance of the words, but were not able to respond to them.

Poets know the truth of this. It is very rare that a listener, or a reader, can truly take in great words on the first listening. Of course this begs another question: How did Lincoln, who had so little formal education, reach such a height of oratorical skill? To the best of our understanding, he slowly and painfully acquired it through laborious practice. Only now, toward the end of his life, did he have the capacity to "throw off" words of such transcendent purpose.

Where did Lincoln the orator go from there?

"But in a larger sense, we can not dedicate—we can not consecrate—we can not hallow this ground. The brave men, living and dead, who struggled here, have consecrated it, far above our poor power to add or detract. The world will little note, nor long remember, what we say here, but it can never forget that they died here."

Here Lincoln stepped beyond even his earlier magnificent prose. Up to this point, what he said could have been anticipated, or even employed, by some other orator. But when he invoked the presence of those "who struggled here," Lincoln did not sound like the commander-in-chief or the leading war strategist. He sounded like the father of a nation, and there was a Biblical feeling that he included the Confederate dead among those who were to be honored. Only someone who anguished over the war, who saw all the telegrams and the casualty lists, could have composed these words, and the only other person who was in that situation was Jefferson Davis. It is no slight to Davis to say that he never rose to this level of image-making prose; very few people ever have.

How did Lincoln head toward his conclusion?

"It is for us the living, rather, to be dedicated here to the unfinished work, which they who fought here have thus far so nobly advanced. It is rather for us to be here dedicated to the great task remaining before us, that from these honored dead we take increased devotion to that cause for which they gave the last full measure of devotion—that we here highly resolve that these dead shall not have died in vain—that this nation, under

God, shall have a new birth of freedom—and that government of the people, by the people, and for the people, shall not perish from the earth."

The crowd was relatively silent when Lincoln finished. Perhaps they were weary after hearing Edward Everett's two-hour speech. Perhaps they were completely overwhelmed by the rich symbolism. Perhaps some of them had not been able to hear all the words. But we—who read it today, or who hear it read aloud—generally concur that it is one of the truly great speeches of history. In ten sentences and 273 words, Lincoln reforged what it means to be an American.

Artist Alfred Waud sketched this drawing of Union troops under General Louis Blenker having a Thanksgiving meal at their camp.

What was the first national Thanksgiving Day like?

Recording the feeling on an individual level was impossible: there were far too many homes and families to accomplish that. But on a national level, the first Thanksgiving was a major triumph. No one planned it—no one could have—but the news of Union triumphs in the Western theater arrived on the front page of the newspapers on Thursday, November 27, 1863.

"Glorious Victory! General Grant's Great Success; Bragg Routed and Driven from Every Point; Successful Battle on Tuesday." These were the headlines in the *New York Times*. Many people commented on the extreme good fortune that Lincoln and his administration enjoyed in public relations. The news of Gettysburg and Vicksburg arrived on or slightly after the Fourth of July, and the news of Lookout Mountain and Missionary Ridge came just as the newspapers were setting their type for Thanksgiving Day.

What was the beginning of the New Year like?

There was a sense, in Washington, D.C., that the great conflict would soon be over. Almost everyone understood how many sacrifices had been made—material as well as human—but there was a belief that the Confederacy would soon implode. How could it be otherwise? How could a people hold on much longer?

In Richmond, which was the only urban place by which to gauge popular opinion, there was a growing sense of despair, but it was the kind that led people to *more* sacrifices, rather than less. How could they do otherwise when the Yankees threatened to grind them into the ground, to destroy their entire way of life?

How did people outside the two capitals view the situation?

Anecdotally, we can employ the words of the carrier boys of the *Rochester Evening Express*; they distributed this circular on the morning of New Year's Day:

When in the circling rounds of time
We hear the low, mysterious chime
Which speaks the dying year,
'Tis well to pause in silent thought
To trace the scenes that year has wrought,
With bended smile and tear,
So reader, I will twine for thee
A wreath for eighteen sixty-three—
A year all stained with blood, and yet,
Who would its record quick forget?

The twenty stanzas that followed were almost entirely concentrated on the scenes of war, which, from the Northern perspective, was going quite well.

Did Lincoln shake as many hands as the previous year?

Yes, it is calculated that roughly eight thousand people passed through the White House on the first of January 1864 and that the President shook hands with nearly all of them. For this occasion, he wore white gloves, but even so, when he removed them, his hands were both worn and even bloody from the exercise.

This New Year's Day at the White House was the first time that any African Americans were in attendance. The record states that four black men—without any wives accompanying them—passed through the executive mansion that day.

What was life for men in the army camps like?

One of our best anecdotes from the winter of 1864 revolves around snowball fights.

In the camps of the Army of Northern Virginia, the soldiers had started a practice of snowball fights, but the one of January 4, 1864, surpassed all earlier endeavors. J. E. B. Stuart and General Heros von Borcke were at their winter quarters that day, watching as hundreds of the men led by General Lafayette McLaws battled with a similar number of General John Bell Hood's division. Stuart and Borcke tried to stay out of it, but the snowball fight swirled around their building, and before long the two cavalrymen were outside, still acting as observers rather than participants. One man had a broken leg; another lost an eye; and there were numerous smaller injuries, but Borcke concluded that the episode "gave ample proof of the excellent spirits of our troops, who, in the wet, wintry weather … were ever ready for any sort of sport or fun that offered itself."

What was the economic situation?

Throughout much—though not all—of the North, it had never been better. There were businessmen who had lost everything in the Panic of 1837 and rebuilt their fortunes, only to lose most of it again in the Panic of 1857. Many of these fortunes were being remade.

An illustration of Wall Street shortly after the Civil War. During the war, stocks and bonds fluctuated considerably depending on the battle successes and failures of the Union army.

At no previous time had there been so many different ways to make money. Then, too, so many different economic enterprises were formed in haste. Even the speed, or haste, did not detract from the moneymaking possibilities. To give just a brief list:

The Union armies needed shoes, shirts, handkerchiefs, pistols, socks, and underwear. The Union transport system needed railroad cars, steam-fitted rails, and all sorts of other instruments and devices. Just to list one that is often overlooked, the Union needed thousands of drums.

What was the situation on Wall Street?

It varied a great deal. Every time the Northern armies suffered a major setback, stocks and bonds declined and there was a consequent rise in the price of gold. With each Confederate defeat or setback, stocks and bonds rose and gold fell.

The number of persons "invested" on the stock market did not resemble that of our world today. There were, perhaps, fewer than ten thousand investors of all kinds and only about one-tenth of that number were truly large-scale investors. But the fortunes that could be made or lost were only growing in number.

What was the economic situation in the South?

It had never been worse. When the war began, there were many Southerners who confidently predicted that King Cotton—as they called it—would defeat all their enemies.

269

England and France would have to intervene just in order to obtain the cotton that their factories so desperately needed. This prediction proved mistaken, however, in large part because England and France both enjoyed a surplus of cotton when the war began. By the time their supplies declined, the cause of the Union was rising so strongly that it was practically impossible for them to intervene.

Also, it must be admitted that the North generally had men of greater skill in its diplomatic posts. Charles Francis Adams, the son of one president (John Quincy Adams) and the grandson of another (John Adams), was the American minister to the Court of St. James. He faced many difficulties, but most observers concluded that he played his hand very well, and never better than where the Laird Rams were concerned.

What were the Laird Rams?

In 1862, the Confederacy entered agreements with British contractors to furnish two ironclad vessels equipped with steel spikes so strong that they would sink practically any wooden-hulled vessel. Built in the Laird shipyards at Liverpool, these rams had the capacity, or potential, to alter the course of the war at sea. Minister Adams held off as long as he could, but in September 1863 he bluntly informed the British foreign secretary that "this means war." Adams did not know it, but the British ministry had already decided—just two days earlier—to prevent the Laird Rams from being delivered to Confederate agents.

What was the attitude of France at this point?

France, led by the Emperor Napoleon III, had, if anything, been even more eager to intervene in the Civil War than was the case with Britain. But France was thoroughly bogged down in its plan to install Maximilian Habsburg of Austria as the new Emperor of Mexico.

Maximilian arrived in Mexico City in the summer of 1863 and established his reign, but it was obvious that he needed French troops to maintain it. The Mexican rebels— or nationalists, as they called themselves—meanwhile retreated to just south of the American border. They set up camp in what is now Ciudad Juárez, named for Benito Juárez, the first person of native blood to become president of Mexico.

What was the attitude, or stance, of Imperial Russia?

Czar Alexander II, often called the Czar Liberator, had freed the Russian serfs one day before Lincoln came into office, and many newspapers—the cartoon sections especially—made comparisons between the two leaders. *Punch*, the most extravagant and popular of the British magazines, made a point of depicting both Lincoln and Czar Alexander as smiling liberators from the front and snarling despots from the back. But relations between the United States and Russia were not all that cozy.

In the summer of 1863, New Yorkers were surprised and pleased that a squadron of ships from the Imperial Russian Navy arrived in their harbor; the people of San Francisco soon were also paid a visit. The people of both cities were surprised; nothing had alerted them to this possibility. For many years, historians believed that Czar Alexander II sent the ships in order to demonstrate his support for the Union cause. If so, this was definitely a secondary motive; his primary reason was to have his fleets at sea so that if a war began with Britain, his ships would not be bottled up in their ports.

TOTAL WAR: MARCH TO SEPTEMBER 1864

THE MAN OF THE HOUR

When did Grant arrive in Washington, D.C.?

On March 7, 1864, Ulysses Grant and his son Frederick arrived in Washington by train. They went straight to the Willard Hotel, the best-known and most popular lodging place in the city. Because of the linen that overhung his shoulders, Grant's general's stars were not visible, and the desk clerk assigned the pair a room in the attic. When the short, mild-mannered fellow signed the register as "Ulysses S. Grant and son," the clerk hastily reassigned them to the best suite in the hotel.

In our day of celebrity worship, one might think such a humble approach was designed to court popularity, but it was, in fact, vintage Grant. He had never cared very much about popularity, or image, and to him it was obvious that one did not call attention to oneself. Later that day, Grant was practically besieged by presidential aides, who asked him to come to the White House for a reception. The chances are that he did not expect the large crowd that turned out to greet him.

What did Lincoln and Grant say to one another?

When they met—for the first time ever—Lincoln extended his hand and practically boomed: "So this is General Grant. What a pleasure." Grant, by contrast, was rather quiet, but he could not help but be the most admired, even adored, man in the room. Fame had caught up with him.

Later that week, when they sat together for two hours, Lincoln explained to his newest and highest-ranking general that he did not need to know the specifics or details of Grant's campaign. What he wanted was to know that Grant would pursue his objectives untiringly and that he would call upon Lincoln for anything and everything he might need (within reason). Pleased and perhaps surprised, Grant agreed with the president that the primary consideration was the Confederate armies. There was little point in fighting an aggressive war if all they did was gain territory: the Confederate forces had to be destroyed.

Was this when the expression "total war" was first employed?

We do not know the precise moment at which those words were used, but no doubt exists that this was the time at which that policy was agreed upon. Every previous Union general in the East had either attempted to capture Richmond or to drive Lee's army south. None—not even "Fighting Joe" Hooker—had declared that he needed to destroy the Army of Northern Virginia. That was precisely what Grant intended to accomplish.

If Grant was to go after Lee, what was Sherman's task?

Sherman had recently performed well on the campaign that culminated in the capture of Meridian, Mississippi. Even so, Sherman had never commanded as many men as the plans now called for, and there were those—in the newspaper business, especially—who doubted whether he could stand the pressure. Grant was determined to put those doubts to rest: he traveled to Cincinnati to confer with his good friend in private.

Grant and Sherman already saw many aspects of the war in a similar fashion, but their task was now to work in complete unison. Grant explained to Sherman that he, and his plans, had the confidence of the president and that the maximum force should be exerted to end the war in the shortest time. Years later, Sherman recalled the conversation with great simplicity: "He was to go for Lee, and I was to go for Johnston."

Was there any doubt that Grant and Sherman would succeed?

To our modern-day view, it does not seem possible they could fail. Between them, Grant and Sherman commanded about 400,000 troops, and they were well supplied. But to the average observer of the war, which was in its fourth year, there was a good deal of doubt. Why should Grant succeed where so many others had failed? Might Sherman prove to be no more than a flash in the pan?

Their Confederate opponents were far from despair. Jefferson Davis had moments when he thought he could take no more, but he always rose and continued his work. Lee had pulled off his professional magic in the past; there seemed no reason he could not do so again. And Joseph Johnston, though he lacked significant victories, had never suffered a serious defeat. If any person could lure Sherman into an untenable situation, it was Joe Johnston.

How about the man or woman on the streets of Richmond?

They were grimly determined. Richmond had roughly doubled in size since the war began, thanks to the great numbers of wounded and refugees, and the cost of living was outrageous, but the people of the Confederate capital were as certain as ever that it was their

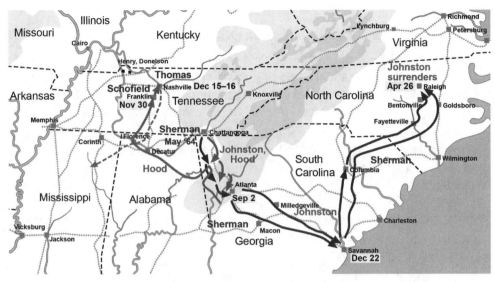

This map shows General Sherman's march through Georgia and the Carolinas as he pursued Johnston (the Savannah Campaign). The scorched-earth tactic was particularly cruel for the South, as Sherman destroyed not only military targets but also infrastructure, farmland, and civilian property.

duty to defy the enemy. And when they spoke of the enemy, they meant the Union, of course, but they were also very angry at the war profiteers, whom they called "hucksters."

What was the first alarm for the people of Richmond in 1864?

The winter had been relatively quiet, albeit filled with bad news from the war front, but Richmonders felt reasonably safe until the first of March, when the alarm bells rang and the government clerks were herded from their offices to man the fortifications. That alarm turned out to be unfounded, but just three days later came the news that Major-General Benjamin "Beast" Butler was bringing yet another Union force up the Peninsula.

General Philip Sheridan and the Union cavalry were also much more aggressive than in the past. In the spring of 1864, Sheridan conducted several raids in Virginia. All told, the people of Richmond felt much less safe than before. They knew, however, that the really big test still had not arrived.

What was Grant and Meade's working relationship like?

Grant was general-in-chief of all the Union armies, and George Meade was still commander of the Army of the Potomac. Meade had graciously stood back, saying that he was content to serve in whatever capacity Grant desired, but the recently arrived man from the West continued Meade in his position. This allowed Grant to direct overall strategy, relieving him of the day-to-day business of running the Army of the Potomac.

Figures vary, but it seems that Meade soon had the Army of the Potomac up to roughly 115,000 men and that these were the most seasoned and professional that

What did the *Richmond Enquirer* say about the "hucksters"?

"The hucksters are a small class of disreputable persons," the *Enquirer* declared, being mostly shirkers of military service, who, combining together, are able to command the market and exact any price they choose from the necessity of the people." Those prices had, indeed, risen sharply.

The beginning of the war was not too bad because ships were still evading the Northern blockade, but as blockade runners succumbed, one by one things became desperate. In the winter of 1864, flour rose to $200 a barrel, and cornfield beans rose as high as $60 per bushel. "How the middle and poor classes of citizens supply themselves with the necessaries of life, is a wonder," the *Enquirer* declared. It did not make it any easier to know that the Northern cities were suffering the reverse: a flood of cheap commodities made the purchases of everyday life easier for all but the poorest of the working people.

the army had ever seen. Equipped with the latest and best rifles, outfitted with the best tents that money could buy, the men of the Army of the Potomac were in, by far, the best shape they had ever experienced. This was the massive force that was to "go for Lee."

How many anecdotes were told of Grant?

There were so many that one can scarcely count them all. The great number was due to the fact that Grant was little known to correspondents, as well as soldiers, in the Eastern theater. One of the best was related by the *Rebellion Record*, published in 1865:

A visitor to the army called on him one morning, and found the General sitting in his tent smoking and talking to one of his staff-officers. The stranger approached the chieftain, and enquired of him as follows: "General, if you flank Lee and get between him and Richmond, will you not uncover Washington, and leave it a prey to the enemy?" General Grant, discharging a cloud of smoke from his mouth, indifferently replied: "Yes, I reckon so." The stranger, encouraged by a reply, propounded question number two: "General, do you not think Lee can detach sufficient force from his army to reinforce Beauregard and overwhelm Butler?" "Not a doubt of it," replied the General. Becoming fortified by his success, the stranger propounded question number three, as follows: "General, is there not danger that Johnston may come up, and reinforce Lee, so that the latter will swing round and cut off your communications, and seize your supplies?" "Very likely," was the cool reply of the General, and he knocked the ashes from the end of his cigar. The stranger, horrified at the awful fate about to befall General Grant and his army, made his exit, and hastened to Washington to communicate the news.

LEE ON THE DEFENSIVE

Where was Lee, and what shape were his men in?

Lee was just south of the Rapidan River, and he had roughly 65,000 men in the Army of Northern Virginia. Their condition was somewhat better than it had been on the Gettysburg campaign because their supply lines were shorter, but there were still plenty of men without shoes. Morale was high, but it was the type of morale brought about by desperation; the soldiers knew that the Union forces were coming their way in great numbers.

Lee, for his part, did not have a strong strategy. Grant, he feared, might be the first Northern general he could not figure out. All Lee could do was block the road to Richmond, and, hopefully, inflict enough casualties that Grant would turn around. This was not Lee's favored or preferred type of strategy; he was confined to the defensive.

When did Grant begin to move?

On the first of May, 1864, the Army of the Potomac began crossing the Rapidan, headed straight for Lee and the Army of Northern Virginia. Grant had to be aware that he was moving in the same direction that "Fighting Joe" Hooker had, one year ago almost to the day, but he let no nerves show.

Grant knew that the Wilderness, which enveloped most of the old Chancellorsville battlefield, was a splendid place for Lee to fight a defensive battle, but he had long since decided to confront Lee at his strongest points. Unlike a chessmaster, who seeks to unmask his opponent's weakness, Grant went straight to his enemy's strength and attempted to break it.

Was Lee ready?

Thanks to J. E. B. Stuart's scouts, Lee knew Grant was coming. Even so, the audacity with which the Army of the Potomac splashed over the Rapidan took Lee by surprise. Grant was, clearly, no Joe Hooker.

What was fighting in the Wilderness like?

Both the newspaper reports of that time and the historians ever since have had a difficult time describing the horrors of the Battle of the Wilderness. They were created by the terrain and the quality of desperation that was growing in the Army of Northern Virginia.

On May 4, 1864, Grant attacked, driving hard to Lee's right. Grant's purpose was to get through the Wilderness to the open terrain that lay beyond. Lee saw this and fought with everything he could bring to bear. There were about seventy thousand men in the Army of Northern Virginia, but only about sixty thousand were effectives at this point, meaning they were outnumbered two to one. If the Confederates had to make a desperate stand, this was the place. The fighting seesawed for several hours until the Union had a decided advantage. At a critical moment, when his center could have caved in,

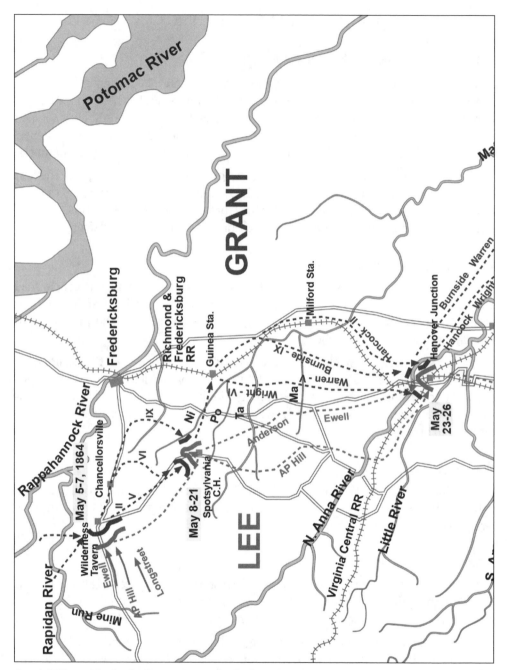

Grant's Wilderness (or Overland) campaign was fought through many parts of Virginia during the spring of 1864. Grant's strategy to hit Lee at his strongest points was daring and costly, but punching into the heart of the Confederate army resulted in a strategic advantage for the North, which overran Richmond and Petersburg.

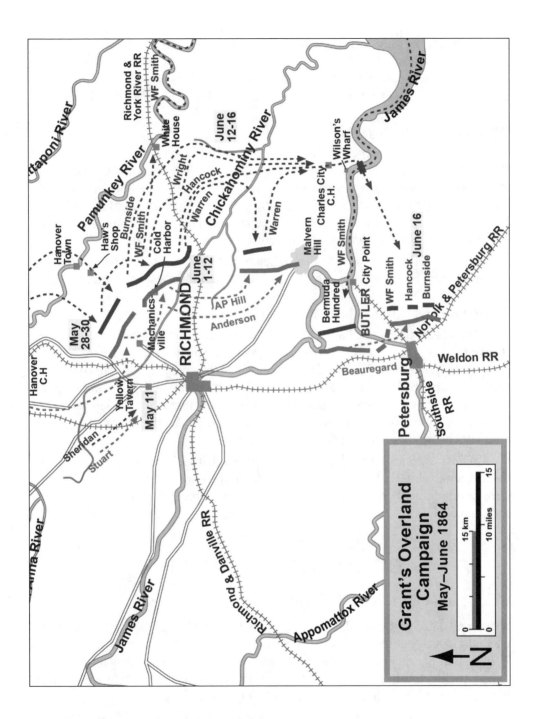

Grant's Overland
Campaign
May–June 1864

Lee galloped to the front and called on the Texans in his presence to "move them." They did, at a massive loss of life. That night, the men of both armies listened in horror to the screams of the wounded, who lay in the no-man's zone in between. Making things much worse was a series of brushfires. Many of the wounded burned to death that night.

What happened to Longstreet?

James Longstreet had, ever since the death of Stonewall Jackson, been the number-one Confederate in the field: Lee affectionately called him his "Old War Horse." Longstreet had always been impassive where enemy fire was concerned: he had a fatalistic attitude made even stronger by the death of three of his children, all of whom succumbed to typhoid fever. During the Battle of the Wilderness, Longstreet reconnoitered, and in a way that was eerily reminiscent of Stonewall Jackson, he was wounded by rifle fire from his own men.

Wounded in the hands and the throat, Longstreet was taken to Richmond. He would be out of action for the next six months, depriving Lee of his best field officer.

Was there a loss of equal importance to the other side?

Yes. Major-General John Sedgwick (1813–1864) had been, for almost three years, the steadiest leader of the Army of the Potomac. Never considered for the top command, and never seeking it, "Father John" had been a godsend to his men; his constant concern for their well-being had been seen and was rewarded with great loyalty. Not unlike James Longstreet, Sedgwick was often contemptuous of enemy fire; at the Wilderness he told his aides not to be concerned, that the enemy could not hit a standing barn. Just seconds later he was hit, and he died soon afterward.

The loss of Major-General Sedgwick paralleled that of James Longstreet. In both cases, this was a loss that could not be replaced. But the Northern men, sensing that they were getting somewhere, dedicated themselves with a ferocity that was not matched by the Confederates.

DEATH OF A CAVALIER

Where, meanwhile, was J. E. B. Stuart?

Stuart's men had participated in the fighting both at the Wilderness and at Spotsylvania Court House, but they were now called on for something even more heroic. On May 7, 1864, Phil Sheridan and 12,000 cavalrymen broke loose from the Army of the Potomac, heading south. There were almost no Confederate army units between them and Richmond, and J. E. B. Stuart, naturally, set off in hot pursuit.

The movements of both cavalry forces took longer than one might expect because they had artillery, as well as some infantry, units with them. But by the morning of May 9, 1864, Sheridan and about ten thousand men were approaching from the west while Stuart and roughly half that number had taken up a defensive position at Yellow Tavern, less than twenty miles from Richmond. To that moment, Stuart had done his duty very well; he had interposed his force, and Richmond had been warned in time. The surprise had yet to be unleashed, however.

Whom was Phil Sheridan after?

He was, in a word, after Stuart. The move south had been a deliberate decoy, an attempt to get Stuart to leave the Army of Northern Virginia. Sheridan, who was no stranger to controversy, had been in a furious argument with George B. Meade, commander of the Army of the Potomac. Sheridan shouted that Meade confused his knowledge of infantry with that of cavalry. Meade reported the shouting match to Ulysses Grant, who, all too typically, took Sheridan at his word. If Sheridan could flush out J. E. B. Stuart, so much the better. Therefore, Stuart mistakenly believed that Sheridan was out for Richmond, when he himself was the target.

Originally an infantry general, Philip Henry Sheridan was transferred to lead the Army of the Potomac's Cavalry Corps. In this position, he defeated Confederates at Shenandoah Valley and later at Appomattox.

The Battle at Yellow Tavern raged for hours, with two significant breaks in between. Stuart's men knew the terrain better, but Sheridan's were on a high, and they were equipped with the new rapid-repeating Spencer carbines. The battle seesawed for hours, and at one point in the midafternoon, Stuart repelled a Yankee attack. Filled with pleasure, standing tall and handsome in the stirrups, Stuart gestured and shouted to his men to begin the pursuit. At that very moment, a federal cavalryman on the run turned back and shot Stuart. The bullet passed through his stomach and went out the other side.

What happened to Stuart?

He was taken on a litter and brought by his grieving men all the way to Richmond, where he was taken to the house of his brother-in-law. Those who were present—and there were many—concurred that here was a genuine hero, one whose countenance and attitude did not alter in the face of death. Stuart had long since promised his mother he would never drink alcohol, and even on his deathbed, he took only a few sips of brandy to dull the pain.

Jefferson Davis came to the house, shook Stuart's hand, and asked if he could be of service. Stuart replied that all he cared about was that he had done his duties and that his family would be cared for. Stuart died on the evening of May 12, 1864. He was thirty-one years old.

What was the reaction in Richmond?

It was the saddest yet recorded. Stonewall Jackson, whose death had, eerily, taken place just a year earlier, had been a major reason for the Confederate belief that they could win the war, but their love and affection for J. E. B. Stuart was a major reason why the war seemed worth winning.

At his best, Stuart had exemplified the code of Southern chivalry. Very likely, his close confidantes kept quiet about some of his escapades and mighty oaths, but the aspects of his character that come through the official record are quite engaging. Stuart was, to some extent, the Erwin Rommel of the Civil War: the enemy general that the winning side fought strongly, but admired at the same time.

What was happening in the Wilderness?

Grant sustained heavy casualties in the Battle of the Wilderness, perhaps 8,000 men killed, wounded, or missing. Two days afterward, when they were ordered to break camp, the men of the Army of the Potomac expected that Grant—like Joe Hooker, Ambrose Burnside, and others—would order them to recross the Rapidan, heading for Washington, D.C. This pattern had been deeply etched in their memories. But at a crucial point in that morning's march, the sergeants and battalion leaders pointed south, rather than north. At that moment, the men of the Army of the Potomac knew that the battle, and the campaign, was to continue. When Grant and his staff came riding by, they cheered him heartily.

What was the progress toward Lincoln's renomination?

There was a major gala event at Cooper Union on May 14, 1864, to drum up support for Lincoln. He had no significant Republican competition, but there were those who claimed the nation would be better served by a compromise candidate who could appeal to Republicans and middle-of-the-road voters. It was to forestall this that the Cooper Union benefit was held.

Several army generals spoke that evening, and the truth of what they said seemed self-evident. Only Lincoln had held the military policy together. There had been times when it seemed that George McClellan—or someone else—would railroad the military agenda; time and again, Lincoln had pulled things together. The Cooper Union event did not guarantee Lincoln the nomination, but it represented an important step in that direction.

What was the attitude of the Northern newspapers in May 1864?

There was a new hardline, which was evidenced by the *New York Times* attack on Robert E. Lee. On May 23, 1864, the *Times* ran a special column entitled "The Chivalry of Robert E. Lee." Readers could see the trend right in the opening sentence, "When monkeys are gods, what must the people be?"

Lee was supposedly the paragon of Southern chivalry, the article declared, but when one traced his bloodlines, he or she found something else entirely. The *Times* mistakenly declared that Lee's father, "Light-Horse" Harry Lee of Revolutionary fame, was his granduncle, but it correctly described his financial and personal woes. Another Lee relative was found, upon some research, to have voted for approval of the Constitution, but to have privately said he hoped it would unravel one day. What is significant about the essay, or column, is that one cannot imagine it having been written three years earlier. The *Times* went as far as to say that when one committed an act of treason—and in Lee's case this meant abandoning the flag under which he was raised—it perverted something in one's character, an irretrievable error. Very likely, this new hardline was the result of the enormous lists of battle casualties.

How many men were lost in May 1864?

Thanks to the pileup of battles—the Wilderness, Spotsylvania Court House, as well as any number of skirmishes—it is difficult to put an exact number on it, but it seems likely that the North suffered 40,000 men killed, wounded, or missing during May. The South probably suffered about 28,000.

Only in retrospect, with 150 years of hindsight, can we say that the North could "afford" such losses. On the human and personal level, no nation or people can ever afford such casualties, but even in the heat of the moment, the lists seemed insupportable. Major-General John Sedgwick was the most prominent casualty, but several brigadier-generals lost their lives, and once one descends to the level of captain, the losses simply become enormous. Most of the newspapers refrained from criticizing General Grant, but they were right on the verge.

What happened to the men who were taken prisoner?

Thousands of men were captured on both sides during May 1864, but—after the Fort Pillow Massacre—prisoner exchanges had been suspended. As a result, many Northern men went to suffer in Southern prisons and vice versa. One of the most interesting comments on the Northern prisoners was made by Mary Chesnut, still living on the Chesnut family plantation in South Carolina.

"In all these years I have seen no Yankees," she wrote on May 8, 1864. "All the prisoners, well or wounded, have been Germans, Scotch regiments, Irish regiments, most German, however."

What was Grant like as a person?

Probably we make too much of it. Grant was a very simple person. To him, it was obvious that the war would only end by stamping out the resistance. Nothing less would do.

Over the next few weeks, as the casualty lists multiplied, Grant would be called "the butcher." Very rarely did he attempt to persuade the public, or any particular person, of the reason for his methods. He had the confidence of the president, and that was what mattered.

How did Lee respond to Grant's move?

The only way he could. As Grant's army moved to its left, Lee and his force had to move to its right, to counter. The two armies clashed at Spotsylvania Court House.

The battle was furious, but at least this time the opponents could see each other. As before, Grant kept turning the Army of the Potomac in a clockwise direction, to the southeast, and Lee and the Army of Northern Virginia continually attempted to keep that clock from moving completely. If the hands of that metaphorical clock ever swung around completely, the Confederates would be smashed.

Spotsylvania Court House was another meat-grinder for the men in the field. Roughly seven thousand men were killed, wounded, or missing on both sides. By now, the men of the Army of the Potomac had great confidence in Grant: they knew he would not turn back, regardless of the casualties. There were many calls in the North for his replacement, however, with the newspapers taking up the call of "Grant the butcher." More temperate newspaper editors questioned the wisdom of his plans. But Grant did the same thing as before.

Where did the Union men move after Spotsylvania?

Just as before, they moved south by southeast, threatening to outflank the Confederates. Lee, again, had to move with great speed and reposition his army, this time along the banks of the North Anna River. Lee was greatly disturbed by the developments; every previous Union general he had faced would have quit by this point. Grant, on the other hand, was sending short, terse, but poignant telegrams to General Halleck, always to the effect that things were going well. Responding to some of the criticisms in the press, Grant wrote: "I propose to fight it out along this line if it takes all summer."

Grant's confidence stemmed from the knowledge that it would not take all summer. One or two more battles such as the ones he had seen would prove the complete ruin of Lee's army, he believed. Most military historians who study the campaign concur that the Confederates were in very bad shape. There had been hundreds of heroic actions, but the Northern men kept coming, and at some point the men of the Army of Northern Virginia would break.

What was the sentiment in Richmond?

The Confederate capital had seen difficult times before, but the spring of 1864 was especially trying. A few prominent persons snuck out of the capital, mostly to flee overseas, but the large majority stayed right where they were. They were confident that Lee and the Army of Northern Virginia would, by some miracle, prevail.

This is the home of President Jefferson Davis in Richmond, Virginia, from 1861 to 1864.

284

The hospitals of Richmond were completely overwhelmed by the number of wounded men brought by ambulance and horse-cart. The Northern prisoners, on Belle Isle, had already gone through privations, but the shortage of everything made matters much worse for them as well. While the Confederates in Richmond hoped and believed that this would be a repeat of the spring of 1862—when McClellan failed—the Yankee prisoners on the island hoped and prayed for the opposite.

DISASTER AT COLD HARBOR

Where is Cold Harbor?

Located about twelve miles northeast of Richmond, Cold Harbor is an undulating series of flatlands mixed with low hills. It was, and is, typical Virginia countryside: delightful in spring and fall and murderous in summer by virtue of the heat. By the end of May 1864, Lee had concentrated his men in a defensive position in and around Cold Harbor with ditches that ran for miles (not for nothing had he been called the "King of Spades"). Grant brought the full Army of the Potomac into position, and for a day or two the armies merely glowered at one another. Then, on June 3, 1864, Grant ordered an attack all along the line.

How was Cold Harbor different from Pickett's Charge?

It was on a much broader front, running slightly more than three miles. All along that line, the Union men advanced, thinking their sheer numbers would overwhelm the Confederates. And in a different kind of situation, perhaps earlier in the war, they might have prevailed. But the men of both sides had become absolute killers when fighting on the defensive. Fredericksburg had proved it, the defeat of Pickett's Charge reiterated the fact, and the Union attack at Cold Harbor should never have been made.

After one hour, roughly seven thousand Northern men were killed, wounded, or missing. Confederate losses were less than half that number. Pulling back to their own ditches, the Union men found that was one of the worst calamities of the war: in terms of absolute casualties, it was worse than Pickett's Charge. Grant was furious with himself and appalled by the slaughter. He did a good job covering up the disaster. Weeks passed before the full story of Cold Harbor was made public.

Why was there such a fuss, or contretemps, about burying the dead?

The war was in such a crisis moment—especially for the South—that Lee did not wish the Federals to see any of his lines. Lee, therefore, rebuffed all attempts to converse with Grant over a truce to remove the wounded and bury the dead. As a result, thousands of wounded men lay between the federal and Confederate lines, sometimes screaming with pain. Some observers claimed that the five days following the Battle of Cold Harbor represented the worst—most horrific—time of the whole war.

General Grant once again charged fully into Lee's strongest point at the Battle of Cold Harbor. This time, it was a mistake, as the South's forces were well fortified and Union casualties ran high.

Was there any possibility Grant would now pull back?

Any other general would have done so. Some would have tendered their resignations. But with Grant, it was entirely different, and by this time Lee and the Confederates knew it. As amazed as they were by their smashing defensive victory, the men of the Army of Northern Virginia knew that this was but the beginning: led by Grant, the men in blue would fight them to the bitter end.

In better days, Lee would have gone on the offensive. There was no chance of that now. He had lost roughly 30,000 men in the past six weeks, and he no longer had J. E. B. Stuart to bring him information of the enemy's movements. Lee, too, was boxed into a situation he could not escape.

What did Grant resolve upon after Cold Harbor?

He decided not to make any more attempts on fortified locations, and, examining his maps, he chose to approach Richmond from a different angle. In 1862, McClellan and the Army of the Potomac had come up the James Peninsula and been stopped; in 1864, Grant would cross over the James River and attack Richmond from the south.

This was one of those brilliant solutions that when it is finally presented, everyone marvels it had not been seen before. But to execute this audacious plan, Grant had to pull back from where his men stared at Lee's, move to his left, and cross a major river, all without alerting the enemy to his intentions. That he even made the attempt indicates his boldness.

When did the move take place?

On June 16, 1864, the Army of the Potomac began pulling back from its positions opposite the Confederates at Cold Harbor. The move was made with great skill and deception. "Dummy" guns were left in place, and handfuls of men kept campfires burning. The wet, damp weather helped in that the Confederates were not very observant, but it made the movement difficult for the Union men. Within a day, however, they had pulled back five miles and were making a dramatic move to the south.

One thing Grant had was plenty of materiel. Three pontoon bridges were constructed in record time, and the Army of the Potomac began crossing the James River. Meanwhile, the Confederates still had not learned of the movement.

How did Grant ever pull off this deception?

Partly it was thanks to the heroic actions of his engineers, but it was also because Lee and the Army of Northern Virginia had lost their "eyes and ears" when J. E. B. Stuart died. The federal cavalry was now everywhere in the ascendant, and Grant had better intelligence than Lee.

Lee was just awakening to Grant's movement, and the danger it posed, when Lincoln sent a congratulatory telegram to his top general. "I begin to see it," Lincoln wrote. "You will succeed." What Lincoln saw was that Grant had completely outmaneuvered Lee and that by crossing the James he could conduct warfare in the open countryside. It seemed a matter of days before Richmond would be taken. To his wife, Julia, Grant wrote that his army had just pulled off one of the true feats of modern warfare, withdrawing in the face of the enemy to make a completely unexpected maneuver.

Who was Grant's other correspondent?

The official papers of Ulysses Grant run to eleven impressive volumes, and the modern-day reader is struck by the terse but accurate composition of this man, who was so quiet in public. Many of the letters are to General-in-Chief William Henry Halleck, but the ones that really catch the reader's eye are those to Lincoln. Grant and the president clearly understood and valued one another. Grant's other major correspondent, however, was his wife.

Ulysses and Julia Grant were an uncommonly close and happy couple. He was a recent graduate of West Point when he courted her at her father's Missouri farm, and once married they were seldom apart (one of the few times they were separated led to his resignation from the U.S. Army in 1854). In his numerous letters, Grant informed Julia of what was happening at the front, but he always asked about personal matters: How was this nephew doing? Was there enough money? The letters between husband and wife show an appealing side to the man whom some people called "the butcher" because of his willingness to shed blood in the cause of the Union.

What, meanwhile, was happening at sea?

The Confederate blockade runners and privateers had enjoyed many notable successes, but the most dramatic were those gained by CSS *Alabama*. Captained by Raphael Semmes (1809–1877), the *Alabama* was a British ship that had been sold to the Confederacy, and—in order to avoid violations of international law—been sent to sea under a British crew before being transferred to Semmes. Once he took command of the *Alabama* in the summer of 1862, Semmes commenced a series of brilliant captures and raids on Northern commerce. For almost two years, Semmes outwitted his Union opponents at sea. But he eventually was cornered in the harbor of Cherbourg, France, by the USS *Kearsarge*.

What was the scene like at Cherbourg, France?

Knowing that Semmes would come out to challenge the *Kearsarge*, most of the population of Cherbourg and half the population of Paris, some claimed, came to observe the action.

Semmes came out of port on June 17, 1864, and the *Alabama* and *Kearsarge* immediately began a series of circular movements. Each captain wished to "cross the T," a naval expression meaning to bring one's guns to bear on the opponent's bow or stern, where the fewest opposing guns were placed. The *Kearsarge* had a heavier complement of guns, and she slowly gained the upper hand. Roughly eight circular movements were made by both ships, and at the end of the last one, the *Alabama* was ready to sink. Semmes and most of his men got off the *Alabama*, some in boats and some in the water. The *Kearsarge* kept a respectful distance to avoid being swamped by the *Alabama*'s sinking, but Semmes later accused the *Kearsage*'s captain of allowing his men to drown. Some did, but the majority, including Semmes, were picked up by neutral boats and ships in the harbor.

Under the command of Captain Raphael Semmes, the CSS *Alabama* helped the South significantly by interrupting Union trade in the Atlantic from 1862 to 1864.

Where did Semmes go after the loss of his ship?

Rescued by an intrepid English yachtsman, Semmes was brought to England, where he found himself something of a hero. Britain indignantly refused all requests for Semmes to be handed over to the Federals, and late in 1864, he made his way back to the Confederacy. Thanks to the Union blockade, Semmes had to enter by way of coastal Texas, and he traced almost the same route as Colonel Arthur Fremantle in 1863. On arriving in Richmond, Semmes was lionized by the populace. Jefferson Davis made him the first rear-admiral of the fledgling Confederate Navy, but it was apparent to most observers that this navy was on its last legs.

Why did Richmond not fall in the summer of 1864?

By all rights it should have fallen. Lee's men were in a rather bad state, and the morale of Grant's men—who still outnumbered them two to one—was at an all-time high. This was one of the key moments of the war, a moment at which the "should" yielded to the "possible."

Once across the James, Grant sent his advance units with great speed. Their mission was to capture the town of Petersburg, twenty miles south of Richmond. Once that key town, blessed with railroad connections, was taken, Grant could choke off Richmond's already tenuous food supply lines. But the Confederates got to Petersburg first. Only about 2,000 men got there in time, with General P. G. T. Beauregard in command, but they fought heroically, well enough to keep Grant's advance force from capturing Petersburg. Knowing the tremendous importance, Grant fired one angry message after another to his subordinates, but they were all in vain: Petersburg held. When he arrived three days later, Grant recognized he would have to reduce the town by means of a siege.

BATTLE OF THE CRATER

How advanced was the art of siege craft?

The art of carrying out sieges had been brought to a very high level a century earlier. One of the best examples of a classic siege was that of Yorktown, Virginia, captured by George Washington, Count Rochambeau, and the combined French and American forces in 1781. But the Napoleonic Wars had brought about a marked bias toward the offense, and the art had languished. It resurfaced during the Civil War at a time when the powerful new weapons of both sides combined to make sieges both longer and more costly in terms of casualties.

The Union was far in advance of the Confederacy in this regard. The Dahlgren gun, the Parrot cannon, and all sorts of mortars would be employed in the Siege of Petersburg. There were times when the regiments of the Army of the Potomac merely provided cover for the engineers, artillerists, and other siege specialists.

Which side was more displeased to have to fight in this way?

Grant, of course, was greatly disappointed in not having captured Petersburg. Instead of a dramatic swift blow that might end the war, he had to settle down to an interminable number of details concerned with the siege: none of them was his specialty. But if Grant was down about having to conduct a siege, Lee was despondent over having to fight in this manner.

From its inception, the Army of Northern Virginia had fought best while on the offensive and had done so with the improvisational skills of its officer corps. Lee and his top commanders provided the tactical and strategic genius, but their orders had to be carried out by the men in the field, and whether it fell harder on the captains and lieutenants or the sergeants and corporals is an interesting question in itself. But Lee and his men were not accustomed to fighting a protracted siege, and Lee confessed to one of his subordinates that being confined to this location meant that it was only a matter of time before the superior Union numbers led to their victory.

What did the siege lines look like?

They ran from the northeast side of Richmond to the James River, then jumped over the James to its southern side, where they slowly extended out to the south and southwest of Petersburg. Roughly thirty-seven miles of offensive and defensive lines were established, and no one can calculate how many metric tons of earth were moved. Throughout these long lines were ditches and trenches, but also temporary housing, which ranged from tents to makeshift shelters to the occasional house. The civilians had, naturally, fled, and the few houses that remained were commandeered. As time passed, the Northern men put up towers, not to use in the style of medieval siege towers, but to observe what happened in the enemy lines.

Who planned "the Crater"?

The idea originated with Lieutenant Colonel Henry Pleasants from Pennsylvania. He proposed to Grant that his Pennsylvania engineers dig a tunnel five hundred feet long, directly under the Confederate defenses. Explosives would be set, and a hole blasted in the enemy lines.

Grant was usually willing to entertain novel ideas, and thousands of men were soon engaged in the hot but quiet work of removing the tons of earth. That this was done without alerting the defenders suggests, yet again, that the Confederate intelligence system had been compromised. All was set for the early morning of July 30, 1864.

What happened when the explosives blew?

At 4:44 A.M. on July 30, 1864, the explosives blew with what must have been the loudest sounds of the entire war. The Pennsylvania miners had done their work well, even expertly. The explosion created a crater twenty feet long and sixty feet wide, and it was—in some places—twenty feet deep.

General Ambrose Burnside—who had commanded at Fredericksburg—had charge of the assault, and three divisions of Northern soldiers attempted to pour into the Crater. The explosion had shaken the Confederate defenders—literally as well as figuratively—and for a few brief moments, it was possible that a breakthrough would be achieved.

What went wrong at "the Crater"?

Almost everything, from the Union point of view. The first men in the Crater were surprised and overwhelmed by the destruction; some even attempted to pull out Confederates from the ruins. But the longer they remained in the Crater, they more they were pushed by the Union men behind them and fired on by the Confederates in front.

The Confederates recovered quickly and began pouring rifle fire into the men jammed into the Crater. It takes an active work of the imagination to see what the Union men trapped in the Crater went through—unless one sees the early part of the movie *Cold Mountain*, which displays the event in all its horror. The Union leaders had deliberately chosen to bring black troops into the Crater; they came in for more than the normal amount of anger and hate from the Confederates. One Confederate nurse believed that the Crater marked a change in relations between Confederates and Yankees, that the former began to detest and even hate the latter. By the time the attack was called off four hours later, the North had suffered 4,500 men killed, wounded, or missing. What might possibly have been the great breakthrough was instead the great disappointment.

What did the Crater look like from the Confederate viewpoint?

The best description was made by Colonel E. P. Alexander, who had commanded the Confederate artillery at Gettysburg a year earlier.

"Into this crater the leading division literally swarmed, until it was packed about as full as it could hold, and what could not get in there, crowded into the adjacent trenches, which the falling earth had caused to be vacated for a short distance on each flank. But, considering the surprise, the novelty of the occasion and the terrific cannonade by 150 guns and mortars which was opened immediately, the coolness and self-possession of the entire brigade was remarkable, and to it is to be attributed the success of the defense."

What did Grant do after the failure of the attack on the Crater?

He could only expand his siege lines and hope that the combined weight of men and materiel would eventually wear down Lee's men. After the failure of the attack, the major initiative for the summer campaign was in Sherman's hands, not Grant's.

FROM DALTON TO ATLANTA

Where, meanwhile, were Sherman and the western armies?

Sherman and Confederate General Joseph Johnston continued their "dance" across northern Georgia. Johnston came in for a lot of criticism from his men, but those who examined the campaign from afar concluded that he was doing the best of all Confederate commanders at this point.

Johnston's desire was to prevent Sherman from taking Atlanta. Given the number of railroad lines that fed into Atlanta, it had suddenly become the second most impor-

> ## What famous painting depicts Farragut at the point when history says he shouted, "Damn the torpedoes! Full speed ahead"?
>
> A magnificent painting, executed by William Heysham Overend, depicts Farragut and the crew of the USS *Hartford* on the morning of August 5, 1864. Seven federal naval officers stand, point, and peer at the enemy, while nearly twenty federal sailors, including one very muscular black man (who has a gold neckerchief on his head), handle the massive cannon that are firing at the Confederates. Admiral Farragut stands grandly atop the scene, leaning with his right arm to one of the ratlines. He looks unconcerned even though the battle is approaching its climax, and the sea is riddled with mines (then called torpedoes).
>
> While the painting naturally takes some artistic liberties, it is not that far from the truth. There were African American sailors in the Union Navy long before there were any black regiments ashore, and the separation between officers and men—as shown in the painting—was a fact of life in nineteenth-century navies. Very likely, Farragut was not standing so unrestrained as in the painting; several reports claim that he ordered his men to tie him into the ratlines so he could watch the battle without being concerned about his footing.

tant city in the Confederacy, a valuation that very few would have expected just three years earlier. Like Richmond, Atlanta was in a state of confusion, but it had not yet become pandemonium.

What was the situation at sea in 1864?

The Union had gained a maritime stranglehold over the Confederacy. Plenty of blockade runners still evaded the Northern ships, but rather few made it back to port: quite a few ended up rotting in the harbors of foreign nations.

David Glasgow Farragut had been out of action far longer than he liked. In the spring of 1864, he practically chomped at the bit to attack Mobile, Alabama, the biggest source for blockade runners. Only in July did Farragut get the go-ahead, and even then he was warned that the Confederates had placed torpedoes around the entrance to the harbor. Farragut had by now assembled seventeen wooden warships and several ironclad monitors, some of which contained not one but two turrets. In terms of overall firepower, his fleet held vastly more than the Confederate defenders. Even so, the attack, which was made on August 5, 1864, was not without risk.

How did the attack on Mobile commence?

Mobile Bay is sheltered by several islands, and Farragut led his fleet in by the closest way, near Fort Morgan, which was on Mobile Point. Farragut went in with all guns blazing,

Visitors can still see Fort Morgan today. It is now a state park by Mobile Bay, Alabama.

but the heart seemed to go out of his men when the lead vessel, the USS *Tecumseh*, hit a mine and exploded. She and her ninety-man crew went to the bottom immediately.

This was a crucial moment in the Battle for Mobile, but also for the entire Union naval effort. Farragut, typically, was not the type to give up. Many observers claim that he shouted "Damn the torpedoes, full speed ahead!" while others state that he merely gave the command for the attack to continue. In either case, the other sixteen ships of the federal attack squadron passed through the torpedo-laden channel without incident. Very likely, the torpedoes had been corrupted by saltwater.

What was the naval battle like?

It was typical for the war in that the Union possessed an overwhelming preponderance of firepower. Several Confederate ships were captured or sunk in half an hour, and the only time of real danger for the Union ships was when the CSS *Tennessee*, a massive ironclad, made a suicidal lunge at them. Rammed, fired upon, and surrounded, the *Tennessee* surrendered, by which time her deck had become a scene of disaster.

Farragut had done it again. At the cost of fewer than 250 men killed, wounded, or missing (Confederate losses were slightly less), he had taken down an entire Confederate port and its squadron, denying the South its last major outlet to the sea. In his telegrams to the navy and war departments, Farragut emphasized his belief that it was not worthwhile to capture Mobile itself. The city of thirty thousand would be difficult to capture, he said, but even more difficult to police. It was much better to keep a squadron of observation and allow the Confederate port to die a slow death from economic hardship, he said.

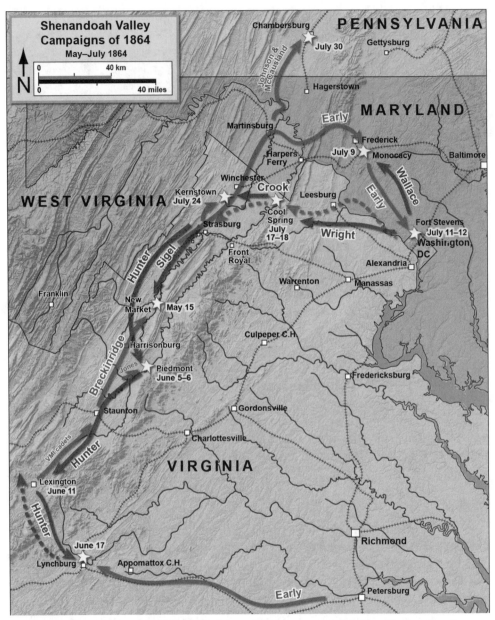

Shenandoah Valley Campaigns of 1864
May–July 1864

0   40 km
0   40 miles

N

PENNSYLVANIA

Chambersburg
July 30

Gettysburg

Johnson & McCausland

Hagerstown

MARYLAND

Martinsburg

Early

Frederick

July 9

Monocacy

Baltimore

Harpers Ferry

Winchester

Crook

Leesburg

Wallace

Early

WEST VIRGINIA

Kernstown
July 24

Cool Spring
July 17–18

Fort Stevens
July 11–12

Strasburg

Hunter

Sigel

Front Royal

Wright

Washington, DC

Alexandria

Franklin

New Market
May 15

Warrenton

Manassas

Breckinridge

Jones

Harrisonburg

Culpeper C.H.

Piedmont
June 5–6

Staunton

Gordonsville

Fredericksburg

Charlottesville

VMI cadets

Hunter

VIRGINIA

Lexington
June 11

Hunter

Richmond

June 17

Lynchburg

Appomattox C.H.

Early

Petersburg

A final push by the South in mid 1864 found Confederates moving once more into Pennsylvania, where they burned Chambersburg, and came dangerously close to Washington, D.C., before being turned back.

Who were Jaquess and Gilmore?

James Jaquess, often called the "fighting parson," helped to recruit a regiment in Illinois. James R. Gilmore was a New York City businessman. Both men wished to see an end to the fighting, and to that end they obtained a pass from Lincoln, allowing them to pass through

General Grant's lines. Jaquess and Gilmore experienced some slight difficulties in passing through the Confederate lines, but upon their repeated description of their mission (as one of peace), they were allowed through to Richmond. On July 17, 1864, they met with Confederate Secretary of State Judah Benjamin, whom they clearly did not like; then that evening they met Benjamin and President Davis. Their description of Davis was as follows:

> He had a broad, massive forehead, and a mouth and chin denoting great energy and strength of will.... His manners were simple, easy, and quite fascinating; and he threw an indescribable charm into his voice, as he extended his hand and said to us, "I am glad to see you gentlemen. You are very welcome to Richmond."

How did the conversation proceed?

Because this was one of the few times that Davis spoke freely in the company of Northern persons, his words are especially important. Both he and his two visitors expressed a profound desire for peace, but they saw different roads toward that end. To Davis, the matter was simple. The Union should cease its invasion and withdraw all its armies from Southern soil.

To Gilmore and Jaquess, the matter was rather different. They asked Davis if he really believed that two peoples who spoke the same language—as well as preserved the same cultural heritage—could really be separated by an imaginary line. Davis replied, with some bitterness, that it was no longer possible. The depredations of the war had caused such ill will that, as he put it: "Our children may forget this war, but *we* cannot."

What did Davis say about the cause of the war and the reason for its continuance?

Because it was such a rare event—a frank talk between the Confederate president and two Northern men who professed goodwill to the South—it may be better to quote Davis precisely:

> "By self-government you mean disunion—Southern independence?" the Northern men asked.
>
> "Yes," Davis replied.
>
> "And slavery you say, is no longer an element in the contest?"
>
> "No, it is not, it never was an *essential* element," Davis answered. "It was only a means of bringing other conflicting elements to an earlier culmination. It fired the musket which was already capped and loaded. There are essential differences between the North and the South that will, however this war may end, make them two nations."

One does not have to agree with Davis, or sympathize with the South, to hear the importance of these words. Very likely, the war was not about slavery, at least not in Jefferson Davis' mind. He could not resist making some more comments on the subject.

What did Davis say about his own slaves?

Here is what Davis said when the commissioners talked of amnesty—the idea that all Confederates would have to apply for it—and emancipation. He dismissed the idea of amnesty, saying that one had to commit a crime in order to require it:

> And emancipation! You have already emancipated nearly two millions of our slaves—and if you will take care of them, you may emancipate the rest. I had a few [slaves] when the war began. I was of some use to them; they never were of any to me. Against their will you "emancipated" them; and you may "emancipate every negro in the Confederacy, but *we will be free*. We will govern ourselves. We will do it, if we have to see every Southern plantation sacked, and every Southern city in flames."

Did Davis really believe it when he said, "I was of some use to them; they never were of any to me"?

It is, naturally, difficult to know when a person is speaking the truth (or the truth as he sees it). A powerful ring of authenticity to this meeting between Davis and the two Northern gentlemen exists, however, and one feels that it is quite possible that Davis—and perhaps other slaveholders—had indeed persuaded themselves of this idea. According to this way of thinking, the enslavement of African Americans was a necessary thing, done in the interests of the slaves. To continue in this vein, Davis believed that he had never needed slaves—he was entirely capable of caring for himself—but that he had accepted the burden of being a slaveholder for the greater good.

Most of us—regardless of party, persuasion, or creed—cringe or are even revolted at this expression, but it is important to take what Davis said at face value. If one accepts his premise that the holding of slaves was more of a burden than a profit, then one can imagine how Davis would react so bitterly to Northern proposals. In his mind, the slaves were better off before the war; the Southern whites were better off; indeed, everyone was better off before the war began.

Where was Sherman at this point?

Sherman left southern Tennessee in May 1864 and almost immediately ran into Joseph Johnston and about sixty thousand Confederate defenders. Johnston was the most experienced officer in the Confederate army at this point, but his critics accurately pointed out that he hardly ever won anything: his career seemed to be based on the principle of retreat.

Sherman was all too happy to oblige. He, too, preferred the advance and retreat

Atlanta's citizens quickly evacuated the city before the Union's General Sherman invaded in 1864.

of flanking maneuvers to brutal, head-on confrontations. Knowing he had the numerical advantage, Sherman could afford to maneuver almost indefinitely.

How important was Atlanta to the Confederate cause?

Atlanta had only about 10,500 people when the war began, but the "Gate City," as it was called, was the hub of three major railroads. If Atlanta fell, the Confederacy would be cut in two.

How long did it take to maneuver Joe Johnston all the way to Atlanta?

It took three long months, during which there were numerous skirmishes but only one major battle, that of Kennesaw Mountain. On June 27, 1864, Sherman made the mistake of a frontal assault on the Confederate position at Kennesaw Mountain; his men ran into rifle fire that was nearly as murderous as what Grant's men experienced at Cold Harbor. Sherman suffered over 2,000 casualties, but he called it cheap at the price, and in the inexorable and remorseless logic of war, his comment made sense. The Confederates kept retreating, and the way to Atlanta became a little clearer all the time.

What did the Confederate population think of Sherman?

They had not, at this point, yet seen all of his remorseless determination. Some Confederates, therefore, underestimated Sherman, as was shown by a conversation between a captain on Sherman's staff and a refined Southern woman:

"May I ask where you intend to go?" he asked.

"To Augusta, where your army can't come," she replied.

"I would not be too sure of that," he replied. "It is a long way from Nashville to Atlanta, and we are here."

"Oh yes," she replied with ineffable scorn, "you will 'flank' us, I suppose?"

"Possibly, madam."

"Look here, sir; there are not two nations on the face of this earth whose language, customs, and histories are [so] different, and who are geographically separated as the poles, but what are nearer to each other than the North and South. There are no two peoples in the world who hate each other more."

Who replaced Joe Johnston?

Up to the third week of July, Jefferson Davis stuck with Joseph Johnston, who could claim one victory, at Kennesaw, and no significant defeats. But pressure built in Richmond for Johnston's removal, and in July Davis telegraphed that General John B. Hood—who had lost an arm at Gettysburg—was to take command of the Army of Tennessee.

Hood was not thrilled with the assignment. He knew that the men were demoralized by the long series of retreats, and he feared the worst. Hood was not a man to back down, however; indeed, when Jefferson Davis asked Lee his opinion of the new commander, Lee replied that Hood was "all lion, and no fox."

How many times did Hood attack Sherman?

Within a week of taking command of the Army of Tennessee, Hood made his first attack, to the southwest of Atlanta. Hood's plan was reasonably good, and his men were keen for a fight, but both the weather—heavy rains—and Sherman's numbers took their toll. The Confederates suffered almost twice as many casualties at the Battle of Peachtree Creek as the Union, and after that failure, Hood's men showed much less spirit.

Why does Hood usually come in for so much blame?

An idea—largely mistaken—exists that Hood was something of a buffoon, unable to draw up good battle plans. As is usually the case, there was some truth to the accusation: Hood certainly was no Robert E. Lee. Hood was a capable, courageous man, however, who was excellent when commanding a division; it was only when he reached the level of commanding general that his deficiencies began to be more apparent. The truth is that Hood was in an impossible situation.

Most of what Hood had learned from three years' service in the Army of Northern Virginia was inapplicable to the Western theater. The distances were longer, the supply lines even creakier, and Hood was outnumbered to a greater extent than Lee and the Army of Northern Virginia. Therefore, when Hood, logically, applied the lessons he had learned from Lee, he leaned toward the attack and played right into Sherman's hands.

Did Sherman understand his adversary?

He understood Hood very well. In Hood's situation, Sherman might have been lured into similar mistakes (both men had fiery tempers). But Sherman knew that the terrain and the numbers both favored him, and he could afford to let Hood make mistakes. One led to another, and by the first day of September 1864, Sherman had a death grip on the city of Atlanta.

Realizing the hopelessness of the situation, Hood evacuated the remains of his army from Atlanta. A set of railway cars intended to carry away the Confederate ordnance had to be abandoned, and Hood ordered them to be set afire. This was the beginning of the destruction that was to mark Atlanta and the rest of the campaign that was bringing "total war" to the Confederacy.

THE FINAL STRUGGLES: SEPTEMBER 1864 TO APRIL 1865

When did Sherman enter Atlanta?

Sherman and his army came into Atlanta on September 2, 1864. Sherman had cleverly outmaneuvered General Hood and won the city with a minimum of lives lost. He immediately telegraphed Lincoln, saying, "Atlanta is ours, and fairly won."

To this point, Sherman and the Army of the Mississippi had, indeed, performed well in the field, and in conquest, but the record was about to become muddied. Perhaps Sherman had already formed the idea in his mind, but his actions, commencing right after the capture of Atlanta, show a callous attitude toward the civilian population.

What was different about the capture of Atlanta from earlier Confederate towns?

To this point in the war, many, if not most, Confederate towns and capitals were still "free" from the Northern foe. New Orleans had fallen early in the war, and Jackson, Mississippi, had been practically destroyed during the Vicksburg campaign, but the majority held out. Atlanta had a population of only about 11,000, but it was one of the most important of all railway towns in the Confederacy; by capturing Atlanta, Sherman practically severed the Confederate States in two.

Another aspect that was different is that Atlanta became memorialized by many of its inhabitants, who sadly contrasted life "before" and "after" the Yankee conquest. These ideas would be enshrined in the novel *Gone with the Wind*, followed by the film of the same name.

What was Sherman's first move?

He ordered that all the civilians remove themselves—or be removed by his soldiers. This was, perhaps, the first time in the war that a civilian population had been treated in so harsh a manner, and there were all sorts of protests. Some of the most articulate came from John Bell Hood, commander of the Army of Tennessee:

"You order into exile the whole population of a city, drive men, women and children from their houses at the point of the bayonet…. You come into our country with your army avowedly for the purpose of subjugating free white men, women and children; and not only intend to rule over them, but you make negroes your allies, and desire to place over us an inferior race, which we have raised from barbarism to its present position."

Sherman replied: "War is cruelty, and you cannot refine it; and those who brought war on our country deserve all the curses and maledictions a people can pour out. I know I had no hand in making this war, and I know I will make more sacrifices today than any of you to secure peace. But you cannot have peace and a division of our country."

Did each man believe that he was right?

While allowing for a bit of hyperbole in the statements of both Hood and Sherman, we can state that they really believed their words. To Hood, it was obvious that Sherman intended to destroy the South he had always known; to Sherman, it was equally apparent that Hood and his fellow Confederates had thrown out the rule book when they seceded from the nation in the first place.

The most bitter part of Hood's letter, the section having to do with making "negroes your allies," was part of the debate that would continue for the rest of the war and for some time thereafter. Many white Southerners, including General Hood, found it difficult to believe that any fellow whites, even if they were Northerners, would really wish to supplant white majority rule in the South with rule by a people that they considered just two steps removed from barbarism.

Was Sherman an ardent abolitionist?

No. Sherman, who was vehemently articulate on most subjects, said little about the blacks during the war, but the few parts of letters that mention the subject indicate that he was a lukewarm abolitionist, at best. That the blacks should be freed from the rule of their Southern masters was apparent to him; what the North, or the nation as a whole, would do with the black population afterward was another matter. To be fair, however, Sherman was not atypical of his army or even the Union leadership as a whole.

Lincoln, right up until the summer of 1862, continued to think there should be a recolonization movement, with most blacks going back to Africa. Ulysses Grant was kind to blacks on a personal level, but he said little or nothing about what their status should be when the war ended. Perhaps the sad truth is that rather few white leaders of the 1860s were really ready for what might come: a South that was transformed racially as well as economically.

When did Sherman first speak of a "march to the sea"?

In telegraphs to the War Department, Sherman spoke of the need to cut loose from his base, meaning Atlanta. General Hood was leading what remained of the Army of Ten-

In his "march to the sea," General Sherman burned everything in his wake to assure the Confederates could not use the land after Union troops had passed through. The "scorched earth" tactic was quite controversial for the harm it did to average Southern citizens.

nessee into the state of that name, threatening to cut the railroad and telegraph lines. Sherman could, of course, pursue Hood, but to do this meant giving up the 150 miles of turf he and his men had fought so hard to win. Much better, Sherman declared, to ignore Hood and strike out for the Atlantic coast.

Doing so would remove Sherman from communications as well as supplies, but he was confident his hard-bitten veterans could live off the land and that in doing so they would "make Georgia howl." Given that Georgia had over one million inhabitants, the 70,000 men of Sherman's army would not suffer, he declared; instead, they would take what they needed, leaving the rebels to suffer during the winter.

Did anyone in Washington, D.C., claim that this was too harsh?

Almost no one. From Lincoln down to Stanton and Grant, the concern revolved around whether Sherman and his men would find enough to eat on their march: little, if any, concern was demonstrated for the plight of the civilians in their path. Grant had some doubts about the whole venture from a military point of view, but he finally gave the go-ahead on October 11, 1864, telegraphing Sherman that "If you are satisfied the trip to the seacoast can be made, holding the line of the Tennessee river firmly, you may make it."

To hold the Tennessee River, Sherman had already dispatched Major-General George Thomas with 20,000 men north to Chattanooga. These and the reinforcements that would come from the North were sufficient to hold Hood at bay, he declared, and he meanwhile would march through the South.

301

What, meanwhile, had Sheridan accomplished in the Shenandoah Valley?

General Philip Sheridan (1831–1888) was only thirty-three, but his recent successes, especially his attack on J. E. B. Stuart in May 1864, had brought him to the forefront where cavalry actions were concerned. Hot-tempered and impulsive, Sheridan was a born fighter, and, according to some observers, the only Union leader whose very physical presence seemed to expand on the battlefield: he looked taller and larger during combat. Some of this sounds like hyperbole to our modern ears, but it is how Sheridan seemed to his contemporaries.

In September 1864, Lincoln asked Grant if Sheridan could be used to attack Jubal Early's men, the ones who had threatened Washington, D.C., just three months earlier. Grant replied that he had the same thought and that he wished to beef up Sheridan's force till it was overwhelming. Grant did not make public his desire to lay the Shenandoah Valley bare of animals and food. The Valley was a major provider of grain and corn to Lee's army.

How did Sheridan's campaign begin?

Grant left his headquarters at City Point, Virginia, and traveled by rail to meet Sheridan in the northern part of the Shenandoah Valley. Typically, Grant carried Sheridan's orders inside his greatcoat, but when the two men spoke, he decided not to pull them out, or even reveal their contents. Grant's reason was that Sheridan had developed an excellent plan of attack, which included an ambitious strike at Jubal Early. When Grant asked if this campaign could begin the following Tuesday, Sheridan answered that he would be ready by Monday.

If Lincoln had labored for years to find his indomitable general in Grant, then Grant had spent some time in finding his endlessly aggressive fighter in Sheridan. Grant gave his blessing to all of Sheridan's plans, parts of which were based on information recently provided him by a Quaker schoolteacher named Rebecca Wright.

Where did the battle begin?

Winchester—now part of West Virginia—had changed hands no fewer than seventy times during the war. As Sheridan and his 35,000 men approached, Jubal Early's (1816–1894) force, estimated at anywhere from 20,000 to 28,000, rushed to make a defense. As it turned out, the fighting began well outside of town, and the battle is called either Opequon or the Third Battle of Winchester.

Sheridan's two columns forced their way through a narrow canyon to find the Confederates awaiting them. The men on both sides had seen plenty of hard fighting before, but there was something especially vicious about the Battle of Opequon. The Confederates had the advantage at the beginning, and among the Union killed was Major-General David Russell, a close friend of Sheridan. But in the furious fighting that followed, the superior Northern numbers allowed them to press, and when Sheridan gathered 7,000 cavalry for the final strike, he was ready to send a shock blow to the entire Confederacy.

What was the most appalling thing that occurred at Opequon?

James E. Taylor was a staff artist for *Frank Leslie's Illustrated Newspaper*, and he had witnessed many shocking things during the war, but none of them prepared him for what he viewed on September 20, 1864. The day after the Battle of Opequon, Taylor was getting ready to move out when he saw ten Northern soldiers stealing from a wounded Confederate officer. This, perhaps, was not so atypical, but the wounded man had had both of his eyes shot out—whether these men were the culprits is not certain—and he was still alive, begging them not to take his possessions. They went right ahead robbing him, and Taylor passed on, realizing that what he had seen indicated the gruesome shape the war was taking.

What was "Sheridan's Ride"?

Sheridan's seven thousand horsemen drew their sabers and began their horses at a walk, which slowly moved to a trot, then finally a canter. They made a magnificent sight, both because of the splendor of their equipment and because the late-afternoon daylight shone behind them. The Confederates who awaited them had been fighting for nearly eight hours, and the assemblage was just too much to take in.

"I never seen any men run faster than the Rebels run last Monday after we got them driving out on the open plain," a Union man wrote his wife. Jubal Early's army collapsed, and he barely maneuvered his men off the field. The total casualties came to about five thousand on the Union side and four thousand for the Confederates, but these numbers disguise the fact that Early's army was a shattered force. He would not face Sheridan again.

What was the political situation in the autumn of 1864?

As late as September 1864, Lincoln continued to think his reelection quite dicey. A master of political arithmetic, he drew up a number of lists that showed how McClellan could win. But to the general public, things looked quite different.

If Sherman had not captured Atlanta, McClellan's candidacy might have caught on more strongly. But with Grant pinning Lee and the Army of Northern Virginia and Atlanta both taken and occupied, it was hard to argue against Lincoln as a successful war leader.

What did the poets think of the election?

The person who wrote this verse is not identified:

> Abram [sic] Lincoln knows the ropes!
> All our hopes
> Centre now about the brave and true;
> Let us help him as we can,
> He's the man,
> Honest for the country through and through.

Others good, perhaps, as he
There may be;
Have we tried them in the war-time's flame?
Do we know if they will stand,
Heart in hand,
Seeking for the Right in Heaven's name?
Let the Nation ask him then,
Once again
To hold the rudder in this stormy sea;
Tell him that each sleepless night,
Dark to light,
Ushers in a morning for the Free.

Let us not forget our rude
Gratitude!
But lend our servant the poor crown as we may!
Give him four more years of toil,
Task and moil,
Knowing God shall crown him in His day!

What was the "Voice from Texas"?

In order to boost morale, the *New York Times* printed a letter from an anonymous writer in Texas, who wrote to the metropolitan newspaper. He or she began with these words: "Perhaps there never was a people more bewitched, beguiled, and befooled than we were when we drifted into this rebellion. We have been kept so to an amazing extent."

When the war began, in 1861, Texas, the writer declared, was on the cusp of full recovery from the Mexican War. The area was becoming settled and industrious, trade was brisk, and the local taxes were next to nothing. Most important of all, "civil law was replacing lynch law." Now, three years into the conflict, the whole male population of Texas was in the war, the ground lay untilled, and sheep and cattle were driven off by marauders. As for civil justice, "Every man relies on his six-shooter." Perhaps the writer exaggerated a little, but not too much. Texas and every other state in the Confederacy was in the midst of a general crisis. Many Southerners lamented that they had begun this war over the issue of states' rights, only to become subject to a dictatorship from Richmond.

How did the countdown to the general election proceed?

Lincoln's aides were, by now, convinced he would win, but he was not sanguine about the margin of his victory. It was all too painful to recall that he had been elected as a minority president in 1860, and he yearned for something better. Neither Lincoln nor McClellan campaigned, in the way that candidates do today, and neither released any

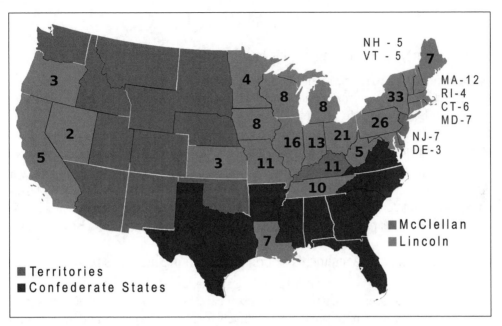

NH - 5
VT - 5
7
3
4
MA-12
8
33
RI-4
8
CT-6
8
26
MD-7
16 13 21
NJ-7
2
5
DE-3
5
3
11
11
10
7

■ McClellan
■ Lincoln

■ Territories
■ Confederate States

Neither Lincoln nor his Democratic opponent, George B. McClellan, ran aggressive campaigns, as the war was still ongoing. Lincoln, this time, won a strong majority of electoral votes: 212 to McClellan's 21.

important policy statements. On November 7, 1864, the *New York Times* pointed to the election the following day with the words "No interference with the Elections" as its leading article. "Raiders and Rebels and Ballot-box Stuffers [are] Warned," the *Times* declared. Two days later came the results.

By what margin did Lincoln lose the Empire City?

Despite all the changes and alterations to his policies, Lincoln lost the Empire City of New York, much as he had in 1860. The twenty-two wards of greater New York City went for McClellan by 73,769 to 36,912. This may well have reflected a continuing urban bias against Lincoln, the man from the rural West; despite all his success, Lincoln was still seen as an unpolished countryperson. The blow was softened by Lincoln's taking the Empire State by a margin of 8,000 votes.

By what margin did Lincoln capture the nation?

The *New York Times* led with "VICTORY! Glorious Result Yesterday." Lincoln won an overwhelming victory in the Electoral College, with 212 to 21. He won the popular vote, nationwide, with a margin of slightly more than 400,000 votes. But perhaps most satisfying of all, Lincoln won the "soldier vote," the votes made in army camps, by a whopping 116,887 to 33,748. McClellan had once been the commanding general of many of these soldiers, but they chose to go with the man from Illinois.

SHERMAN'S PLAN

When did Sherman cut loose from his base?

On November 10, 1864, Sherman headed south-by-southeast, moving toward the coast. His brigade and division commanders understood their orders, which were simple and to the point. They were to destroy whatever infrastructure they saw—houses, barns, factories: anything that could contribute to the Confederate war effort was to be wrecked. One of Sherman's aides described the scene as they departed:

"A brigade of Massachusetts soldiers are now the only ones left in the town: they will be the last to leave it. To-night I heard the really fine band of the Thirty-Third Massachusetts playing 'John Brown's soul goes marching on,' by the light of the burning buildings. I have never heard that noble anthem when it was so grand, so solemn, so inspiring."

How many Confederate regiments or brigades stood in Sherman's path?

Almost none. When he went north to attack Nashville, General John Hood took most of the Army of Tennessee: those who did not accompany him soon deserted. Southern and central Georgia had been, to this point, relatively free from the war, and there were no local troops to resist Sherman. Practically all the men of military age were either with Hood or with General Robert E. Lee.

Sherman, therefore, enjoyed a nearly unique opportunity. That he intended to wreck the countryside was understood by his superiors; that he had no one in his path was becoming apparent. Not only was there little resistance, but Sherman's men were among the most battle hardened of all the Union troops. If ever there was a chance for "reconstructing" the South, this was it.

Where were John B. Hood and the Army of Tennessee?

Hood soon realized that Sherman would not turn around and follow him north, but he continued on his way just the same. Hood was one of the most relentless of all Confederate fighters, and if there was a way to hurt the Union cause, he would find it.

What was the first major town Sherman reached?

On November 24, 1864, Sherman and the center of his army entered Milledgeville, the capital of Georgia. The state legislature had fled just a few hours earlier, and Sherman's men conducted a mock "session" in the capitol building.

Where did Hood go?

Hood and the Army of Tennessee were on their last legs. These Confederates had not won a battle, let alone a campaign, in fourteen months' time. Hood unwisely led them north, hoping against hope that Sherman would be drawn into pursuit. Sherman, for his part, kept right on going.

Hood fought the Battle of Franklin against Major-General George Thomas' Army of the Cumberland in November. In frontal assaults, Hood lost over 6,000 men killed, wounded, or missing and several general officers, including Patrick Cleburne, who many observers believed was the most promising of the younger officers in the Western theater. Hood actually pushed on and laid a very tentative siege to Nashville, Tennessee, but when Thomas attacked him in mid-December, the Confederates were bowled over. Following that defeat, it could be questioned whether there was any remaining Army of Tennessee.

What was Christmas Day 1864 like in New York City?

The winter was a cold one, and the ice skaters were already out. The *New York Times* commented on the overall situation in the metropolis:

> Tomorrow is Christmas, the merriest of all holidays…. A walk through Broadway or the Bowery at this time would not convey to a stranger the idea that we were a people impoverished by an exhausted [sic] war, overburdened with taxes and oppressed with woe. Gaily decorated shops, filled with articles of convenience and luxury, crowded with eager customers, attest the prosperity of the people.

Of course, these were not all the people. There were some who shivered in the cold and others who had nowhere to sleep. But New York City then—as now—reflected the image that the upper-class, white American wished to see. And even if all was not perfect in the Empire City, things there were certainly a good deal better than those in the Confederate capital.

What was Christmas Day 1864 in Richmond like?

Mrs. Judith Brockenbrough McGuire described it thus:

> The sad Christmas has passed away. J. and C. were with us, and very cheerful. We exerted ourselves to be so too…. When we got home [from church] our family circle was small, but pleasant. The Christmas turkey and ham were not. We had aspired to a turkey, but finding the prices range from $50 to $100 in the market on Saturday, we contented ourselves with roast beef and the various little dishes which Confederate times have made us believe are tolerable substitutes for the viands of better days. At night I treated our little party to tea and ginger cakes—two very rare indulgences; and but for the sorghum, grown in our own fields, the cakes would be an impossible indulgence.

How much worse were things for people out of town or down on their luck?

Hardship was present throughout the Confederacy in December 1864, but the people on the farms probably did better than their relatives in the city, at least so long as no Union forces were in the neighborhood. Few, if any, records of outright starvation exist, but the Confederate people, as a whole, experienced serious malnutrition during the winter of

1864 to 1865. It did not help that they could sometimes read Northern newspapers and see the luxuries and conveniences of the population that was making war upon them.

What was New Year's Day like in Washington, D.C.?

The scene was much the same as the previous two years, but the crowd was a little smaller than before. Roughly five thousand people came to the White House for the afternoon reception.

TO MAKE MEN FREE

How did the path to the Thirteenth Amendment begin?

U.S. Representative James M. Ashley from Ohio brought up his motion that Congress should outlaw slavery throughout the nation. Ashley had done so before, in 1864, and the measure had passed the Senate, but failed to obtain the two-thirds necessary in the House.

Even at this late date, when slaves were either running away or being freed directly by Union intervention, there were congressmen who doubted either the wisdom or the efficacy of freeing all slaves everywhere in the nation. They pointed to Lincoln's Emancipation Proclamation, saying correctly that it was a piecemeal move and that it was not their task to complete what the president had left undone. There was still concern that some men might desert the Union armies if Congress announced that the end of slavery was the single greatest reason for the war. And there was legitimate concern about what would happen when four million suddenly freed persons appeared on the labor market.

James M. Ashley, a representative from Ohio, brought up the motion in Congress that slavery be formally abolished throughout the country.

What role did Lincoln play in the fight for the Thirteenth Amendment?

A substantial one. He had, by now, learned that it was better to let his men in Congress do most of the work, but he could effect change from behind the scenes. And Lincoln, ever an astute politician, was willing to use all sorts of patronage—the dispensing of federal appointments—to gain votes in the House of Representatives. His political men told him it would be a close, narrow fight, and they would need every single vote.

By January 20, 1865, the cause looked stalled. Many Democrats had been swept out of office in the 1864 elections, but enough remained to block passage of the bill. Former New York City Mayor Fernando Wood was one of the leaders of the opposition. Thaddeus Stevens, of Pennsylvania, was the leader of the Radical Republicans, who pressed the most strongly for passage.

How accurate is the portrayal of Thaddeus Stevens in the 2012 film *Lincoln*?

As far as his character and attitudes go, actor Tommy Lee Jones achieves a remarkably good portrayal. Stevens was, indeed, an irascible and tyrannical person who ran his section of the Republican Party—the Radicals—very much like a dictator. He was also one of the few congressmen who had a virulent, almost violent, repulsion to slavery.

As is shown at the very end of *Lincoln*, Stevens had a mistress, or perhaps what we would call a common-law wife. She was a black woman, a seamstress in Washington, D.C. They lived together for many years, but did so quietly. How many of Stevens' congressional colleagues knew about this is not certain, but the subject was never brought up or used on the House floor.

How accurate is the portrayal of Mary Todd Lincoln in *Lincoln*?

Sally Field, an actress with many credits over a long career, won high praise for her portrayal of the difficult first lady. About the only criticism that can be offered is that she, and the movie scriptwriters, did not go far enough.

Lincoln's marriage was difficult all the way, but after the tragic death of his son Willie in 1862, Mary Todd Lincoln began to fall apart. Her grief was real, not feigned, but she used it to tyrannize her husband and many other people. Perhaps the most accurate, and painful, moment in *Lincoln* is when the president shouts at his wife: "*Your* grief, *your* grief, always *your* grief!" In one of the final scenes of the film, Lincoln and his wife talk of going away, of traveling to see Jerusalem when the war, and his presidency, are over. This vision, or hope, was a real one. Lincoln also spoke of moving to California when he left the White House.

How accurate is the portrayal of the president in *Lincoln*?

Most critics and moviegoers agree that Daniel Day-Lewis turned in a magnificent performance as the chief executive. A seasoned actor who took on relatively few roles, but then devoted himself wholeheartedly, Day-Lewis had shone in previous films such as *My Left Foot* and *Last of the Mohicans*. In *Lincoln*, he did a remarkable job of presenting the soft, human side of the nation's sixteenth president.

There were the jokes, always made in good humor, and the casual asides, as well as the profound statements. There was the awkward relationship with the eldest son, Robert Lincoln, and the ongoing turmoil of the relationship between husband and wife. And there was, occasionally, the moment when Lincoln turned into steel. When one of his political handlers suggested that the vote be put off, Lincoln turned on him with words that bite, even now. "I am clothed in power. You will get me those votes!"

How accurate is the scene on the floor of the House of Representatives in *Lincoln*?

Again, it is well done. The House was a chummier place in 1865 than it is today, but party lines were also sharply drawn. *Ad hominen* attacks took place frequently, as people on all sides of the chamber pursued the policies they believed were correct.

Members of Congress celebrate after the passage of the Thirteenth Amendment in this *Harper's Weekly* illustration.

The roll call, as depicted in *Lincoln*, is especially revealing of the technologies and the presentation from that time. Unlike our time, in which senators and representatives file their votes electronically, there was both a paper ballot and a voice vote. This, too, was an accurate depiction of elections and politics at that time.

What and when was the final vote for the Thirteenth Amendment?

On January 31, 1865, the House of Representatives passed the Thirteenth Amendment. The vote was 119 in favor, 56 opposed, and 8 not voting, giving the bill the two-thirds majority by a slim margin.

How close did the end of the war seem to Lincoln and his Cabinet?

Very close indeed, but the end was not predictable. No one could know which direction Lee and the Army of Northern Virginia might take, for example, and no one could be sure that all Confederates would ever lay down their arms.

LINCOLN'S SECOND INAUGURAL ADDRESS

What was the scene at Lincoln's second inauguration?

On March 4, 1865, Lincoln and his Cabinet came before an immense crowd outside the newly completed Capitol to witness an extraordinary change. Though the war was not over, public sentiment was different from a year ago, and when compared to the scene on March 4, 1861, it was vastly different.

If Lincoln had been a vainglorious person given to boasting and pride, this was his opportunity to make the most of it. Over the preceding four years, he had presided over the greatest gathering of strength—military, political, and financial—ever seen in America, perhaps even in the Western world. No previous military contest—not even those of the Napoleonic Wars—had involved so many men fighting so fiercely. The final victory was not far off, and Lincoln could have basked in a mild orgy of self-congratulation. That he did not do so is yet another proof of his greatness *and* shrewdness as a statesman.

Who swore Lincoln into office?

Chief Justice Roger Taney—the man who wrote the infamous *Dred Scott* decision—died a year earlier, and the oath of office was, therefore, administered by the new chief justice, Salmon P. Chase. There was a great irony in the moment, and it was not lost on most of the observers. Chase had long coveted Lincoln's job and sincerely believed he would have made a better wartime president than the man from Illinois. Lincoln had asked for his resignation as secretary of the treasury in 1864, but had then vaulted him by nominating him to the Supreme Court.

Whether Chase ever fully realized his own error is not known. He may have gone to his deathbed sincerely believing he was the better leader of men. But the comparison is not made to belittle Salmon Chase, or any of the other fine leaders of that time. They were, simply and absolutely, upstaged by the man with crude, homespun manners.

How did Lincoln begin his second inaugural address?

Lincoln began by calmly observing that this second inaugural address was not as pressing as the first had been. He meant that matters within the nation were moving in a more predictable fashion and that the great crisis of the past four years was beginning to recede. He declined to speculate on when or how the war would end, saying only that there was "high hope for the future."

In the second paragraph, Lincoln turned to the situation as it was four years ago. He pointed out that, in 1861, no one was eager for war. The North and the South alike wished to attain their objectives by more peaceful means, but when they found this impossible, they turned to war. There was little, if any, recrimination in these remarks. Lincoln could certainly have taken the South to task, but he chose not to.

What was the thickest, or most dense, part of Lincoln's second inaugural address?

In his third paragraph, Lincoln turned to the matter of slavery. He did so in the most deft of ways, speaking of it in the third person, and not casting blame. Some abolitionists in the crowd doubtless were disappointed by the calm way in which Lincoln approached the subject: "These slaves constituted a peculiar and powerful interest. All knew that this interest was somehow the cause of the war."

Even at this late date, four years into the war, there were still plenty of Southerners who would choose to disagree with Lincoln's second sentence. To them, the war had

L et us count the ways he did it: "Both read the same Bible, and prayed to the same God." "It may seem strange that any men should dare to ask a just God's assistance...." "If we shall suppose that American slavery is one of those offenses which, in the providence of God...." "Yet, if God wills that it continue...." This was a very different Lincoln from the one who delivered the first inaugural address in 1861.

Those who trace Lincoln's religious or spiritual development are often convinced that he was a profound skeptic in youth and still something of a doubter in middle age. Sometime before he became president, however, Lincoln went through a long self-examination, and with the help of a Springfield, Illinois, pastor, he became a self-professed Christian. Even then, it must be admitted that his Christianity was not of a linear or conventional type. Four years in the White House had changed Lincoln in many ways, however, and if it was true what he said to the crowd in Springfield as he departed (see page 62), it was much more true in 1865.

always been about the right of the states to determine their own future. But to Lincoln's overwhelmingly Northern audience, the wording was just right. He did not blame the slaveholders for what had taken place: he merely observed that slavery itself was the root cause of the war.

When did Lincoln move in the direction of poetry rather than prose?

The fourth and final paragraph is a triumph of the written word: a masterful use of rhetoric backed by an unswerving belief that the Almighty favored the Northern cause.

"With malice toward none, with charity for all, with firmness in the right as God gives us to see the right, let us strive on to finish the work we are in." This, of course, begs yet another question: Could anyone else have delivered an address with words and sentiments like these?

Yes. Another person, who had been through four years of agonizing self-doubt and soul-searching, could have done so. No one could have done it without that kind of rigorous self-examination, however. Here, in these words, Lincoln set the tone for his second administration and for what the reconstruction of the nation would be.

How was the second inaugural address received?

Like those who heard the Gettysburg Address, Lincoln's listeners at the Capitol would have benefited from a second reading. Lincoln's rhetorical style was so spare, so straight to the point, that it could not all be taken in one listening. The numerous references to the Almighty were so different from earlier Lincoln speeches that they would have to be examined in detail. But the tone was unmistakable. Lincoln saw mutual forgiveness as the only way for the nation to move forward.

Not everyone in Washington or the nation as a whole desired forgiveness. The Radical Republicans, who were soon to become even more "radical," disliked talk of mercy and forgiveness. To them, it was obvious that the Confederacy had broken all the rules of conduct and that its leaders, at the very least, would have to suffer retribution.

What, meanwhile, had happened to Vice President Andrew Johnson?

Before Lincoln stepped out of the Capitol to deliver his second inaugural address, the new Vice President, Andrew Johnson (1808–1875), delivered a speech in the Senate chamber. He was preceded by the outgoing Vice President, Hannibal Hamlin (1809–1891).

Johnson had been ill before coming to Washington, and he was very nervous about the speech. He took two strong drinks the night before, to fortify his nerves, then made the mistake of taking two more that morning. Red faced and angry looking, Johnson rose to deliver his remarks, which were a complete disaster. Rather than speaking to the larger issues of the day, or the war, Johnson spoke primarily about himself, his struggles as a young man, and his relentless battles against the slave-holding oligarchy in Tennessee. Had his speech been even mildly coherent, it would at least have won him some plaudits from the Radical Republicans, but even they were ashamed of "Andy" Johnson this day. People observed Lincoln holding his head in his hands. Others in the Senate chamber believed that Johnson might self-destruct at any moment. His was, beyond any doubt, the worst beginning for a person in national office before or since.

An April 8, 1865, illustration from the *Illustrated London News* shows the inaugural ball celebration held at the Great Hall of the Patent Office in Washington, D.C.

What was the high point of the inaugural celebrations??

Thanks to the *London Illustrated Times*, we have a good idea of what the inaugural ball looked like. Hundreds of superbly dressed men and women danced in high spirits in the largest section of the U.S. Patent building. Gauging by the size and height of the windows, the room was twenty feet high and almost two hundred feet in length, meaning that it was, perhaps, the grandest venue for such a celebration that could possibly be found. The British observers did not comment directly, but implicit in the drawing was the acknowledgement that the Americans had come a long way in terms of refinement and elegance.

What, meanwhile, was happening in the Confederacy?

To some extent, it could be doubted whether the Confederacy still existed. There was still a military presence, a strong one, in parts of Virginia, but most of the other Confederate states east of the Mississippi were under Union control. The two states that showed the most remaining fight were at the two extremes: Virginia and Texas.

Only one other measure could be taken to bolster the failing Confederate manpower, and Jefferson Davis and Robert E. Lee were on the cusp of doing it. Both men had long agonized, as well as hesitated, over the idea of putting black slaves in arms, but by March 1865 they saw there was no other alternative. Either the Confederacy would arm black men and use them in its defense, or it would be overrun. Recruiting for the first black Confederate regiments began in mid-March 1865.

What was Lee's last offensive move?

On March 25, 1865, Lee unleashed his last offensive, an attack on federal Fort Stedman. It was part of the grand encirclement that the Federals had been drawing for months, and Lee saw this as his only hope for a victory—however small—that might bolster the Confederate cause. The attack did not go well, however.

There was a significant Confederate movement early in the day, but by afternoon the Confederates were in full retreat, and Lee lost roughly four thousand men killed, wounded, or missing, a solid ten percent of his remaining force.

BEGINNING OF THE END

When did Richmond fall?

On the morning of April 2, 1865, hundreds of well-to-do Richmonders were worshipping at St. Paul's Church when a telegraph messenger entered. He went straight to Jefferson Davis, who rose from his pew and—with an ashen face—walked briskly out of the church and to the Confederate White House. Though he said nothing, the people at St. Paul's guessed the worst: Lee's lines around Petersburg had been broken by the Union forces.

The telegraph was from Lee, informing the president that Richmond would soon fall. Jefferson Davis and his family escaped Richmond a few hours before the end, but

An illustration from the book *Richmond, Its People and Its Story* shows the evacuation of Richmond, Virginia.

most of the civilians were not so lucky. They heard the cannon fire from the south, then from the west, and guessed—correctly—that Grant and the Union forces had finally completed their death grip on the Confederate capital. By nightfall, Jefferson Davis, most of the Cabinet, and most of the higher levels of the Confederate government had escaped, but, as many Richmonders asked, where could they go? Richmond was the heart and soul of the Confederacy.

Did Mrs. Robert E. Lee accompany her husband?

She did not. Lee's wife had been ill for some time, and she remained at their house on Franklin Street in downtown Richmond.

How did the major newspapers track the excitement as the war neared its end?

The *New York Times* was most interested in the Union attack on Mobile, Alabama, until Monday, April 3, 1865, when its front page practically screamed: VICTORY. An enormous American eagle appeared on that front page, and the headline declared that 12,000 rebels had been taken prisoner. That was followed by, if anything, an even bolder headline on Tuesday, April 4: GRANT, RICHMOND AND VICTORY. If anyone has discounted the effect of the war's end, believing that Americans were too jaded to care, the *Times'* headlines would rebut that idea on the spot.

"The capture of Richmond plucks out the very heart of the rebellion," The *Times* declared. "It is not enough to say that a rebel capital has been taken. Richmond bore a much more important relation to the rebellion than that term would express." Americans throughout the North and the West gave way to a round of rejoicing, the likes of which had never before been seen.

How did Grant take Richmond?

The final part was easy, made possible by all the heroic exertions of the previous nine months. By the first of April 1865, the Union siege lines ran thirty-seven miles in a nearly complete circle of Richmond and Petersburg. The Confederates, too, had fought heroically, but the game was clearly up.

Lee did not reveal all his decision making, but he let Jefferson Davis know that the capital could be held no longer. Throughout the first of April, Lee and the Army of Northern Virginia made good their escape, heading due west. What little hope remained was that Lee would effect a meeting with Johnston and that the two combined forces would somehow overcome Sherman's army. Even the most die-hard Confederate knew this was a forlorn hope, but in desperate times people often cling to what has been and will make all sorts of sacrifices to attempt to maintain it.

How did Lincoln react to the fall of Richmond?

The president expressed great satisfaction over Richmond's fall. He told Admiral David Porter—the man who had done so much to capture Vicksburg two years earlier—that he wanted to see the Confederate capital. Porter knew it was hopeless to try to prevent Lincoln from this, but Secretary of War Stanton telegraphed from Washington, saying it was premature. Richmond had fallen, but there was no way of knowing how many Confederates remained in the city or their sentiments. Lincoln went right ahead.

How did Lincoln get *to* Richmond?

This was something of a saga. The president's party began that morning with the steamer *River Queen* and with Admiral Porter's flagship, the USS *Malvern*. The closer they came to Richmond, the more hazards presented themselves, however, and eventually Admiral Porter found he could take the two large vessels no farther. At that point, Lincoln insisted that they travel in the admiral's barge, which, under normal circumstances, was rowed by twelve sailors. Climbing into the barge were Lincoln, his son Tad, Admiral Porter, and one journalist. That was all.

As they passed the turn at Drewry's Bluff, a turn that had baffled and bedeviled the federal navy for three years, the people aboard the barge could see the smoke above Richmond, and they gained some sense of how desperate the condition of the fallen capital was. Not until they came closer, however, did Lincoln and the group see the sheer devastation. Just to complete the sequence of nautical mishaps, the admiral's barge ran aground, and Lincoln and the group had to be helped up to the wharf. But then they were there: in Confederate Richmond.

How did the people act toward Lincoln?

There were two very different receptions. Confederate and *white* Richmond largely remained indoors, while Union, and recently emancipated, *black* Richmond turned out to hail the deliverer, as many blacks called Lincoln. A number fell on their knees before him, but he said they must stand and kneel only to God. That action only endeared Lincoln more to the African Americans, who were coming to realize, moment by moment, that the Confederacy was finished and they were free.

Moving through the city, Lincoln was protected only by the twelve sailors, each of whom carried a short naval carbine. Had a group of Confederates organized themselves as cavalry, they might have overwhelmed the group and had a lone assassin take aim from a second-story window, who might have succeeded in killing the president. Lincoln appeared unperturbed, however. Arriving at the Confederate White House, he asked merely for a drink of water, while some of the sailors took shots of brandy, toasting the Confederate president who had fled.

Did Lincoln recognize the importance of the moment?

To be sure. No previous American president had ever toured a surrendered capital, and no previous American chief executive had ever received the thanks of so many people. To top it all off, Lincoln roamed the streets, showing little concern for his personal safety. This alarmed some of his bodyguards, but it delighted the people of Richmond.

The South's capital, Richmond, lay in ruins after the Union captured it. President Lincoln later toured the city and talked to its people, a brave act that many of the residents admired.

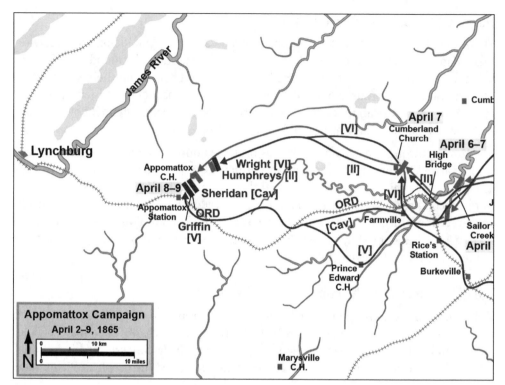

The final troop movements of the war had Confederate forces retreating from Richmond and Petersburg, eventually ending up in Appomattox, Virginia.

At that moment, in the first week of April 1865, Lincoln stood atop a mountain, figuratively speaking. He had reached the summit of his long battle to preserve the Union, and the Confederacy—if it had any life remaining—was about to be consigned to the dustbin. Just as important, Lincoln had done it his way: his emphasis on mercy and forgiveness seemed to be doing the trick. No one could be unmoved by the sight of such success, and Lincoln certainly was not. He did realize, however, how much work remained to be accomplished.

What was on Lincoln's mind as he returned to Washington, D.C.?

There had to be a score of things, but the three that topped the list had to do with the Confederate soldiers, the freed African Americans, and the status of the states. What, for example, was to be done with the hundreds of thousands of former Confederate soldiers? Were they to be punished, even slightly, for their actions? As to the newly freed black Americans, how were they to be integrated into a nation, and an economy, that had previously scorned them? And what of the eleven states that had seceded from the Union? Were they to be readmitted? Did they have to be reorganized? And would the Radical Republicans in Congress allow the president the leeway he desired to make these decisions?

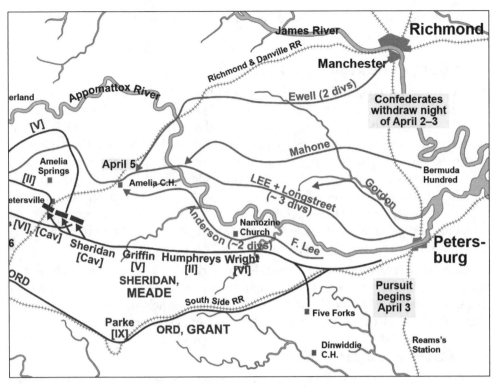

When one contemplates the number of challenges that faced Lincoln in April 1865, it is easy to become overwhelmed. One wonders how the president prevented himself from being overwhelmed. And the answer can only be found in a remark he made to a friend two years earlier. He had no grand strategy, Lincoln replied. He was forever putting out fires and erecting tent poles to prevent things from blowing away. This had served him very well during the war, but it is not clear as to whether it would serve him—or the nation—during the peace.

Where, at this point, was Lee?

Lee and about forty thousand men—by the best, most optimistic estimate—were escaping by way of the roads that led west from Richmond. It was all a forlorn hope, but then again, that was what Lee had specialized in from the very beginning.

On April 6, 1865, the advance units of the Army of the Potomac caught up with the Army of Northern Virginia, which turned out for one last confrontation. By most accounts, the Battle of Sayler's Creek was one of the most intense and vicious of the war. Realizing they were at the end of the road did not make the Confederates tame; rather, they turned and fought like lions. The sailors from the ruined ships at Richmond fought with special vigor: accounts describe them wielding rifle butts and ruined weapons. But the conclusion was inescapable: there were now three times as many men in pursuit.

By the end of the day, six thousand Confederates had been taken prisoner; Lee's son, William Lee, was one of them.

Who pulled the bayonet from Samuel Eddy's chest?

Practically every town in the United States has a Civil War hero, but Chesterfield, Massachusetts—the author's hometown—is especially proud of Samuel Eddy, a private in the 37th Massachusetts Volunteers. A blacksmith, the forty-three-year-old Eddy had already served in at least a dozen engagements, but the Battle of Sayler's Creek is where he showed his mettle to the extreme. A Confederate plunged his bayonet into Eddy's chest and then twisted it. Using his Spencer rifle, Eddy killed his assailant, then pulled the bayonet out. The pain from the thrust was not so bad, he claimed, but the rebel had twisted the bayonet after thrusting it. Eddy was in bad shape that afternoon, and one of his fellows, Sergeant William Shaw, thought this might be the last of him. But Eddy survived and lived another forty-odd years.

Eddy was awarded the Congressional Medal of Honor for his service, but by one of those odd chances, it was never given to him. Therefore, in 1982, a special ceremony, as well as a reenactment of the Battle of Sayler's Creek, was held in Eddy's hometown of Chesterfield. The Medal of Honor was finally bestowed, 117 years after the fact!

What was left to do at this point?

Though Lee had entertained some hopes of escaping, and perhaps prolonging the war with a guerrilla conduct, the end was clearly in front of him. Therefore, when Grant initiated a conversation via letter, Lee was receptive. He did not immediately indicate a willingness to surrender.

Knowing his opponent's reputation as "Unconditional Surrender" Grant, Lee wished to come to the peace table with some semblance of dignity. He, therefore, proposed that they should meet in person, and when aides made the arrangements, they found that Appomattox Court House was the best place to be found. It was close to the headquarters of both armies, and it was the only thing close to a town center. The meeting was arranged for the afternoon of April 9, 1865, which just happened to be Palm Sunday.

LEE'S SURRENDER

Where did the two leaders meet? Is it true that the house had a connection to the Battle of Bull Run?

Again, strictly by chance, the meeting was to be at Appomattox Court House, and the house that fit the purposes best was the two-story home of Wilmer McLean. He had, indeed, lived in Manassas, Virginia, before the war, and just prior to the Battle of Bull Run, his house in Manassas had been commandeered to serve as the headquarters of General Pierre T. Beauregard.

Soon after the Battle of Bull Run, Wilmer McLean had moved farther south, vowing he wished to have nothing to do with the war. Though it was not an immediate or "clean" move (he went back to Manassas for a time), it was again Wilmer McLean's house that was chosen for the meeting between Grant and Lee. Of the many odd coincidences of the long war, this is one that is commented on, perhaps, the most.

What did Lee look like?

Lee knew that his reputation preceded him, and he wished to live up to it. He dressed in the uniform of a full general, and he rode his well-known horse, Traveller, to the meeting. Lee went with a few aides, but when he dismounted to enter the McLean house, he was pretty much alone. There he found everything in readiness: everything except General Grant, who, as usual, was running late.

It is often commented that both men ran true to form that day, and when Grant and a dozen aides reined up to the McLean house, the Union general looked mud splattered. He had, throughout the war, been indifferent to appearance; in this, as in so many other ways, he and Lee were diametrically opposed. Entering the house, Grant walked over to shake Lee's hand. That first handshake had to have been a little stiff, but before long the two great commanders of the era were sitting at a square table and discussing events past and present.

Who spoke first?

It is believed that Grant was the more talkative and the friendlier. He mentioned that he remembered Lee's appearance from the War with Mexico and commented that the Confederate general looked as splendid now as he had then. Lee, by contrast, said nothing about Mexico: he may not have remembered Lieutenant Grant from those days. Before too much time passed, Lee reminded Grant that they had come to discuss the terms of surrender. Grant then went to business.

What authority did Grant possess at that moment?

Everything Grant did was conditional upon Lincoln's approval, but the two men had been in such concert for the past year that there was little chance of a mishap. In his last meeting with Grant, Lincoln had expressed his desire that the defeated Confederates be let up easy, as he put it.

That Lee would surrender the Army of Northern Virginia was beyond dispute: there was no turning back at this point. But what Grant would allow Lee and his men to retain was another matter entirely. As they talked, Colonel Ely Parker—a Seneca Indian—wrote out the terms on blank pieces of paper. There was a tense moment when Lee asked what his men could keep and a sigh of relief when Grant said that the men could keep their horses and mules and that the officers could retain their side-arms. Lee admitted that these generous conditions would have a sizeable effect on his men.

Union soldiers stand in wait at Appomattox Court House, where General Robert E. Lee finally surrendered to General Ulysses S. Grant.

Who signed first?

Grant signed first, and Lee—after examining the document at length—did the same. The two men rose, and their aides made some brief conversation. Grant would almost surely have wished to continue the conversation, but Lee was eager to get away, to avoid the specter of humiliation. Perhaps two hours after he rode up to the McLean house, Lee rode off again.

The thing was done. No one could truly claim that the war was over because Joseph Johnston still had a small army in the field and there were Confederate forces in Texas. The mainstay of the Confederate cause had given way, however, and there was not the slightest doubt of the Union triumph. What did Grant say as Lee rode away? Neither he nor the members of his staff ever revealed that. Knowing Grant, he may well have taken some puffs from his cigar, nodded his head, and simply ridden back to his own encampment.

Who was the odd man out in the room at the McLean house?

Numerous portrait painters attempted to capture the scene, and many did plausible acts of recreating the dramatic moments at the McLean house. The odd man out was Colonel Ely S. Parker, an Indian—a Seneca, to be precise—who was on Grant's staff. When Grant and Lee had scratched out the terms of the capitulation, Grant handed the rough copy over to Parker, who turned out the transcribed copy. Lee said nothing to Parker, but there was a moment—noticed by several men—during which he looked at Parker, and seemed astonished, because he believed that Grant had made an *African American* a member of his staff.

When did the two great military leaders meet again?

Tradition has it that Lee and Grant never met again after Palm Sunday 1865, but tradition is in error. They met again on the afternoon of April 10, 1865, and on this occasion not only their staffs but a large number of officers from both armies were present. The work was, of course, finished; this was merely the pleasant afterlude.

In the conversation they held while on horseback, Lee mentioned that it was well that all had been settled. A guerrilla war would have taken a long time, he said, mentioning the vast extent of territory that the Union would have to conquer. Grant said little to that because he did not have to. The awesome strength of the Union had already been presented for all the world to see. After that second meeting, they never saw one other again.

When did the surrender ceremony take place?

It took place on Wednesday, April 12, 1865. General Joshua Chamberlain (1828–1914) of Maine was assigned the honor of being the first man of general rank to receive the defeated Confederates (he was the man who, while still a colonel, had defended Little Round Top on the second day of the Battle of Gettysburg). General John B. Gordon, who had also been at Gettysburg, was chosen to lead the Confederates as they stacked their arms. The scene was described many times, but the single best description comes from the pen of General Chamberlain, who wrote his sister one day after the event:

"I took post on the right," he wrote, "with my staff and the old flag, the red maltese cross on the white field with blue border. We received them with the honor due to troops, at a shoulder and in silence. They came to a shoulder on passing my flag, and preserved perfect order. When the head of their column reached our left, they halted faced toward our line and close upon it, say 4 or 6 yards, and stacked their arms and piled their colors. Poor fellows. I pitied them from the bottom of my heart."

How many men remained of the Army of Northern Virginia?

According to the records of General Chamberlain and his staff, 28,231 Confederates were fed and paroled. This, of course, begs the question of what had happened to the 15,000 or so others who had been with Lee when the retreat from Richmond began. Some 4,000 had been taken prisoner, and perhaps 2,000 had died at the Battle of Sayler's Creek, but another 8,000 or 9,000 had simply disappeared. In their haste to pursue Lee, the Union forces had not swept up stragglers, and it was easy for many Confederates to melt away and make their way home.

What were the feelings expressed in and following the surrender ceremony?

They can be best summarized with the expression employed by General Joshua Chamberlain: "Honor answering honor."

LINCOLN'S DEATH, NEW NATION: APRIL 1865 TO 1877

LINCOLN ON THE MOUNTAINTOP

What was Lincoln's state of mind?

He was transported. Time and again, Lincoln had been required to rein himself in, to stay cautiously optimistic. Now, however, he knew the end result.

Lincoln quickly confirmed all that Grant had done: there would be no take-back of the generous terms that were offered at Appomattox. Lincoln then turned his attention to the thousand and one details that required his attention. There were bills and checks to sign and orders to be sent. Lincoln was anxious that General Sherman catch and force General Johnston to surrender, making a complete sweep of all the Confederate armies. But there was celebration, too, as well as an acknowledgment of all that had transpired. Considering all that could have happened, it was an amazing admission that so much had gone well. As he made his plans, Lincoln expressed his desire to go to the theatre that weekend. His first choice for companions was General and Mrs. Grant.

How did the newspapers respond to Lee's surrender?

On Monday, April 10, 1865, the *New York Times* outdid itself with: "Hang out your Banners! Union! Victory! Peace!" Labeling the surrender "The Work of Palm Sunday," the *Times* hailed the surrender ceremony, saying it boded well for reconciliation between the North and the South. The *Times* announced that a two-hundred-gun salute would be fired by every army, department, post, and arsenal in the nation.

The Confederacy still had, perhaps, a dozen newspapers, but only one of them reported Lee's surrender in all its rich detail. The *Columbia Carolinian* had been forced to move north to Charlotte, North Carolina, after Columbia was taken by Sherman's army, but its pages reported the end of the Army of Northern Virginia. The *Augusta*

Constitutionalist kept up a defiant tone, saying, "The End is not in Sight." Other Southern newspapers either glossed over the event or did not report it at all.

What did Lincoln do on Tuesday, April 11, 1865?

Throughout the previous two summers, Lincoln had become accustomed to being serenaded on summer evenings. Sometimes it was the Marine Corps Band; at other times it was unofficial music groups that performed on the White House lawn. Because of the excitement and joy in Washington, D.C., another such performance was scheduled for the evening of April 11.

When the music finished, Lincoln pulled out sheets of paper and spoke from the portico. "We meet this evening not in anxiety but in gladness of heart," he began. The crowd began chanting, expecting a victory speech. But Lincoln soon transitioned to the difficult processes that lay ahead. How would the former Confederate states be reintegrated, he asked? The most reasonable course of action, he declared, was to follow what had begun in Louisiana the previous year. When 12,000 Unionists turned out to vote in the federally sponsored elections of 1864, Lincoln declared that Louisiana had resumed its former statehood.

Was this what the people of Washington wished to hear?

Given the excitement and joy, they would have cheered almost anything, but there were some who were disappointed by the clemency inherent in Lincoln's approach. Should the former Confederate states not suffer some type of punishment for their misdeeds? Was the vote of 12,000 people—just ten percent of those who had voted in 1860—sufficient to bring a state back into the Union?

Lincoln was persuaded that the task would be difficult.

What did Lincoln do on Good Friday?

Good Friday fell on April 14, and Lincoln was in an unusually cheerful mood. He met with his Cabinet for several hours, discussing and debating the approach the federal government should take to the defeated Confederacy. Lincoln was already setting the tone, but he and his officials had to establish parameters of conduct as well. There was concern that the Radical Republicans in Congress would do their best to prevent the former Confederate states from being readmitted to the Union. Lincoln, as ever, hoped this could be bypassed by simply stating that those states had never departed it in the first place, but members of his Cabinet were less hopeful. Late that afternoon, Lincoln expressed regret that General Grant and his wife could not accompany him and Mrs. Lincoln to the theater. The Grants were already on a train for Philadelphia.

What dream did Lincoln relate to his Cabinet?

Members of Lincoln's Cabinet were well accustomed to his idiosyncrasies. He had a habit of telling jokes just when the mood was most solemn, for example. But on April 14,

Did Lincoln foresee his own death?

He seems to have had a major premonition. A week before the assassination, he told his wife and some staff members of an eerie dream. In it, he wandered through the White House, seeing signs of mourning and distress, and upon making inquiries, he learned that the president was dead.

Deeply upset, Mary Todd Lincoln upbraided her husband, saying he should not talk about such things. He attempted to calm her, saying that it was merely a dream, but some historians believe that Lincoln—who had little fear of death—actually teased his wife on such matters.

1865, he surprised them a little by telling them of a dream he had—perhaps the night before—of a mighty ship under full sail. He told them he was certain that great and good news would soon arrive because he had had this dream before each of the major Union victories of the war.

Who accompanied the president and first lady to Ford's Theatre?

Major Henry Rathbone and Miss Clara H. Harris were the first, and only, persons to accept the president's invitation. Lincoln had asked as many as four different couples, and all had—for one reason or another—declined. Finally there was a party of four, and the presidential carriage took them to the theatre.

Lincoln was an earnest theatre lover, and he was eager to see the production of *Our American Cousin*. Ford's Theatre was well accustomed to having the president and first lady in attendance: the "presidential" box was ready for the Lincoln couple. There was even the special chair that Lincoln had become accustomed to over the previous four years.

LINCOLN'S ASSASSINATION

How did the play begin?

Our American Cousin was a pleasant comedy about an English couple eager to advance their cause with American relatives. Lincoln was nodding; the first lady was engrossed. All seemed well. And then, at about 9:45, people in the audience were surprised to hear the explosion of a gun: that it was a pistol could not immediately be determined. Believing that this was part of the play, they continued to watch till they noticed that the actors were also in a state of shock. There was a shout, then a scream, then the sound of a thud as a man leapt from the president's box all the way to the stage. Standing there for one brief moment, he shouted, *Sic semper tyrannis!* ("Thus always to tyrants"). Then he was gone.

Minutes later, the audience learned that the president had been shot.

A lithograph depicting the assassination takes some artistic license, such as Lincoln holding onto the flag and, at far left, Henry Rathbone (a military officer who accompanied the president along with his fiancée, Clara), trying to stop the murder when, in fact, he did not see anything until after Booth pulled the trigger.

Why do we remember and dwell on Lincoln's assassination to so great an extent?

For three reasons. The first is that he was shot on Good Friday and died on the morning of Holy Saturday. Americans of 1865 were much more religiously observant than they are today, and the coincidence of the events with Holy Week was too much for them to merely pass over. Second, John Wilkes Booth killed Lincoln when he was in his prime, not physically, but as a moral force around which Americans could cohere. And the third reason that the Lincoln assassination remains with us is the charitable, open-hearted spirit that Lincoln held toward the defeated South. Those Southerners who thought Lincoln was their great foe were about to learn that he was MUCH better than the man who succeeded him in that respect.

Who was John Wilkes Booth?

Born in Maryland on May 10, 1838, Booth was the son of Junius Brutus Booth and Mary Ann Booth. Their story, and that of his siblings, is every bit as colorful as his own.

Early in the 1820s, Junius Brutus Booth and his wife Mary Ann arrived from England. He had been a very successful stage actor in London, and he now took up his vocation in America, which suffered from a dearth of native-born actors (some historians believe there were almost no native-born Americans performing on the American stage till about 1815). Junius Brutus Booth became a true sensation; he eventually gave over 2,800 performances in sixty-eight American cities and towns. But at the same time, there was tragedy, which seemed to surround his family.

Where did the Booths live? How many children did they have?

Junius Brutus Booth and Mary Ann Booth settled just outside of Bel Air, Maryland, where they lived in considerable comfort. As a matter of principle, they did not own slaves, but they did "rent out" slaves from neighbors from time to time. And as the family grew—they eventually had nine children—"The Farm," as they called it, grew larger and larger.

Of the first five children, four died in a relatively short time (three died in the cholera epidemic of 1833, and a fourth died from smallpox in 1837). When the younger children were born, their heart-stricken parents showered them with affection, and, in one of those remarkable coincidences with which the family was filled, their son Edwin Booth was born during the amazing meteor shower of

John Wilkes Booth (far left) is seen here in a production of Shakespeare's *Julius Caesar*, along with his brothers Edwin (center) and Junius Jr.

1835. Their second-youngest son, John Wilkes Booth, was born in 1838 and was named for the eccentric, patriotic, and colorful mayor of London, John Wilkes.

That sounds bad enough for any family, in terms of losses. Were there more?

In 1850 a woman appeared in Maryland and claimed she was the true wife of Junius Brutus Booth. She became a naturalized citizen and presented papers in court that appeared to justify her claim. Junius Brutus Booth had abandoned her and their two children in London many years ago and run off to America with Mary Ann.

Junius Brutus Booth did not contest the charges. He and his first wife were divorced in 1851, and that same year he married Mary Ann for the second, and legal, time. Junius Brutus Booth died a year later, but the effects of the family drama, or nightmare, were long lasting on all the children, perhaps on John Wilkes Booth the most.

Where was John Wilkes Booth when the Civil War commenced?

He was living in Maryland, but he had a peripatetic life, often traveling to New York City or Boston to give a performance, then hastening back. By sheer chance, he was one of the militiamen summoned to observe while John Brown was hanged in December 1859, and Booth sometimes traced his affection for the South to that event. As the Civil War gained momentum, John Wilkes' Southern sympathies became more pronounced. By the end of 1864, he was engaged in discussions and conversations

Who was the "Prince of Players"?

Born on November 13, 1833, in the middle of the Leonid meteor shower which lit up most of the Atlantic Coast—Edwin Booth was clearly destined for great things. His parents had just lost three children to the cholera epidemic of that year, and they earnestly desired that this child would survive and repay his parents' love. Very likely Edwin Booth felt the pressure to excel, and he followed in his father's footsteps.

By his mid-twenties, Edwin Booth was the most renowned of all Shakespearean actors in America, and his reputation eventually proceeded to other lands. He took his younger brother, John Wilkes Booth, on an acting tour in California, and the younger sibling showed considerable talent, but also an ungovernable temper. The elder brother, who was all for the Union in the Civil War, lamented his younger brother's actions so much that he never spoke of him after 1865.

and conspiracies, most of which revolved around a plan to kidnap, rather than kill, the president.

Was Booth as great a womanizer as the stories indicate?

Darkly handsome and quite daring—he was constantly injuring himself on stage—John Wilkes Booth was a successful womanizer. No one knows how many women he bedded, but given his predilection for prostitutes, as well as a desire to marry "up," there were probably quite a few. When he was down on his luck, especially where money was concerned, John Wilkes Booth was bailed out by his female admirers. He was with one of them on the evening of April 11, 1865, when Lincoln gave a speech at the White House. On hearing Lincoln's words, Booth said, "That means nigger citizenship. Now I'll finish him."

Why did the plan change from kidnapping to assassination?

Booth had not expected Richmond to fall so quickly, and he did not believe that the South was truly finished: as some Southerners said, "There's life in the old land yet!" But the speed of Grant's victories caused Booth to alter his plans. Right down to the last hour or two, he seemed to have entertained some doubts, but he overcame them and went to Ford's Theatre, a place he knew very well (he and other Booth family members had performed there many times). The guard outside the theatre saw nothing strange in the entry of a Booth family member, and John Wilkes went up the back stairs. He thought he would have to kill the guard at the door to the president's box, but the chair was unoccupied, and Booth, using the spyhole, peered through to see Lincoln, Mary Lincoln, Major Rathbone, and Miss Harris watching the play. From Booth's vantage point, Lincoln was the closest person to him, and Miss Harris was the farthest away.

How did Booth strike?

Only he, who stood there in that moment, could relate the full tale. Our best surmise is that Booth stole into the president's box, snuck up behind Lincoln, and fired his Colt derringer from a very short distance, perhaps less than a foot.

Why didn't the entire audience rise in a fury?

Because they believed that the pistol shot they heard was part of the performance. For the next two minutes, no one in the general audience understood what had happened. What they saw, however, was a dark-haired, very athletic man make a twelve-foot leap from the president's box to the stage. This man held aloft a dagger that seemed to have blood on it, and he shouted, *Sic semper tyrannis!* ("Thus always to tyrants"). Some in the audience knew that this was the state motto of Virginia, others knew it only as a Latin expression, but in either case it seemed to fit almost perfectly with the play. The audience, therefore, did not rise for another sixty seconds, and in that time Booth made his escape by stage left.

When did everyone realize that Lincoln had been hurt?

They weren't certain until members of the audience went up the stairs and forced open the door to the president's box. Booth had cleverly placed a chair under the doorknob, and it was some time before they entered, whereupon they found the president slumped over in his cozy chair and Major Rathbone bleeding profusely. The major had to wait for medical attention because all eyes were on the president. A twenty-three-year-old physician was in the audience; he was quickly drafted to do the painful work of administering to the president, who was unconscious.

How did Major Rathbone come by his wound?

A split second after Booth fired his pistol into the back of Lincoln's head, Major Rathbone was on his feet and crossing the box. Booth anticipated him, lunging with his knife, and he wounded Rathbone severely in the arm. Reeling from the pain, Rathbone stood by and watched for the next several hours as Lincoln hovered between life and death. When the doctors finally ministered to Rathbone, they found he had lost a great deal of blood, but he did not lose his arm. Something else, however, proved his undoing.

Guilt followed Rathbone for the rest of his life. Most of us, with our twenty-first century mindset, would absolve him of any weakness or guilt: he had jumped when the call of duty arrived. But Rathbone was a thoroughly nineteenth-century person, and it seemed to him that he had signally failed to protect the president. Though he later married Clara Harris and though they had three children, Rathbone still seemed ill at ease. Appointed U.S. consul to Hanover, Germany, in 1882, he went there with his family, and on December 23, 1883, he murdered his wife. Rathbone shot Clara dead, then stabbed her many times. When the police arrived, they found that Rathbone had attempted to stab himself. Found insane, he was confined to an asylum, where he died in July 1911.

Why do most of the Lincoln death pictures not look like he is in a theatre?

Policemen and theatre-goers carried the wounded, unconscious president to a nearby boarding house. Brought to a room on the first floor of the Petersen house, Lincoln remained unconscious but still breathing for many hours. The men that gathered around him were from the top of Washington's government, but not all could be present because attempts had also been made on the lives of Vice President Andrew Johnson and Secretary of State William H. Seward.

Most of the black-and-white prints that were made of the deathbed scene are accurate in most of the details, but there was an attempt, on the part of many of the sketch artists, to make Lincoln appear Christlike. He may, indeed, have seemed that way to some of those who stood, knelt, and prayed by the bedside. To many of them, Lincoln had once been the rubelike man from the Midwest, but he now personified the nation. It was hard to imagine the United States without him.

What was the scene in Ford's Theatre?

It was little short of pandemonium. Miss Laura Keene, the star of the play, attempted to obtain silence from the crowd, but found it impossible. Many persons struggled up the stairs and to the president's box, only to find it barred. When Major Rathbone managed to free the chair Booth had set under the doorknob, they flooded in. Fortunately, there were several physicians in the audience. The youngest of the group, a twenty-three-year-old surgeon, tended to Lincoln first.

Some people wanted to pick Lincoln up and take him to the White House, but the physicians believed he would not survive such a trip. Far better, they declared, to bring him to the nearest house. By this time, they had identified the bullet wound in the back of Lincoln's head. Using a .44 caliber derringer, Booth had made his mark quite well. Lincoln was brought to Petersen's boarding house, where he was tended by the physicians and watched over by members of his Cabinet. Not all could be present, however.

When did Lincoln die?

The president died at 7:22 A.M. on Saturday, April 15.

What was the first reaction?

Secretary of War Stanton said, "Now he belongs to the ages."

When did Andrew Johnson become the seventeenth president of the United States?

He was sworn into office within the hour.

What was the response around the nation?

There was deep grief in the North, but there was also anger. For the next few weeks, it was extremely dangerous for anyone in a Northern city or town to say anything negative about the fallen president. Lincoln, in death, had taken on a saintly aura.

In the South, the real sentiment was much more difficult to determine. Many Southerners had loathed Lincoln since his first appearance on the public stage in 1858, but quite a few of them had recently concluded, however reluctantly, that Lincoln was better than most of the alternatives. Now there was a sudden firestorm of danger because it seemed quite likely that the North would inflict punishment on the South.

How did Robert E. Lee take the news of Lincoln's death?

By an odd chance, Lee arrived home in Richmond on the afternoon of Holy Saturday, the day Lincoln died. Lee did not yet know the news, but the small crowd that awaited him at his Franklin Street house clearly wished him to—in some way—lift their spirits. He chose not to do so. Acknowledging their presence with a wave of his hat, Lee went inside to his ill wife. When he learned of Lincoln's death, perhaps the next day, Lee was appalled. He realized the potential for more strife.

Who took the famous photographs of Lee?

Lee and Lincoln were the two most photogenic persons of the war: the former because of his handsomeness, and the latter because of his humanness. Far more photographs had been taken of the Northern president than the Southern general, but Lee had one more opportunity when Mathew B. Brady knocked on his door on April 20, 1865. The two men knew each other well, and Lee consented to a series of photographs, all to be taken outside the house.

What does Lee look like in these photographs?

The danger in this description is that every viewer will find one thing or another on which to fasten and "peg" his analysis. The two most famous of the photographs show Lee alone, outside the door, and Lee with his son and his aide-de-camp, Colonel Walter H. Taylor, flanking him. To this viewer, the author, the thing that strikes most forcibly is the magnificent shine on Robert E. Lee's shoes. The man had just come home from campaigns and battles that lasted for four years, and his demeanor suggests great weariness, but the shoes are immaculately shined. Whether Lee shined them himself or had a slave do so is unknown, but it indicates the extent to which a person does not give up the habits of a lifetime (Lee was always known for his cleanliness).

Beyond the shoes, is, of course, the face, and Lee's countenance suggests quiet defiance. He was far too intelligent to stir up trouble, and he knew that Grant had been extremely generous in the terms of peace, but Lee's expression feels stonelike, as if he might do it all over again. One can observe, as well, from the photograph why Lee was considered one of the handsomest men of the South.

Where was Secretary of State Seward?

By one of those odd coincidences with which the Lincoln assassination is replete, Secretary of State Seward was confined to his bed on Good Friday, April 14, 1865. Two weeks earlier, he had been in a carriage when the horses made a getaway run; anxious to escape the carriage, Seward jumped out, taking severe wounds to his shins and face. He was, therefore, in bed when someone came to kill him on the evening of April 14.

Where was Vice President Andrew Johnson?

Johnson had not been attacked the night before. He was shaken, however, both by the assassination and the duties that now devolved upon him. Those who brought him the news, and continually updated it, feared he might repeat his woeful performance on Inauguration Day, but Johnson's first response was swift and to the point: "The duties are mine," he said. "I will perform them, trusting in God."

Johnson was, in several ways, an unknown quantity. Lincoln had trusted him because of the way he governed Tennessee, but many members of Congress barely knew him.

How did Booth get out of the presidential box, and, for that matter, out of the theatre?

He shouted, *Sic semper tyrannis!* ("Thus always to tyrants") and leapt from the box to the floor of the stage, breaking part of his tibia bone in the fall. Booth then held his dagger—with which he had stabbed Major Rathbone—aloft, and shouted, "The South shall be free!" Seconds later, he was out the back door, running or hobbling as the case may be, to his own freedom.

There were dozens of military men in Ford's Theatre, many of whom had faced much more dangerous and difficult situations over the previous four years, but virtually all of them were too stunned to respond. Major Rathbone was in agony from the wound to his arm, and virtually all the other men who might have sprung to attention were either lulled to complacency by the idea that the gunshot was part of the play or simply too stunned to act. As a result, Booth got out that door and to his horse.

How did Booth get out of Washington, D.C.?

During wartime, it would have been more difficult, but on April 14, Washington was a city in the midst of constant celebrations. The guards at all ends of the city were more relaxed than usual, and the one at the bridge leading to Maryland allowed Booth to pass through. Another of the conspirators passed a few minutes later.

Booth was in considerable pain. In his last note, clearly intended to be discovered, he wrote, "[I] rode sixty miles that night, with the bone of my leg tearing the flesh at every jump." Even so, it was remarkable he made his escape, and the next day he went to the home of Dr. Samuel Mudd—whom he had met five months earlier—and asked to have the broken bone set. Dr. Mudd did not recognize Booth, who kept his face turned to the wall, and once the bone was set there was a real chance that the assassin would get free. He had to cross the Potomac, however.

Who spoke at Lincoln's funeral?

The service was held in the East Room of the Executive Mansion on April 17. Several men of the cloth spoke, but the most significant words were uttered by George Bancroft. Secretary of the Navy under James K. Polk, a former preparatory school teacher and now the most prominent historian in the United States, Bancroft gave a lengthy eulogy that culminated with these words:

The "Old Nashville" train carried Abraham Lincoln from Washington, D.C., to his burial place in Springfield, Illinois.

> To that Union Abraham Lincoln has fallen a martyr. Peace to the ashes of our departed friend, the friend of his country and his race. Happy was his life, for he was the restorer of the republic; he was happy in his death, for the manner of his end will plead forces for the union of the States....

Where did Lincoln's body travel after the funeral?

Andrew Johnson's Cabinet, which was composed of the same men who had served Lincoln, agreed that the president's body should be returned home, to Springfield, Illinois, by way of the same train route he had taken to Washington, D.C., in 1861. Three other stops were added, making it a very long and eventful journey.

The stops in Philadelphia and New York City were the longest. Thousands of people came to see the body, and every person who did probably told three others of the experience. Quite a few Americans who were young at the time remembered the event for the rest of their lives (the artist Grandma Moses was one). Lincoln's body was buried in Springfield on May 1, 1865.

LINCOLN'S POSTHUMOUS FAME

What did the foreign press say?

Punch, the number-one popular magazine in Great Britain, had often taken pot-shots at the American president. The magazine had lampooned and caricatured Lincoln unmercifully in 1861 and 1862, and only began to slowly change its attitude in 1863. Right around the time of Lincoln's death, *Punch* came out with a tribute (we are not certain whether the news of his assassination had yet reached London):

> Beside this corpse, that bears for winding-sheet
> The Stars and Stripes he liv'd to rear anew,

335

Between the mourners at his head and feet,
Say, scurrile jester, is there room for you?

Yes: he had liv'd to shame me from my sneer,
To lame my pencil and confute my pen;
To make me own this hind of princes peer,
This rail-splitter a true-born king of men.

What were some of the later comments, those made in the months that followed?

There were a vast number of comments, about ninety-nine percent of which were complimentary, if not laudatory, to Lincoln. But the most poignant words, almost certainly, came from the pen of Walt Whitman:

O Captain! My Captain! Our fearful trip is done,
The ship has weather'd every rack, the prize we sought is won.
The port is near, the bells I hear, the people all exulting,
While follow eyes the steady keel, the vessel grim and daring:
But O heart! Heart! Heart!
O the bleeding drops of red,
Where on the deck my Captain lies,
Fallen cold and dead.

Whom do we remember more: Lincoln or the hundreds of thousands of soldiers who died?

We remember Lincoln because it is easier to concentrate our grief on one person. Those of us who have Civil War ancestors and know their stories may give great attention to their stories, but it is—for most of us—easier, indeed more possible, to look at the figure of the fallen president.

How did Lincoln come to assume this role as father of the nation?

The best answer to this comes from the extremely able pen of Michael Burlingame, the most prolific Lincoln scholar of our time. In Burlingame's estimation, Lincoln's rather sad personal story allowed him to become the *paterfamilias*, the father of the nation.

Having endured a very painful relationship with his own father, and a rather difficult marriage, Lincoln devoted himself to the tasks of parenthood. He was a loving parent to Willie, who was something of a carbon copy of himself. He had a distant relationship with Robert, who, as many writers see it, was "all Todd and no Lincoln." When Willie died, Lincoln devoted himself to Tad, but he also became the father of the people.

Could anyone else have filled this role?

Here, as so often, we run into the difficulties because of our lack of knowledge. There may well have been undiscovered "Lincolns" in his time period, just as there may have

How many people died during the Civil War?

For a long time, the general consensus was that 626,000 Americans died between 1861 and 1865, making the Civil War by far the most deadly conflict of all American history. Recently, however, new statistical analysis and extrapolation of data suggest that the number may be closer to 750,000. Even if we take the former figure of 626,000 and divide it into the total population of roughly thirty-two million, we come up with 1.9 percent of the total population killed. No other war or conflict in American history compares in terms of mortality and destruction, to put it simply.

been undiscovered "FDRs" during the Great Depression. But when we examine the people at or near the top, of whom we have certain knowledge, we feel reasonably confident in saying "no."

When we look at Lincoln, we examine William Seward, Edwin M. Stanton, Montgomery Blair, and Salmon P. Chase, as well as active wartime governors such as John A. Andrew of Massachusetts. We also bring into play persons such as Frederick Douglass, Ulysses Grant, William T. Sherman, and so forth. As we go through this list, giving proper respect and acknowledgement to each of these persons, we conclude that none of them was on Lincoln's level: they could not have filled his role as father of the nation and the people.

How important, then, is John Wilkes Booth?

He is the single most underestimated person of the Civil War. No one admires him; no one wishes to be like him; but we have to admit his importance. In April 1865, there was one person who had a genuine possibility of reconciling the North and the South: only Lincoln could fulfill that role (and even he would have had a hard time doing it). By striking Lincoln down at the prime of his intellectual and social power, Booth made reconciliation much more difficult, and it would take much longer to achieve.

How many people's lives were altered by the war?

On an anecdotal level, everyone's lives were altered by the war. Practically no one that we know of came out of the war in 1865 and said that his or her life was the same as it had been in 1861. For many people, the war had been a benefit, financially speaking. Fortunes had been made on Wall Street, but also on Main Street, where those engaged in the buying and selling of anything connected to the war generally received a major boost. Many of these new fortunes were, necessarily, fragile, and they would not survive the first big stock market swoon, which came in 1869.

Millions of other people could—quite rightly—claim that the war had ruined their lives. No one can truly count the cost in the rural South, where for the next two gener-

337

ations, white women outnumbered white men in almost every county, making it difficult to find a husband. No one can really assess the total damage to the infrastructure of the South, to Georgia and South Carolina most especially. This naturally begs the next question.

Why do we remember the gallantry and heroism of combat so much better than the death and destruction that accompanied it?

The answer lies in human nature. People often have to forget the worse parts of an experience in order to get up and move; so it was with Americans—white and black, rich and poor—when the Civil War ended. It was—and remains—much easier to concentrate on the heroism of Pickett's Charge than to really contemplate that seven thousand men were killed, wounded, or went missing that afternoon. To use a statistical approach, those seven thousand men represented roughly one-tenth of one percent of the entire white population of the Confederate States!

Was Lincoln as remarkable a person and a president as we are led to believe?

Beyond a doubt. Lincoln had the greatest range of talents of any person ever to occupy the White House. He had depth of feeling, strength of character, enormous perseverance, and, as one person of his time expressed it, "the intellect of a giant."

How Lincoln gained all this capability is somewhat mysterious. He did not have any higher education, and he had no brilliant tutors that we know of: he was, and remains, the most truly "self-taught" of all American presidents. But before attempting to dissect his path to the top, let us look—just for a moment—at what he accomplished. There were times, in 1863 and 1864, when he acted as chief executive, commander-in-chief, friend to the men who ran the War Department telegraph, father to Tad and Robert, and consoler to his wife over the loss of their beloved son Willie, *all at the same time*. American history records no similar set of demands on one person.

LINCOLN COMPARED TO
OTHER GREAT PRESIDENTS

Could not the same be said of Franklin D. Roosevelt, or perhaps of George Washington?

No. Washington had enormous official duties, including the setting of many important precedents, but his personal life—during the 1790s—was relatively untroubled. Franklin D. Roosevelt had overcome many adversities by the time the Japanese attacked Pearl Harbor in 1941, but he had almost no personal trials concerning family or friends during the four years that he was the active commander-in-chief. Then, too, Franklin D. Roosevelt had the advantage of a first-class education.

There have been other great presidents in American history, including those memorialized on Mount Rushmore—Washington, Jefferson, and Theodore Roosevelt—but of them all Abraham Lincoln surmounted the most trying time in American history as well as great personal hardships. Even on Mount Rushmore, he stands apart.

George Washington carried out the immense work of setting the nation on a course. Woodrow Wilson guided the nation through the First World War and attempted to navigate the free world through the peace that followed. Franklin D. Roosevelt carried the economic struggles of the nation during the 1930s and the military struggles of the 1940s, but he did not have to do them at the same time. No, Lincoln stands alone, at the top of his august company.

Was there ever a time—even a moment—when Jefferson Davis was the equal of Abraham Lincoln?

There was greatness within the man, and there were moments when he acted with a spirit of greatness, but he was not able to sustain it for long. This does not mean he was an inferior person (far from it), rather that few people have that capacity. When one compares, for instance, the inaugural addresses of Jefferson Davis and Abraham Lincoln in 1861, one is struck by the insistent humble tone of the former and the gradually confident tone of the latter. Reading these addresses, one might think that Lincoln was the person who might be tempted by overconfidence when, in fact, it was the reverse. Listening to the words of these two addresses, one might think that Jefferson Davis' greater experience in worldly affairs would make him a superior war leader to Lincoln: we know that this was not the case.

339

Was there any other person who could have filled Lincoln's shoes and guided the nation through the Civil War?

Very likely. In every generation, persons of great, undiscovered talents exist, and it is quite likely that someone else could have done all that Lincoln did. But when we examine the character and the actions of the men who were close to him—Secretary of State Seward, Secretary of War Stanton, Secretary of the Treasury Salmon Chase—not one of them even comes close. All of them brought special skills and talents, but not one of them possessed Lincoln's range of interests, humor, and everlasting tenacity. Therefore, if we look for "the" man, the person who could have done what Lincoln did, we have to look outside the narrow, accepted range of candidates.

How does Lincoln stand in comparison to other great world leaders of his time?

At the very top. There were two that we know of who had qualities similarly great, and we might place them—on a good day—as his equals. These were Otto von Bismarck, the Chancellor of the Kingdom of Prussia, and Benito Juárez, the embattled president of the Republic of Mexico.

Historians do not usually make comparisons between Lincoln and Bismarck because the former was so clearly the leader of a democratic nation and the latter is seen as the embodiment of Prussian militarism, which later turned into the German militarism that helped bring about not one, but two, world wars. When one compares the two on a level playing field, however, Bismarck is found to be the equal of Lincoln in intellect and in the making of strategy: where he falls below Lincoln is on the level of humor and forgiveness. Benito Juárez's was a remarkably capable and courageous man, who battled the French invasion of Mexico and eventually threw out the Emperor Maximilian. We wish we knew more of Juárez's personal qualities, but we suspect that—like almost all other world leaders of that time—his would lag behind those of Lincoln.

Are you saying that Lincoln had no faults?

He had few. His primary fault was that of ambition. It was not by accident that he rose from log-cabin boy to president, or that he persisted in politics after some early setbacks. Lincoln was extraordinarily ambitious, but his greatness of soul is revealed by the fact that power did not corrupt him; he retained the traits of compassion and mercy right to the end. On a personal level, we suspect that he was not always a kind husband to Mary Todd: he may even have enjoyed seeing her, on occasion, make a fool of herself. As a father, Lincoln was too permissive, but this is one of the lesser faults that one can level at a parent.

If we rate Lincoln as an "A plus," how do we rate, or rank, Jefferson Davis?

We give him a "C." Anyone who studies Davis' career is struck by how many problems he confronted on the day he became president of the Confederate States. He had to create a government, an army, a navy on the spot, and he had to establish precedents, much like George Washington had done seventy years earlier. Once we acknowledge Davis' difficulties, however, we have to add that he created many others.

Was Robert E. Lee the paragon of virtue we have been led to know?

Yes. If one puts aside the fact that he and his wife owned slaves—and this is, of course, difficult to do—it is nearly impossible to find a stain on his character. Regardless of whether he made the right or wrong decision in battle, Lee took responsibility. Regardless of whether his cause prospered or failed, he maintained a formidable belief in God, and that included God's will as far as the war was concerned. Great leaders are often best evaluated by looking at their relations with subordinates, the people beneath them, and in this regard Lee shines on almost every occasion. He was, with very few exceptions, gracious, courteous, and self-sacrificing. One of the most wonderful true stories is of a Union soldier, wounded and captured at the Battle of Gettysburg. The young man was lying on the ground, in great pain, and when he saw that the Confederate leader was close by, he jumped up, just for a moment, to shout, "Hurrah for the Union!" Lee came close, and the young man feared that he might strike him, but the older one took his hand and said, "My son, I hope you will soon be well."

Davis was quarrelsome. He believed himself a fine military mind, and he feuded with his generals (his relationship with Robert E. Lee was one notable exception). Davis did not inspire confidence among his generals or among the rank-and-file. Where he did shine was as the wartime leader of Richmond. That he possessed great courage is beyond dispute, and at times—when examining his poor physical health— one feels quite sorry for the man.

How about Lee's great adversary, Ulysses Grant?

The truly wonderful thing about Grant is that he did not take himself all that seriously. His task—that of winning the war—was all-important, and his letters to subordinates are models of clear, effective planning, but Grant never puffed himself up or put on airs. No phrenologist, or pseudoscientific analyst, ever determined the reason for Grant's singular success; we suspect that it derived from the ability to drop all else from his mind and concentrate on whatever task was at hand. There was, as well, a deeply fatalistic part of Grant: he did his best and did not concern himself whether the odds were in his favor. At one time during the Wilderness Campaign of 1864, some of his top subordinate generals mused over what Lee might do next to thwart them, and Grant stifled them with these words: "You're always gabbling about what Lee might do; you seem to think he's going to turn a somersault and land in our lines. Concentrate on what we're going to do next."

What happened to Lee after the war?

From the day that he returned to Richmond—April 15, 1865—Lee made it plain, through actions rather than words, that the Lost Cause was the Lost Cause. He allowed no one to build a movement around him; instead, he acted like a man who had come through four terrible years and wanted to go back to life as normal. Of course, there were ways in which he could not do so.

Lee lived quietly in Richmond, knowing that his former estate, Arlington House, had been taken over by the federal government. He became president of the Washington College and wrote his memoirs. Though he was a good writer who could turn a phrase well, Lee never saw much success from his memoirs; the reason is that there were so many hundreds, perhaps even thousands, of his soldiers who would always claim that the words on paper could never match the executions in the flesh. To them, the Battles of Malvern Hill, of Second Bull Run, and of Chancellorsville could not come alive in the words of any participant: they had to be lived to be believed. Lee died of heart disease in 1870.

What did Grant do after the war?

Grant might have liked to retire, but his immense popularity practically assured he would be a candidate for the presidency in 1868. He ran for, and easily won, the office, but he soon found that running the nation from the Executive Mansion was quite different from managing the armies in the field. Always good natured and generous to a fault, Grant promoted friends and relatives to positions they did not deserve, and he reaped the consequence: his two-term presidency was rife with corruption and intrigue. After leaving Washington, D.C., in 1869, Grant and his wife made a round-the-world journey by steamship and railroad and returned to live in New York City. Some ill-timed financial adventures left them nearly penniless, and at about the time that Grant learned he had cancer of the throat, his family fortunes were at an extremely low ebb.

Knowing he had but a few months to live, Grant hastened to write his military memoirs, which, when published by Mark Twain, were hailed as one of the greatest literary achievements within a military context seen in a very long time. Grant finished the two-volume work just before he died in upstate New York. He was buried on the northernmost part of Manhattan Island, and a joke began to go around: "Who is buried in Grant's tomb?" Many, many people have been stumped, but the answer is quite simple: "Ulysses and Julia Grant."

President Grant in a c. 1872 photo with his son, Jesse, and wife, Julia.

A lot of the great persons involved in the war seem to have died rather young. Was that common?

Lincoln was assassinated at fifty-six. Lee died of heart disease at sixty-two. Grant died of throat cancer at sixty-three. Jefferson Davis reached seventy-one, but had all manner of physical infirmities well before then. William T. Sherman died one week after his seventy-first birthday. His old rival in the field, General Joseph Johnston, was in poor health, but he went to Sherman's funeral and insisted on standing bareheaded in the rain. He died a month later, at the age of eighty-four.

To the majority of people at that time, to reach one's mid-sixties was a real achievement. Anything beyond that point was seen as grace, or as icing on the cake.

Speaking of old age and sickness, what did the Census of 1870 reveal about the population?

First, and most striking, is the fact that the total United States population increased from 31,443,000 in 1860 to 38,558,000 in 1870, an increase of seventeen percent. This happened despite the fact that 750,000 men—by our best estimate—died in the four years of war. Even when one accounts for the level of foreign migration, this represents a surprising, even staggering, achievement.

Second, and to few people's surprise, the ratio of men to women in the total population fell significantly between 1860 and 1870. This was especially the case in the Southern states, where the image of the well-bred "Southern widow" remained for decades. A woman of the working class could, and usually did, marry, regardless of the man's prospects, but a proper Southern lady had to find her equal. He was increasingly difficult to find because so many of that class and station had perished during the war.

Did women yet outnumber men in the United States?

Here is a surprise: no. Throughout the Colonial, Revolutionary, and early National periods, men consistently outnumbered women. Today we know that women have genetic "backups" that favor them to live longer lives, but in the Civil War, and for a full fifty years thereafter, most American women continued to experience great dangers in childbirth. Not till the appearance of the hospital, in the early part of the twentieth century, did American women begin to outnumber men: this was first recorded in the Census of 1920.

What about state-by-state overall population?

Virginia lost population. In 1860 there were 1,596,000 people in the Old Dominion, while in 1870 there were only 1,225,000. South Carolina barely escaped losing population in the war and the five years that followed: the Palmetto State went from a population of 703,000 to 705,000. Missouri suffered greatly during the war as a result of the bitter partisan feelings and actions, but the Show-Me State increased from 1,182,000 to 1,721,000.

There were many, even most, states in the winners column, but none expanded with the same incredible vitality that had been seen between 1850 and 1860. New York State, for example, went from 3,880,000 persons to 4,382,000 between 1860 and 1870. Pennsylvania increased from 2,906,000 to 3,521,000. The biggest winner in relative, as opposed to absolute, terms was California. Spared the effects of the Civil War, the Golden State's population increased from 379,000 to 560,000.

How about the number of work animals?

Given the great number of animals that were used, with many being killed during the war, we might expect the overall numbers to fall. But the Census of 1870 showed that the number of horses in the United States rose from 6,249,174 in 1860 to 7,145,370 in 1870. The number of mules and asses fell somewhat, from 1,151,148 in 1860 to 1,125,415 in 1870. The number of milch cows rose from 8,585,735 in 1860 to 8,935,332 in 1870, but the number of working oxen fell considerably, from 2,254,911 in 1860 to 1,319,271 in 1870.

Which parts of the nation rebounded more easily after the war's end?

The farther north a state was, the more likely that its population and material resources recovered quickly. The farther west a state was, the more likely that its population would rebound swiftly. And the converse was also true. The farther south a state was, the more slowly—sometimes agonizingly so—it recovered from the war.

What happened to the enormous Union Navy?

During the war, the Union showed that it had all the requisites for maritime greatness, even supremacy. Plenty of English visitors fretted over the size of the new American Navy, fearing it might be used against their own, but the Union Navy was scaled back almost at once. That the United States felt confident enough to do this shows how well-off the nation was; it could afford to let down its guard, where many other nations could not.

What happened to the immense Union armies?

Ninety, perhaps even ninety-five, percent of the soldiers were demobilized in a very short time. There simply was no need for their presence: the North had shown its mighty power on the battlefield.

For many, if not most, of the Northern soldiers, the Civil War was the defining experience of their lives, the moment to which all other events were designated as "before" or "after." Many soldiers had kept diaries: many of them now turned those into book form. There were reunions and reviews on almost an ongoing basis for the next thirty years. And, perhaps most importantly, almost every man who wished to run for high officer—from U.S. congressman to U.S. president—had to answer that all-important question: What had he done during the war?

Which Union regiments suffered the highest rate of casualties during the war?

The Union records were better kept than the Confederate ones, and thanks to the tireless efforts of a lieutenant-colonel, we have the precise numbers of killed, wounded, and missing for many, but not all, of the regiments that served on the Northern side. The top five, in terms of percentage of losses, are as follows:

- The First Minnesota lost 82% of its men, killed, wounded, or missing, at the Battle of Gettysburg.
- The 141st Pennsylvania lost 75.7%, killed wounded, or missing, at Gettysburg.
- The 101st New York lost 73.8%, killed, wounded, or missing, at the Second Battle of Bull Run.
- The 25th Massachusetts lost 70.00%, killed, wounded, or missing, at Cold Harbor.
- The 36th Wisconsin lost 69%, killed, wounded, or missing, at Bethesda Church.

(See Appendix G for a full list.)

MODERN–DAY REENACTMENTS

What is the difference between a reenactor and a revisionist?

Let's talk about the similarity first. Both a reenactor and a revisionist are fascinated by the past and believe it contains power to help shape the future. The chances are good that either of these two types grew up in a family where museums were valued more than television and where out-of-doors experiences were seen as preferable. But surprises happen, too, including the pudgy young person who turns into an athletic adult and becomes a serious reenactor.

The difference is that the reenactor wishes to bring to life that which transpired, and to do so with a maximum of accuracy, while the revisionist wishes to change, or alter, the way an event is perceived. For example, the reenactor who goes to Gettysburg generally wants to see Pickett's Charge, or Chamberlain's defense of Little Round Top, redone with great accuracy. The revisionist, more likely, wishes to examine Pickett's Charge and to determine if it was really as important as we usually believe.

When did the reenacting movement begin?

The desire to enact scenes from the Civil War has been with us almost from the day the war ended. Countless returning veterans were asked by family and friends to perform skits, to demonstrate what it was really like to serve in the trenches. To the best of our knowledge, the majority of returning men, even if they had witnessed horrific scenes, tended to oblige their family and friends. Then came the Grand Army of the Republic (known as the GAR; Union vets).

Reenacting the American Civil War is not a hobby only in the United States. Here, volunteers at the American Museum in Bath, England, put on a demonstration.

During the 1880s and 1890s, hundreds of thousands of surviving veterans enlisted in the Grand Army of the Republic. They put on parades, large and small, around the nation, enacting scenes from the past. Many, if not most, of these men believed that their task was complete, and that the nation would never be troubled by so large an event in the future (they could not envision the new equipment and casualty lists of the First World War, for example). There may have been some surviving veterans who scorned the whole thing as a waste of time, but for many persons, it was reenacting the highlight of their lives.

What difference was made by the First World War?

As late as 1910, there were still some Grand Army of the Republic units, and there were the occasional plays or set-pieces. But as the veterans kept dying off, and as America entered the twentieth century, the Civil War past began to seem remote. The appearance of the automobile, for example, persuaded many Americans—young ones, especially—to look forward to the future, not back to the past. Civil War reenactments therefore fell off dramatically, and when the First World War began in 1914, Americans looked at military events from very different eyes.

The Civil War had, of course, represented a vast leap forward in the development of military technology. Many units and not a few individual soldiers moved from muskets to rifles and from single-shot brass cannon to multiple-shot steel ones in the course of a year or two. But even the transition to Civil War technology was dwarfed by the changes that appeared in World War One. The machine gun, the massive use of the railroad, the appearance of the tank and the first airplanes, all made World War One seem even more overpowering a change than the Civil War. For years after 1918, American boys played with First World War memorabilia rather than Civil War artifacts.

Where were the revisionists at about that time (the 1920s)?

They were just beginning to emerge. It takes longer for Americans, and perhaps any other population, to develop the powers of revisioning a war than it does for them to reenact scenes from that war. Therefore, the 1920s represented the first attempt of the revisionists to see the Civil War anew and to argue over which causes and motives were most powerful. One can suggest that we have been doing the same ever since.

Thanks to the writings of a small number of revisionist historians (W. E. B. Du Bois is one of the first that comes to mind), Americans began reexamining the Civil War. Was it all about saving the Union? Was it primarily about freeing the slaves? Persons on both sides of the argument could find plenty of documentary evidence to back up either claim. At least with persons such as Lincoln and Jefferson Davis, a paper trail exists in which an historian or journalist can trace their thinking. But when it comes to many, perhaps the majority of the three million men who served, we are left in the dark.

MODERN–DAY MOVIES

What is the finest Civil War movie ever made?

Although every movie-goer will have his or her favorite, little doubt exists that *Glory*, released to the wide screen in 1989, is the best made of all Civil War films. The film takes the viewer on a trip into the still segregated Boston of 1862 as the men of the Massachusetts 54th get ready to play their part in the great conflict. One can see, visibly at times, the tension between the ideals of the abolitionist movement and the doubts that sometimes assailed the men who led it.

An all-star cast includes Matthew Broderick, Morgan Freeman, and Denzel Washington, but *Glory*, clearly, is not the work of one star or even several. The cast and crew combine to create marvelous effects, most notably the terrible battle as the 54th attempts to capture Battery Wagner, just outside of Charleston. Some have criticized the film, saying that it does too much to 'glorify' the actions of one side, but this is similar to the reviewers of 1939 declaring that *Gone with the Wind* did not say enough about the Northern point of view. Although *Lincoln*, released in 2012, was almost as persuasive to millions of viewers, *Glory* still stands all alone at the top of its genre.

What about *Gone with the Wind*? Was it as important as *Glory*?

In its time, yes. *Gone with the Wind* never attempted to undertake a major act of verisimilitude (the recreation of the past as it happened). *Gone with the Wind* attempted, and in some ways succeeded, in showing a way of life that disappeared with the last months of the war: the freestyle, happy life of the truly rich plantation owners.

This home in Madison, Georgia, which still stands today, is a good example of the antebellum mansions that were the center of plantations in the South before the war.

Such a film would never succeed today because the movie-goers would accurately claim that it did not do enough to depict the lives of the slaves, but in 1939 it represented a significant achievement. Enough time—seventy-five years—had passed since the destruction of Atlanta that Southern movie-goers could be counted on to see it; the romance of the antebellum South was still strong enough—in memory—to guarantee that millions of Northerners would go as well. He or she who sees the reruns today can usually take it as it was: a magnificent period piece that lacked historical sophistication.

What about *Lincoln*?

In November 2012, Steven Spielberg's long-awaited *Lincoln* was released to theatres around the nation. Knowing that Spielberg had produced it brought many viewers; knowing that Daniel Day-Lewis—often called the finest actor of his generation—would play the nation's sixteenth president was another major reason they came. To top it off was the knowledge that Sally Field—a longtime favorite of many—would play Mary Todd Lincoln.

No one can criticize the stage, the set, or the acting. Lewis was remarkable; he studied his role and played it to perfection. Sally Field's performance was a little uneven, but most people recognized that she had a tough act to perform. Where the film was weak was in the narrowness of its concept; the viewer only got to see Lincoln and the Congress during January of 1865, the month that culminated in the passage of the Thirteenth Amendment. Given the monumental amount of work Spielberg and his studio had done, one imagines a film with broader applications could have been the result.

How about *Gettysburg*?

Released to the public in 1993, *Gettysburg* may have put to work more actors and extras than any other Civil War film. The casting was excellent, with Martin Sheen as Robert E. Lee, Tom Berenger as James Longstreet, and Stephen Lang as George Pickett. Some critics complained that the film went on too long, but those who had already invested three hours were not reluctant to spend one more.

The battle scenes were often splendid; the fight for Little Round Top has never been surpassed in terms of dramatic intensity. But the lead-up to Pickett's Charge did go on a long time, and the viewer was—perhaps necessarily—spared some of the worst of the blood and gore. It might have been too much to see how much suffering was caused during that one hour on July 3, 1863. Where the film falls short, however, is with the lack of female roles. Of course, 99.5 percent of all the people on a battlefield were men, but that did not prevent the filmmakers from using the wonderful story of Jennie Wade, the only civilian casualty of Gettysburg. Then, too, the amazing story of John Burns was not used at all.

What about the numerous "made-for-television" series on the Civil War?

John Jakes' novels were made into series during the 1980s, and several other attempts have been made, but the Civil War does not, generally speaking, thrive on the small

What was so special about *Cold Mountain*?

For an answer, ask any of the millions of Americans who purchased the novel, especially those who snapped it up from 1997 to 1998. It had been a long time since any war novel had attracted such attention, but the story of a Civil War deserter, on his way home to Appalachia, was irresistible to many readers. Not until 2005 was the book made into a film, and those who had read the book with such keen interest were often disappointed by the wide-screen results.

Partly this was because the novel had such a surprising end to it: it was difficult to translate that complete surprise to the big screen. On another level, however, one wonders if the film's mediocre success has to do with the discouraging portrayal of the war. Rather than well-uniformed men moving out to the sighs and cheers of beautiful ladies, the book—and the film—devoted a good deal of attention to the "sorry" aspects of the war.

screen. The battle scenes, as well as the romantic partings of friends and lovers, fairly cry out for the wide-angle lens and the ability to let the camera linger.

If that is true, then how do we account for the amazing success of Ken Burns' *The Civil War*?

For four nights in October 1990, the American television audience was seized by a fever, almost a mania, for the war. Ken Burns had already developed a reputation as a solid filmmaker, but his four-part series exceeded expectations and confounded the critics. Who wanted to see one more rerun of all the terrors of the events of 1861 to 1865, the critics asked. 'Almost everybody' was the answer.

The still-life photography, accompanied by sounds that were both lonesome and stirring, was part of the reason. Another was the fine narration by the seasoned historian David McCullough. He was already known as the author of several well-received books, but he had not yet written *John Adams*, *Truman*, or *1776*, all of which enhanced his standing even more. Yet another, often overlooked reason was that the United States was, in that very month, girding itself in preparation for what would become known as the Persian Gulf War. Many soldiers and their families took time out to view Ken Burns' masterpiece just before departing for the Middle East.

How many young people became drummer boys as a result?

We really don't know the answer, but we can say with great confidence that the release of *Glory* in 1989, the release of *The Civil War* in 1990, and that of *Gettysburg* in 1993 turned thousands, perhaps scores of thousands, of everyday Americans into Civil War reenactors. The reenactment movement hit its peak sometime in the 1990s and remained strong till the early part of the next decade, but it was fading by 2010. Part of the reason was that there were few young persons to stand in for those who were becoming "old in the trenches." Another is that the dramatic events of September 11, 2001, had the effect of riveting the attention of many Americans on the here and now as opposed to the distant, however magnificent it might have been.

What was the most important of all Civil War songs?

It has to be a tie between "John Brown's Body" and "Dixie." Both were fantastic marching songs, and they seemed to echo the different lifestyles of the opponents. "John Brown's Body" fairly reeks of masculine endeavor, of action, while "Dixie" appeals to a gentler sensibility. This is not to say that the same person cannot enjoy both songs. Far from it. Lincoln, for example, lamented that the South had such a wonderful song in "Dixie" and wanted the North to appropriate at least some of it.

What is the most important of all Civil War photographs?

Everyone, of course, will have their own favorites, but the one that tells us the most about the time has no generals or politicians. This is the photograph of a Civil War soldier and, we suspect, his family.

The soldier stands dead center, facing the camera. Bearded and ruggedly handsome, he looks to be in his late twenties. Immediately to his right is a woman in the midst of doing laundry or cooking: it is difficult to say which. She faces the camera with what can only be called a determined expression: here is a woman who has seen much of the worst that life has to offer. Two children (we cannot automatically assume that they belong to the soldier and woman) are in front of the soldier and to his left. The boy, who looks about five years old, holds a dog which looks rather afraid. The girl, who looks about six or seven, holds a doll that is stunningly lifelike. Behind the soldier and the woman sit or stand about six other men, all wearing caps, which suggests they belong to the Union cause.

The photograph, overall, is indicative both of the trials of the soldier life and the fortitude of humans under stress. One wonders what the two children will be like as adults, and one marvels at the power of the photograph to illumine a situation.

What is the most important of all Civil War paintings?

Again, each person may have his or her favorite, but the one that tells the greatest part of the story is Winslow Homer's "Prisoners from the Front."

A Union officer, dressed in black rather than blue, stands at the extreme right and points his head sideways, in the direction of four Confederates who have recently surrendered. The Confederate at the extreme left is dressed in grayish green and looks, for all the world, like many later depictions of "poor white trash." The Confederate in the middle is an old man with a face and countenance that can only be described as Biblical. He may be the father of the soldier previously mentioned, but we cannot be certain. The third of the Confederates wears cavalryman's boots and has his hand on his hip in

This photo by the well-known Civil War photographer Mathew Brady captures the determination and spirit of a soldier and his family at an Army of the Potomac camp. Wives sometimes insisted on accompanying their husbands during the long campaigns.

a jaunty physical expression. To the right is a Union soldier in blue, who has brought these prisoners forward.

Is it possible to determine what Winslow Homer's painting means?

Like most truly good art, the painting can be read on different levels. At first one simply sees the Confederates brought forward and the likelihood that the war will soon be over: this is shown in the handsome uniform of the Union officer as well as the ragged clothing of the Southern men. But when we delve deeper, we see other meaning encased in layers. The old man, for example, seems as if he may be a civilian, with no stake or participation in the war. Why has he been made a prisoner? The confidence of the Union officer sets him apart, not only from the prisoners, but even from the private who has brought them forward. One senses that reconciliation will be needed on several different levels.

Who gave the most sons to either side in the war?

We hesitate to include this as fact because it seems so incredible and no corroborating evidence exists. Still, the story was reported in the *Harrisburg Telegraph* and from there found its way into Frank Moore's remarkable collection of stories and songs connected with the Civil War.

William Henry Fon Rodd was a German living in the little town of Butztown, Pennsylvania. He lost nine sons in the war: eight were killed in battle, and the ninth died of starvation at the Confederate prison in Salisbury, North Carolina. The tenth and youngest son in the family was John Fon Rodd, who was also in the Confederate prison, and he was released at the war's end.

Who was the youngest person to serve in the Civil War?

He seems to have been Johnny Clem of Licking County, Ohio. Christened John Joseph Clem, he was born in August 1851 and was just under ten years of age when the war began. His mother died at about that time, and young Johnny Clem determined on a life of adventure. He was mustered into the 22nd Michigan on May 1, 1863.

Harper's Weekly ran an image of Johnny Clem in February 1864, with the twelve-year-old boy wearing the uniform of a sergeant. He had a sad expression, but this was typical of many photographs and images from that time: nineteenth-century Americans did not "smile" for the camera in the style of their descendants. When the war was over, Johnny Clem petitioned President Grant, who made him a second lieutenant in the 24th U.S. Infantry. Clem lived to a ripe old age.

How many foreign-born persons served in the war?

Many. If one counts those who were born in other countries and then migrated to the United States, it runs past the hundred thousand mark. But if one rephrases the question and applies it only to those who came to the United States to serve in the war, then it is a much smaller number.

How many Chinese persons served in the Civil War?

Far more than we might think! One of the best estimates is that something like twenty-five Chinese fought at one time or another. The single best-known case, thanks to reporting in the *New York Times* in March 1864, is that of John Fouenty (of course, this is a transliteration of his actual Chinese name).

Though he came from a well-to-do family in China, John Fouenty was kidnapped (or shanghaied) and made to serve as a coolie on a ship to Cuba. Four years later, at about the age of twelve, his four-year forced service was over, and he made his way to Savannah, where he worked in a cigar manufactory. Sometime in 1862, when he was still quite young, Fouenty was persuaded to serve in the Confederate army. He served one year, then made his way to St. Augustine, and from there to Washington, D.C. He showed no desire to serve in the Union Army, and may—like many other foreigners—have been confused about the reasons for which the war was fought.

THE CIVIL WAR IN MEMORY: 1877 TO 2013

Who won the war?

The North, upholding the causes of Union and Emancipation, won the war. The South, which fought for disunion and slavery, lost.

Did any particular social or economic class win the war?

This one is trickier because there were divisions within the social and economic classes. On the whole, however, one can argue that the Northern industrial and commercial classes—those that made, bought, and sold goods—benefited, while the agricultural classes of the South suffered. If there was any obvious economic winner, it was the group (class is too strong a word) of newly made rich men in the North, especially those who invested in arms making during the war.

Did anyone experience any doubt as to who had won and who had lost?

Not in the immediate aftermath. From 1865 until about 1877, it was abundantly clear that the North had won and that the Union was preserved. But after roughly 1877, some people, especially blacks, began to ask whether the war had indeed been won so far as emancipation was concerned.

These doubts were raised by the resurgence of white supremacy in the former Confederate states. Virtually all of those states were prostrate when the war ended and could not resist the efforts of the North to impose new voting requirements and systems in the South. But within seven or eight years, most of the former Confederate states began to emerge from their devastated condition, and the white populations of those states began to discover ways to deprive the recently freed African Americans from exercising their right to vote. Of course it was an uneven process, with blacks faring better in some states than others, but by 1877—the year the last federal troops were withdrawn from the military districts in the South—the former Confederate states were well on their way to instituting white supremacy.

What is, or was, the difference between slavery and white supremacy?

It was considerable, both on a material and a psychological level. The blacks were freed by the Emancipation Proclamation, and many of them experienced a wonderful sense of release when the war ended. Economic and social conditions worked against most of the recently emancipated persons, however, and a majority began to fall into what some historians call the "second slavery" of the late nineteenth century.

It is difficult to throw off the effects of a system that has been in place for generations, and those blacks that remained in the South—about ninety percent—were subjected to all sorts of harassment and discouragement by those whites interested in keeping them "down." To be sure, this experience was not uniform. There were Southern whites who wanted to see the blacks succeed, and there were blacks who got out of the South and thereby gave themselves a better chance at success. But at least three-quarters of all the blacks who lived in the South and were freed by the Civil War soon experienced conditions that led them to question whether they, and the Union, had in fact won the war.

How did men and women in the North experience the decade that followed the war?

Men and women in the Northern states generally considered the issues of Union, disunion, slavery, and emancipation to be finished. There was now one federal union, in-

What was, and is, the Ku Klux Klan?

Part of the answer lies buried under the subterfuge of a generation of angry white Southerners and their actions, but the Klan was, beyond doubt, established in order to bring white supremacy to the South. General Nathan Forrest, the famous general of cavalry who won so many victories during the war, was the founder—or at least the leading founder—of the Klan.

Right from the beginning, the intention was to keep blacks from becoming "uppity" and to ensure that the white man and his family were seen as the embodiment of all that was "right" with the South. Had the Klan restricted itself to the outer attempt at these goals, it might have been obnoxious, but not terrible; instead, the Klan used any and all methods—including nighttime raids that involved the burning of crosses and the terrorizing of black families—to achieve its goals. Seldom has so vicious an organization lasted for so long, and seldom has one been so successful at keeping a population subject to its anger. The Klan was outlawed in the 1870s but it thrived underground, and it went through a major revival in the 1920s. This time, the Klan was against not only blacks but also foreigners of all types, Catholics, and anyone who did not seem to be a descendant of the early, "pure" immigrant population.

divisible, and slavery had been eradicated. That seemed sufficient to the great majority of people in the North. They were, therefore, surprised and disturbed to learn of the appearance of the Ku Klux Klan and the battle for white supremacy. The issues of the 1860s had been very intense for most people in the North, but they wanted to let go of them and tend to other ones.

A minority of white people in the North recognized the need to complete the work that had been begun, but they were seen as troublemakers, both by white Southerners and by their fellows in the North. Known as "carpetbaggers" and "scallywags," the well-meaning Northern-

A 1928 Ku Klux Klan march in Washington, D.C.

ers received a frosty reception in the South. Many of them achieved notable results until the last federal troops were removed in 1877.

How were national politics affected by the war?

From 1865 until 1900, the single most important question that could be asked of each and every major political candidate was: What did you do during the war? It is no surprise that a slew of high-ranking Union Army officers won presidential elections: Ulysses Grant in 1868 and 1872; Rutherford B. Hayes in 1876; William McKinley in 1896 and 1900. What was true on the national level was also true in local, county, and state elections. A man who had been adult and able-bodied during the war was expected to have served; anyone who did not was considered suspect where political office was concerned.

The Republican Party, too, was seen as the party of Lincoln, of Union, and of victory. For almost forty years, the Republican Party remained the most powerful element in American politics, and it had nearly a stranglehold on the vote in the industrial North. The Democratic Party, conversely, became known as the party of the South, the Confederacy, and the Lost Cause. The "Solid South," as politicians and pundits call it, emerged in the years following the war.

What was, or is, the Solid South?

In the fifty years that followed the war, the Democratic Party nearly always won all the states that had been part of the Confederacy. The "Solid South" shows up on electoral maps from those years. During the four-term presidency of Franklin D. Roosevelt, some of the Southern states began to defect from the Democratic fold, but it was not until the Civil Rights struggle of the mid-1960s that the switch became permanent. When he signed the Civil Rights Act of 1964, President Lyndon B. Johnson was reported to have said, "There goes the South." If so, he was right. Ever since the late 1960s, the South has been solidly Republican, with a few small countertrends.

That the South tends to vote as a bloc gives it political power, and no politician, Republican or Democratic, can ignore its importance. By contrast, the North, the Midwest, and the Far West have alternated, sometimes favoring one party or the other.

What was the Grand Army of the Republic?

The GAR was a veterans organization formed to maintain solidarity between former Union soldiers. It was especially strong and prominent during the 1880s, with frequent marches and celebrations. By the mid-1890s, the GAR was beginning to fade.

Leaders of the GAR lamented the change, but they missed the fact that many veterans were turning to other causes and concerns. The politics of the 1890s revolved around urban reform, immigration, and the animosity between Midwestern farmers and big-city bosses, all of which tended to obscure the former contests between the North and the South.

Was there any point at which the Civil War suddenly became "old news"?

It took a long time for that to happen. Even at the beginning of the Spanish-American War, the newspapers made much of the fact that this new conflict would have the happy side effect of reconciling the North and the South. Much was made of the fact that Joseph Wheeler, a major-general of Confederate cavalry, served in the Spanish-American War. Therefore, even when one turned the corner to the new, twentieth century, the Civil War remained strong in people's minds. The White House was occupied by men—Theodore Roosevelt and Woodrow Wilson—whose childhoods had been affected by the Civil War. It took, therefore, until roughly 1920 for the Civil War to really fade into the background.

The Grand Army of the Republic holds a march in Detroit, Michigan, in this 1914 photo.

What happened at the 50ᵗʰ anniversary of the Battle of Gettysburg?

As so often happened, Gettysburg overshadowed Vicksburg; practically all the attention in the newspapers went to the commemoration of the former battle. Thousands of veterans arrived at Gettysburg in time for the event, which featured a tent so large that 15,000 people could fit underneath.

The opening ceremonies were, perhaps, the most touching. Seven "Gettysburg girls," now in their seventies, came forth to say that they were among those who sang patriotic songs to General Buford's cavalrymen back in 1863. Some of those cavalrymen were also present, and their leader, Major Jerome Wheeler, gave a moving tribute. "If absence makes the heart grow fonder, how our hearts go out to you today as we look into your dear faces after an absence of fifty years." All seemed well, except for the blistering heat, which the veterans declared was about the same as what they remembered from 1863. Not everything went so smoothly, however.

What did Mrs. Longstreet have to say?

Helen D. Longstreet was the widow of General James Longstreet, the man who had led the First Confederate Corps at the Battle of Gettysburg. While the newspapers extolled Mrs. Longstreet for making it to Gettysburg in 1913, she sharply reminded them—in words printed in the *New York Times*—that the women of the Civil War never received the honors they deserved. It was difficult to argue with the nation's most prominent Civil War widow, but Mrs. Longstreet stumbled badly a day or two later when she expressed her view that "Pickett's Charge" should really be called "Longstreet's Charge." Not only had her husband been *against* that charge, but he would surely have wished to separate himself from a disaster of that magnitude.

Battles of words were not the only battles at Gettysburg in 1913, however.

What happened at the Gettysburg Hotel?

Right from the beginning of the commemoration, there were calls—sometimes anxious ones—for local authorities to close the saloons. Some of the veterans were imbibing to excess, it was claimed. The truth of this was revealed at the Gettysburg Hotel on the second night of the commemoration, when seven men—most of them veterans—received nasty knife wounds. The trouble began when an old veteran heard disparaging words about President Lincoln. He rose to challenge the man who spoke, and a whole row of men—some his friends and others unknown to him—rose to fight. The knives came out in an instant, the *New York Times* declared, and the stab wounds were serious. Of the seven men injured that evening, one was a local man, and another was from Harrisburg. The others had come from far off.

Did the 50ᵗʰ anniversary have any good results?

Many people applauded the reenactment of Pickett's Charge. At its end, the Confederate and Union veterans stood at the stone wall—the very one where Lewis Armistead had crossed at the height of the battle on July 3, 1863—and shook hands. Cameras caught the moment, and reconciliation seemed the order of the day.

Almost no one commented on the dearth of African-American participants at Gettysburg in 1913. There had, it is true, been very few blacks on the field in 1863, but it is still surprising to us today to learn that the only way blacks could participate in 1913 was to sell blankets to the veterans. Reenactment and reconciliation, clearly, did not include African Americans.

How did the First World War affect sentiment, or feeling, about the Civil War?

Almost no person that we know of served in both the Civil War and the First World War: to do so, he would have to have been a teenager in 1861 and an octogenarian in 1917! The First World War, therefore, became the new great marker for millions of Americans who divided their lives into "before" and "after" sections. One can, of course, ask what was the great "before" and "after" moment for the two generations that grew to maturity between 1865 and 1917. The answer is that they did not have one.

Just as many Americans alive today lament that they "missed" the 1960s by virtue of being too young to participate, there were millions of Americans between 1865 and 1917 who were sad that they "missed" the Civil War. With the benefit of hindsight, we can assert that they were probably fortunate to have missed the blood and destruction, but that was not the way they saw it. Quite a few of those Americans also decried the fact that America was changing before their eyes because of immigration.

How did the immigrants of the 1890s and early 1900s view the Civil War?

They had almost no connection to it. The great majority of these immigrants arrived either in Northern cities like New York and Philadelphia or in Western ones such as Seattle and San Francisco. To them, it was as if the Civil War had never taken place.

In reaction, or response, many Americans whose ancestors had been in the United States for a long time organized educational experiences to instruct a new generation about the importance of the Civil War. Many of these efforts fell flat on their face because the times had changed so greatly.

How did Southerners of the early twentieth century view the Civil War?

They were very proud of what their parents and grandparents had done, and they were bitter over the economic disparities between the North and the South. The Southern population changed very little in its ethnic composition between 1865 and 1910; Southerners, therefore, felt much more connected to the events of 1861–1865.

The advent of the First World War was more welcomed in the South than the North. Southerners, on the whole, enlisted in greater percentages than Northerners and felt a stronger connection to a military heritage. By 1920, a year that was a marker in so many ways, quite a few Southerners were willing to let "bygones be bygones" so far as relations with the North were concerned.

Why is 1920 one of the grand landmark years of American history?

1920 is not a "red-letter" date in the way 1776, 1812, 1861, and 1941 are. Rather, it is one of those "quiet" years that saw an enormous transition. For example, the federal census of 1920 revealed that for the first time more Americans lived in localities of two thousand persons and more than lived in smaller towns and villages. The United States was not yet a truly urban nation, but it was on its way toward that reality. The year 1920 was also when full demobilization of the World War One forces was complete and when the nation went back to a peacetime footing. And, perhaps most important, 1919–1920 was when the nation rejected its international obligations, saying it preferred to live in neutrality.

President Woodrow Wilson attempted to persuade Americans to sign on to the Versailles Treaty that ended the war, and that established the League of Nations, the world's first true international political organization. When the U.S. Senate, the prominent leaders of which were mainly Southern, rejected the treaty, the United States embarked on almost twenty years of self-chosen isolation; 1920 also witnessed a powerful resurgence of the Ku Klux Klan.

What happened to interest in the Civil War during the 1930s and 1940s?

It almost disappeared. Plenty of white Southerners were still raised with stories of Vicksburg and Gettysburg, but in the North the war attracted little memory. The Great Depression of the 1930s, and the onset of the Second World War in 1939, were collectively so momentous that Americans of those decades thought little of the far past. Then, too, the experience of many African Americans serving in the Second World War led to improvements on the material and economic side for many of their families. And then, with the onset of the Cold War from 1946 to 1947, the international side of affairs seemed so large, indeed overwhelming, that Americans paid little attention to the struggle they had once waged against each other. By the time that Dwight Eisenhower became the first commanding general since Ulysses Grant to be elected to the presidency, the Civil War seemed very far away and bound to fade into insignificance. But it all began to change two years later.

What was so important about 1954?

To Americans who continued to think about the Civil War, it was the one hundredth anniversary of the Kansas-Nebraska Act and of the Anthony Burns episode in Boston. But to the average American—white or black—it was a very normal year, and time, until the Supreme Court handed down its decision in *Brown v. Board of Education*. In that decision, the Court ruled that the doctrine of "separate but equal," established in the *Plessy v. Ferguson* case of 1895, was inherently unconstitutional. As a result, many public schools throughout the United States faced the possibility, even the probability, of enforced desegregation. All of a sudden, many Americans—white and black—remembered that it was precisely a century since the landmark events of 1854 and that the struggles for racial equality were not completed.

Who represented the Civil War to mid-twentieth century Americans?

Born in Michigan in 1899, Bruce Catton was a journalist who turned historian around the age of fifty. Gifted with a prose that lifted and sang as well as crashed and burned, he wrote over a dozen books, all on the Civil War. *Mr. Lincoln's Army* came out in 1951 and was followed by *Glory Road* in 1952 and *A Stillness at Appomattox*. Catton was a marvelous writer who did more with the personal stories of the boys in blue and gray than any previous author. It helped that he was essentially a nineteenth-century person, comfortable with the technology of that time.

Author Bruce Catton was a journalist who became popular for writing books about the Civil War, earning him the nickname "Mr. Civil War."

Some critics bashed the sentimental nature of Catton's prose, but few could dispute his mastery of the facts. As the one hundredth anniversary of the Civil War approached, he was "Mr. Civil War" to millions of Americans, and to his faithful readers he remained in that post till the end of his days.

Where did things go from there?

The unhealed wounds from the Civil War were reopened, and it would be a long time before they could be stitched up. To be sure, not everyone—North or South, white or black—realized that they were reenacting the struggles of a previous century: this became evident with the passage of time. But the Civil Rights struggles of the 1960s grew out of the unresolved disputes following the Civil War.

The height of the ugliness was between 1964 and 1968. In the former year, the Civil Rights Bill became law, allowing for federal monitoring of elections in the South. In that same year, Martin Luther King Jr. spent time in jail for his efforts to desegregate Southern cities. And, in a truly interesting coincidence, the forty-four-year-old Nelson Mandela was given a life sentence for crimes against the state of South Africa.

How did the Centennial of Gettysburg go?

Remarkably, the heat was as oppressive as ever. Both July 1863 and July 1913 had been oppressive, but July 1963 was even worse, with the mercury hitting ninety-eight degrees in New York City.

What happened to the centennial celebrations of the Civil War?

Between 1961 and 1965, the nation celebrated the hundredth anniversary of the Civil War, but the events were anything but harmonious. Some Americans, misunderstanding how the war played into their current concerns, dismissed the celebrations as irrelevant, while others criticized them for being one-sided, meaning they concentrated only on the experience of white people.

In retrospect, it is easy to criticize the hundredth anniversary celebrations. They waxed eloquent where Gettysburg and Vicksburg were concerned and did almost nothing to commemorate the actions of black soldiers. The "Lost Cause" was paraded endlessly, while there was little talk of the importance of emancipation. Was it completely by accident that Martin Luther King Jr. chose August 1963 as the time for the March on Washington? No, indeed; he was commemorating the actions of an earlier Civil Rights leader, who attempted the same thing. Generally speaking, however, a majority of Americans considered the centennial either unimportant or too one-sided.

This time there were, of course, no veterans: most of the people who came to Gettysburg in 1963 came with fresh eyes. There was, equally, a determination not to let the Centennial be overshadowed by the things that had plagued the celebrations of 1961. To that end, the Centennial organizers went out of their way to establish connections between the Battle of Gettysburg in 1863 and the world of 1963. Several speakers waxed about the Cold War with the Soviet Union, declaring that American values had been demonstrated in 1863 and would prove sufficient for the task a century later. Pennsylvania Governor Scranton added a rather dark note, saying that one hundred years after Gettysburg, America still was not truly integrated. When the pounding rains came a day later—yet another way that history repeated itself—most people agreed that the Centennial had gone off rather well.

Where did the Civil War "go" during the 1970s?

It was, again, nearly forgotten. The nation, which was attempting to put both the Vietnam War and the Civil Rights struggle behind it, was much more interested in celebrating the American Revolution. Seventeen seventy-six was the date most often mentioned, not 1861. There was a "feel-good" experience to the Revolution that was seldom found with the Civil War because in the former Americans had not—for the most part—fought and killed each other. Some scholars pointed to the eventual 150th anniversary of the Civil War, pointing out it was not that far off, but the public as a whole banished the Civil War from its mind.

The early 1980s took American minds even further away from the Civil War. Heightened tensions between the U.S.A. and the Soviet Union made a nuclear war seem possible, and present-day concerns trumped the past. The 125th anniversary celebrations of the Civil War were muted, to say the least. But a series of events was about to alter that situation.

How did the end of the decade alter perceptions of the Civil War?

In November 1989, the film *Glory* was released to select theatres: it went into broader release in February 1990. *Glory* was, quite likely, the finest Civil war film ever made, and millions of Americans suddenly became more conscious of the roles played by black soldiers. And then, by sheer happenstance, came one of the landmark events of that time, which helped connect Americans to their own past.

How important was the sudden release of Nelson Mandela from jail?

To Mandela himself, it was the event of a lifetime, the culmination of his twenty-seven-year quest to demonstrate the evils of the system of apartheid. To millions of black South Africans, it was a vivid demonstration of the coming end of apartheid. And to hundreds of millions of people around the globe, Mandela's release seemed to justify some of the fonder feelings that humans have for their own species, something that Lincoln would have called "the better angels of our nature."

Martin Luther King had been dead for twenty-one years, but many Americans quickly perceived a link between their Civil Rights struggle of the 1960s and the human rights struggle that went on in South Africa. And, though the highbrow news organizations did not comment, the release of the film *Glory* at almost the same time helped establish a connection.

Did Mandela ever seek to establish a connection between the Civil War and the struggle against apartheid in South Africa??

Mandela was such a far-seeing, truly global statesman that he was more interested in establishing connections to freedom and liberation movements around the globe. But as he worked to bring about reconciliation in South Africa, and impressed millions of people with his willingness to forgive, it became apparent that Mandela was one of the truly "great" persons of modern world history, and it was natural to look for others to compare. Mohandas Gandhi, the man who ejected the British imperialists from India, was one person on the same level as Mandela, and he paid a stiff price, falling to an assassin's bullet in 1948. Another was Lincoln.

There were plenty of fears that Mandela would pay the same price as Lincoln and Gandhi, but he was fortunate—both in the men of his security team and in the different times—to avoid any assassination attempts. When Mandela stepped down from office in 1998, he left South Africa more peaceful than he found it.

What was the height of the Civil War reenacting fever?

It ran strong for many years. The late 1980s and early 1990s probably represented the peak, and it is no accident that the Turner Company film *Gettysburg* was filmed in 1993, employing thousands of reenactors. By the beginning of the twenty-first century, the rage had abated somewhat, and by 2010 some of the reenactors' regiments had difficulty filling their rosters.

Computers were usually listed as the culprit. The reenactor groups depended on a certain age group of Americans, primarily men in their thirties and forties, who wanted to get away from modern technology and comforts to "rough it" for a period of time. The newer generation, however, those people who grew up with computers from their first days, were less inclined to head for the trees and the reenactment camp grounds.

How many books were being written, and published, on the Civil War?

There were so many that one could not keep track. Some were sweeping narratives, attempting to relate the war in all its complexity, while others concentrated on a month, a week, sometimes even a day, in the war. The Lincoln bibliography grew to such proportions that he became the second-most discussed person in human history, second only to Jesus Christ.

The struggle for human rights for all races and all people is still continuing long after the Civil War. In South Africa, Nelson Mandela (seen here with President Bill Clinton) sacrificed his freedom to help liberate his country of the apartheid system.

Academics, popular historians, and journalists all had a field day with the Civil War in the early part of the twenty-first century, each group attempting to claim a piece of the turf. There was no single person who "spoke" for and about the Civil War in the way that Bruce Catton had in the 1960s. But if there was one person listened to more than any other, it was probably David W. Blight, a distinguished professor of history who won numerous grants and wrote numerous books, most of them to do with the Civil War and its place in the national story.

What did Blight say?

His words were informed by his own personal story. Like many young people in the 1960s, he had been inspired by the writings of Bruce Catton, and he felt something very large was left out: the black presence. In *American Oracle: The Civil War in the Civil Rights Era*, published in 2011, Blight pointed out the discrepancies between the promises of the 1860s and the disillusionment of the 1960s.

At the beginning of the Civil War Centennial in 1961, blacks could not even stay at the same hotels as whites, and even if this had not been the case, only two or three blacks were given any roles during the opening ceremonies in Charleston. It was, to

Blight, as if the African Americans had not been present, as if the Civil War had been fought between two white peoples, with the blacks merely holding the bags and watching till the event was over. Blight captured the depth of his feeling, and that of many of his generation, when he wrote: "As a broad culture Americans seem incapable of completely shucking this event from its protective shells of sentimentalism, pathos, romance, in order to see to its heart of tragedy."

Was there a broader consensus, perhaps in the public at large?

Americans, as of 2011, the year of the Civil War's 150th anniversary, continue to revere the boys in blue and gray. They continue to be astonished by the sacrifices their ancestors made and marvel at the hardships they endured. Many Americans of our present time say that the war is long over and the issues it raised are resolved, but they wish to experience—sometimes vicariously and sometimes up-front and personal—the struggles of their great-great-great-grandparents.

Whether the *other* boys in blue—those whose skins were of a different color—will ever get the full credit for what they accomplished is uncertain. Whether the girls of the Union and Confederacy will ever be fully appreciated is not clear. And whether Americans as a whole will ever fully comprehend both the triumph and the tragedy of the Civil War remains one of the great questions of our time.

Appendix A: Jefferson Davis' First Inaugural Address, February 18, 1861

Gentlemen of the Congress of the Confederate States of America, Friends, and Fellow-citizens. Called to the difficult and responsible station of Chief Magistrate of the Provisional Government which you have instituted, I approach the discharge of the duties assigned to me with humble distrust of my abilities, but a sustaining confidence in the wisdom of those who are to guide and aid me in the administration of public affairs, and an abiding faith in the virtue and patriotism of the people. Looking forward to the speedy establishment of a permanent government to take the place of this, which by its greater moral and physical power will be better able to combat with many difficulties that arise from the conflicting interests of separate nations, I enter upon the duties of the office to which I have been chosen with the hope that from the beginning of our career, as a Confederacy, may not be obstructed by hostile opposition to our enjoyment of the separate existence and independence we have asserted, and which, with the blessing of Providence, we intend to maintain.

Our present political position has been achieved in a manner unprecedented in the history of nations. It illustrates the American idea that governments rest on the consent of the governed, and that it is the right of the people to alter or abolish them at will whenever they have become destructive of the ends for which they were established. The declared purpose of the compact of the Union from which we have withdrawn was to "establish justice, insure domestic tranquility, provide for the common defense, promote the general welfare, and secure the blessings of liberty to ourselves and for our posterity"; and when, in the judgment of the sovereign States, composing this Confederacy, it has been perverted from the purpose for which it was ordained, and ceased to answer the ends for which it was established, a peaceful appeal to the ballot box declared that, so far as they are concerned, the Government created by that compact should cease to exist. In this they merely asserted the right which the Declaration of Independence of July 4, 1776 defined to be "inalienable." Of the time and occasion of its exercise they as sovereigns were the final judges, each for itself. The impartial and enlightened verdict of mankind will vindicate the rectitude of our conduct; and He who knows the hearts of men will judge of the sincerity with which we have labored to preserve the Government or our fathers in its spirit.

The right solemnly proclaimed at the birth of the United States, and which has been solemnly affirmed and reaffirmed in the Bill of Rights of the States subsequently admitted into the Union of 1789, undeniably recognizes in the people the power to resume the authority delegated for the purposes of government. Thus the sovereign States here represented have proceeded to form this Confederacy; and it is by abuse of language that their act has been denominated a revolution. They formed a new alliance, but within each State its government has remained; so that the rights of person and property have not been disturbed. The agent through which they communicated with foreign nations is changed, but this does not necessarily interrupt their international relations. Sustained by the consciousness that the transition from the former Union to the present Confederacy has not proceeded from a disregard on our part of just obligations, or any, failure to perform every constitutional duty, moved by no interest or passion to invade the rights of others, anxious to cultivate peace and commerce with all nations, if we may not hope to avoid war, we may at least expect that posterity will acquit us of having needlessly engaged in it. Doubly justified by the absence of wrong on our part, and by wanton aggression on the part of others, there can be no cause to doubt the courage and patriotism of the people of the Confederate States will be found equal to any measure of defense which their honor and security may require. An agricultural people, whose chief interest is the export of commodities required in every manufacturing country our true policy is peace, and the freest trade which our necessities will permit. It is alike our interest and that of all those to whom we would sell, and from whom we would buy, that there should be the fewest practicable restrictions upon the interchange of these commodities. There can, however, be but little rivalry between ours and any manufacturing or navigating community, such as the Northeastern States of the American Union. It must follow, therefore, that mutual interest will invite to good will and kind offices on both parts. If, however, passion or lust of dominion should cloud the judgment or inflame the ambition of those States, we must prepare to meet the emergency and maintain, by the final arbitration of the sword, the position which we have assumed among the nations of the earth.

We have entered upon the career of independence, and it must be inflexibly pursued. Through many years of controversy with our late associates of the Northern States, we have vainly endeavored to secure tranquility and obtain respect for the rights to which we were entitled. As a necessity, not a choice, we have resorted to the remedy of separation, and henceforth our energies must be directed to the conduct of our own affairs, and the perpetuity of the Confederacy which we have formed. If a just perception of mutual interest shall permit us peaceably to pursue our separate political career, my most earnest desire will have been fulfilled. But if this be denied to us, and the integrity of our territory and jurisdiction be assailed, it will but remain for us with firm resolve to appeal to arms and invoke the blessings of Providence on a just cause.

As a consequence of our new condition and relations, and with a vicar to meet anticipated wants, it will be necessary to provide for the speedy and efficient organization of branches of the Executive department having special charge of foreign intercourse, finance, military affairs, and the postal service. For purposes of defense, the Confederate States may, under ordinary circumstances, rely mainly upon the militia, but it is deemed advisable, in the present condition of affairs, that there should be a well-instructed and disciplined army, more numerous than would usually be required on a peace establishment. I also suggest that, for the protection of our harbors and commerce on the high seas, a navy be adapted to those objects will be required. But this, as well as other subjects appropriate to our necessities, have doubtless engaged the attention of Congress.

With a Constitution differing only from that of our fathers in so far as it is explanatory of their well-known intent, freed from sectional conflicts, which have interfered with the pursuit of the general welfare, it is not unreasonable to expect that States from which we have recently parted may seek to unite their fortunes to ours under the Government which we have instituted. For this your Constitution makes adequate provision; but beyond this, if I mistake not the judgment and will of the people, a reunion of the States from which we have separated is neither practicable nor desirable. To increase the power, develop the resources, and promote the happiness of the Confederacy, it is requisite that there should be so much of homogeneity that the welfare of every portion shall be the aim of the whole. When this does not exist, antagonisms are engendered which must and should result in separation.

Actuated solely by the desire to preserve our own rights, and promote our own welfare, the separation by the Confederate States has been marked by no aggression upon others, and followed by no domestic convulsion. Our industrial pursuits have received no check, the cultivation of our fields has progressed as heretofore, and even should be involved in war, there would be no considerable diminution in the production of the staples which have constituted our exports, and in which the commercial world has an interest scarcely less than our own. This common interest of the producer and the consumer can only be interrupted by exterior force which would obstruct the transmission of our staples to foreign markets—a course of conduct which would be as unjust, as it would be detrimental, to manufacturing and commercial interests abroad.

Should reason guide the action of the Government from which we have separated, a policy so detrimental to the civilized world, the Northern States included, could not be dictated by even the strongest desire to inflict injury upon us; but if the contrary should prove true, a terrible responsibility will rest upon it, and the suffering of millions will bear testimony to the folly and wickedness of our aggressors. In the meantime there will remain to us, besides the ordinary means before suggested, the well-known resources of retaliation upon the commerce of an enemy.

Experience in public stations, of subordinating grade to this care and disappointment are the price of official elevation. You will see many errors to forgive, many deficiencies to tolerate; but you shall not find in me either want of zeal or fidelity to the cause that is to me the highest in hope, and of most enduring affection. Your generosity has bestowed upon me an undeserved distinction, one which I neither sought nor desired. Upon the continuance of that sentiment, and upon your wisdom and patriotism, I rely to direct and support me in the performance of the duties required at my hands.

We have changed the constituent parts, but not the system of government. The Constitution framed by our fathers is that of these Confederate States. In their exposition of it, and in the judicial construction, we have a light which reveals its true meaning.

Thus instructed as to the true meaning and interpretation of that instrument, and ever remembering that all officers are but trusts held for the people, and that powers designated are to be strictly construed, I will hope by due diligence in the performance of my duties, though I may disappoint your expectations, yet to retain, when retiring, something of the good will and confidence which welcome my entrance into office.

It is joyous in the midst of perilous times to look around upon a people united in heart, where one purpose of high resolve animates and actuates the whole; where the sacrifices to be made are not weighed in the balance against honor and right and liberty and equality. Obstacles may retard, but they cannot long prevent, the progress of a movement sanctified by its justice and sustained by a virtuous people. Reverently let us invoke the God of our fathers to guide and protect us in our efforts to perpetuate the principles which by his blessing they were able to vindicate, establish, and transmit to their posterity. With the continuance of his favor ever gratefully acknowledged, we may hopefully look forward to success, to peace, and to prosperity.

Appendix B: Abraham Lincoln's First Inaugural Address, March 4, 1861

Fellow citizens of the United States:

In compliance with a custom as old as the government itself, I appear before you to address you briefly, and to take, in your presence, the oath prescribed by the Constitution of the United States, to be taken by the President "before he enters on the execution of his office."

I do not consider it necessary, at present, for me to discuss those matters of administration about which there is no special anxiety, or excitement.

Apprehension seems to exist among the people of the Southern States, that by the accession of a Republican Administration, their property, and their peace, and personal security, are to be endangered. There has never been any reasonable cause for such apprehension. Indeed, the most ample evidence to the contrary has all the while existed, and been open to their inspection. It is found in nearly all the published speeches of him who now addresses you. I do but quote from one of those speeches when I declare that "I have no purpose, directly or indirectly, to interfere with the institution of slavery in the States where it exists. I believe I have no lawful right to do so, and I have no inclination to do so." Those who nominated and elected me did so with full knowledge that I had made this, and many similar declarations, and had never recanted them. And more than this, they placed in the platform, for my acceptance, and as a law to themselves, and to me, the clear and emphatic resolution which I now read.

"Resolved, That the maintenance inviolate of the rights of the States, and especially the right of each State to order and control its own domestic institutions according to its own judgment exclusively, is essential to that balance of power on which the perfection and endurance of our political fabric depend; and we denounce the lawless invasion by armed force of the soil of any State or Territory, no matter under what pretext, as among the gravest of crimes."

I now reiterate these sentiments: and in doing so, I only press upon the public attention the most conclusive evidence of which the case is susceptible, that the property, peace and security of no section are to be in anywise endangered by the now incoming Administration. I add, too, that all the protection which, consistently with the Constitu-

369

tion and the laws, can be given, will be cheerfully given to all the States when lawfully demanded, for whatever cause—as cheerfully to one section, as to another.

There is much controversy about the delivering up of fugitives from service or labor. The clause I now read is as plainly written in the Constitution as any other of its provisions:

"No person held to service or labor in one State under the laws thereof, escaping into another, shall, in consequence of any law or regulation therein, be discharged from such service or labor, but shall be delivered up on claim of the party to whom such service or labor may be due."

It is scarcely questioned that this provision was intended by those who made it, for the reclaiming of what we call fugitive slaves; and the intention of the law-giver is the law. All members of Congress swear their support to the whole constitution—to this provision as much as to any other. To the proposition then, that slaves whose cases come within the terms of this clause, "shall be delivered up," their oaths are unanimous. Now, if they would make the effort in good temper, could they not, with nearly equal unanimity, frame and pass a law, by means of which to keep good that unanimous oath?

There is some difference of opinion whether this clause should be enforced by national or by state authority; but surely that difference is not a very material one. If the slave is to be surrendered, it can be of but little consequence to him, or to others, by which authority it is done. And should any one, in any case, be content that his oath shall go unkept, on a merely unsubstantial controversy as to how it shall be kept?

Again, in any law upon this subject, ought not all the safeguards of liberty known in civilized and humane jurisprudence to be introduced, so that a free man be not, in any case, surrendered as a slave? And might it not be well, at the same time, to provide by laws for the enforcement of that clause in the Constitution which guarantees that "The citizens of each State shall be entitled to all privileges and immunities of citizens in the several States"?

I take the official oath today, with no mental reservations, and with no purpose to construe the Constitution or laws, by any hypercritical rules. And while I do not choose now to specify particular acts of Congress as proper to be enforced, I do suggest, that it will be much safer for all, both in official and private stations, to conform to, and abide by, all those acts which stand unrepealed, than to violate any of them, trusting to find impunity in having held them to be unconstitutional.

It is seventy-two years since the first inauguration of a President under our national Constitution. During that period fifteen different and greatly distinguished citizens have, in succession, administered the executive branch of the government. They have conducted it through many perils; and, generally, with great success. Yet, with all this scope for precedent, I now enter upon the same task for the brief constitutional term of four years, under great and peculiar difficulty. A disruption of the Federal Union heretofore only menaced, is now formidably attempted.

I hold, that in contemplation of universal law, and of the Constitution, the Union of these States is perpetual. Perpetuity is implied, if not expressed, in the fundamental law of all national governments. It is safe to assert that no government proper, ever had a provision in its organic law for its own termination. Continue to execute all the express provisions of our national Constitution, and the Union will endure forever—it being impossible to destroy it, except by some action not provided for in the instrument itself.

Again, if the United States be not a government proper, but an association of States in the nature of contract merely, can it, as a contract, be peaceably unmade, by less than all the parties who made it? One party to a contract may violate it—break it, so to speak; but does it not require all to lawfully rescind it?

Descending from these general principles, we find the proposition that, in legal contemplation, the Union is perpetual, confirmed by the history of the Union itself. The Union is much older than the Constitution. It was formed, in fact, by the Articles of Association in 1774. It was matured and continued by the Declaration of Independence in 1776. It was further matured and the faith of all the then thirteen States expressly plighted and engaged that it should be perpetual, by the Articles of Confederation in 1778. And finally, in 1787, one of the declared objects for ordaining and establishing the Constitution, was "to form a more perfect union."

But if destruction of the Union, by one, or by a part only, of the States, be lawfully possible, the Union is less perfect than before the Constitution, having lost the vital element of perpetuity.

It follows from these views that no State, upon its own mere motion, can lawfully get out of the Union—that resolves and ordinances to that effect are legally void; and that acts of violence, within any State or States, against the authority of the United States, are insurrectionary or revolutionary, according to circumstances.

I therefore consider that, in view of the Constitution and the laws, the Union is unbroken; and to the extent of my ability, I shall take care, as the Constitution itself expressly enjoins upon me, that the laws of the Union be faithfully executed in all the States. Doing this I deem to be only a simple duty on my part; and I shall perform it, so far as practicable, unless my rightful masters, the American people, shall withhold the requisite means, or, in some authoritative manner, direct the contrary. I trust this will not be regarded as a menace, but only as the declared purpose of the Union that it will constitutionally defend, and maintain itself.

In doing this there needs to be no bloodshed or violence; and there shall be none, unless it is forced upon the national authority. The power confided to me, will be used to hold, occupy, and possess the property and places belonging to the government, and to collect the duties and imposts; but beyond what may be necessary for these objects, there will be no invasion—no using of force against, or among the people anywhere. Where hostility to the United States, in any interior locality, shall be so great and so universal, as to prevent competent resident citizens from holding the Federal offices, there will be no attempt to force obnoxious strangers among the people for that object. While the strict legal right may exist in the government to enforce the exercise of these offices, the attempt to do so would be so irritating, and so nearly impractical with all, that I deem it better to forego, for the time, the uses of such offices.

The mails, unless repelled, will continue to be furnished in all parts of the Union. So far as possible, the people everywhere shall have that sense of perfect security which is most favorable to calm thought and reflection. The course here indicated will be followed, unless current events and experience, shall show a modification, or change, to be proper; and in every case and exigency, and with a view and a hope of a peaceful solution of the national troubles, and the restoration of fraternal sympathies and affections.

That there are persons in one section, or another who seek to destroy the Union at all events, and are glad of any pretext to do it, I will neither affirm nor deny; but if there really be such, I need address no word to them. To those, however, who really love the Union, may I not speak?

Before entering upon so grave a matter as the destruction of our national fabric, with all its benefits, its memories, and its hopes, would it not be wise to ascertain precisely why we do it? Will you hazard so desperate a step, while there is any possibility that any portion of the ills you fly from, have no real existence. Will you, while the certain ills you fly to, are greater than all the real ones you fly from? Will you risk the commission of so fearful a mistake?

All profess to be content in the Union, if all constitutional rights can be maintained. Is it true, then, that any right, plainly written in the Constitution, has been denied? I think not. Happily the human mind is so constituted, that no party can reach to the audacity of doing this. Think, if you can, of a single instance in which a plainly written provision of the Constitution has ever been denied. If, by the mere force of numbers, a majority should deprive a minority of any clearly written constitutional right, it might, in a moral point of view, justify revolution—certainly would, if such right were a vital one. But such is not our case. All the vital rights of minorities, and of individuals, are so plainly assured to them, by affirmations and negations guarantees and prohibitions in the Constitution, that controversies never arise concerning them. But no organic law can ever be framed with a provision specifically applicable to every question which may occur in practical administration. No foresight can anticipate, nor any document of reasonable length contain provisions for all possible questions. Shall fugitives from labor be surrendered by national or by State authority? The Constitution does not expressly say. May Congress prohibit slavery in the territories? The Constitution does not expressly say. Must Congress protect slavery in the territories? The Constitution does not expressly say.

From questions of this class spring all our constitutional controversies, and we divide upon them into majorities and minorities. If the minority will not acquiesce, the majority must, or the government must cease. There is no other alternative; for continuing the government, is acquiescence on one side or the other. If a minority, in such case, will secede rather than acquiesce, they make a precedent which, in turn, will divide and ruin them; for a minority of their own will secede from them, whenever a majority refuses to be controlled by such minority. For instance, why may not any proportion of a new confederacy, a year or two hence, arbitrarily secede again, precisely as portions of the present Union now claim to secede from it. All who cherish disunion sentiments, are now being educated to the exact temper of doing this.

Is there any such perfect identity of interests among the States to compose a new Union, as to produce harmony only, and prevent renewed secession?

Plainly, the central idea of secession, is the essence of anarchy. A majority, held in restraint by constitutional checks and limitations, and always changing easily, with deliberate changes of popular opinion and sentiments, is the only true sovereign of a free people. Whoever rejects it, does of necessity, fly to anarchy or to despotism. Unanimity is impossible; the rule of a minority as a permanent arrangement, is wholly inadmissible; so that rejecting the majority principle, anarchy or despotism in some form, is all that is left.

I do not forget the position assumed by some, that constitutional questions are to be decided by the Supreme Court; nor do I deny that such decisions must be binding in any case upon the parties to a suit, as to the object of that suit, while they are also entitled to very high respect and consideration, in all parallel cases, by all other departments of the government. And while it is obviously possible that such decisions may be erroneous in any given case, still the evil effect following it, being limited to that particular case, with the chance that it may be over-ruled, and never become a precedent for other cases, can better be borne than could the evils of a different practice. At the same time the candid citizen must confess that if the policy of the government, upon vital questions, affecting the whole people, is to be irrevocably fixed by decisions of the Supreme Court, the instant they are made, in ordinary litigation between parties, in personal actions the people will have ceased to be their own rulers, having, to that extent, practically resigned their government into the hands of that eminent tribunal. Nor is there, in this view, any assault upon the court or the judges. It is a duty, from which they may not shrink, to decide cases properly brought before them; and it is no fault of theirs if others seek to turn their decisions to political purposes.

One section of our country believes slavery is right, and ought to be extended, while the other believes it is wrong, and ought not to be extended. This is the only substantial dispute. The fugitive slave clause of the Constitution, and the law for the suppression of the foreign slave trade, are each as well enforced, perhaps, as any law can ever be in a community where the moral senses of the people imperfectly supports the law itself. The great body of the people abide by the dry legal obligation in both cases, and a few break over in each. This, I think, cannot be perfectly cured; and it would be worse in both cases after the separation of the sections, than before. The foreign slave trade, now imperfectly suppressed, would be ultimately revived without restriction, in one section; while fugitive slaves, now only partially surrendered, would not be surrendered at all, by the other.

373

Physically speaking, we cannot separate. We cannot remove our respective sections from each other, nor build an impassable wall between them. A husband and wife may be divorced, and go out of the presence, and beyond the reach of each other; but the different sections of our country cannot do this. They cannot but remain face to face; and intercourse, either amicable or hostile, must continue between them. Is it possible then to make that intercourse more advantageous or more satisfactory after separation than before? Can aliens make treaties easier than friends can make laws? Can treaties be more faithfully enforced between aliens than laws can among friends? Suppose you go to war, you cannot fight always; and when, after much loss on both sides, and no gain on either, you cease fighting, the identical old questions, as to terms of intercourse, are again upon you.

This country, with its institutions, belongs to the people who inhabit it. Whenever they shall grow weary of the existing government, they can exercise their constitutional right of amending it, or their revolutionary right to dismember, or overthrow it. I can not be ignorant of the fact that many worthy and patriotic citizens are desirous of having the national constitution amended. While I make no recommendation of amendments, I fully recognize the rightful authority of the people over the whole subject, to be exercised in either of the modes prescribed in the instrument itself; and I should, under existing circumstances, favor, rather than oppose, a fair opportunity being afforded the people to act upon it.

I will venture to add that, to me, the convention mode seems preferable, in that it allows amendments to originate with the people themselves, instead of only permitting them to take or reject propositions originated by others, not especially chosen for the purpose, and which might not be precisely such, as they would wish to either accept or refuse. I understand a proposed amendment to the Constitution—which amendment, however, I have not seen, has passed Congress, to the effect that the federal government shall never interfere with the domestic institutions of the States, including that of persons held to service. To avoid misconstruction of what I have said, I depart from my purpose not to speak of particular amendments so far as to say that, holding such a provision to now be implied constitutional law, I have no objection to its being made express and irrevocable.

The Chief Magistrate derives all his authority from the people, and they have conferred none upon him to fix terms for the separation of the States. The people themselves can do this also if they choose; but the executive, as such, has nothing to do with it. His duty is to administer the present government, as it came to his hands, and to transmit it, unimpaired by him, to his successor.

Why should there not be a patient confidence in the ultimate justice of the people? Is there any better, or equal hope, in the world? In our present differences, is either party without faith of being in the right? If the Almighty Ruler of nations, with his eternal truth and justice, be on your side of the North, or on yours of the South, that truth, and that justice, will surely prevail, by the judgment of this great tribunal, the American people.

By the frame of the government under which we live, this same people have wisely given their public servants but little power for mischief; and have, with equal wisdom, provided for the return of that little to their own hands at very short intervals.

While the people retain their virtue and vigilance, no administration, by any extreme of wickedness or folly, can very seriously injure the government in the short space of four years.

My countrymen, one and all, think calmly and well, upon this whole subject. Nothing valuable can be lost by taking time. If there be an object to hurry any of you, in hot haste, to a step which you would never take deliberately, that object will be frustrated by taking time; but no good object can be frustrated by it. Such of you as are now dissatisfied, still have the old Constitution unimpaired, and on the sensitive point, the laws of your own framing under it; while the new administration will have no immediate power, if it would, to change either. If it were admitted that you who are dissatisfied hold the right side in the dispute, there still is no single good reason for precipitate action. Intelligence, patriotism, Christianity, and a firm reliance upon Him, who has never yet forsaken this favored land, are still competent to adjust, in the best way, all our present difficulty.

In your hands, my dissatisfied fellow countrymen, and not in mine, is the momentous issue of civil war. The government will not assail you. You can have no conflict without being yourselves the aggressors. You have no oath registered in Heaven to destroy the government, while I shall have the most solemn one to "preserve, protect and defend" it.

I am loathe to close. We are not enemies, but friends. We must not be enemies. Though passion may have strained, it must not break our bonds of affection. The mystic chords of memory, stretching from every battlefield and patriot grave, to every living heart and hearthstone, all over this broad land, will yet swell the chorus of the Union, when again touched, as surely they will be, by the better angels of our nature.

Appendix C: The Emancipation Proclamation, January 1, 1863

Whereas, on the twenty-second day of September, in the year of our Lord one thousand eight hundred and sixty-two, a proclamation was issued by the President of the United States, containing, among other things, the following, to wit:

"That on the first day of January, in the year of our Lord one thousand eight hundred and sixty-three, all persons held as slaves within any State or designated part of a State, the people whereof shall then be in rebellion against the United States, shall be then, thenceforward, and forever free; and the Executive Government of the United States, including the military and naval authority thereof, will recognize and maintain the freedom of such persons, and will do no act or acts to repress such persons, or any of them in any efforts they may make for their actual freedom.

"That the Executive will, on the first day of January aforesaid, designate the States and parts of States, if any, in which the people thereof, respectively, shall then be in rebellion against the United States; and the fact that any State, or the people thereof, shall on that day be, in good faith, represented in the Congress of the United States by members chosen thereto at elections wherein a majority of the qualified voters of such State shall have participated, shall, in the absence of strong countervailing testimony, be deemed conclusive evidence that such State, and the people thereof, are not then in rebellion against the United States."

Now, therefore I, Abraham Lincoln, President of the United States, by virtue of the power in me vested as Commander-in-Chief of the Army and Navy of the United States in time of actual armed rebellion against the authority and government of the United States, and as a fit and necessary war measure for suppressing said rebellion, do, on this first day of January, in the year of our Lord one thousand eight hundred and sixty-three, and in accordance with my purpose so to do publicly proclaimed for the full period of one hundred days, from the day first above mentioned, order and designate the States and parts of States wherein the people thereof respectively, are in this day in rebellion against the United States, the following, to wit:

Arkansas, Texas, Louisiana (except the Parishes of St. Bernard, Plaquemines, Jefferson, St. John, St. Charles, St. James, Ascension, Assumption, Terrebonne, Lafourche, St. Mary, St. Martin, and Orleans, including the City of New Orleans), Mississippi, Alabama, Florida, Georgia, South Carolina, North Carolina, and Virginia (except the forty-eight counties designated as West Virginia, and also the counties of Berkeley, Accomac, Northampton, Elizabeth City, York, Princess Ann, and Norfolk, including the cities of Norfolk and Portsmouth, and which excepted parts, are for the present, left precisely as if this proclamation were not issued.

And by virtue of the power, and for the purpose aforesaid, I do order and declare that all persons held as slaves within said designated States, and parts of States, are, and henceforward shall be free; and that the Executive government of the United States, including the military and naval authorities thereof, will recognize and maintain the freedom of said persons.

And I hereby enjoin upon the people so declared to be free to abstain from all violence, unless in necessary self-defense; and I recommend to them that, in all cases when allowed, they labor faithfully for reasonable wages.

And I further declare and make known, that such persons of suitable condition, will be received into the armed service of the United States to garrison forts, positions, stations, and other places, and to man vessels of all sort in said service.

And upon this act, sincerely believed to be an act of justice, warranted by the Constitution, upon military necessity, I invoke the considerate judgment of mankind, and the gracious favor of Almighty God.

In witness whereof, I have hereunto set my hand and caused the seal of the United States to be affixed.

Done at the City of Washington, this first day of January, in the year of our Lord one thousand eight hundred and sixty-three, and of the Independence of the United States of America the eighty-seventh.

Appendix D: The Gettysburg Address, November 23, 1863

Four score and seven years ago our fathers brought forth on this continent a new nation, conceived in liberty and dedicated to the proposition that all men are created equal. Now we are engaged in a great civil war, testing that nation or any nation so conceived and so dedicated can long endure. We are met on a great battlefield of that war. We have come to dedicate a portion of that field as a final resting-place for those who here gave their lives that this nation might live. It is all together fitting and proper that we should do this. But in a larger sense we cannot dedicate, we cannot consecrate, we cannot hallow this ground. The brave men, living and dead who struggled here have dedicated it far beyond out poor power to add or detract. The world will little note nor long remember what we say here, but it can never forget what they did here. It is for us the living rather to be dedicated here to the unfinished work which they who fought here have thus far so nobly advanced. It is rather for us to be here dedicated to the great task remaining before us—that from these honored dead we take increased devotion to that cause for which they gave the last full measure of devotion—that we here highly resolve that these dead shall not have died in vain, that this nation under God shall have a new birth of freedom, and that government of the people, by the people, for the people shall not perish from the earth.

Appendix E: Abraham Lincoln's Second Inaugural Address, March 4, 1865

At this second appearing to take the oath of the Presidential office there is less occasion for an extended address than there was at the first. Then a statement somewhat in detail of a course to be pursued seemed fitting and proper. Now, at the expiration of four years, during which public declarations have been constantly called forth on every point and phrase of the great contest which still absorbs the attention and engrosses the energies of the nation, little that is new could be presented. The progress of our arms, upon which all else chiefly depends, is as well known to the public as to myself, and it is, I trust, reasonably satisfactory and encouraging to all. With high hope for the future, no predication in regard to it is ventured.

On the occasion corresponding to this four years ago all thoughts were anxiously directed to an impending civil war. All dreaded it, all sought to avert it. While the inaugural address was being delivered from this place, devoted altogether to saving the Union without war, insurgent agents were in the city seeking to destroy it without war—seeking to dissolve the Union and divide effects by negotiation. Both parties deprecated war, but one of them would make war rather than let the nation survive, and the other would accept war rather than let it perish, and the war came.

One-eighth of the whole population were colored slaves, not distributed generally over the Union, but centralized in the southern part of it. These slaves constituted a peculiar and powerful interest. All knew that this interest was somehow the cause of the war. To strengthen, perpetuate, and extend this interest was the object for which the insurgents would rend the Union even by war, while the Government claimed no right to do more than to restrict the territorial enlargement of it. Neither party expected for the war the magnitude or the duration which it has already attained. Neither anticipated that the *cause* of the conflict might cease with or even before the conflict itself should cease. Each looked for an easier triumph, and a result less fundamental and astounding. Both read the same Bible and pray to the same God, and each invoked His aid against the other. It may seem strange that any men should dare to ask a just God's assistance in wringing their bread from the sweat of other men's faces, but let us judge not, that we be not judged. The Almighty has His own purposes. "Woe unto the world because of offenses; for it must needs be that offenses come, but woe to that man by whom the offense cometh." If we shall suppose that American slavery is one of those offenses, which in the providence of God must needs come, but which, having continued through His appointed time, He now wills to remove, and that He gives to both North and South this terrible war as the woe due to those by whom the offense came, shall we discern therein any departure from those divine attributes which the believers in a living God always ascribe to Him? Fondly do we hope, fervently do we pray, that this mighty scourge of war shall speedily pass away. Yet if God wills that it continue until all the wealth piled by the bondsman's two hundred and fifty years of unrequited toil shall be sunk, and until every drop of blood drawn with the lash shall be paid by another drawn with the sword, as was said three thousand years ago, so still it must be said "the judgments of the Lord are true and righteous altogether."

With malice toward none, with charity for all, with firmness in the right as God gives us to see the right, let us strive on to finish the work we are in, to bind up the nation's wounds, to care for him who shall have borne the battle and for his widow and his orphan, to do all which may achieve and cherish a just and lasting peace among ourselves and with all nations.

Appendix F: The Thirteenth Amendment

Section 1. Neither slavery nor involuntary servitude, except as a punishment for crime whereof the party shall have been duly convicted, shall exist within the United States, or any place subject to their jurisdiction.

Section 2. Congress shall have power to enforce this article by appropriate legislation.

Appendix G: Union Regiments That Suffered the Highest Percentage of Total Casualties

Regiment	Action	No. of Men	Percent
1st Minnesota	Gettysburg	262	82.0
141st Pennsylvania	Gettysburg	198	75.7
101st New York	Manassas	310	73.8
25th Massachusetts	Cold Harbor	310	70.0
36th Wisconsin	Bethesda Church	240	69.0
20th Massachusetts	Fredericksburg	238	68.4
8th Vermont	Cedar Creek	156	67.9
81st Pennsylvania	Fredericksburg	261	67.4
12th Massachusetts	Antietam	334	67.0
1st Maine, H.A.	Petersburg	950	66.5
9th Louisiana Colored	Milliken's Bend	300	64.0
111th New York	Gettysburg	390	63.8
24th Michigan	Gettysburg	496	63.7
5th New Hampshire	Fredericksburg	303	63.6
9th Illinois	Shiloh	578	63.3
9th New York (8 cos)	Antietam	373	63.0
15th New Jersey	Spotsylvania	432	62.9
15th Massachusetts	Gettysburg	239	61.9
69th New York	Antietam	317	61.8
51st Illinois	Chickamauga	209	61.2
19th Indiana	Manassas	423	61.2
121st New York	Salem Church	453	60.9
5th New York	Manassas	490	60.6
93rd New York	Wilderness	433	60.0
2nd Wisconsin	Gettysburg	302	59.9
41st Illinois	Jackson	338	59.7
148th Pennsylvania	Gettysburg	210	59.5
15th Indiana	Missionary Ridge	334	59.5
7th Ohio	Cedar Mountain	307	59.2
80th New York	Gettysburg	287	59.2
63rd New York	Antietam	341	59.2
3rd Wisconsin	Antietam	340	58.8
114th New York	Opequon	315	58.7

Regiment	Action	No. of Men	Percent
59th New York	Antietam	381	58.7
26th Ohio	Chickamauga	362	58.5
2nd Wisconsin	Manassas	511	58.3
3rd Maine	Gettysburg	210	58.0
17th U.S. Infantry	Gettysburg	260	57.6
126th New York	Gettysburg	402	57.4
45th Pennsylvania	Cold Harbor	315	57.4
49th Pennsylvania	Spotsylvania	478	57.3
6th U.S. Colored	Chaffin's Farm	367	56.9
15th Massachusetts	Antietam	606	56.7
26th New York	Fredericksburg	300	56.6
14th Indiana	Antietam	320	56.2
96th Illinois	Chickamauga	401	56.1
26th Pennsylvania	Gettysburg	382	55.7
11th New Jersey	Gettysburg	275	55.6
1st Michigan	Manassas	320	55.6
19th Indiana	Gettysburg	288	55.5
12th New Hampshire	Cold Harbor	301	55.4
61st Pennsylvania	Fair Oaks	574	55.4
25th Illinois	Chickamauga	337	54.9
14th Ohio	Chickamauga	449	54.5
2nd New Hampshire	Gettysburg	354	54.5
8th Kansas	Chickamauga	406	54.1
16th Maine	Fredericksburg	427	54.0
16th United States	Stone's River	308	53.8
55th Illinois	Shiloh	512	53.7
69th New York	Fredericksburg	238	53.7
35th Illinois	Chickamauga	299	53.5
22nd Indiana	Chaplin Hills	303	52.4
11th Illinois	Fort Donelson	500	50.1

Chronology

Date	Event
Sept. 1850	The Compromise of 1850 is forged and enacted through a series of separate pieces of Congressional legislation. Mood in the nation is upbeat; many people believe that the questions of slavery and Union have been settled.
1850–1852	Jenny Lind, the "Swedish Nightingale," tours the United States
Nov. 1852	Franklin Pierce, Democrat, defeats General Winfield Scott, Whig, for the presidency
March 1853	*Uncle Tom's Cabin; or, Life among the Lowly* is published in Boston
May 24, 1853	Anthony Burns apprehended in Boston; he is eventually returned to Maryland
Summer 1853	Anthony Burns' freedom is purchased
March 20, 1854	Republican Party formed
May 30, 1854	Kansas–Nebraska Act passed by Congress
May 21, 1856	Sack of Lawrence, Kansas, carried out by Border Ruffians
May 22, 1856	Senator Charles Sumner attacked and nearly killed in Senate chamber
May 24, 1856	John Brown and sons carry out Pottawatomie Massacre
Nov. 4, 1856	James C. Buchanan, Democrat, defeats John C. Frémont, Republican, in presidential election
March 4, 1857	James C. Buchanan inaugurated
March 5, 1857	Dred Scott decision announced
Autumn 1857	Economic recession begins
1858	Lincoln declares for U.S. Senate seat from Illinois
	Lincoln–Douglas debates in summer and fall
	Douglas is selected by Illinois legislature

Oct. 16–17, 1859	John Brown and accomplices attack federal arsenal at Harpers Ferry
Oct. 17–18, 1859	Robert E. Lee and U.S. marines capture Harpers Ferry
Nov. 1859	Trial of John Brown
Dec. 2, 1859	John Brown is executed
Jan. 1860	Lincoln declares candidacy for Republican nomination
Feb. 22, 1860	Lincoln delivers speech at Cooper Union in Manhattan
Feb. 23, 1860	Famous Matthew Brady photograph of Lincoln is published
Feb. 1860	Lincoln tours New England
April 1860	Democratic Party splits into Northern and Southern sections
Summer 1860	Constitutional Union Party is formed
Nov. 6, 1860	Lincoln wins general election with plurality of 41 percent
Nov. 7, 1860	South Carolina calls special convention
Dec. 20, 1860	Special convention votes unanimously to secede from the Union
Dec. 26, 1860	Garrison at Fort Moultrie moves, on initiative of its commander, to Fort Sumter
Jan. 9, 1861	Mississippi secedes
Jan. 10, 1861	Florida secedes
Jan. 11, 1861	Alabama secedes
Jan. 19, 1861	Georgia secedes
Jan. 26, 1861	Louisiana seceded
Feb. 1, 1861	Texas secedes
Feb. 4, 1861	Provisional government of Confederate States of America established
Feb. 11, 1861	Lincoln departs Springfield, Illinois
Feb. 11, 1861	Jefferson Davis departs Brierfield, Mississippi
Feb. 18, 1861	Jefferson Davis inaugurated in Montgomery, Alabama
March 4, 1861	Lincoln inaugurated in Washington, D.C.
March 1861	Confederate preparations against Fort Sumter
April 12, 1861	War begins with bombardment of Fort Sumter
April 13, 1861	Fort Sumter surrenders
April 15, 1861	Lincoln calls for 75,000 volunteers
April 17, 1861	Virginia secedes
April 20, 1861	Massive pro-Union rally in lower Manhattan
April 24, 1861	Elmer Ellsworth killed as federal troops occupy Alexandria, Virginia

April 1861	Virginia military forces seize numerous installations
	General Benjamin Butler utters his famous words regarding black contrabands
May 6, 1861	Arkansas and Tennessee secede
July 4, 1861	Lincoln delivers memorable Fourth of July message to the nation
Summer 1861	First use of aerial balloons
July 21, 1861	Battle of Bull Run, also called Manassas
August 10, 1861	Battle of Wilson Creek, Missouri
Sept.–Nov. 1861	Preparation for Federal naval offensive against South Carolina
Oct. 24, 1861	Transcontinental Telegraph complete; messages transmitted between San Francisco and New York City
Nov. 8, 1861	USS *San Jacinto* stops British mail steamer *Trent*; takes commissioners into custody
Nov.–Dec. 1861	The *Trent* Affair threatens to bring about a war between the North and Great Britain
Dec. 26, 1861	*Trent* Affair blows over when Lincoln orders release of the commissioners
New Year's 1862	Celebration at White House; Lincoln shakes hands with thousands
Jan. 10, 1862	Bad news from Western theatre; Washington, D.C., in gloom
Feb. 1862	Brigadier-General Grant captures Fort Henry (Feb. 6) and then Fort Donelson (Feb. 16)
Feb. 20, 1862	Willie (William Wallace) Lincoln dies at the White House
Spring 1862	Union forces succeed in taking more than half the Confederate positions along the Mississippi River
March 1862	Confederate forces gather at Corinth, Mississippi
April 6, 1862	Battle of Shiloh
April 24, 1862	Farragut passes the Confederate forts south of New Orleans
	Farragut captures (April 25) and Butler's men occupy (May 1) city of New Orleans
April 1862	General McClellan brings most of the Army of the Potomac to Fort Monroe at bottom of the James Peninsula
May 5, 1862	Mexicans defeat French invaders at Battle of Puebla, leading to national holiday of Cinquo de Mayo
May 5, 1862	Battle of Williamsburg fought on James Peninsula
May 1862	General Joseph Johnston conducts an elegant defense of the James Peninsula

June 10, 1862	Federal forces come within seven miles of Richmond, Virginia
June 25–July 1, 1862	Seven Days' Battle rages east and southeast of Richmond
July 1862	McClellan withdraws the Army of the Potomac
August 1862	Lee, Stonewall Jackson, and James Longstreet move north
August 29, 1862	Confederates win the Second Battle of Bull Run, also known as Second Manassas
Sept. 4, 1862	Lee and the Army of Northern Virginia cross into Maryland
Sept. 5–12, 1862	Great anxiety at the White House and the War Department
Sept. 13, 1862	One of Lee's dispatches is found by two Federal soldiers
Sept. 13–14, 1862	Armed with the dispatch, McClellan concentrates the Army of the Potomac
Sept. 15, 1862	McClellan forces make it through the passes of South Mountain in Maryland; Stonewall Jackson takes Harpers Ferry
Sept. 17, 1862	Battle of Antietam
Oct. 1862	Clara Barton, who later founds the American Red Cross, is first noticed by the press
Sept. 22, 1862	Lincoln issues first Emancipation Proclamation
Nov. 7, 1862	Ambrose Burnside replaces McClellan as leader of the Army of the Potomac
Dec. 11, 1862	Army of the Potomac crosses the Rapidan River at Fredericksburg
Dec. 13, 1862	Battle of Fredericksburg
Dec. 29, 1862	Sherman repulsed in attack at Chickasaw Bayou near Vicksburg
Jan. 1–2, 1863	Battle of Murfreesboro, also known as Stones' River, in Tennessee
	Lincoln signs Emancipation Proclamation
Feb. 1863	Grant and Sherman's men begin digging canals to cut off Vicksburg
April 1863	Grant abandons canal effort; resolves to cross Mississippi below Vicksburg
	Colonel Arthur Fremantle of Queen Victoria's Coldstream Guards arrives in Texas
April 16, 1863	Rear-Admiral David Porter's squadron passes Vicksburg at night
April 18–27, 1863	Grant and Sherman's men march down west side of Mississippi River
April 29, 1863	General Joseph Hooker brings Army of the Potomac to south side of Rapidan River
April 30, 1863	Grant's army crosses to Bruinsburg, Mississippi; Battle of Port Hudson

May 1, 1863	Army of the Potomac reaches Chancellorsville and halts
May 2, 1863	Stonewall Jackson leads brilliant flanking maneuver; is shot by his own men at the height of victory
May 2–5, 1863	Battle of Chancellorsville ends in debacle for Federals
May 10, 1863	Stonewall Jackson dies
May 14, 1863	Grant enters and wrecks Jackson, Mississippi
May 16, 1863	Grant wins Battle of Champion Hill
May 1863	Lee decides to invade the North
May 18, 1863	Grant bottles Pemberton up at Vicksburg
June 9, 1863	Daring Federal raid throws J. E. B. Stuart off balance
June 16, 1863	Lee crosses the Potomac, enters Maryland
June 22, 1863	Advance units of Army of Northern Virginia enter Pennsylvania
June 27, 1863	General Joe Hooker replaced by General Gordon Meade
July 1, 1863	Climax of the Siege of Vicksburg approaches
	Lee's men approach Gettysburg from the north; Meade's men from the south
	First Day of Battle of Gettysburg; heroism of John Burns
July 2, 1863	Second Day of Battle of Gettysburg; tremendous fight for Little Round Top
July 3, 1863	Third Day of Battle of Gettysburg: Pickett's Charge fails
July 3, 1863	Pemberton asks Grant for terms
July 4, 1863	Confederate garrison at Vicksburg surrenders
July–August 1863	General William Rosecrans advances through southern Tennessee
Sept. 1863	Jefferson Davis sends Longstreet's corps to Western theatre
Sept. 9, 1863	General Braxton Bragg retreats, yielding town of Chattanooga
Sept. 19–20, 1863	Battle of Chickamauga near border between Tennessee and Georgia
Sept. 23, 1863	Confederates occupy Lookout Mountain and Missionary Ridge
Oct. 16, 1863	Ulysses Grant chosen to lead all Federal forces west of Appalachian Mountains
Oct. 23. 1863	Grant arrived in Chattanooga
Oct. 25, 1863	The "cracker line" is opened
Oct. 29, 1863	Jefferson Davis arrives in Marietta, Georgia; confers with Bragg and his generals
Nov. 18, 1863	Lincoln travels to Gettysburg to help dedicate a new cemetery

Nov. 19, 1863	Edward Everett delivers two-hour speech; Lincoln delivers Gettysburg Address in five minutes
Nov. 24, 1863	Union forces capture Lookout Mountain and Orchard Knob
Nov. 25, 1863	Army of the Cumberland captures Missionary Ridge; puts Confederates to flight
Nov. 26, 1863	Thanksgiving celebrated as national holiday for first time
Dec. 14, 1863	Longstreet attacks, but fails to capture Knoxville
Jan. 1864	Lincoln holds New Year's Day reception at White House
	Major cold front develops over Midwest, keeping Midwest and East Coast very cold for two weeks
	Confederates fight with snowballs in their winter camp
Feb. 1864	Hunger plagues Confederate winter camps
March 8–9, 1864	Ulysses Grant arrives in Washington, is made nation's first lieutenant-general since George Washington
March 1864	Grant and Sherman confer in Cincinnati
May 1864	Richmond threatened by surprise attacks by Union cavalry
May 4, 1864	Grant crosses the Rapidan
May 5–6, 1864	Battle of the Wilderness
May 1864	Grant moves on the North Anna River; Lee's men go into fortifications
May 8–21, 1864	Battle of Spotsylvania Court House
May 10, 1864	Death of J. E. B. Stuart at Battle of Yellow Tavern
May 12, 1864	Sherman captures Dalton; Johnston retreats
June 1–3, 1864	Battle of Cold Harbor
June 19, 1864	CSS *Alabama* is defeated and sunk by USS *Kearsarge* off coast of France
June 27, 1864	Battle of Kennesaw Mountain
June 1864	Grant brings his men over the James River and threatens Petersburg, Virginia
June 1864	Petersburg saved by heroic actions of P. T. Beauregard
June 1864	Siege of Richmond and Petersburg begins
July 30, 1864	Battle of the Crater near Petersburg
July–August, 1864	Sherman defeats Hood in three separate engagements
Sept. 1, 1864	Hood evacuates Atlanta; Sherman occupies it
Sept. 1864	Lincoln's re-election campaign begins in earnest
Oct. 1864	Sherman asks permission to march to the sea
Nov. 1864	Grant gives permission to Sherman, who departs Atlanta with 70,000 men on Nov. 16

Nov. 24, 1864	Second national Thanksgiving is celebrated
Dec. 10–20, 1864	Sherman besieges Savannah
Dec. 21, 1864	Sherman enters Savannah
Jan. 15, 1865	Federal forces besiege and capture Fort Fisher and then move on Wilmington, Delaware
Jan. 31, 1865	Thirteenth Amendment passed by House of Representatives
Feb. 1865	Robert Todd Lincoln becomes a captain on Grant's staff
Feb. 17, 1865	Sherman takes and nearly destroys Columbia, South Carolina
Feb.–March 1865	Confederate Congress contemplates arming Negro slaves
March 1865	Deprivation in Richmond
March 13, 1865	Confederate Congress approves arming of black slaves
March 19–21, 1865	Battle of Bentonville
March 29, 1865	Lee attempts to capture Fort Stedman, but is repulsed
April 2, 1865	Confederate forces abandon Richmond and Petersburg
April 3, 1865	Richmond suffers from a tremendous fire
April 4, 1865	Lincoln visits Richmond, accompanied by twelve sailors, Admiral Porter, and his son Tad
April 5, 1865	Army of the Potomac in full pursuit of Army of Northern Virginia
April 6, 1865	Battle of Sayler's Creek, Virginia, ends in Northern victory
April 9, 1865	Lee surrenders to Grant at Appomattox Court House
April 10, 1865	Lincoln receives news of Lee's surrender
April 11, 1865	Lincoln delivers speech on Reconstruction from White House portico
April 14, 1865	General Robert Anderson raises U.S. flag over Fort Sumter
	Lincoln holds three-hour meeting of his cabinet
	Lincoln is shot at Ford's Theatre, around 9:30 P.M.
April 15, 1865	Lincoln dies at 7:22 A.M.
	Andrew Johnson sworn in as seventeenth president
	Lee arrives at his house on Franklin Street in Richmond
April 17, 1865	Rumors of Lincoln's death spread
April 18, 1865	Lincoln's funeral in East Room of the White House
April 20, 1865	Photographer Matthew Brady meets and takes pictures of Robert E. Lee
May 1, 1865	Lincoln buried in Springfield, Illinois
May 21, 1865	Review of Army of the Potomac in Washington, D.C.
May 22, 1865	Review of Sherman's army in Washington, D.C.

Bibliography

A Richmond Lady (pseudonym for Sallie Putnam). *Richmond during the War*. New York: G.W. Carleton & Company, 1867.

Alexander, E.P. *Military Memoirs of a Confederate: A Critical Narrative*. New York: Charles Scribner's Sons, 1907.

Allen, Thomas B., and Roger MacBride Allen. *Mr. Lincoln's High-Tech War: How the North used the Telegraph, Railroads, Surveillance Balloons, Iron-Clads, High-Powered Weapons and More to Win the Civil War*. Washington, D.C.: National Geographic, 2009.

Andrews, Matthew Page. *The Women of the South in War Times*. Baltimore: The Norman, Remington Company, 1920.

Bernard, Kenneth A. *Lincoln and the Music of the Civil War*. Caldwell, ID: The Caxton Printers, 1966.

Bill, Alfred Hoyt. *The Beleaguered City: Richmond, 1861–1865*. New York: Knopf, 1946, reprinted, Greenwood Press, 1980.

Blight, David W. *Race and Reunion: The Civil War in American Memory*. Cambridge: Harvard University Press, 2001.

———. *American Oracle: The Civil War in the Civil Rights Era*. Cambridge: Harvard University Press, 2011.

Bowman, Kent A. *Voices of Combat: A Century of Liberty and War Songs, 1765–1865*. Westport, CT: Greenwood Press, 1987.

Buchanan, Lamont. *A Pictorial History of the Confederacy*. New York: Bonanza Books, 1951.

Bucklin, Sophronia E. *In Hospital and Camp: A Woman's Record of Thrilling Incidents among the Wounded in the Late War*. Philadelphia: John E. Potter, 1869.

Burlingame, Michael. *The Inner World of Abraham Lincoln*. University of Illinois Press, 1994.

Bushong, Millard K. *Old Jube: A Biography of General Jubal A. Early*. Boyce, VA: Carr Publishing Company, 1955.

Campbell, John Francis. *A Short American Tramp in the Fall of 1864*. Edinburgh, UK: Edmonston & Douglas, 1865.

Century Company. *Battles and Leaders of the Civil War*, 4 vols. New York: The Century Company, 1884–1888.

DeLeon, T.C. *Belles Beaux and Brains of the '60s*. Reprint, New York: Arno Press, 1974.

Detzer, David. *Donnybrook: The Battle of Bull Run, 1861*. New York: Harcourt, 2004.

Eckert, Ralph Lowel. *John Brian Gordon: Soldier, Southerner, American*. Baton Rouge: Louisiana State University Press, 1989.

Flood, Charles Bracelen. *Grant and Sherman: The Friendship That Won the Civil War*. New York: Harper Perennial, 2005.

———. *1864: Lincoln at the Gates of History*. New York: Simon & Schuster, 2009.

Fox, William F. *Regimental Losses in the American Civil War*. Albany: Albany Publishing Company, 1889.

Gordon, John B. *Reminiscences of the Civil War*. New York: Charles Scribner's Sons, 1903.

Harwell, Richard B. *The Confederate Reader: How the South Saw the War*. New York: Dover Publications, 1989.

———. *Honor Answering Honor*. Brunswick, ME: Bowdoin College, 1965.

Holzer, Harold, and the New York Historical Society. *The Civil War in 50 Objects*. New York: Viking, 2013.

Hood, J.B. *Advance and Retreat: Personal Experiences in the United States and Confederate States Armies*. New Orleans: G.T. Beauregard, 1880.

Horan, James D. *Mathew Brady: Historian with a Camera*. New York: Crown Publishers, 1955.

Jordan, Robert Paul. *The Civil War*. New York: National Geographic Society, 1969.

Kauffman, Michael W. *American Brutus: John Wilkes Booth and the Lincoln Conspiracies*. New York: Random House, 2004.

Lafantasie, Glenn W. *Gettysburg Requiem: The Life and Lost Cause of Confederate Colonel William C. Oates*. New York: Oxford University Press, 2006.

Levine, Bruce. *The Fall of the House of Dixie: The Civil War and the Social Revolution That Transformed the South*. New York: Random House, 2013.

Lossing, Benson J. *Pictorial History of the Civil War*. Mansfield, OH: Estill & Company, 1866, reprinted, Carlisle, MA: Applewood Books, 2008.

Marten, James. *The Children's Civil War*. Chapel Hill: University of North Carolina Press, 1998.

McDonough, James Lee. *Chattanooga: A Death Grip on the Confederacy*. Knoxville: University of Tennessee Press, 1984.

McGuire Judith W. *Diary of a Southern Refugee during the War*. New York: E. J. Hale & Son, 1867, reprint, New York: Arno Press, 1972.

McMurry, Richard M. *John Bell Hood and the War for Southern Independence*. Lexington: University Press of Kentucky, 1982.

McPherson, James M. *War on the Waters: The Union & Confederate Navies, 1861–1865*. Chapel Hill: University of North Carolina Press, 2012.

Moore, Frank, ed. *The Rebellion Record: A Diary of American Events and Documents, Narratives, Illustrative Incidents, Poetry, Etc.,* 11 vols. New York: D. Van Nostrand, 1868.

———, ed. *The Civil War in Song and Story, 1860–1865*. New York: P. F. Collier, 1889.

Morris, B. F., ed. *Memorial Record of the Nation's Tribute to Abraham Lincoln*. Washington, D.C.: W. H. & O. H. Morrison, 1865.

New York Times. *The Most Fearful Ordeal: Original Coverage of the Civil War by Writers and Reporters of the New York Times*. New York: St. Martin's Press, 2004.

Nichols, George Ward. *The Story of the Great March, from the Diary of a Staff Officer*. New York: Harper & Brothers, 1865, reprint, Williamstown, MA: Corner House Publishers, 1972.

Pember, Phoebe Yates. *A Southern Woman's Story: Life in Confederate Richmond*, edited by Bell I. Wiley. St. Simons Island, Georgia: Mockingbird Books, 1974.

Ramold, Steven J. *Across the Divide: Union Soldiers View the Northern Home Front*. New York: New York University Press, 2013.

Sandburg, Carl. *Abraham Lincoln: The War Years*, 4 vols. New York: Harcourt, Brace & World, 1939.

Schultz, Duane. *The Most Glorious Fourth: Vicksburg and Gettysburg, July 4, 1863*. New York: W. W. Norton, 2002.

Sears, Stephen W. *Landscape Turned Red: The Battle of Antietam*. Boston: Houghton Mifflin, 1983.

Semmes, Raphael. *Service Afloat or the Remarkable Careers of the Confederate Cruisers Sumter and Alabama*. London: Sampson, Low, Marston, Searle & Rivington, 1887.

Smith, Gene. *Lee and Grant: A Dual Biography*. New York: McGraw Hill, 1984.

Stephens, John Richard. *Commanding the Storm: Civil War Battles in the Words of the Generals Who Fought Them*. Guilford, CT: Lyons Press, 2012.

Stout, Harry S. *Upon the Altar of the Nation: A Moral History of the Civil War*. New York: Viking, 2006.

Townsend, E. D. *Anecdotes of the Civil War in the United States*. New York: D. Appleton & Company, 1884.

Trudeau, Noah Andre. *Like Men of War: Black Troops in the Civil War, 1862–1865*. Boston: Little, Brown & Company, 1998.

Victor, Orville J. *The History, Civil, Political, & Military of the Southern Rebellion*. New York: J. D. Torrey, 1861.

Watkins, Sam R. *Co Aytch: A Confederate Memoir of the Civil War*. New York: Touchstone, 2003.

Wert, Jeffry D. *Cavalryman of the Lost Cause: A Biography of J. E. B. Stuart*. New York: Simon & Schuster, 2008.

———. *A Glorious Army: Robert E. Lee's Triumph, 1862–1863*. New York: Simon & Schuster, 2011.

Winik, Jay. *April 1865: The Month That Saved America*. New York: Harper Collins, 2001.

Winther, Oscar Osborn, ed. *With Sherman to the Sea: The Civil War Letters Diaries and Reminiscences of Theodore P. Upson*. Baton Rouge: Louisiana State University Press, 1943.

Index

Note: (ill.) indicates photos and illustrations.

402

reaction to Confederate launching of *Virginia*, 105
rebounds after Bull Run, 98
response to Lee's invasion, 214
soldiers in Washington, D.C., 88–89
in St. Louis, 88
technical advantage, 98
West in 1863, 151–52
United States, geographic boundaries, 3
U.S. Sanitary Commission, 168
USS *Galena*, 117
USS *Kearsarge*, 288
USS *Monitor*, 117

V

Velsor, Louisa Van, 182
Versailles Treaty, 359
Vicksburg, 153, 158
Grant, Ulysses S., 151–52
Vicksburg, Siege of, 207 (ill.), 209 (ill.)
action begins to move forward, 201–2
attack, 209–10
Battle of Champion Hill, 207–8
conditions at, 239
Confederate cannons, 204
Confederate overconfidence after early Union assault failure, 203
Confederate soldiers at, 202
Confederate surrender, 238–39
Grant decides on frontal assault, 208
Grant's digging plan, 203–4
Grant's men come ashore at Bruinsburg, Mississippi, 206
Jackson, Mississippi, occupation of, 206–7
newspapers' accounts of Union victory, 239
newspapers' response to Jackson destruction, 207
Port Gibson, 205–6
status of war after, 240
Union approach on west side of Mississippi, 204
Union march southward, 205
Union pummels Confederacy, 237

Union ships succeed in making passage of Vicksburg, 204–5
Union soldiers at, 202–3
Vicksburg as a town, 201
Victoria, Queen, 81, 170–71
Vincent, Strong, 228
Virginia
population, 343–44
secession, 78, 83
Virginia, Army of. *See* Army of Virginia
Virginia, CSS, 105–6, 107, 107 (ill.)
"Voice from Texas," 304

W

Wade, Jennie, 348
Walker, Mary Edward, 175
Wall Street, 269, 269 (ill.)
Wallace, William, 104
Washington, Denzel, 347
Washington, George
compared to Lincoln, 338–39
electoral vote sweep, 55
grand-nephew as central figure in Harpers Ferry raid, 35
Harpers Ferry federal arsenal, 33
inaugural, 68
Lee, Light Horse Harry, 41
sword of, 39
universally admired figure, 171
Yorktown, 109, 289
Washington, Lewis, 35, 38, 39, 40
Washington, Martha Custis, 41
Watkins, Sam, 112–13, 256, 260, 261
Waud, Alfred Rudolf, 223 (ill.), 267 (ill.)
Webster, Daniel, 9–10, 20, 26
Welles, Gideon, 140 (ill.), 150
West
census, 51–52
fighting in, 95
New Mexico Territory, 94–95
in 1850s, 6–8
Wheeler, Jerome, 357
Whig Party, 24, 46
White, Julius, 131
white supremacy, 354, 355, 355 (ill.)
Whitman, Edward, 182, 184
Whitman, George, 183
Whitman, Hannah, 184
Whitman, Jeff, 184

Whitman, Jesse, 182, 184
Whitman, Walt, 176, 183 (ill.), 183–84, 336
Whitman, Walter, Sr., 182
Wide Awakes, 53
Wigfall, Louis T., 26, 73
Wilderness, Battle of the, 161 (ill.)
casualties, 282, 283
fighting in, 277, 278–79 (ill.), 280
Lee does not attempt to fight in, 160
location of, 159
Longstreet wounded, 280
Sedgwick killed, 280
Wilson, Woodrow, 195, 339, 356, 359
Wise, Henry, 215
women
Alcott, Louisa May, 175–77, 176 (ill.)
Barton, Clara, 174, 174 (ill.)
Bickerdyke, "Mother" Ann, 174
Davis, Varina, 170, 170 (ill.)
in 1850s, 3
foreigners' views on condition of American, 168
helping Confederate soldiers, 182
lack of prominence of, 171
Lincoln, Mary Todd, 169, 169 (ill.)
McGuire, Judith Brockenbrough, 178
Northern stereotypes, 197–98
Pember, Phoebe Yates, 179 (ill.), 179–82
roles of, 167–68
Southern stereotypes, 197
Walker, Mary Edward, 175
Wood, Fernando, 309
Wool, John, 192
work animals, 52, 344
World War I, 346, 358, 359
World War II, 135, 359
Wright, Rebecca, 302

Y–Z

Yancey, William, 63
Yellow Tavern, 280–81
Yorktown, Siege of, 92 (ill.)
Zouaves, 80, 86–87